Boston Symphony Orchestra

Boston Pops Orchestra

Boston Symphony Orchestra

Boston Pops Orchestra

ISBN/EAN: 9783741137914

Manufactured in Europe, USA, Canada, Australia, Japa

Cover: Foto ©Angelika Wolter / pixelio.de

Manufactured and distributed by brebook publishing software (www.brebook.com)

Boston Symphony Orchestra

Boston Pops Orchestra

THE MUSIC HALL
PROMENADE CONCERTS

PUBLISHED BY
C. A. ELLIS,
MUSIC HALL.

BOSTON, MONDAY, MAY 8, 1899.

SUMMER SEASON.
Vol. XIV. No. 1.

THE MUSIC HALL... Promenade Concerts
FOURTEENTH SEASON.

C. A. ELLIS, Manager.   F. R. COMEE, Assistant Manager.

Mr. MAX ZACH, Conductor.

MONDAY, MAY 8.

PROGRAMME.

1. POLONAISE, from "Eugene Onéguin" . . . . . Tschaikowsky
 (First Time.)
2. WALTZ, "Gross-Wien" . . . . Strauss
3. OVERTURE, "Orpheus aux Enfers" . . . . Offenbach
 Violin Obligato, Mr. KARL ONDRICEK.
4. ORIENTAL MARCH . . . . Zach
5. BALLET MUSIC from "Coppelia" . . . . . Delibes
 (a) Dance of the Automatons.
 (b) Valse.
 (c) Czardas.
6. (a) SPRING SONG . . . . Mendelssohn
 (b) SEVILLANA . . . . Massenet
7. VALSE CAPRICE, "Honeymoon" . . . . . Stix
 For String Orchestra.
 (First Time.)
 The audience is respectfully requested to preserve silence during the performance of this number.
8. OVERTURE, "Mignon" . . . . . . Ambroise Thomas
9. TWO SLAVONIC DANCES . . . . . . Dvorak
10. POLKA, "Tic-tac" . . . . Strobl
11. WALTZ, "Grubenlichter" . . . . Zeller
12. MARCH, "Stars and Stripes Forever" . . . . Sousa

THE TWO MOST POPULAR TWO-STEPS
OF THE SEASON.

THE RUNAWAY GIRL, by Van Baar, ... 60c.
THE CECIL, by Megone, ... 50c.
FOR ORCHESTRA OR PIANO SOLO.

BOOSEY & CO.,
9 EAST 17TH STREET,   NEW YORK.

YOU CAN
Have your last season's outfit dyed or cleansed and refinished so it will look like new, by our French process. Why discard soiled clothing when it can be overhauled and worn as second best? You can

RELY ON
Our methods of cleansing, and need not hesitate to trust us with articles of the most delicate textures.
We dye or cleanse and refinish PROPERLY, all materials of household use and clothing of all kinds.

LEWANDO'S
W. L. Crosby, General Manager.
French Cleansers, Fancy Dyers, Fine Launderers.

PRINCIPAL OFFICES:
17 Temple Place, Boston,
470 Fifth Avenue, New York.
Established 70 years.
Largest in America.
Bundles called for and delivered.
Telephones in all offices.

Save half your money
do not throw it away in half-smoked cigars! You will find that 50% of your cigar money is thrown away every day if you recall how few cigars you really have time to smoke "up."

BETWEEN THE ACTS
Little Cigars
are pure—clean—all good tobacco, and are in every way a very satisfactory short smoke. While you are listening to the music to-night, try a 10-cent box. The waiter will get them for you as they are for sale here. You will enjoy them!

DRINK VAN NOSTRAND'S BOSTON CLUB LAGER
SOLD AT THESE CONCERTS

NORFOLK CABINET

LAGER BEER
A Particularly Fine Lager for Family Use and Clubs.
Bottled in the most careful manner at our own bottling department, and sold by the N. R. Pierce Co. and all other leading grocers in New England.
Other Brands in Bottles:
"Norfolk India Pale Stock Ale."
"Norfolk Extra Golden Ale" (blue label).
"Norfolk Standard Lager."
Our "Cabinet" and "Bismarck Braeu" are the most popular refreshments at these concerts.

HABICH & CO.
H. W. HABICH,   Telephone, 56 Roxbury
EDWARD BUHL.   or 1192 Boston.

ESTABROOK & EATON'S MARGUERITE PERFECTOS, 10c. EACH,
CONCHAS, 10c., 3 FOR 25c., SOLD AT THE "POPS."

THE ICE-CREAM SERVED AT THESE CONCERTS IS FURNISHED BY WEBER, 25 Temple Place and 33 West Street.

MUSIC HALL PROMENADE PROGRAMME.

PUBLISHED EVERY EVENING DURING THE SUMMER SEASON.

NOTICE TO ADVERTISERS.

The advertising columns in the Programme are controlled SOLELY by F. R. Comee, Boston Music Hall Box Office, to whom all communications should be addressed.

The United States Hotel,

SARATOGA SPRINGS, N.Y.

Under a continuous management for 25 years.

Without a peer in its appointments, service, and liberal management.

The largest structure of its kind in the world.

Built entirely of brick.

The Hotel and court cover over seven acres.

For further information, rates, etc., etc., address

GAGE & PERRY,
Proprietors,
UNITED STATES HOTEL,
Saratoga Springs, N.Y.

Colonial Beer...

The Beer that's Brewed in Glass.

PURE, CLEAN, PALATABLE.

Order a Bottle.

SOUTHER BREWING CO.,
919 Parker Street,
Roxbury, Mass.

All The **IMPORTED CIGARS**

Sold At These Concerts Are Supplied By The

S. S. PIERCE COMPANY.

The MONOPOLE CIGARETTES,

"CASINO GOLD TIPS,"

— AND —

"PRINCESS LILLIAN" (Turkish).

SOLD AT THESE CONCERTS.

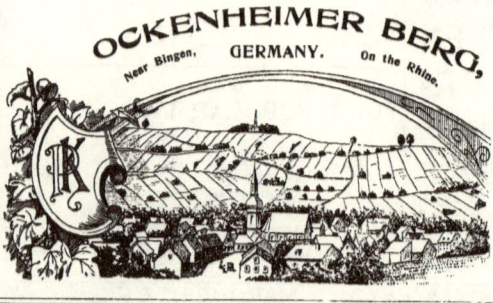

OCKENHEIMER BERG, Near Bingen, GERMANY. On the Rhine.

PHILIP KRIM'S OWN IMPORTATION OF **Rhine Wines,** FOR 30 YEARS AT **163 Shawmut Avenue.**

OUR WINES SOLD AT THESE CONCERTS.

HERRICK, COPLEY SQUARE, Telephones 608 and 950 (Back Bay), CHOICE TABLES for Music Hall "Pops."

GREAT WESTERN CHAMPAGNE

———A natural, genuine champagne, of the finest quality produced in America.

Sold by Wine Merchants, Grocers, and Druggists.

TUESDAY, MAY 9.

PROGRAMME.

1. MARCH, "Under the Double Eagle" . . . Wagner
2. OVERTURE, "Light Cavalry" . . . . Suppé
3. WALTZ, "Snowballs" . . . . . Ziehrer
4. PEARLS FROM THE OPERAS OF . . Meyerbeer

5. MARCH from "El Capitan" . . . . Sousa
6. WALTZ, "Emperor" . . . . . . Strauss
7. BOSNIAN SONG AND KOLO (National Dance) . Komzak
(First Time.)
The audience is respectfully requested to preserve silence during the performance of this number.
8. FINALE from Act I, "Lohengrin" . . . Wagner

9. TWO SPANISH DANCES . . . . Moszkowski
10. LARGO . . . . Handel
    Violin Solo, Mr. K. ONDRICEK.
11. WALTZ, "Jolly Fellows" . . . . . Vollstedt
12. TEUFELSMARSCH . . . . . . Suppé

Handsomest Dining Hotel in New England.

THE HAYWARD

20 Private Dining-rooms.

Beer and Ale drawn direct from wood in THE DUTCH TAP.

SMITH & KERRISSEY, Proprietors.

"M. S." GINGER ALE.

An epicurean beverage, made with Myles Standish Spring Water and compounded with scrupulous care from the highest grade materials.

To be had at the Promenade Concerts.

L. BOYER'S SONS,
Proprietors,
No. 27 Devonshire St., Boston.

MAIN OFFICE.
No. 90 Wall St., New York.

"AMERICA'S FINEST PRODUCT."

Bartholomay's "APOLLO"

LAGER BEER IN BOTTLES.

Sold at these Concerts.

ALBRECHT & KOELLNER,
SOLE AGENTS,
Telephone, Boston 1751.   295-305 A Street.

Also Agents for the "Crystal Rock" Mineral Water.

PURE BEER

Harvard

BREW. CO'S $1000.00

PURE BEER

Sold at these Concerts
IN BOTTLES ONLY
20¢ PER BOTTLE.

TABLE LINEN USED AT THESE CONCERTS THE L. K. HUSTED LAUNDERING COMPANY. 27 and 29 BROADWAY, CHELSEA, MASS.

Inglenook Vineyard.

The only California Wines sold at these Concerts.

THE CODMAN & HALL CO.,
Opposite the South Union Station.

Sole Agents for New England.

IND. COOPE & CO.'S English Ale.

THE SECOND LARGEST BREWERY IN ENGLAND.

Brewers of the finest *light quality* ale. Very highly endorsed by the medical profession. : : : : :

THE CODMAN & HALL CO.,
Opposite South Union Station.

Sole Agents for the United States.

Instruct your waiter to bring a bottle of

Pfaff's "Monogram" Lager.

If you will do this, it will not be necessary for us to expatiate upon the good qualities of our production.
YOU CAN JUDGE FOR YOURSELF.

H. & J. PFAFF BREWING COMPANY,
Telephone 2608.   16 ARCH STREET, BOSTON.

They cannot sell you here
Canadian Club Whisky,
Ruinart Champagne,
Royal Liqueur Scotch,
Carstair's Philadelphia Rye,
Fort Hill Bourbon,
Alhambra Sherry,
All of which you will find
of excellent quality;

But you can get

Kaiser Water,

the most refreshing of all
table waters.

*Chateau d' Arsac Claret,
N. Johnston & Sons' Medoc,*
and
California Inglenook Clarets.

SUPPLIED BY

CODMAN & HALL
COMPANY,
WINE MERCHANTS,
Opposite New South
Station.

WEDNESDAY, MAY 10.

PROGRAMME.

1. PERSIAN MARCH . . . Strauss
2. OVERTURE, " Merry Wives of Windsor " Nicolai
3. WALTZ, " Nachtschwärmer " . Zichrer
   (First Time.)
4. SELECTION from " The Serenade " Victor Herbert

---

5. WALTZ, "Du und Du," from "The Bat" . Strauss
6. EN RÊVE . . . Gabriel Marie
   (First Time.)
   The audience is respectfully requested to preserve silence during the performance of this number.
7. TWO MOVEMENTS from "Feramors" . Rubinstein
8. OVERTURE to " The Mastersingers " Wagner

---

9. GAVOTTE for String Orchestra Bach
10. SELECTION from " Erminie " Jakobowsky
11. WALTZ, " España " . Waldteufel
12. MARCH, " Vienna Dude " Wagner

THE WILSON, AMERICA'S PUREST
Mineral Spring Water,

Is used in making our celebrated Belfast Ginger Ale, Champagne Kola, Lemon Soda, Club Soda, Vichy, etc. Hotels and Families supplied. Try a sample order of these goods, and be convinced of their superiority, purity, and medicinal qualities..........

All of our beverages bottled at the spring. We ship only in glass, and all bottles and demijohns are sterilized before being filled..........

Wilson Spring and Hotel Co.,
Tel., 3129 Boston. | 45 ARCH STREET.

"THE RECOGNIZED FAVORITE OF ALL BEERS."
Schlitz
THE BEER THAT MADE MILWAUKEE FAMOUS.
HIGHEST AWARD FOR PURITY.
Sold at these Concerts. JOS. GAHM & CO., N.E. AGENTS, 125-127 PURCHASE ST.

THE ONLY BEER ON DRAUGHT AT THESE CONCERTS.
"the beer that's brewed"
SOLD AT THESE CONCERTS
ROCHESTER BREWING CO'S
NOTED THE WORLD OVER FOR ITS PURITY.
FAMOUS BOTTLED BEER
HOME OFFICE & BREWERY ROCHESTER, N.Y.
295-305 LAND BRANCH
A STREET BOSTON
free delivery in city and Suburbs
RIENZI, PREMIER, BOHEMIAN, BAVARIAN, STANDARD.

THE FALL RIVER LINE

OCCUPYING THE
LONG ISLAND SOUND ROUTE
BETWEEN

Boston and New York

Has the finest quintette of great steamboats that the world has ever seen. The

Priscilla, Puritan, Plymouth, Pilgrim, and Providence

Are the largest, best equipped, safest, and handsomest steamboats ever constructed. This route is one of the most attractive and naturally beautiful traversed by any transportation agency in the world.

Trips of the Fall River Line are made throughout the year.

Each steamboat has its own orchestra, and the service on each member of the fleet is maintained at the highest possible standard.

Tickets via this route are on sale at all of the principal Ticket Offices in the United States.

From BOSTON. Trains, connecting with steamers at Fall River in 80 minutes, leave Park Square Station, New York, New Haven & Hartford Railroad (Old Colony System), daily at 6 p.m.

From NEW YORK. Steamers leave Pier 19, North River, foot of Warren Street, daily at 5.30 p.m.

S. A. GARDNER, Superintendent, NEW YORK.
GEO. L. CONNOR, Passenger Traffic Manager, NEW HAVEN, CONN.
O. H. TAYLOR, General Passenger Agent, NEW YORK CITY.

HOTEL LANGWOOD,

Middlesex Fells Reservation.

P.O. Address, Melrose, Mass.   Wyoming Station, B. & M. R. R.

Twenty minutes by rail from Boston. Sixty trains daily. Hotel coaches meet trains each way. Four hundred feet above sea level. Beautiful rides, drives, and walks. Golf links, tennis courts, and ball grounds.

OPENS ABOUT MAY 20.

For plans and prices address:

F. W. GASKILL, Manager.

BOSTON OFFICE:
Hemenway Building, 10 Tremont Street, Room 29.

Third Season.

3 Ideal Outings

Personally conducted by
F. R. COMEE, Music Hall, Boston.

S.S. "Howard." Boston to Norfolk, 522 miles. Norfolk to Baltimore, 200 miles.

	1.	2.	3.
Boston	Leave July 2	July 15	August 19
	Arrive July 12	July 31	September 4

S.S. "Toronto." Toronto to Montreal, through the "Thousand Islands" and the "Rapids," 376 miles.

No. 1. Ten days. Saratoga, Lake George, 2,136 miles from Buffalo to Duluth, and return on the steamer "North-Land" through the Great Lakes, Erie, Huron, St. Clair, and Superior.

Nos. 2 and 3. Sixteen days. Exactly alike. 700 miles' ocean sail to Norfolk and Baltimore. Over Alleghany Mountains and a day in Chicago. Up Lake Michigan and three days at Mackinac Island. 1,560 miles on steamer "North-West" to Duluth and return to Buffalo through the Great Lakes. Niagara Falls to Toronto. Across Lake Ontario, through the Thousand Islands, and down the St. Lawrence River to Montreal and Boston.

SEND FOR CIRCULARS.

S.S. "Manitou." Chicago to Mackinac Island, across Lake Michigan, 350 miles.

"North-West." Mackinac Island to Duluth and return to Buffalo, 1,555 miles.

Ask for....

ALLSOPP'S INDIA PALE ALE
TRADE MARK

It has been known for over 130 years as the best. Bottled at the brewery, Burton-on-Trent, England, under the personal supervision of the Messrs. Allsopp.

Sold at these concerts.

If you want the best, ask for

Allsopp's

"The Red Hand Brand."

THURSDAY, MAY 11.

PROGRAMME.

1. MARCH, "Princess Ninetta" . . . . Strauss
2. OVERTURE, "Le roi l'a dit" . . . . Delibes
3. WALTZ, "Arlequin en Voyage" . . . . Zach
4. SELECTION from "Aïda" . . . . Verdi

5. NARCISSUS . . . . Nevin
6. WALTZ, "Landeskinder" . . . . E. Strauss
7. INTRODUCTION to "Lohengrin" . . . . Wagner
8. POLKA, "Tyrolean" . . . . Zeller

9. ANDANTE, for String Orchestra . . . Tschaikowsky
    The audience is respectfully requested to preserve silence during the performance of this number.
10. WALTZ, "Meerleuchten" . . . . Ziehrer
11. PIZZICATI, from "Sylvia" . . . . Delibes
12. MARCH from "The Serenade" . . . . V. Herbert

The *only* Lithia Water sold at these concerts.

Hygeia Lithia Water

Sparkling and Still.

By its use you will avoid the germs of disease which natural MINERAL WATERS are liable to contain.

For Sale at these concerts and by

S. S. PIERCE CO.

The purity and keeping quality of the Tannhaeuser Export under all changes of temperature, its uniform excellence being guaranteed, together with its nutritious properties, make it the most pleasant, delicious, and convenient beverage for home consumption.
Put up in corked bottles, and packed in casks of 10 dozen white flint pints, and 6 dozen amber quarts.

Highest Awards wherever exhibited.

FOR SALE AT THESE CONCERTS.

FAMOUS **TANNHAEUSER** EXPORT BEER

The finest Light Beer Extant.   Brewery Bottling.   Favorite of Connoisseurs.

Pure,   Palatable,   Perfect.

B. & E. Philadelphia Ale on Draught.
FOR SALE AT THESE CONCERTS.

The BERGNER & ENGEL BREWING CO.'S N.E. Depot,
508 and 510 Atlantic Avenue, Boston.
Telephone 3805.   SOL. BACHARACH, Manager.

M. Steinert & Sons Co.,

STEINERT HALL BUILDING,

No. 162 Boylston Street, corner Carver, Boston.

STEINWAY & SONS,

HARDMAN, GABLER,
EMERSON, HOLMSTROM,
SINGER,

PIANOS.

The Æolian, Aeriol, Orchestrelle, and Pianola,

AND THE

STEINERTONE.

THE ÆOLIAN

AND

THE PIANOLA

FOR SUMMER HOMES.

At this season of the year we receive many orders for these instruments for Summer Residences, and therefore beg to call attention to our extensive assortment now on display, especially suited for this purpose.

The ÆOLIAN meets the requirements of country homes, furnishing, as it does, music suitable for every occasion. It practically takes the place of an orchestra — music for dancing — orchestral concerts, — in short, music of every style and description is always available.

The PIANOLA will appeal to many on account of the very little space it occupies. It will play any kind of a piano, and can also be used upon a rented piano without the slightest injury. For the above reasons it is bound to be very popular for small cottages.

We are glad to be able to announce that we can furnish PIANOLAS with no more than a week's delay, and, at times, the day the order is given.

Persons not familiar with these instruments are cordially invited to call at our warerooms and hear them, or a descriptive catalogue will be mailed free upon application.

M. STEINERT & SONS CO.,
Steinert Hall, 162 Boylston Street, Boston.

ANHEUSER-BUSCH BREWING ASS'N,

ST. LOUIS, MO., U.S.A.

BREWERS OF HIGH=GRADE BEERS EXCLUSIVELY.

Black and Tan.		Faust.
Michelob.		Pale Lager.
Muenchener.		Anheuser Standard.

Served at the Music Hall Concerts.

Also at all first-class hotels, clubs, and bars, and on all Pullman and Wagner cars and ocean and lake steamers.

JACOB WIRTH, Wholesale Dealer, Boston, Mass.

THE MUSIC HALL PROMENADE CONCERTS

PUBLISHED BY C. A. ELLIS, MUSIC HALL.

BOSTON, TUESDAY, MAY 9, 1899.

SUMMER SEASON. Vol. XIV. No. 2.

YOU CAN
Have your last season's outfit dyed or cleansed and refinished so it will look like new, by our French process. Why discard soiled clothing when it can be overhauled and worn as second best? You can

RELY ON
Our methods of cleansing, and need not hesitate to trust us with articles of the most delicate textures. We dye or cleanse and refinish PROPERLY, *all* materials of household use and clothing of all kinds.

LEWANDO'S
W. L. Crosby, General Manager.
French Cleansers, Fancy Dyers, Fine Launderers.
PRINCIPAL OFFICES:
17 Temple Place, Boston.
470 Fifth Avenue, New York.
Largest in America.
Established 70 years.
Bundles called for and delivered.
Telephones in all offices.

In no other way
are men as wasteful and extravagant as in cigar smoking — because cigars are thrown away half smoked half the time.

BETWEEN THE ACTS
Little Cigars
are just right for all short smokes. They light right, they burn right, and taste right. Have you ever seen them? At all stores: 10 for 10 cts., or, as they are for sale here, you can try them to-night. Tell the waiter to bring you a 10-cent box of "Between the Acts." They will add to your enjoyment of this concert.

THE MUSIC HALL :: Promenade Concerts

FOURTEENTH SEASON.

C. A. ELLIS, Manager.   F. R. COMEE, Assistant Manager.

Mr. MAX ZACH, Conductor.

TUESDAY, MAY 9.

PROGRAMME.

1. MARCH, "Under the Double Eagle" . . . Wagner
2. OVERTURE, "Light Cavalry" . . . . Suppé
3. WALTZ, "Snowballs" . . . . . Ziehrer
4. PEARLS FROM THE OPERAS OF . . . Meyerbeer
5. MARCH from "El Capitan" . . . . Sousa
6. WALTZ, "Emperor" . . . . . Strauss
7. BOSNIAN SONG AND KOLO (National Dance) . Komzak
   (First Time.)
   The audience is respectfully requested to preserve silence during the performance of this number.
8. FINALE from Act I., "Lohengrin" . . . Wagner
9. TWO SPANISH DANCES . . . . Moszkowski
10. LARGO . . . . Händel
    Violin Solo, Mr. K. ONDRICEK.
11. WALTZ, "Jolly Fellows" . . . . Vollstedt
12. TEUFELSMARSCH . . . . . Suppé

Now the rage of the LONDON Concerts and Drawing-rooms:

YOU AND I, by Liza Lehmann, . . . 60c.
KING CHARLES, by M. V. White, . . 60c.
LIKE VIOLETS PALE, by F. Allitsen, . . 60c.
WHEN THE WORLD IS FAIR, by F. H. Cowen, 60c.
QUEEN OF MY LIFE, by E. T. Lloyd, . . 60c.

BOOSEY & CO.,
9 East 17th Street,   New York.

DRINK VAN NOSTRAND'S BOSTON CLUB LAGER
SOLD AT THESE CONCERTS

NORFOLK CABINET

LAGER BEER
A Particularly Fine Lager for Family Use and Clubs.
Bottled in the most careful manner at our own bottling department, and sold by the S. S. Pierce Co. and all other leading grocers in New England.

Other Brands in Bottles:
"Norfolk India Pale Stock Ale"
"Norfolk Extra Golden Ale" (blue label).
"Norfolk Standard Lager"
Our "Cabinet" and "Bismarck Brau" are the most popular refreshments at these concerts.

HABICH & CO.
H. W. HABICH,   Telephone, 56 Roxbury
EDWARD BUHL,   or 1134 Boston.

ESTABROOK & EATON'S MARGUERITE   PERFECTOS, 10c. EACH. CONCHAS, 10c., 3 FOR 25c.   SOLD AT THE "POPS."

THE ICE-CREAM SERVED AT THESE CONCERTS IS FURNISHED BY WEBER, 25 Temple Place and 33 West Street.

MUSIC HALL PROMENADE PROGRAMME.
PUBLISHED EVERY EVENING DURING THE SUMMER SEASON.

NOTICE TO ADVERTISERS.
The advertising columns in the Programme are controlled SOLELY by F. R. Comee, Boston Music Hall Box Office, to whom all communications should be addressed.

The United States Hotel,
SARATOGA SPRINGS, N.Y.

Under a continuous management for 25 years.

Without a peer in its appointments, service, and liberal management.

The largest structure of its kind in the world.

Built entirely of brick.

The Hotel and court cover over seven acres.

For further information, rates, etc., etc., address

GAGE & PERRY,
Proprietors,
UNITED STATES HOTEL,
Saratoga Springs, N.Y.

Colonial Beer...

The Beer that's Brewed in Glass.

PURE, CLEAN, PALATABLE.

Order a Bottle.

SOUTHER BREWING CO.,
919 Parker Street,
Roxbury, Mass.

VEUVE CHAFFARD

PURE OLIVE OIL.
IN HONEST BOTTLES.

The MONOPOLE CIGARETTES,
"CASINO GOLD TIPS,"
— AND —
"PRINCESS LILLIAN" (Turkish).

SOLD AT THESE CONCERTS.

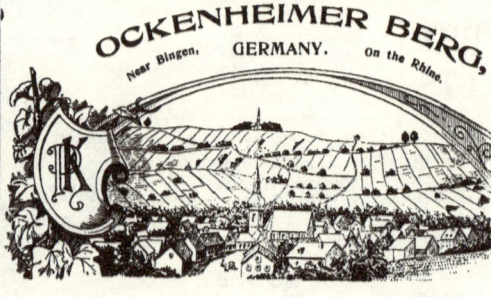

OCKENHEIMER BERG, Near Bingen, GERMANY. On the Rhine.

PHILIP KRIM'S
OWN IMPORTATION OF
Rhine Wines.
FOR 30 YEARS
AT
163 Shawmut Avenue.
OUR WINES SOLD AT THESE CONCERTS.

HERRICK, COPLEY SQUARE, Telephones 608 and 950 (Back Bay), CHOICE TABLES for Music Hall "Pops

SHINNECOCK

The Perfection of

SCOTCH WHISKY.

Sold by
S. S. PIERCE COMPANY.

WEDNESDAY, MAY 10.

PROGRAMME.

1. PERSIAN MARCH . . . . . Strauss
2. OVERTURE, "Merry Wives of Windsor" . Nicolai
3. WALTZ, "Nachtschwärmer" . . . Ziehrer
   (First Time.)
4. SELECTION from "The Serenade" . Victor Herbert

5. WALTZ, "Du und Du," from "The Bat" . . Strauss
6. EN RÊVE . . . . . Gabriel Marie
   (First Time.)
   The audience is respectfully requested to preserve silence during the performance of this number.
7. TWO MOVEMENTS from "Feramora" . Rubinstein
8. OVERTURE to "The Mastersingers" . . Wagner

9. GAVOTTE for String Orchestra . . Bach
10. SELECTION from "Erminie" . . Jakobowsky
11. WALTZ, "España" . . . Waldteufel
12. MARCH, "Vienna Dude" . . . Wagner

Handsomest Dining Hotel in New England.

THE HAYWARD

20 Private Dining-rooms.

Beer and Ale drawn direct from wood in THE DUTCH TAP.

SMITH & KERRISSEY, Proprietors.

"M. S." GINGER ALE.

An epicurean beverage, made with Myles Standish Spring Water and compounded with scrupulous care from the highest grade materials.

To be had at the Promenade Concerts.

L. BOYER'S SONS,
Proprietors,
No. 27 Devonshire St., Boston.

MAIN OFFICE.
No. 90 Wall St., New York.

"AMERICA'S FINEST PRODUCT."

Bartholomay's "APOLLO"

LAGER BEER IN BOTTLES.

Sold at these Concerts.

ALBRECHT & KOELLNER,
SOLE AGENTS,
Telephone, Boston 1751.   295-305 A Street.

Also Agents for the "Crystal Rock" Mineral Water.

PURE BEER

Harvard BREW. CO'S **$1000.00**

PURE BEER

Sold at these Concerts
IN BOTTLES ONLY
20¢ PER BOTTLE.

Inglenook Vineyard.

The only California Wines sold at these Concerts.

❧❧

THE CODMAN & HALL CO.,
Opposite the South Union Station.

Sole Agents for New England.

IND. COOPE & CO.'S English Ale.

THE SECOND LARGEST BREWERY IN ENGLAND.

Brewers of the finest *light quality* ale. Very highly endorsed by the medical profession. : : : :

❧❧

THE CODMAN & HALL CO.,
Opposite South Union Station.

Sole Agents for the United States.

DRINK only the

PUREST

WHISKY

If you want pur and richness flavor, try o only genui and original

OLD KENTUCK TAYLOR,

Eight years old, o own distillation a guaranteed pur Bottled and shipp direct from o warehouses by u None genuine wit out our signatu on both labels. B ware of imitatio For consumptio indigestion, and a ailments requiri stimulants, OL KENTUCKY TA LOR has n superior.

Sold by all firs class Druggist grocers, and liqu dealers.

Wright & Taylor
Distillers,
Fine Kentucky
Whiskies,
Louisville, Ky.

Hirshfield & Co.
New England
Agents,
31 Doane Street,
Boston.

Instruct your waiter to bring a bottle of

Pfaff's "Monogram" Lager.

If you will do this, it will not be necessary for us to expatiate upon the good qualities of our production.
YOU CAN JUDGE FOR YOURSELF.

H. & J. PFAFF BREWING COMPANY,
Telephone 2608.   16 ARCH STREET, BOSTON.

They cannot sell you here
Canadian Club Whisky,
Ruinart Champagne,
Royal Liqueur Scotch,
Carstair's Philadelphia Rye,
Fort Hill Bourbon,
Alhambra Sherry,
All of which you will find
of excellent quality;

But you can get

Kaiser Water,

the most refreshing of all
table waters.

*Chateau d'Arsac Claret,
N. Johnston & Sons' Medoc,*
and
California Inglenook Clarets.

SUPPLIED BY

CODMAN & HALL COMPANY,

WINE MERCHANTS,

Opposite New South Station.

THURSDAY, MAY 11.

PROGRAMME.

1. MARCH, "Princess Ninetta" — Strauss
2. OVERTURE, "Le roi l'a dit" — Delibes
3. WALTZ, "Arlequin en Voyage" — Zach
4. SELECTION from "Aida" — Verdi
5. NARCISSUS — Nevin
6. WALTZ, "Landeskinder" — E. Strauss
7. INTRODUCTION to "Lohengrin" — Wagner
8. POLKA, "Tyrolean" — Zeller
9. ANDANTE for String Orchestra — Tschaikowsky
    The audience is respectfully requested to preserve silence during the performance of this number.
10. WALTZ, "Meerleuchten" — Ziehrer
11. PIZZICATI, from "Sylvia" — Delibes
12. MARCH from "The Serenade" — V. Herbert

THE WILSON,
AMERICA'S PUREST
Mineral Spring Water,

Is used
in making
our celebrated
**Belfast
Ginger Ale,
Champagne
Kola,**
Lemon Soda, Club Soda,
Vichy, etc. Hotels and Families supplied. Try a sample order of these goods, and be convinced of their superiority, purity, and medicinal qualities.........

All of our beverages bottled at the spring. We ship only in glass, and all bottles and demijohns are sterilized before being filled.........

Wilson Spring and Hotel Co.,
Tel., 3129 Boston. | 45 ARCH STREET.

"THE RECOGNIZED FAVORITE OF ALL BEERS."

Schlitz
THE BEER THAT MADE MILWAUKEE FAMOUS.
HIGHEST AWARD FOR PURITY.
Sold at these Concerts. JOS. GAHM & CO., N.E. AGENTS. 125-127 PURCHASE ST.

THE ONLY BEER ON DRAUGHT AT THESE CONCERTS.
"the beer that's brewed"

Rochester Brewing Co's.
SOLD AT THESE CONCERTS
HOME OFFICE & BREWERY
ROCHESTER, N.Y.
NEW ENGLAND BRANCH
295-305 A STREET BOSTON
Free delivery in city and suburbs

FAMOUS BOTTLED BEER
RIENZI, PREMIER, BOHEMIAN, BAVARIAN, STANDARD.

THE FALL RIVER LINE

OCCUPYING THE
LONG ISLAND SOUND ROUTE
BETWEEN

Boston and New York

Has the finest quintette of great steamboats that the world has ever seen. The

Priscilla, Puritan, Plymouth, Pilgrim, and Providence

Are the largest, best equipped, safest, and handsomest steamboats ever constructed. This route is one of the most attractive and naturally beautiful traversed by any transportation agency in the world. Trips of the Fall River Line are made throughout the year. Each steamboat has its own orchestra, and the service on each member of the fleet is maintained at the highest possible standard.

Tickets via this route are on sale at all of the principal Ticket Offices in the United States.

From BOSTON. Trains connecting with steamers at Fall River in 80 minutes, leave Park Square Station, New York and New Haven & Hartford Railroad (Old Colony System), daily at 6 p.m.

From NEW YORK. Steamers leave Pier 19, North River, foot of Warren Street, daily at 5.30 p.m.

S. A. GARDNER,	GEO. L. CONNOR,	O. H. TAYLOR,
Superintendent,	Passenger Traffic Manager,	General Passenger Agent,
NEW YORK.	NEW HAVEN, CONN.	NEW YORK CITY.

HOTEL LANGWOOD,

Middlesex Fells Reservation.

P.O. Address, Melrose, Mass.   Wyoming Station, B. & M. R.R.

Twenty minutes by rail from Boston. Sixty trains daily. Hotel coaches meet trains each way. Four hundred feet above sea level. Beautiful rides, drives, and walks. Golf links, tennis courts, and ball grounds.

OPENS ABOUT MAY 20.

For plans and prices address:

F. W. GASKILL, Manager.

BOSTON OFFICE:
Hemenway Building, 10 Tremont Street, Room 29.

S.S. "Howard." Boston to Norfolk, 522 miles. Norfolk to Baltimore, 200 miles.

	1.	2.	3.
Boston	Leave July 2	July 16	August 13
	Arrive July 12	July 31	September 4

S.S. "Toronto." Toronto to Montreal, through the "Thousand Islands" and the "Rapids," 376 miles.

Third Season.

3 Ideal Outings

Personally conducted by F. R. COMEE, Music Hall, Boston.

No. 1. Ten days. Saratoga, Lake George. 2,130 miles from Buffalo to Duluth, and return on the steamer "North-Land" through the Great Lakes, Erie, Huron, St. Clair, and Superior.

Nos. 2 and 3. Sixteen days. Exactly alike. 700 miles' ocean sail to Norfolk and Baltimore. Over Alleghany Mountains and a day in Chicago. Up Lake Michigan and three days at Mackinac Island. 1,846 miles on steamer "North-West" to Duluth and return to Buffalo through the Great Lakes. Niagara Falls to Toronto. Across Lake Ontario, through the Thousand Islands, and down the St. Lawrence River to Montreal and Boston.

SEND FOR CIRCULARS.

S.S. "Manitou." Chicago to Mackinac Island, across Lake Michigan, 350 miles.

"North-West." Mackinac Island to Duluth and return to Buffalo, 1,555 miles.

Ask for ....

ALLSOPP'S
INDIA PALE ALE
TRADE MARK

It has been known for over 130 years as the best. Bottled at the brewery, Burton-on-Trent, England, under the personal supervision of the Messrs. Allsopp.

Sold at these concerts.

If you want the best, ask for

Allsopp's
"The Red Hand Brand."

FRIDAY, MAY 12.

PROGRAMME.

1. MARCH, "Trial Kiss" . . . . Millöcker
2. OVERTURE, "Black Domino" . . . . . . Auber
3. WALTZ, "Freut euch des Lebens" . . . . Strauss
4. SELECTION from "The Fortune-teller" . . V. Herbert
    (First Time.)

5. TWO ENTR'ACTES from "Carmen" . . . . Bizet
6. INTRODUCTION to Act III., "Lohengrin" . Wagner
7. SELECTION from "Cavalleria Rusticana" . Mascagni
8. GALOP CHROMATIQUE . . . . Liszt

9. POTPOURRI, "The Brigands" . . . . . . Offenbach
10. RONDE D'AMOUR . . . . Westerhout
    The audience is respectfully requested to preserve silence during the performance of this number.
11. WALTZ, "Pomone" . . . . Waldteufel
12. MARCH, "Boccaccio" . . . . Suppé

The *only* Lithia Water sold at these concerts.

Hygeia Lithia Water

Sparkling and Still.

By its use you will avoid the germs of disease which natural MINERAL WATERS are liable to contain.

For Sale at these concerts and by

S. S. PIERCE CO.

The purity and keeping quality of the Tannhaeuser Export under all changes of temperature, its uniform excellence being guaranteed, together with its nutritious properties, make it the most pleasant, delicious, and convenient beverage for home consumption.
Put up in corked bottles, and packed in casks of 10 dozen white flint pints, and 6 dozen amber quarts.

Highest Awards wherever exhibited.

FOR SALE AT THESE CONCERTS.
FAMOUS TANNHAEUSER EXPORT BEER
The finest Light Beer Extant. Brewery Bottling. Favorite of Connoisseurs.

Pure, Palatable, Perfect.
B. & E. Philadelphia Ale on Draught.
FOR SALE AT THESE CONCERTS.

The BERGNER & ENGEL BREWING CO.'S N.E. Depot,
508 and 510 Atlantic Avenue, Boston.
Telephone 3805.   **SOL. BACHARACH, Manager.**

M. Steinert & Sons Co., STEINERT HALL BUILDING, No. 162 Boylston Street, corner Carver, Boston. **STEINWAY & SONS,** HARDMAN, GABLER, EMERSON, HOLMSTROM, SINGER, **PIANOS.** The Æolian, Aeriol, Orchestrelle, and Pianola, AND THE **STEINERTONE.**	**THE ÆOLIAN** AND **THE PIANOLA** **FOR SUMMER HOMES.** At this season of the year we receive many orders for these instruments for Summer Residences, and therefore beg to call attention to our extensive assortment now on display, especially suited for this purpose. The ÆOLIAN meets the requirements of country homes, furnishing, as it does, music suitable for every occasion. It practically takes the place of an orchestra — music for dancing — orchestral concerts,— in short, music of every style and description is always available. The PIANOLA will appeal to many on account of the very little space it occupies. It will play any kind of a piano, and can also be used upon a rented piano without the slightest injury. For the above reasons it is bound to be very popular for small cottages. We are glad to be able to announce that we can furnish PIANOLAS with no more than a week's delay, and, at times, the day the order is given. Persons not familiar with these instruments are cordially invited to call at our warerooms and hear them, or a descriptive catalogue will be mailed free upon application. **M. STEINERT & SONS CO.,** Steinert Hall, 162 Boylston Street, Boston.

ANHEUSER-BUSCH BREWING ASS'N,

ST. LOUIS, MO., U.S.A.

BREWERS OF HIGH-GRADE BEERS EXCLUSIVELY.

Black and Tan.	Faust.
Michelob.	Pale Lager.
Muenchener.	Anheuser Standard.

Served at the Music Hall Concerts.

Also at all first-class hotels, clubs, and bars, and on all Pullman and Wagner cars and ocean and lake steamers.

JACOB WIRTH,   **Wholesale Dealer,**   **Boston, Mass.**

SMOKE THE POPULAR "BARRISTER" CIGARS AT THE POPULAR CONCERTS.
SMOKE "LA CELESTINA," THE BEST ALL-HAVANA CIGAR. DANIEL FRANK & CO.

THE MUSIC HALL
PROMENADE CONCERTS

PUBLISHED BY
C. A. ELLIS,
MUSIC HALL.

BOSTON, WEDNESDAY, MAY 10, 1899.

SUMMER SEASON.
Vol. XIV. No. 3.

YOU CAN

Have your last season's outfit dyed or cleansed and refinishd so it will look like new, by our French process. Why discard soiled clothing when it can be overhauled and worn as second best? You can

RELY ON

Our methods of cleansing, and need not hesitate to trust us with articles of the most delicate textures.
We dye or cleanse and refinish PROPERLY, *all* materials, of household use and clothing of all kinds.

LEWANDO'S

W. L. Crosby, General Manager.
French Cleansers, Fancy Dyers, Fine Launderers.

PRINCIPAL OFFICES:
17 Temple Place, Boston.
479 Fifth Avenue, New York.
Established 70 years.
Largest in America.
Bundles called for and delivered.
Telephones in all offices.

Knowledge differs from Experience.

You may know "all about"

BETWEEN THE ACTS
Little Cigars

but have you ever tried them yourself? Do you know how desirable they really are—how good they are—how economical they are—how convenient they are—how satisfactory they are? You can know—once for all—by having the waiter bring you a 10 cent box of ten—to smoke now—to-night—while you are enjoying this concert. They are for sale here.

THE MUSIC HALL... Promenade Concerts
FOURTEENTH SEASON.

C. A. ELLIS, Manager.   F. R. COMEE, Assistant Manager.
Mr. MAX ZACH, Conductor.

WEDNESDAY, MAY 10.

PROGRAMME.

1. PERSIAN MARCH . . . . . . Strauss
2. OVERTURE, " Merry Wives of Windsor " . Nicolai
3. WALTZ, " Nachtschwärmer " . . . Ziehrer
   (First Time.)
4. SELECTION from " Wizard of the Nile " . Victor Herbert
5. WALTZ, " Du und Du," from " The Bat " . Strauss
6. EN RÊVE . . . . Gabriel Marie
   (First Time.)
   The audience is respectfully requested to preserve silence during the performance of this number.
7. TWO MOVEMENTS from " Feramors " . Rubinstein
8. OVERTURE to " The Mastersingers " . Wagner
9. GAVOTTE for String Orchestra . . Bach
10. SELECTION from " Erminie " . . Jakobowsky
11. WALTZ, " España " . . . . Waldteufel
12. MARCH, " Vienna Dude " . . . Wagner

HERE ARE A FEW NAMES FROM OUR LIST OF COMPOSERS:

ENGLISH.— Stephen Adams, F. H. Cowen, S. Liddle, C. V. Stanford, A. C. Mackenzie, R. H. Walthew, H. R. Shelley, Goring Thomas, Frances Alltsen, Maude V. White, Edward German, Mary Carmichael, Liza Lehmann, etc.

FRENCH.— C. Chaminade, Jane Vieu, L. Denza, P. Delmet, Bemberg, Guy d'Hardelot, De Leva, F. P. Tosti, etc.

ITALIAN.— F. P. Tosti, P. Mascagni, G. Puccini, G. Verdi, Don Lorenzo Perosi, etc.

THE MOST REPRESENTATIVE PUBLISHING HOUSE IN AMERICA.

BOOSEY & CO., 9 East 17th Street, New York.

BEST BEER BREWED

"OH BE JOLLY"

DRINK VAN NOSTRAND'S P.B. ALE

SOLD AT THESE CONCERTS

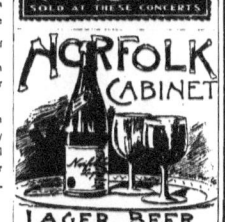

LAGER BEER

A Particularly Fine Lager for Family Use and Clubs.

Bottled in the most careful manner at our own bottling department, and sold by the S. S. Pierce Co. and all other leading grocers in New England.

Other Brands in Bottles:
" Norfolk India Pale Stock Ale."
" Norfolk Extra Golden Ale " (blue label).
" Norfolk Standard Lager "
Our " Cabinet " and " Bismarck Brau " are the most popular refreshments at these concerts.

HABICH & CO.

H. W. HABICH.   Telephone, 56 Roxbury
EDWARD BUHL.   or 1152 Boston.

ESTABROOK & EATON'S MARGUERITE PERFECTOS, 10c. EACH.
CONCHAS, 10c., 3 FOR 25c. **SOLD AT THE "POPS."**

THE ICE-CREAM SERVED AT THESE CONCERTS IS FURNISHED BY WEBER, 25 Temple Place and 33 West Street.

MUSIC HALL PROMENADE PROGRAMME.
PUBLISHED EVERY EVENING DURING THE SUMMER SEASON.

NOTICE TO ADVERTISERS.
The advertising columns in the Programme are controlled SOLELY by F. R. Comee, Boston Music Hall Box Office, to whom all communications should be addressed.

The United States Hotel,
SARATOGA SPRINGS, N.Y.

Under a continuous management for 25 years.

Without a peer in its appointments, service, and liberal management.

The largest structure of its kind in the world.

Built entirely of brick.

The Hotel and court cover over seven acres.

For further information, rates, etc., etc., address

GAGE & PERRY,
Proprietors,
UNITED STATES HOTEL,
Saratoga Springs, N.Y.

COLONIAL BEER
The Beer that's Brewed in Glass.

Colonial Beer...

PURE, CLEAN, PALATABLE.

Order a Bottle.

SOUTHER BREWING CO.,
919 Parker Street,
Roxbury, Mass.

All The IMPORTED CIGARS

Sold At These Concerts Are Supplied By The

S. S. PIERCE COMPANY.

The MONOPOLE CIGARETTES, "CASINO GOLD TIPS,"
— AND —
"PRINCESS LILLIAN" (Turkish).

SOLD AT THESE CONCERTS.

OCKENHEIMER BERG,
Near Bingen, GERMANY. On the Rhine.

PHILIP KRIM'S
OWN IMPORTATION OF
Rhine Wines,
FOR 30 YEARS AT
163 Shawmut Avenue.

OUR WINES SOLD AT THESE CONCERTS.

HERRICK, COPLEY SQUARE, Telephones 608 and 950 (Back Bay), CHOICE TABLES for Music Hall "Pops."

GREAT WESTERN CHAMPAGNE

———— A natural, genuine champagne, of the finest quality produced in America.

Sold by Wine Merchants, Grocers, and Druggists.

THURSDAY, MAY 11.

PROGRAMME.

1. MARCH, "Princess Ninetta" . . . Strauss
2. OVERTURE, "Le roi l'a dit" . . . Delibes
3. WALTZ, "Arlequin en Voyage" . . Zach
4. SELECTION from "Aïta" . . . Verdi

5. NARCISSUS . . . . . Nevin
6. WALTZ, "Landeskinder" . . . E. Strauss
7. INTRODUCTION to "Lohengrin" . Wagner
8. POLKA, "Tyrolean" . . . . Zeller

9. ANDANTE for String Orchestra . . Tschaikowsky
   The audience is respectfully requested to preserve silence during the performance of this number.
10. WALTZ, "Meerleuchten" . . . Ziehrer
11. PIZZICATI, from "Sylvia" . . . Delibes
12. MARCH from "The Serenade" . . V. Herbert

Handsomest Dining Hotel in New England.

THE HAYWARD

20 Private Dining-rooms.

Beer and Ale drawn direct from wood in THE DUTCH TAP.

SMITH & KERRISSEY, Proprietors.

"M. S." GINGER ALE.

An epicurean beverage, made with Myles Standish Spring Water and compounded with scrupulous care from the highest grade materials.

To be had at the Promenade Concerts.

L. BOYER'S SONS, Proprietors, No. 27 Devonshire St., Boston.

MAIN OFFICE. No. 90 Wall St., New York.

"AMERICA'S FINEST PRODUCT."

Bartholomay's "APOLLO"

LAGER BEER IN BOTTLES.

Sold at these Concerts.

ALBRECHT & KOELLNER, SOLE AGENTS,

Telephone, Boston 1751.   295-305 A Street.

Also Agents for the "Crystal Rock" Mineral Water.

PURE BEER

Harvard BREW. CO'S $1000.00

PURE BEER

Sold at these Concerts, IN BOTTLES ONLY 20¢ PER BOTTLE.

TABLE LINEN USED AT THESE CONCERTS LAUNDERED BY THE L. K. HUSTED LAUNDERING COMPANY, 27 and 29 BROADWAY, CHELSEA, MASS.

Inglenook Vineyard.

The only California Wines sold at these Concerts.

❧❧

THE CODMAN & HALL CO.,
Opposite the South Union Station.

Sole Agents for New England.

IND. COOPE & CO.'S English Ale.

THE SECOND LARGEST BREWERY IN ENGLAND.

Brewers of the finest *light quality* ale. Very highly endorsed by the medical profession. : : : : :

❧❧

THE CODMAN & HALL CO.,
Opposite South Union Station.

Sole Agents for the United States.

DRINK only the PURE WHISK

If you want pu and richness flavor, try only cenui and origina

OLD KENTUC TAYLOR,

Eight years old, own distillation guaranteed pu Bottled and ship direct from warehouses by None genuine wi out our signat on both labels. ware of imitatio For consumpti indigestion, and ailments requir stimulants, O L KENTUCKY TA LOR has superior.

Sold by all fir class druggi grocers, and liqu dealers.

Wright & Taylo Distillers, Fine Kentucky Whiskies. Louisville, Ky.

Hirshfield & Co New England Agents, 31 Doane Street Boston.

Instruct your waiter to bring a bottle of

Pfaff's "Monogram" Lager.

If you will do this, it will not be necessary for us to expatiate upon the good qualities of our production.
YOU CAN JUDGE FOR YOURSELF.

H. & J. PFAFF BREWING COMPANY,
Telephone 2608.   16 ARCH STREET, BOSTON.

FRIDAY, MAY 12.

PROGRAMME.

1. MARCH, "Trial Kiss" — Millöcker
2. OVERTURE, "Black Domino" — Auber
3. WALTZ, "Freut euch des Lebens" — Strauss
4. SELECTION from "The Fortune-teller" — V. Herbert
   (First Time.)
5. TWO ENTR'ACTES from "Carmen" — Bizet
6. INTRODUCTION to Act III., "Lohengrin" — Wagner
7. SELECTION from "Cavalleria Rusticana" — Mascagni
8. GALOP CHROMATIQUE — Liszt

9. POTPOURRI, "The Brigands" — Offenbach
10. RONDE D'AMOUR — Westerhout
    The audience is respectfully requested to preserve silence during the performance of this number.
11. WALTZ, "Pomone" — Waldteufel
12. MARCH, "Boccaccio" — Suppé

THE WILSON, AMERICA'S PUREST Mineral Spring Water,

Is used in making our celebrated **Belfast Ginger Ale, Champagne Kola,** Lemon Soda, Club Soda, Vichy, etc. Hotels and Families supplied. Try a sample order of these goods, and be convinced of their superiority, purity, and medicinal qualities.

All of our beverages bottled at the spring. We ship only in glass, and all bottles and demijohns are sterilized before being filled.

Wilson Spring and Hotel Co.,
al., 3128 Boston. | 45 ARCH STREET.

BEER MADE E FAMOUS.
AWARD FOR PURITY.
GAHM & CO., N.E. AGENTS. 125-127 PURCHASE ST.

THE ONLY BEER ON DRAUGHT AT THESE CONCERTS.
"the beer that's brewed"
SOLD AT THESE CONCERTS.
ROCHESTER BREWING CO'S. NOTED THE WORLD OVER FOR ITS PURITY.
FAMOUS BOTTLED BEER
HOME OFFICE & BREWERY ROCHESTER, N.Y.
NEW ENGLAND BRANCH 295-305 A STREET BOSTON
Free delivery in city and Suburbs
RIENZI, PREMIER, BOHEMIAN, BAVARIAN, STANDARD.

TRY THE "COLUMBIA BRAND" VIENNA SAUSAGES. SERVED HOT OR COLD AT THESE CONCERTS.

THE FALL RIVER LINE

OCCUPYING THE
LONG ISLAND SOUND ROUTE
BETWEEN

Boston and New York

Has the finest quintette of great steamboats that the world has ever seen. The

Priscilla, Puritan, Plymouth, Pilgrim, and Providence

Are the largest, best equipped, safest, and handsomest steamboats ever constructed. This route is one of the most attractive and naturally beautiful traversed by any transportation agency in the world.

Trips of the Fall River Line are made throughout the year.

Each steamboat has its own orchestra, and the service on each member of the fleet is maintained at the highest possible standard.

Tickets via this route are on sale at all of the principal Ticket Offices in the United States.

From BOSTON. Trains, connecting with steamers at Fall River in 80 minutes, leave Park Square Station, New York, New Haven & Hartford Railroad (Old Colony System), daily at 6 p.m.

From NEW YORK. Steamers leave Pier 19, North River, foot of Warren Street, daily at 5.30 p.m.

S. A. GARDNER, Superintendent, NEW YORK.
GEO. L. CONNOR, Passenger Traffic Manager, NEW HAVEN, CONN.
O. H. TAYLOR, General Passenger Agent, NEW YORK CITY.

HOTEL LANGWOOD,

Middlesex Fells Reservation.

P.O. Address, Melrose, Mass.   Wyoming Station, B. & M. R.R.

Twenty minutes by rail from Boston. Sixty trains daily. Hotel coaches meet trains each way. Four hundred feet above sea level. Beautiful rides, drives, and walks. Golf links, tennis courts, and ball grounds.

OPENS ABOUT MAY 20.

For plans and prices address:

F. W. GASKILL, Manager.

BOSTON OFFICE:
Hemenway Building, 10 Tremont Street, Room 29.

Third Season.

3 Ideal Outings

Personally conducted by
F. R. COMEE, Music Hall, Boston.

S.S. "Howard." Boston to Norfolk, 522 miles. Norfolk to Baltimore, 200 miles.

	1.	2.	3.
Boston	Leave July 2	July 15	August 19
	Arrive July 12	July 31	September 4

S.S. "Toronto." Toronto to Montreal, through the "Thousand Islands" and the "Rapids", 376 miles.

No. 1. Ten days. Saratoga, Lake George, 2,130 miles from Buffalo to Duluth, and return on the steamer "North-Land" through the Great Lakes, Erie, Huron, St. Clair, and Superior.

Nos. 2 and 3. Sixteen days. Exactly alike. 700 miles ocean sail to Norfolk and Baltimore. Over Alleghany Mountains and a day in Chicago. Up Lake Michigan and three days at Mackinac Island. 1,546 miles on steamer "North-West" to Duluth and return to Buffalo through the Great Lakes. Niagara Falls to Toronto. Across Lake Ontario, through the Thousand Islands, and down the St. Lawrence River to Montreal and Boston.

SEND FOR CIRCULARS.

S.S. "Manitou." Chicago to Mackinac Island, across Lake Michigan, 350 miles.

"North-West." Mackinac Island to Duluth and return to Buffalo, 1,555 miles.

Ask for....

It has been known for over 130 years as the best. Bottled at the brewery, Burton-on-Trent, England, under the personal supervision of the Messrs. Allsopp.

Sold at these concerts.

If you want the best, ask for

Allsopp's

"The Red Hand Brand."

SATURDAY, MAY 13.

PROGRAMME.

1. MARCH, "Bride Elect" — Sousa
2. OVERTURE, "Pique Dame" — Suppe
3. WALTZ, "Grubenlichter" — Zeller
4. SELECTION from "The Gondoliers" — Sullivan
5. OVERTURE, "Prince pro Tem." — Thompson
6. TWO MOVEMENTS from Suite "Peer Gynt" — Grieg
7. AMERICAN PATROL — Meecham
8. OVERTURE, "Tannhäuser" — Wagner
9. INTERMEZZO, "Forget me not" — McBeth
10. SELECTION from "The Belle of New York" — Kerker
11. LOVE'S DREAM AFTER THE BALL — Czibulka
12. GEORGIA CAMP-MEETING — Mills

The *only* Lithia Water sold at these concerts.

Hygeia Lithia Water

Sparkling and Still.

By its use you will avoid the germs of disease which natural MINERAL WATERS are liable to contain.

For Sale at these concerts and by

S. S. PIERCE CO.

FOR SALE AT THESE CONCERTS.

FAMOUS TANNHAEUSER EXPORT BEER

The finest Light Beer Extant.   Brewery Bottling.   Favorite of Connoisseurs.

Pure,   Palatable,   Perfect.

B. & E. Philadelphia Ale on Draught.

FOR SALE AT THESE CONCERTS.

The purity and keeping quality of the Tannhaeuser Export under all changes of temperature, its uniform excellence being guaranteed, together with its nutritious properties, make it the most pleasant, delicious, and convenient beverage for home consumption.
Put up in corked bottles, and packed in casks of 10 dozen white flint pints, and 6 dozen amber quarts.

Highest Awards wherever exhibited.

The BERGNER & ENGEL BREWING CO.'S N.E. Depot,

508 and 510 Atlantic Avenue, Boston.

Telephone 3805.   SOL. BACHARACH, Manager.

M. Steinert & Sons Co.,

STEINERT HALL BUILDING,

No. 162 Boylston Street, corner Carver, Boston.

STEINWAY & SONS,

HARDMAN, GABLER,
EMERSON, SINGER,

PIANOS.

The Æolian, Aeriol, Orchestrelle,
and Pianola,

AND THE

STEINERTONE.

THE ÆOLIAN
AND
THE PIANOLA
FOR SUMMER HOMES.

At this season of the year we receive many orders for these instruments for Summer Residences, and therefore beg to call attention to our extensive assortment now on display, especially suited for this purpose.

The ÆOLIAN meets the requirements of country homes, furnishing, as it does, music suitable for every occasion. It practically takes the place of an orchestra — music for dancing — orchestral concerts, — in short, music of every style and description is always available.

The PIANOLA will appeal to many on account of the very little space it occupies. It will play any kind of a piano, and can also be used upon a rented piano without the slightest injury. For the above reasons it is bound to be very popular for small cottages.

We are glad to be able to announce that we can furnish PIANOLAS with no more than a week's delay, and, at times, the day the order is given.

Persons not familiar with these instruments are cordially invited to call at our warerooms and hear them, or a descriptive catalogue will be mailed free upon application.

M. STEINERT & SONS CO.,
Steinert Hall,   162 Boylston Street,   Boston.

ANHEUSER-BUSCH BREWING ASS'N,

ST. LOUIS, MO., U.S.A.

BREWERS OF HIGH-GRADE BEERS EXCLUSIVELY.

Black and Tan.   Faust.

Michelob.   Pale Lager.

Muenchener.   Anheuser Standard.

Served at the Music Hall Concerts.

Also at all first-class hotels, clubs, and bars, and on all Pullman and Wagner cars and ocean and lake steamers.

JACOB WIRTH,   Wholesale Dealer,   Boston, Mass.

THE MUSIC HALL
PROMENADE CONCERTS

PUBLISHED BY } C. A. ELLIS, MUSIC HALL.

BOSTON, THURSDAY, MAY 11, 1899.

SUMMER SEASON. Vol. XIV. No. 4.

SMOKE THE POPULAR "BARRISTER" CIGARS AT THE POPULAR CONCERTS.

SMOKE "LA CELESTINA," THE BEST ALL-HAVANA CIGAR. DANIEL FRANK & CO.

YOU CAN
Have your last season's outfit dyed or cleansed and refinished so it will look like new, by our French process. Why discard soiled clothing when it can be overhauled and worn as second best? You can

RELY ON
Our methods of cleansing, and need not hesitate to trust us with articles of the most delicate textures. We dye or cleanse and refinish PROPERLY, *all* materials of household use and clothing of all kinds.

LEWANDO'S
W. L. Crosby, General Manager. French Cleansers, Fancy Dyers, Fine Launderers.

PRINCIPAL OFFICES:
17 Temple Place, Boston.
479 Fifth Avenue, New York.
Established 70 years.
Largest in America.
Bundles called for and delivered.
Telephones in all offices.

If you are open to conviction, to-night try one 10-cent box of

BETWEEN THE ACTS
Little Cigars

to smoke now — or at any time when you want a short smoke and haven't time for a long one. They are real cigars, but small ones.

They cost so little that you can use them every day as well as not and actually save on your daily cigar expense by substituting them for larger cigars.

FOR SALE HERE.

THE MUSIC HALL... Promenade Concerts
FOURTEENTH SEASON.

C. A. ELLIS, Manager.   F. R. COMEE, Assistant Manager.

Mr. MAX ZACH, Conductor.

THURSDAY, MAY 11.

PROGRAMME.

1.	MARCH, " Princess Ninetta"	Strauss
2.	OVERTURE, " Le roi l'a dit "	Delibes
3.	WALTZ, " Arlequin en Voyage "	Zach
4.	SELECTION from " Aida "	Verdi
5.	NARCISSUS	Nevin
6.	WALTZ, " Landeskinder "	E. Strauss
7.	INTRODUCTION to " Lohengrin "	Wagner
8.	POLKA, ' Tyrolean "	Zeller
9.	ANDANTE for String Orchestra	Tschaikowsky
	The audience is respectfully requested to preserve silence during the performance of this number.	
10.	WALTZ, " Meerleuchten "	Ziehrer
11.	PIZZICATI, from " Sylvia "	Delibes
12.	MARCH from " The Serenade "	V. Herbert

ALBUMS OF SONGS,
Containing many popular compositions not published in single form.

IRISH FOLK SONGS, by Charles Wood,	$2.00
RUSSIAN SONGS, by F. Wishaw (2 vols.),	1.00
NINE SONGS, by S. Liddle,	1.00
NINE SONGS, by Liza Lehmann,	1.00
FIVE SONGS, by Francis Korbay,	2.00

Beautifully illustrated by J. S. SARGENT, R.A.

BOOSEY & CO.,
9 East 17th Street,   New York.

DRINK VAN NOSTRAND'S
BOSTON CLUB LAGER
SOLD AT THESE CONCERTS

NORFOLK CABINET
LAGER BEER

A Particularly Fine Lager for Family Use and Clubs.

Bottled in the most careful manner at our own bottling department, and sold by the S. S. Pierce Co. and all other leading grocers in New England.

Other Brands in Bottles:
" Norfolk India Pale Stock Ale."
" Norfolk Extra Golden Ale " (blue labels).
" Norfolk Standard Lager."

Our " Cabinet " and " Bismarck Brand " are the most popular refreshments at these concerts.

HABICH & CO.

H. W. HABICH, | Telephone, 56 Roxbury
EDWARD BUHL. | or 1132 Boston.

ESTABROOK & EATON'S MARGUERITE PERFECTOS, 10c. EACH. CONCHAS, 10c., 3 FOR 25c. **SOLD AT THE "POPS."**

THE ICE-CREAM SERVED AT THESE CONCERTS IS FURNISHED BY WEBER, 25 Temple Place and 33 West Street.

MUSIC HALL PROMENADE PROGRAMME.
PUBLISHED EVERY EVENING DURING THE SUMMER SEASON.

NOTICE TO ADVERTISERS.
The advertising columns in the Programme are controlled SOLELY by F. R. Comee, Boston Music Hall Box Office, to whom all communications should be addressed.

The United States Hotel,
SARATOGA SPRINGS, N.Y.

Under a continuous management for 25 years.

Without a peer in its appointments, service, and liberal management.

The largest structure of its kind in the world.

Built entirely of brick.

The Hotel and court cover over seven acres.

For further information, rates, etc., etc., address

GAGE & PERRY,
Proprietors,
UNITED STATES HOTEL,
Saratoga Springs, N.Y.

COLONIAL BEER

The Beer that's Brewed in Glass.

Colonial Beer...

PURE, CLEAN, PALATABLE.

Order a Bottle.

SOUTHER BREWING CO.,
919 Parker Street,
Roxbury, Mass.

VEUVE CHAFFARD

PURE OLIVE OIL,
IN HONEST BOTTLES.

The **MONOPOLE CIGARETTES,**
"CASINO GOLD TIPS,"
—AND—
"PRINCESS LILLIAN" (Turkish).

SOLD AT THESE CONCERTS.

OCKENHEIMER BERG, Near Bingen, GERMANY, on the Rhine.

PHILIP KRIM'S
OWN IMPORTATION OF
Rhine Wines.
FOR 30 YEARS AT
163 Shawmut Avenue.
OUR WINES SOLD AT THESE CONCERTS.

HERRICK, COPLEY SQUARE, Telephones 608 and 950 (Back Bay), CHOICE TABLES for Music Hall "Pops."

D. LEIDEN'S
SPARKLING
MOSELLE,
The only Sparkling Wine sold at these Concerts.

SHINNECOCK
The Perfection of

Scotch Whisky

Sold by
S. S. PIERCE COMPANY.

FRIDAY, MAY 12.

PROGRAMME.

1. MARCH, "Trial Kiss" . . . Millöcker
2. OVERTURE, "Black Domino" . . Auber
3. WALTZ, "Freut euch des Lebens" . Strauss
4. SELECTION from "The Fortune-teller" . V. Herbert
   (First Time.)
5. TWO ENTR'ACTES from "Carmen" . Bizet
6. INTRODUCTION to Act III., "Lohengrin" . Wagner
7. SELECTION from "Cavalleria Rusticana" Mascagni
8. GALOP CHROMATIQUE . . . Liszt

9. POTPOURRI, "The Brigands" . . Offenbach
10. RONDE D'AMOUR . . . . . Westerhout
    The audience is respectfully requested to preserve silence during the performance of this number.
11. WALTZ, "Pomone" . . . Waldteufel
12. MARCH, "Boccaccio" . . . Suppé

Handsomest Dining Hotel in New England.

THE HAYWARD
20 Private Dining-rooms.
Beer and Ale drawn direct from wood in THE DUTCH TAP.
SMITH & KERRISSEY, Proprietors.

"M. S."
GINGER ALE.

An epicurean beverage, made with Myles Standish Spring Water and compounded with scrupulous care from the highest grade materials.

To be had at the Promenade Concerts.

L. BOYER'S SONS,
Proprietors,
No. 27 Devonshire St., Boston.

MAIN OFFICE.
No. 90 Wall St., New York.

"AMERICA'S FINEST PRODUCT."
Bartholomay's "APOLLO"
LAGER BEER IN BOTTLES.

Sold at these Concerts.

ALBRECHT & KOELLNER,
SOLE AGENTS,
Telephone, Boston 1751.   295-305 A Street.

Also Agents for the "Crystal Rock" Mineral Water.

PURE BEER
Harvard
BREW. CO'S $1000.00
PURE BEER
Sold at these Concerts
IN BOTTLES ONLY
20¢ PER BOTTLE.

Inglenook Vineyard.

The only California Wines sold at these Concerts.

※ ※

THE CODMAN & HALL CO.,
Opposite the South Union Station.

Sole Agents for New England.

IND. COOPE & CO.'S English Ale.

THE SECOND LARGEST BREWERY IN ENGLAND.

Brewers of the finest *light quality* ale. Very highly endorsed by the medical profession. : : : : :

※ ※

THE CODMAN & HALL CO.,
Opposite South Union Station.

Sole Agents for the United States.

DRINK only the PURE WHISKIES

If you want purity and richness of flavor, try only genuine and original

OLD KENTUCKY TAYLOR,

Eight years old own distillation, guaranteed pure. Bottled and shipped direct from warehouses by us. None genuine without our signature on both labels. Beware of imitations. For consumptives, indigestion, and all ailments requiring stimulants, OLD KENTUCKY TAYLOR has no superior.

Sold by all first class druggists, grocers, and hotel dealers.

Wright & Taylor
Distillers,
Fine Kentucky
Whiskies,
Louisville, Ky.

Hirshfield & Co.
New England
Agents,
31 Doane Street
Boston.

Instruct your waiter to bring a bottle of

Pfaff's "Monogram" Lager.

If you will do this, it will not be necessary for us to expatiate upon the good qualities of our production.
YOU CAN JUDGE FOR YOURSELF.

H. & J. PFAFF BREWING COMPANY,
Telephone 2608.   16 ARCH STREET, BOSTON.

TABLE LINEN USED AT THESE CONCERTS LAUNDERED BY THE L. K. HUSTED LAUNDERING COMPANY. 27 and 29 BROADWAY, CHELSEA, MASS.

TRY THE "COLUMBIA BRAND" VIENNA SAUSAGES. SERVED HOT OR COLD AT THESE CONCERTS.

They cannot sell you here
Canadian Club Whisky,
Ruinart Champagne,
Royal Liqueur Scotch,
Carstair's Philadelphia Rye,
Fort Hill Bourbon,
Alhambra Sherry,
All of which you will find
of excellent quality;

But you can get

Kaiser Water,

the most refreshing of all table waters.

Chateau d'Arsac Claret,
N. Johnston & Sons' Medoc,
and
California Inglenook Clarets.

SUPPLIED BY

CODMAN & HALL COMPANY,

WINE MERCHANTS,

Opposite New South Station.

SATURDAY, MAY 13.

PROGRAMME.

1. MARCH, "Bride Elect" . . . . Sousa
2. OVERTURE, "Pique Dame" . . . . Suppé
3. WALTZ, "Grubenlichter" . . . . Zeller
4. SELECTION from "The Gondoliers" . Sullivan

5. OVERTURE, "Prince pro Tem." . . . . Thompson
6. TWO MOVEMENTS from Suite "Peer Gynt" . Grieg
7. AMERICAN PATROL . . . . Meacham
8. OVERTURE, "Tannhäuser" . . . . Wagner

9. INTERMEZZO, "Forget me not" . . . McBeth
10. SELECTION from "The Belle of New York" . Kerker
11. LOVE'S DREAM AFTER THE BALL . Czibulka
12. GEORGIA CAMP-MEETING . . . . . . Mills

THE WILSON,
AMERICA'S PUREST
Mineral Spring Water,

Is used in making our celebrated
Belfast Ginger Ale,
Champagne Kola,
Lemon Soda, Club Soda, Vichy, etc. Hotels and Families supplied. Try a sample order of these goods, and be convinced of their superiority, purity, and medicinal qualities.

All of our beverages bottled at the spring. We ship only in glass, and all bottles and demijohns are sterilized before being filled.

Wilson Spring and Hotel Co.,
Tel., 3129 Boston. | 45 ARCH STREET.

THE FALL RIVER LINE

OCCUPYING THE LONG ISLAND SOUND ROUTE BETWEEN

Boston and New York

Has the finest quintette of great steamboats that the world has ever seen. The

Priscilla, Puritan, Plymouth, Pilgrim, and Providence

Are the largest, best equipped, safest, and handsomest steamboats ever constructed. This route is one of the most attractive and naturally beautiful traversed by any transportation agency in the world.

Trips of the Fall River Line are made throughout the year. Each steamboat has its own orchestra, and the service on each member of the fleet is maintained at the highest possible standard.

Tickets via this route are on sale at all of the principal Ticket Offices in the United States.

From BOSTON. Trains, connecting with steamers at Fall River in 80 minutes, leave Park Square Station, New York, New Haven & Hartford Railroad (Old Colony System), daily at 6 p.m.

From NEW YORK. Steamers leave Pier 19, North River, foot of Warren Street, daily at 5.30 p.m.

S. A. GARDNER, Superintendent, NEW YORK.
GEO. L. CONNOR, Passenger Traffic Manager, NEW HAVEN, CONN.
O. H. TAYLOR, General Passenger Agent, NEW YORK CITY.

HOTEL LANGWOOD,

Middlesex Fells Reservation.

P.O. Address, Melrose, Mass.   Wyoming Station, B. & M. R.R.

Twenty minutes by rail from Boston. Sixty trains daily. Hotel coaches meet trains each way. Four hundred feet above sea level. Beautiful rides, drives, and walks. Golf links, tennis courts, and ball grounds.

OPENS ABOUT MAY 20.

For plans and prices address:

F. W. GASKILL, Manager.

BOSTON OFFICE:
Hemenway Building, 10 Tremont Street, Room 29.

Third Season.

3 Ideal Outings

Personally conducted by F. R. COMEE, Music Hall, Boston.

S.S. "Howard." Boston to Norfolk, 522 miles. Norfolk to Baltimore, 200 miles.

	1.	2.	3.
Boston {	Leave July 2	July 15	August 19
	Arrive July 12	July 31	September 4

S.S. "Toronto." Toronto to Montreal, through the "Thousand Islands" and the "Rapids," 376 miles.

No. 1. Ten days. Saratoga, Lake George, 2,120 miles from Buffalo to Duluth, and return on the steamer "North-Land" through the Great Lakes, Erie, Huron, St. Clair, and Superior.

Nos. 2 and 3. Sixteen days. Exactly alike. 700 miles' ocean sail to Norfolk and Baltimore. Over Alleghany Mountains and a day in Chicago. Up Lake Michigan and three days at Mackinac Island. 1,546 miles on steamer "North-West" to Duluth and return to Buffalo through the Great Lakes. Niagara Falls to Toronto. Across Lake Ontario, through the Thousand Islands, and down the St. Lawrence River to Montreal and Boston.

SEND FOR CIRCULARS.

S.S. "Manitou." Chicago to Mackinac Island, across Lake Michigan, 350 miles.

"North-West." Mackinac Island to Duluth and return to Buffalo, 1,555 miles.

Ask for ....

ALLSOPP'S INDIA PALE ALE

It has been known for over 130 years as the best. Bottled at the brewery, Burton-on-Trent, England, under the personal supervision of the Messrs. Allsopp.

Sold at these concerts.

If you want the best, ask for

Allsopp's

"The Red Hand Brand."

The purity and keeping quality of the Tannhaeuser Export under all changes of temperature, its uniform excellence being guaranteed, together with its nutritious properties, make it the most pleasant, delicious, and convenient beverage for home consumption.
Put up in corked bottles, and packed in casks of 10 dozen white flint pints, and 6 dozen amber quarts.

Highest Awards wherever exhibited.

MONDAY, MAY 15.

PROGRAMME.

1. MARCH, "For the Country" — Millöcker
2. WALTZ, "Les Patineurs" — Waldteufel
3. OVERTURE, "Donna Diana" — Reznicek
4. SELECTION from "The Serenade" — Herbert
5. FANTASIE, "Il Trovatore" — Verdi
6. ENTR'ACTE, "La Colombe" — Gounod
   The audience is respectfully requested to preserve silence during the performance of this number.
7. WALTZ, "Jolly Fellows" — Vollstedt
8. RIDE OF THE HUSSARS — Spindler

9. OVERTURE, "Poet and Peasant" — Suppé
   'Cello Obligato, Mr. KELLER.
10. RETRAITE CROATE — G. Marie
11. LOIN DU BAL — Gillet
12. AUSTRIA MARCH — Zach

FOR SALE AT THESE CONCERTS.

FAMOUS **TANNHAEUSER** EXPORT BEER

The finest Light Beer Extant. Brewery Bottling. Favorite of Connoisseurs.

Pure, Palatable, Perfect.

B. & E. Philadelphia Ale on Draught.

FOR SALE AT THESE CONCERTS.

The **BERGNER & ENGEL BREWING CO.'S** N.E. Depot,
508 and 510 Atlantic Avenue, Boston.
Telephone 3805. SOL. BACHARACH, Manager.

The *only* Lithia Water sold at these concerts.

Hygeia Lithia Water

Sparkling and Still.

By its use you will avoid the germs of disease which natural MINERAL WATERS are liable to contain.

For Sale at these concerts and by

S. S. PIERCE CO.

M. Steinert & Sons Co.,
STEINERT HALL BUILDING,
No. 162 Boylston Street, corner Carver, Boston.

STEINWAY & SONS,
HARDMAN, GABLER,
EMERSON, SINGER,
PIANOS.

The Æolian, Aeriol, Orchestrelle, and Pianola,

AND THE

STEINERTONE.

THE ÆOLIAN
AND
THE PIANOLA
FOR SUMMER HOMES.

At this season of the year we receive many orders for these instruments for Summer Residences, and therefore beg to call attention to our extensive assortment now on display, especially suited for this purpose.

The ÆOLIAN meets the requirements of country homes, furnishing, as it does, music suitable for every occasion. It practically takes the place of an orchestra — music for dancing — orchestral concerts, — in short, music of every style and description is always available.

The PIANOLA will appeal to many on account of the very little space it occupies. It will play any kind of a piano, and can also be used upon a rented piano without the slightest injury. For the above reasons it is bound to be very popular for small cottages.

We are glad to be able to announce that we can furnish PIANOLAS with no more than a week's delay, and, at times, the day the order is given.

Persons not familiar with these instruments are cordially invited to call at our warerooms and hear them, or a descriptive catalogue will be mailed free upon application.

M. STEINERT & SONS CO.,
Steinert Hall, 162 Boylston Street, Boston.

ANHEUSER-BUSCH BREWING ASS'N,
ST. LOUIS, MO., U.S.A.

BREWERS OF HIGH-GRADE BEERS EXCLUSIVELY.

Black and Tan.	Faust.
Michelob.	Pale Lager.
Muenchener.	Anheuser Standard.

Served at the Music Hall Concerts.
Also at all first-class hotels, clubs, and bars, and on all Pullman and Wagner cars and ocean and lake steamers.

JACOB WIRTH, Wholesale Dealer, Boston, Mass.

THE MUSIC HALL
PROMENADE CONCERTS

PUBLISHED BY
C. A. ELLIS,
MUSIC HALL.

BOSTON, FRIDAY, MAY 12, 1899.

SUMMER SEASON.
Vol. XIV. No. 5.

THE MUSIC HALL... **Promenade Concerts**

FOURTEENTH SEASON.

C. A. ELLIS, Manager.   F. R. COMEE, Assistant Manager.

Mr. MAX ZACH, Conductor.

FRIDAY, MAY 12.

PROGRAMME.

1. MARCH, "Trial Kiss" . . . . Millöcker
2. OVERTURE, "Black Domino" . . . . . Auber
3. WALTZ, "Freut euch des Lebens" . . . Strauss
4. SELECTION from "The Fortune-teller" . V. Herbert
   (First Time.)
5. TWO ENTR'ACTES from "Carmen" . . Bizet
6. INTRODUCTION to Act III., "Lohengrin" . Wagner
7. SELECTION from "Cavalleria Rusticana" . Mascagni
8. GALOP CHROMATIQUE . . . . Liszt

9. POTPOURRI, "The Brigands" . . . . . Offenbach
10. RONDE D'AMOUR . . . . Westerhout
    The audience is respectfully requested to preserve silence during the performance of this number.
11. WALTZ, "Pomone" . . . . Waldteufel
12. MARCH, "Boccaccio" . . . . Suppé

THE TWO MOST POPULAR TWO-STEPS
OF THE SEASON.

THE RUNAWAY GIRL, by Van Baar, ... 60c.
THE CECIL, by Megone, ... 50c.
FOR ORCHESTRA OR PIANO SOLO.

BOOSEY & CO.,
9 EAST 17th STREET,   NEW YORK.

YOU CAN Have your last season's outfit dyed or cleansed and refinished so it will look like new, by our French process. Why discard soiled clothing when it can be overhauled and worn as best? You can **RELY ON** Our methods of cleansing, and need not hesitate to trust us with articles of the most delicate textures. We dye or cleanse and refinish PROPERLY, *all* materials of household use and clothing of all kinds.

LEWANDO'S
W. L. Crosby, General Manager.
French Cleansers, Fancy Dyers,
Fine Launderers.

PRINCIPAL OFFICES:
17 Temple Place, Boston.
479 Fifth Avenue, New York.
Established 70 years.
Largest in America.
Bundles called for and delivered.
Telephones in all offices.

Save half your money
do not throw it away in half-smoked cigars! You will find that 50% of your cigar money is thrown away every day if you recall how few cigars you really have time to smoke "up."

BETWEEN THE ACTS
Little Cigars

are pure — clean — all good tobacco, and are in every way a very satisfactory short smoke. While you are listening to the music to-night, try a 10-cent box. The waiter will get them for you as they are for sale here. You will enjoy them!

BEST BEER BREWED

OH BE JOLLY!
DRINK VAN NOSTRAND'S
P. B. ALE
SOLD AT THESE CONCERTS

NORFOLK CABINET
LAGER BEER
A Particularly Fine Lager for Family Use and Clubs.
Bottled in the most careful manner at our own bottling department, and sold by the S. S. Pierce Co. and all other leading grocers in New England.
Other Brands in Bottles:
"Norfolk India Pale Stock Ale."
"Norfolk Extra Golden Ale" (blue label).
"Norfolk Standard Lager."
Our "Cabinet" and "Bismarck Brau" are the most popular refreshments at these concerts.
HABICH & CO.
H. W. HABICH.   Telephone, 56 Roxbury
EDWARD BUHL.   or 1132 Boston.

SMOKE "LA CELESTINA," THE BEST ALL-HAVANA CIGAR. DANIEL FRANK & CO.

SMOKE THE POPULAR "BARRISTER" CIGARS AT THE POPULAR CONCERTS.

ESTABROOK & EATON'S MARGUERITE PERFECTOS, 10c. BAJA CONCHAS, 10c., 3 FOR 25c. SOLD AT THE "POPS."

THE ICE-CREAM SERVED AT THESE CONCERTS IS FURNISHED BY WEBER, 25 Temple Place and 33 West Street.

MUSIC HALL PROMENADE PROGRAMME.
PUBLISHED EVERY EVENING DURING THE SUMMER SEASON.

NOTICE TO ADVERTISERS.
The advertising columns in the Programme are controlled SOLELY by F. R. Comee, Boston Music Hall Box Office, to whom all communications should be addressed.

The United States Hotel,
SARATOGA SPRINGS, N.Y.

Under a continuous management for 25 years.

Without a peer in its appointments, service, and liberal management.

The largest structure of its kind in the world.

Built entirely of brick.

The Hotel and court cover over seven acres.

For further information, rates, etc., etc., address

GAGE & PERRY,
Proprietors,
UNITED STATES HOTEL,
Saratoga Springs, N.Y.

Colonial Beer...
The Beer that's Brewed in Glass.
PURE, CLEAN, PALATABLE.
Order a Bottle.
SOUTHER BREWING CO.,
919 Parker Street,
Roxbury, Mass.

All The
IMPORTED CIGARS

Sold At These Concerts Are Supplied By The

S. S. PIERCE COMPANY.

The MONOPOLE CIGARETTES,
"CASINO GOLD TIPS,"
— AND —
"PRINCESS LILLIAN" (Turkish).

SOLD AT THESE CONCERTS.

OCKENHEIMER BERG,
Near Bingen, GERMANY. On the Rhine.

PHILIP KRIM'S
OWN IMPORTATION OF
Rhine Wines,
FOR 30 YEARS
AT
163 Shawmut Avenue.
OUR WINES SOLD AT THESE CONCERTS.

HERRICK, COPLEY SQUARE, Telephones 608 and 950 (Back Bay), CHOICE TABLES for Music Hall "Pops."

GREAT WESTERN CHAMPAGNE

——A natural, genuine champagne, of the finest quality produced in America.

Sold by Wine Merchants, Grocers, and Druggists.

SATURDAY, MAY 13.

PROGRAMME.

1. MARCH, "Bride Elect" . . . Sousa
2. OVERTURE, "Pique Dame" . . Suppé
3. WALTZ, "Grubenlichter" . . . Zeller
4. SELECTION from "The Gondoliers" . Sullivan

5. OVERTURE, "Prince pro Tem." . . Thompson
6. TWO MOVEMENTS from Suite "Peer Gynt" . Grieg
7. AMERICAN PATROL . . . Meecham
8. OVERTURE, "Tannhäuser" . . . Wagner

9. INTERMEZZO, "Forget me not" . . McBeth
10. SELECTION from "The Belle of New York" . Kerker
11. LOVE'S DREAM AFTER THE BALL . Czibulka
12. GEORGIA CAMP-MEETING . . . Mills

Handsomest Dining Hotel in New England.

THE HAYWARD

20 Private Dining-rooms.

Beer and Ale drawn direct from wood in THE DUTCH TAP.

SMITH & KERRISSEY, Proprietors.

"M. S." GINGER ALE.

An epicurean beverage, made with Myles Standish Spring Water and compounded with scrupulous care from the highest grade materials.

To be had at the Promenade Concerts.

L. BOYER'S SONS,
Proprietors,
No. 27 Devonshire St., Boston.

MAIN OFFICE.
No. 90 Wall St., New York.

"AMERICA'S FINEST PRODUCT."

Bartholomay's "APOLLO"

LAGER BEER IN BOTTLES.

Sold at these Concerts.

ALBRECHT & KOELLNER,
SOLE AGENTS,

Telephone, Boston 1751. 295-305 A Street.

Also Agents for the "Crystal Rock" Mineral Water.

PURE BEER

Harvard BREW. CO'S $1000.00

PURE BEER

Sold at these Concerts,
IN BOTTLES ONLY
20¢ PER BOTTLE.

Inglenook Vineyard.

The only California Wines sold at these Concerts.

❧❧

THE CODMAN & HALL CO.,
Opposite the South Union Station.

Sole Agents for New England.

IND. COOPE & CO.'S English Ale.

THE SECOND LARGEST BREWERY IN ENGLAND.

Brewers of the finest *light quality* ale. Very highly endorsed by the medical profession. : : : : :

❧❧

THE CODMAN & HALL CO.,
Opposite South Union Station.

Sole Agents for the United States.

DRINK only the PUREST WHISK

If you want pure and richness flavor, try our only genuine and original

OLD KENTUCKY TAYLOR,

Eight years old, our own distillation and guaranteed pure. Bottled and shipped direct from our warehouses by us. None genuine without our signature on both labels. Beware of imitation. For consumption, indigestion and ailments requiring stimulants, OLD KENTUCKY TAYLOR has no superior.

Sold by all first class druggists, grocers, and liquor dealers.

Wright & Taylor,
Distillers,
Fine Kentucky Whiskies,
Louisville, Ky.

Hirshfield & Co.
New England Agents,
31 Doane Street,
Boston.

Instruct your waiter to bring a bottle of

Pfaff's "Monogram" Lager.

If you will do this, it will not be necessary for us to expatiate upon the good qualities of our production.
YOU CAN JUDGE FOR YOURSELF.

H. & J. PFAFF BREWING COMPANY,
Telephone 2608.   16 ARCH STREET, BOSTON.

TABLE LINEN USED AT THESE CONCERTS LAUNDERED BY THE L. K. HUSTED LAUNDERING COMPANY. 27 and 29 BROADWAY, CHELSEA, MASS.

TRY THE "COLUMBIA BRAND" VIENNA SAUSAGES. SERVED HOT OR COLD AT THESE CONCERTS.

They cannot sell you here
Canadian Club Whisky,
Ruinart Champagne,
Royal Liqueur Scotch,
Carstair's Philadelphia Rye,
Fort Hill Bourbon,
Alhambra Sherry,
All of which you will find of excellent quality;

But you can get

Kaiser Water,

the most refreshing of all table waters,

Chateau d' Arsac Claret,
N. Johnston & Sons' Medoc,
and
California Inglenook Clarets.

SUPPLIED BY

CODMAN & HALL COMPANY,

WINE MERCHANTS,

Opposite New South Station.

MONDAY, MAY 15.

PROGRAMME.

1. MARCH, "For the Country" . . . . Millocker
2. WALTZ, "Les Patineurs" . . . . Wahlteufel
3. OVERTURE, "Donna Diana" . . . . Reznicek
4. SELECTION from "The Serenade" . . . . Herbert
5. FANTASIE, "Il Trovatore" . . . . Verdi
6. ENTR'ACTE, "La Colombe" . . . . Gounod
   The audience is respectfully requested to preserve silence during the performance of this number.
7. WALTZ, "Jolly Fellows" . . . . Vollstedt
8. RIDE OF THE HUSSARS . . . . Spindler
9. OVERTURE, "Poet and Peasant" . . . . Suppé
   Cello Obligato, Mr. KELLER.
10. RETRAITE CROATE . . . . G. Marie
11. LOIN DU BAL . . . . Gillet
12. AUSTRIA MARCH . . . . Zach

THE WILSON, AMERICA'S PUREST

Mineral Spring Water,

Is used in making our celebrated

Belfast Ginger Ale, Champagne Kola,

Lemon Soda, Club Soda, Vichy, etc. Hotels and Families supplied. Try a sample order of these goods, and be convinced of their superiority, purity, and medicinal qualities.

All of our beverages bottled at the spring. We ship only in glass, and all bottles and demijohns are sterilized before being filled

Wilson Spring and Hotel Co.,

Tel., 3129 Boston. | 45 ARCH STREET.

"THE RECOGNIZED FAVORITE OF ALL BEERS."

Schlitz

THE BEER THAT MADE MILWAUKEE FAMOUS.

HIGHEST AWARD FOR PURITY.

Sold at these Concerts. JOS. GAHM & CO., N.E. AGENTS, 125-127 PURCHASE ST.

THE FALL RIVER LINE

OCCUPYING THE
LONG ISLAND SOUND ROUTE
BETWEEN

Boston and New York

Has the finest quintette of great steamboats that the world has ever seen. The

Priscilla, Puritan, Plymouth, Pilgrim, and Providence

Are the largest, best equipped, safest, and handsomest steamboats ever constructed. This route is one of the most attractive and naturally beautiful traversed by any transportation agency in the world.

Trips of the Fall River Line are made throughout the year. Each steamboat has its own orchestra, and the service on each member of the fleet is maintained at the highest possible standard.

Tickets via this route are on sale at all of the principal Ticket Offices in the United States.

From BOSTON. Trains, connecting with steamers at Fall River in 80 minutes, leave Park Square Station, New York, New Haven & Hartford Railroad (Old Colony System), daily at 6 p.m.

From NEW YORK. Steamers leave Pier 19, North River, foot of Warren Street, daily at 5.30 p.m.

S. A. GARDNER, Superintendent, NEW YORK.
GEO. L. CONNOR, Passenger Traffic Manager, NEW HAVEN, CONN.
O. H. TAYLOR, General Passenger Agent, NEW YORK CITY.

HOTEL LANGWOOD,

Middlesex Fells Reservation.

P.O. Address, Melrose, Mass.   Wyoming Station, B. & M. R.R.

Twenty minutes by rail from Boston. Sixty trains daily. Hotel coaches meet trains each way. Four hundred feet above sea level. Beautiful rides, drives, and walks. Golf links, tennis courts, and ball grounds.

OPENS ABOUT MAY 20.

For plans and prices address:

F. W. GASKILL, Manager.

BOSTON OFFICE:
Hemenway Building, 10 Tremont Street, Room 29.

S.S. "Howard." Boston to Norfolk, 522 miles. Norfolk to Baltimore, 200 miles.

	1.	2.	3.
Boston	Leave July 2 Arrive July 12	July 15 July 31	August 18 September 4

S.S. "Toronto." Toronto to Montreal, through the "Thousand Islands" and the "Rapids," 376 miles.

Third Season.

3 Ideal Outings

Personally conducted by F. R. COMEE, Music Hall, Boston.

No. 1. Ten days. Saratoga, Lake George. 2,130 miles from Buffalo to Duluth, and return on the steamer "North-Land" through the Great Lakes, Erie, Huron, St. Clair, and Superior.

Nos. 2 and 3. Sixteen days. Exactly alike, 700 miles' ocean sail to Norfolk and Baltimore. Over Alleghany Mountains and a day in Chicago. Up Lake Michigan and three days at Mackinac Island. 1,546 miles on steamer "North-West" to Duluth and return to Buffalo through the Great Lakes. Niagara Falls to Toronto. Across Lake Ontario, through the Thousand Islands, and down the St. Lawrence River to Montreal and Boston.

SEND FOR CIRCULARS.

S.S. "Manitou." Chicago to Mackinac Island, across Lake Michigan, 350 miles.

"North-West." Mackinac Island to Duluth and return to Buffalo, 1,555 miles.

Ask for ....

It has been known for over 130 years as the best.

Bottled at the brewery, Burton-on-Trent, England, under the personal supervision of the Messrs. Allsopp.

Sold at these concerts.

If you want the best, ask for

Allsopp's

"The Red Hand Brand."

TUESDAY, MAY 16.

PROGRAMME.

1. MARCH, "Am I a Wiz?" . . . Herbert
2. WALTZ, "Artists' Life" . . . Strauss
3. OVERTURE, "Le Brasseur de Preston" . Adam
4. SELECTION, "La Fille de Madame Angot" Lecocq
5. OVERTURE to "Zampa" . . . Herold
6. (a) ENTR'ACTE, "Rosamunde" . . Schubert
   (b) GAVOTTE from "Mignon" . . . Thomas
   The audience is respectfully requested to preserve silence during the performance of this number.
7. WALTZ, "Gil Blas" . . . . Czibulka
   (First Time)
8. ENTREE TRIOMPHALE DES BOYARDS . Halvorsen
9. OFFENBACHIANA . . . . Conradi
10. SERENADE ROCOCO . . . Meyer-Helmund
11. POLKA, "Papa-Mama" . . . Bayer
12. MARCH from "Puppenfee" . . . Bayer

The *only* Lithia Water sold at these concerts.

Hygeia Lithia Water

Sparkling and Still.

By its use you will avoid the germs of disease which natural MINERAL WATERS are liable to contain.

For Sale at these concerts and by

S. S. PIERCE CO.

The purity and keeping quality of the Tannhaeuser Export under all changes of temperature, its uniform excellence being guaranteed, together with its nutritious properties, make it the most pleasant, delicious, and convenient beverage for home consumption.

Put up in corked bottles, and packed in casks of 10 dozen white flint pints, and 6 dozen amber quarts.

Highest Awards wherever exhibited.

FOR SALE AT THESE CONCERTS.

FAMOUS TANNHAEUSER EXPORT BEER

The finest Light Beer Extant.   Brewery Bottling.   Favorite of Connoisseurs.

Pure,   Palatable,   Perfect.

B. & E. Philadelphia Ale on Draught.

FOR SALE AT THESE CONCERTS.

The BERGNER & ENGEL BREWING CO.'S N.E. Depot,

508 and 510 Atlantic Avenue, Boston.

Telephone 3805.   SOL. BACHARACH, Manager.

M. Steinert & Sons Co.,

STEINERT HALL BUILDING,

No. 162 Boylston Street, corner Carver, Boston.

STEINWAY & SONS,

HARDMAN,   GABLER,
EMERSON,   SINGER,

PIANOS.

The Æolian, Aeriol, Orchestrelle, and Pianola,

AND THE

STEINERTONE.

THE ÆOLIAN
AND
THE PIANOLA
FOR SUMMER HOMES.

At this season of the year we receive many orders for these instruments for Summer Residences, and therefore beg to call attention to our extensive assortment now on display, especially suited for this purpose.

The ÆOLIAN meets the requirements of country homes, furnishing, as it does, music suitable for every occasion. It practically takes the place of an orchestra — music for dancing — orchestral concerts,— in short, music of every style and description is always available.

The PIANOLA will appeal to many on account of the very little space it occupies. It will play any kind of a piano, and can also be used upon a rented piano without the slightest injury. For the above reasons it is bound to be very popular for small cottages.

We are glad to be able to announce that we can furnish PIANOLAS with no more than a week's delay, and, at times, the day the order is given.

Persons not familiar with these instruments are cordially invited to call at our warerooms and hear them, or a descriptive catalogue will be mailed free upon application.

M. STEINERT & SONS CO.,
Steinert Hall,   162 Boylston Street,   Boston.

ANHEUSER-BUSCH BREWING ASS'N,

ST. LOUIS, MO., U.S.A.

BREWERS OF HIGH=GRADE BEERS EXCLUSIVELY.

Black and Tan.   Faust.

Michelob.   Pale Lager.

Muenchener.   Anheuser Standard.

Served at the Music Hall Concerts.

Also at all first-class hotels, clubs, and bars, and on all Pullman and Wagner cars and ocean and lake steamers.

JACOB WIRTH,   **Wholesale Dealer,**   **Boston, Mass.**

THE MUSIC HALL
PROMENADE CONCERTS

BOSTON, SATURDAY, MAY 13, 1899.

PUBLISHED BY C. A. ELLIS, MUSIC HALL.

SUMMER SEASON. Vol. XIV. No. 6.

THE MUSIC HALL Promenade Concerts
FOURTEENTH SEASON.

C. A. ELLIS, Manager.   F. R. COMEE, Assistant Manager.

Mr. MAX ZACH, Conductor.

SATURDAY, MAY 13.

PROGRAMME.

1. MARCH, "Bride Elect" . . . . . Sousa
2. OVERTURE, "Pique Dame" . . . . Suppé
3. WALTZ, "Grubenlichter" . . . . Zeller
4. SELECTION from "The Gondoliers" . Sullivan

---

5. OVERTURE, "Prince pro Tem." . . . Thompson
6. TWO MOVEMENTS from Suite "Peer Gynt" . Grieg
7. AMERICAN PATROL . . . . . Meacham
8. OVERTURE, "Tannhäuser" . . . . Wagner

---

9. INTERMEZZO, "Forget me not" . . . McBeth
10. SELECTION from "The Belle of New York" . Kerker
11. LOVE'S DREAM AFTER THE BALL . . Czibulka
12. GEORGIA CAMP-MEETING . . . . Mills

Now the rage of the LONDON Concerts and Drawing-rooms:

YOU AND I, by Liza Lehmann, . . . 60c.
KING CHARLES, by M. V. White, . . 60c.
LIKE VIOLETS PALE, by F. Allitsen, . 60c.
WHEN THE WORLD IS FAIR, by F. H. Cowen, 60c.
QUEEN OF MY LIFE, by E. T. Lloyd, . 60c.

BOOSEY & CO.,
9 East 17th Street,   New York.

YOU CAN
Have your last season's outfit dyed or cleansed and refinished so it will look like new, by our French process. Why discard soiled clothing when it can be overhauled and worn as second best? You can

RELY ON
Our methods of cleansing, and need not hesitate to trust us with articles of the most delicate textures. We dye or cleanse and refinish PROPERLY, *all* materials of household use and clothing of all kinds.

LEWANDO'S
W. L. Crosby, General Manager.
French Cleansers, Fancy Dyers, Fine Launderers.
PRINCIPAL OFFICES:
17 Temple Place, Boston.
473 Fifth Avenue, New York.
*Established 70 years.
Largest in America.*
Bundles called for and delivered.
Telephones in all offices.

In no other way
are men as wasteful and extravagant as in cigar smoking — because cigars are thrown away half smoked half the time.

BETWEEN THE ACTS
Little Cigars
are just right for all short smokes. They light right, they burn right, and taste right. Have you ever seen them? At all stores: 10 for 10 cts., or, as they are for sale here, you can try them to-night. Tell the waiter to bring you a 10-cent box of "Between the Acts." They will add to your enjoyment of this concert.

DRINK VAN NOSTRAND'S BOSTON CLUB LAGER
SOLD AT THESE CONCERTS

NORFOLK CABINET LAGER BEER
A Particularly Fine Lager for Family Use and Clubs.
Bottled in the most careful manner at our own bottling department, and sold by the S. S. Pierce Co. and all other leading grocers in New England.
Other Brands in Bottles:
"Norfolk India Pale Stock Ale."
"Norfolk Extra Golden Ale" (blue label).
"Norfolk Standard Lager."
"Our 'Cabinet' and 'Bismarck Brau'" are the most popular refreshments at these concerts.
HABICH & CO.
H. W. HABICH, Telephone, 56 Roxbury
EDWARD BUHL. or 1152 Boston.

SMOKE THE POPULAR "BARRISTER" CIGARS AT THE POPULAR CONCERTS.

SMOKE "LA CELESTINA," THE BEST ALL-HAVANA CIGAR. DANIEL FRANK & CO.

ESTABROOK & EATON'S MARGUERITE PERFECTOS, 10c. EACH. CONCHAS, 10c., 3 FOR 25c. **SOLD AT THE "POPS."**

THE ICE-CREAM SERVED AT THESE CONCERTS IS FURNISHED BY WEBER, 25 Temple Place and 33 West Street.

MUSIC HALL PROMENADE PROGRAMME.
PUBLISHED EVERY EVENING DURING THE SUMMER SEASON.

NOTICE TO ADVERTISERS.
The advertising columns in the Programme are controlled SOLELY by F. R. Comee, Boston Music Hall Box Office, to whom all communications should be addressed.

The United States Hotel,
SARATOGA SPRINGS, N.Y.

Under a continuous management for 25 years.

Without a peer in its appointments, service, and liberal management.

The largest structure of its kind in the world.

Built entirely of brick.

The Hotel and court cover over seven acres.

For further information, rates, etc., etc., address

GAGE & PERRY,
Proprietors,
UNITED STATES HOTEL,
Saratoga Springs, N.Y.

Colonial Beer...
The Beer that's Brewed in Glass.

PURE, CLEAN, PALATABLE.

Order a Bottle.

SOUTHER BREWING CO.,
919 Parker Street,
Roxbury, Mass.

VEUVE CHAFFARD

PURE OLIVE OIL.
IN HONEST BOTTLES.

The Peer of all Cigarettes.
Save the band-label on each box for valuable premiums.

::: ALSO :::

Monopol
High-grade Egyptian Cigarettes

No. 8A Khedive,
No. 66A Nakim,
No. 9A Egyptian Belles,
No. 70A Princess Lillian

On sale at these concerts and all first-class dealers.

OCKENHEIMER BERG,
Near Bingen, GERMANY. On the Rhine.

PHILIP KRIM'S
OWN IMPORTATION OF
Rhine Wines.
FOR 30 YEARS AT
163 Shawmut Avenue.
OUR WINES SOLD AT THESE CONCERTS.

HERRICK, COPLEY SQUARE, Telephones 608 and 950 (Back Bay), CHOICE TABLES for Music Hall "Pops."

D. LEIDEN'S SPARKLING MOSELLE,

The only Sparkling Wine sold at these Concerts.

SHINNECOCK

The Perfection of

Scotch Whisky

Sold by
S. S. PIERCE COMPANY.

MONDAY, MAY 15.

PROGRAMME.

1. MARCH, "For the Country" . . . Millöcker
2. WALTZ, "Les Patineurs" . . . Waldteufel
3. OVERTURE, "Donna Diana" . . . Reznicek
4. SELECTION from "The Serenade" . . . Herbert

5. FANTASIE, "Il Trovatore" . . . Verdi
6. ENTR'ACTE, "La Colombe" . . . Gounod
   The audience is respectfully requested to preserve silence during the performance of this number.
7. WALTZ, "Jolly Fellows" . . . Vollstedt
8. RIDE OF THE HUSSARS . . . Spindler

9. OVERTURE, "Poet and Peasant" . . . Suppé
   Cello Obligato, Mr. KELLER.
10. RETRAITE CROATE . . . G. Marie
11. LOIN DU BAL . . . Gillet
12. AUSTRIA MARCH . . . Zach

Handsomest Dining Hotel in New England.

THE HAYWARD

20 Private Dining-rooms.

Beer and Ale drawn direct from wood in THE DUTCH TAP.

SMITH & KERRISSEY, Proprietors.

"M. S." GINGER ALE.

An epicurean beverage, made with Myles Standish Spring Water and compounded with scrupulous care from the highest grade materials.

To be had at the Promenade Concerts.

L. BOYER'S SONS,
Proprietors,
No. 27 Devonshire St., Boston.

MAIN OFFICE.
No. 90 Wall St., New York.

"AMERICA'S FINEST PRODUCT."

Bartholomay's "APOLLO"

LAGER BEER IN BOTTLES.

Sold at these Concerts.

ALBRECHT & KOELLNER,
SOLE AGENTS,
Telephone, Boston 1751.   295-305 A Street.

Also Agents for the "Crystal Rock" Mineral Water.

PURE BEER

Harvard BREW. CO'S $1000.00

PURE BEER

Sold at these Concerts.
IN BOTTLES ONLY
20¢ PER BOTTLE.

Inglenook Vineyard.

The only California Wines sold at these Concerts.

THE CODMAN & HALL CO.,
Opposite the South Union Station.

Sole Agents for New England.

IND. COOPE & CO.'S English Ale.

THE SECOND LARGEST BREWERY IN ENGLAND.

Brewers of the finest *light quality* ale. Very highly endorsed by the medical profession. : : : : :

THE CODMAN & HALL CO.,
Opposite South Union Station.

Sole Agents for the United States.

DRIN
only th
PURE
WHIS

If you want pu
and richnes
flavor, try
only genu
and origin

**OLD KENTU
TAYLOR,**

Eight years old,
own distillation
guaranteed pu
Bottled and ship
direct from
warehouses by
None genuine w
out our signat
on both labels.
ware of imitati
For consumpti
indigestion, and
ailments requir
stimulants, OL
KENTUCKY TA
LOR has n
superior.
Sold by all fir
class druggi
grocers, and liqu
dealers.

Wright & Tayl
Distillers,
Fine Kentucky
Whiskies,
Louisville, Ky.

Hirshfield & C
New England
Agents,
31 Doane Street
Boston.

Instruct your waiter to bring a bottle of

Pfaff's "Monogram" Lager.

If you will do this, it will not be necessary for us to expatiate upon the good qualities of our production.
YOU CAN JUDGE FOR YOURSELF.

H. & J. PFAFF BREWING COMPANY,
Telephone 2608. 16 ARCH STREET, BOSTON.

TRY THE "COLUMBIA BRAND" VIENNA SAUSAGES. SERVED HOT OR COLD AT THESE CONCERTS.

They cannot sell you here
Canadian Club Whisky,
Ruinart Champagne,
Royal Liqueur Scotch,
Carstair's Philadelphia Rye,
Fort Hill Bourbon,
Alhambra Sherry,
All of which you will find
of excellent quality;

But you can get

Kaiser Water,

the most refreshing of all table waters.

Chateau d'Arsac Claret,
N. Johnston & Sons' Medoc,
and
California Inglenook Clarets.

SUPPLIED BY

CODMAN & HALL COMPANY,

WINE MERCHANTS,

Opposite New South Station.

TUESDAY, MAY 16.

PROGRAMME.

1. MARCH, "Am I a Wiz?" . . . Herbert
2. WALTZ, "Artists' Life" . . . Strauss
3. OVERTURE, "Le Brasseur de Preston" . . . Adam
4. SELECTION, "La Fille de Madame Angot" . . . Lecocq

5. OVERTURE to "Zampa" . . . Herold
6. (a) ENTR'ACTE, "Rosamunde" . . . Schubert
   (b) GAVOTTE from "Mignon" . . . Thomas

   The audience is respectfully requested to preserve silence during the performance of this number.

7. WALTZ, "Gil Blas" . . . Czibulka
   (First Time)
8. ENTRÉE TRIOMPHALE DES BOYARDS . . . Halvorsen

9. OFFENBACHIANA . . . Conradi
10. SERENADE ROCOCO . . . Meyer-Helmund
11. POLKA, "Papa-Mama" . . . Bayer
12. MARCH from "Puppenfee" . . . Bayer

THE WILSON,
AMERICA'S PUREST

Mineral Spring Water,

Is used in making our celebrated Belfast Ginger Ale, Champagne Kola, Lemon Soda, Club Soda, Vichy, etc. Hotels and Families supplied. Try a sample order of these goods, and be convinced of their superiority, purity, and medicinal qualities.

All of our beverages bottled at the spring. We ship only in glass, and all bottles and demijohns are sterilized before being filled.

Wilson Spring and Hotel Co.,

Tel., 3129 Boston. | 45 ARCH STREET.

"THE RECOGNIZED FAVORITE OF ALL BEERS."

HIGHEST AWARD FOR PURITY.

Sold at these Concerts. JOS. GAHM & CO., N.E. AGENTS, 125-127 PURCHASE ST.

THE ONLY BEER ON DRAUGHT AT THESE CONCERTS.

"the beer that's brewed"

Free delivery in city and Suburbs

THE FALL RIVER LINE
OCCUPYING THE
LONG ISLAND SOUND ROUTE
BETWEEN
Boston and New York

Has the finest quintette of great steamboats that the world has ever seen. The

Priscilla, Puritan, Plymouth, Pilgrim, and Providence

Are the largest, best equipped, safest, and handsomest steamboats ever constructed. This route is one of the most attractive and naturally beautiful traversed by any transportation agency in the world.

Trips of the Fall River Line are made throughout the year.

Each steamboat has its own orchestra, and the service on each member of the fleet is maintained at the highest possible standard.

Tickets via this route are on sale at all of the principal Ticket Offices in the United States.

From BOSTON. Trains, connecting with steamers at Fall River in 80 minutes, leave Park Square Station, New York, New Haven & Hartford Railroad (Old Colony System), daily at 6 p.m.

From NEW YORK. Steamers leave Pier 19, North River, foot of Warren Street, daily at 5.30 p.m.

| S. A. GARDNER, Superintendent, NEW YORK. | GEO. L. CONNOR, Passenger Traffic Manager, NEW HAVEN, CONN. | O. H. TAYLOR, General Passenger Agent, NEW YORK CITY. |

HOTEL LANGWOOD,
Middlesex Fells Reservation.

P.O. Address, Melrose, Mass.   Wyoming Station, B. & M. R.R.

Twenty minutes by rail from Boston. Sixty trains daily. Hotel coaches meet trains each way. Four hundred feet above sea level. Beautiful rides, drives, and walks. Golf links, tennis courts, and ball grounds.

OPENS ABOUT MAY 20.

For plans and prices address:

F. W. GASKILL, Manager.

BOSTON OFFICE:
Hemenway Building, 10 Tremont Street, Room 29.

S.S. "Howard." Boston to Norfolk, 522 miles. Norfolk to Baltimore, 200 miles.

	1.	2.	3.
Boston	Leave July 2 Arrive July 12	July 15 July 31	August 19 September 2

S.S. "Toronto." Toronto to Montreal, through the "Thousand Islands" and the "Rapids," 376 miles.

Third Season.
3 Ideal Outings

Personally conducted by
F. R. COMEE, Music Hall, Boston.

No. 1. Ten days. Saratoga, Lake George, 2,130 miles from Buffalo to Duluth, and return on the steamer "North-Land" through the Great Lakes, Erie, Huron, St. Clair, and Superior.

Nos. 2 and 3. Sixteen days. Exactly alike. 700 miles' ocean sail to Norfolk and Baltimore. Over Alleghany Mountains and a day in Chicago. Up Lake Michigan and three days at Mackinac Island. 1,846 miles on steamer "North-West" to Duluth and return to Buffalo through the Great Lakes. Niagara Falls to Toronto. Across Lake Ontario, through the Thousand Islands, and down the St. Lawrence River to Montreal and Boston.

SEND FOR CIRCULARS.

S.S. "Manitou." Chicago to Mackinac Island, across Lake Michigan, 350 miles.

"North-West." Mackinac Island to Duluth and return to Buffalo, 1,555 miles.

Ask for ....

ALLSOPP'S INDIA PALE ALE
TRADE MARK

It has been known for over 130 years as the best. Bottled at the brewery, Burton-on-Trent, England, under the personal supervision of the Messrs. Allsopp.

Sold at these concerts.

If you want the best, ask for

Allsopp's

"The Red Hand Brand."

WEDNESDAY, MAY 17.

PROGRAMME.

1. MARCH, "Der flotte Reservist" — Sabathil
2. OVERTURE, "Martha" — Flotow
3. WALTZ, "Arabian Nights" — Strauss
4. SELECTION from "Faust" — Gounod

5. HUNGARIAN MARCH, "Szeghenyi" — Fahrbach
   (First Time.)
6. QUINTETTE from the "Mastersingers," arranged for String Orchestra by . . . . . . G. Sandre
   (First Time.)
   The audience is respectfully requested to preserve silence during the performance of this number.
7. WALTZ, "Barcarolle" — Waldteufel
8. ENTR'ACTE from "Philemon and Baucis" — Gounod

9. TWO HUNGARIAN DANCES — Brahms
10. HYMN TO ST. CECILIA . . . . — Gounod
    Violin Obligato, MR. K. ONDRICEK.
11. WALTZ from "Puppenfee" — Bayer
12. MARCH, "Obersteiger" — Zeller

The *only* Lithia Water sold at these concerts.

Hygeia Lithia Water

Sparkling and Still.

By its use you will avoid the germs of disease which natural MINERAL WATERS are liable to contain.

For Sale at these concerts and by

S. S. PIERCE CO.

The purity and keeping quality of the Tannhaeuser Export under all changes of temperature, its uniform excellence being guaranteed, together with its nutritious properties, make it the most pleasant, delicious, and convenient beverage for home consumption. Put up in corked bottles, and packed in casks of 10 dozen white flint pints, and 6 dozen amber quarts.

Highest Awards wherever exhibited.

FOR SALE AT THESE CONCERTS.

FAMOUS **TANNHAEUSER** EXPORT BEER

The finest Light Beer Extant.   Brewery Bottling.   Favorite of Connoisseurs.

Pure,   Palatable,   Perfect.

B. & E. Philadelphia Ale on Draught.

FOR SALE AT THESE CONCERTS.

The **BERGNER & ENGEL BREWING CO.'S N.E. Depot,**

508 and 510 Atlantic Avenue, Boston.

Telephone 3805.   SOL. BACHARACH, Manager.

M. Steinert & Sons Co.,

STEINERT HALL BUILDING,

No. 162 Boylston Street, corner Carver, Boston.

STEINWAY & SONS,

HARDMAN,   GABLER,
EMERSON,   SINGER,

PIANOS.

The Æolian, Aeriol, Orchestrelle, and Pianola,

AND THE

STEINERTONE.

THE ÆOLIAN
AND
THE PIANOLA
FOR SUMMER HOMES.

At this season of the year we receive many orders for these instruments for Summer Residences, and therefore beg to call attention to our extensive assortment now on display, especially suited for this purpose.

The ÆOLIAN meets the requirements of country homes, furnishing, as it does, music suitable for every occasion. It practically takes the place of an orchestra — music for dancing — orchestral concerts, — in short, music of every style and description is always available.

The PIANOLA will appeal to many on account of the very little space it occupies. It will play any kind of a piano, and can also be used upon a rented piano without the slightest injury. For the above reasons it is bound to be very popular for small cottages.

We are glad to be able to announce that we can furnish PIANOLAS with no more than a week's delay, and, at times, the day the order is given.

Persons not familiar with these instruments are cordially invited to call at our warerooms and hear them, or a descriptive catalogue will be mailed free upon application.

M. STEINERT & SONS CO.,
Steinert Hall,   162 Boylston Street,   Boston.

ANHEUSER-BUSCH BREWING ASS'N,

ST. LOUIS, MO., U.S.A.

BREWERS OF HIGH=GRADE BEERS EXCLUSIVELY.

Black and Tan.		Faust.
Michelob.		Pale Lager.
Muenchener.		Anheuser Standard.

Served at the Music Hall Concerts.

Also at all first-class hotels, clubs, and bars, and on all Pullman and Wagner cars and ocean and lake steamers.

JACOB WIRTH,   **Wholesale Dealer,**   **Boston, Mass.**

THE MUSIC HALL
PROMENADE CONCERTS

BOSTON, MONDAY, MAY 15, 1899.

SUMMER SEASON. Vol. XIV. No. 7.

THE MUSIC HALL... Promenade Concerts

FOURTEENTH SEASON.

C. A. ELLIS, Manager.   F. R. COMEE, Assistant Manager.

Mr. MAX ZACH, Conductor.

MONDAY, MAY 15.

PROGRAMME.

1. MARCH, "For the Country" . . . . . Millöcker
2. WALTZ, "Les Patineurs" . . . . . Waldteufel
3. OVERTURE, "Donna Diana" . . . . . Reznicek
4. SELECTION from "The Serenade" . . . . . Herbert

5. FANTASIE, "Il Trovatore" . . . . . Verdi
6. ENTR'ACTE, "La Colombe" . . . . . Gounod
   The audience is respectfully requested to preserve silence during the performance of this number.
7. WALTZ, "Jolly Fellows" . . . . . Vollstedt
8. RIDE OF THE HUSSARS . . . . . Spindler

9. OVERTURE, "Poet and Peasant" . . . . . Suppé
   'Cello Obligato, Mr. KELLER.
10. RETRAITE CROATE . . . . . G. Marie
11. LOIN DU BAL . . . . . Gillet
12. AUSTRIA MARCH . . . . . Zach

HERE ARE A FEW NAMES FROM OUR LIST OF COMPOSERS:

ENGLISH.— Stephen Adams, F. H. Cowen, S. Liddle, C. V. Stanford, A. C. Mackenzie, R. H. Walthew, H. R. Shelley, Goring Thomas, Frances Allitsen, Maude V. White, Edward German, Mary Carmichael, Liza Lehmann, etc.

FRENCH.— C. Chaminade, Jane Vieu. L. Denza, P. Delmet, Hemberg, Guy d'Hardelot, De Leva, F. P. Tosti, etc.

ITALIAN.— F. P. Tosti, P. Mascagni, G. Puccini, G. Verdi, Don Lorenzo Perosi, etc.

THE MOST REPRESENTATIVE PUBLISHING HOUSE IN AMERICA.

BOOSEY & CO., 9 East 17th Street, New York.

THE ICE-CREAM SERVED AT THESE CONCERTS IS FURNISHED BY WEBER, 25 Temple Place and 33 West Street.

MUSIC HALL PROMENADE PROGRAMME.
PUBLISHED EVERY EVENING DURING THE SUMMER SEASON.

NOTICE TO ADVERTISERS.
The advertising columns in the Programme are controlled SOLELY by F. R. Comee, Boston Music Hall Box Office, to whom all communications should be addressed.

The United States Hotel,

SARATOGA SPRINGS, N.Y.

Under a continuous management for 25 years.

Without a peer in its appointments, service, and liberal management.

The largest structure of its kind in the world.

Built entirely of brick.

The Hotel and court cover over seven acres.

For further information, rates, etc., etc., address

GAGE & PERRY,
Proprietors,
UNITED STATES HOTEL,
Saratoga Springs, N.Y.

Colonial Beer...

PURE, CLEAN, PALATABLE.

Order a Bottle.

The Beer that's Brewed in Glass.

SOUTHER BREWING CO.,
919 Parker Street,
Roxbury, Mass.

The Peer of all Cigarettes.
Save the band-label on each box for valuable premiums.

::: ALSO :::

Monopol

High-grade Egyptian Cigarettes.

No. 8a Khedive,
No. 8½ Nakine,
No. 9a Egyptian Belles,
No. 70a Princess Lillian

On sale at these concerts and all first-class dealers.

All The **IMPORTED CIGARS**

Sold At These Concerts Are Supplied By The **S. S. PIERCE COMPANY.**

OCKENHEIMER BERG, Near Bingen, GERMANY, On the Rhine.

PHILIP KRIM'S OWN IMPORTATION OF **Rhine Wines,** FOR 30 YEARS AT **163 Shawmut Avenue.**

OUR WINES SOLD AT THESE CONCERTS.

HERRICK, COPLEY SQUARE, Telephones 608 and 950 (Back Bay), CHOICE TABLES for Music Hall "Pops."

GREAT WESTERN CHAMPAGNE

——— A natural, genuine champagne, of the finest quality produced in America.

Sold by Wine Merchants, Grocers, and Druggists.

TUESDAY, MAY 16.

PROGRAMME.

1. MARCH, "Am I a Wiz?" . . . Herbert
2. WALTZ, "Artists' Life" . . . Strauss
3. OVERTURE, "Ruy Blas" . . . Mendelssohn
4. SELECTION, "La Fille de Madame Angot" . Lecocq

5. OVERTURE to "Zampa" . . . Hérold
6. (a) ENTR'ACTE, "Rosamunde" . . . Schubert
   (b) GAVOTTE from "Mignon" . . . Thomas
   The audience is respectfully requested to preserve silence during the performance of this number.
7. WALTZ, "Gil Blas" . . . Czibulka
   (First Time.)
8. ENTRÉE TRIOMPHALE DES BOYARDS . Halvorsen

9. OFFENBACHIANA . . . Conradi
10. SERENADE ROCOCO . . . Meyer-Helmund
11. POLKA, "Papa-Mama" . . . Bayer
12. MARCH from "Puppenfee" . . . Bayer

Handsomest Dining Hotel in New England.

THE HAYWARD

20 Private Dining-rooms.

Beer and Ale drawn direct from wood in THE DUTCH TAP.

SMITH & KERRISSEY, Proprietors.

"M. S." GINGER ALE.

An epicurean beverage, made with Myles Standish Spring Water and compounded with scrupulous care from the highest grade materials.

To be had at the Promenade Concerts.

L. BOYER'S SONS,
Proprietors,
No. 27 Devonshire St., Boston.

MAIN OFFICE.
No. 90 Wall St., New York.

"AMERICA'S FINEST PRODUCT."

Bartholomay's "APOLLO"

LAGER BEER IN BOTTLES.

Sold at these Concerts.

ALBRECHT & KOELLNER,
SOLE AGENTS,
Telephone, Boston 1751.   295-305 A Street.

Also Agents for the "Crystal Rock" Mineral Water.

PURE BEER

Harvard BREW. CO'S $1000.⁰⁰

PURE BEER

Sold at these Concerts, IN BOTTLES ONLY

20¢ PER BOTTLE.

Inglenook Vineyard.

The only California Wines sold at these Concerts.

❧❧

THE CODMAN & HALL CO.,
Opposite the South Union Station.

Sole Agents for New England.

IND. COOPE & CO.'S English Ale.

THE SECOND LARGEST BREWERY IN ENGLAND.

Brewers of the finest *light quality* ale. Very highly endorsed by the medical profession. : : : : :

❧❧

THE CODMAN & HALL CO.,
Opposite South Union Station.

Sole Agents for the United States.

DRIN
only th
PURE
WHIS

If you want p
and richne
flavor, try
only genu
and origin

OLD KENTU
TAYLOR,

Eight years old
own distillation
guaranteed pu
Bottled and shi
direct from
warehouses by
None genuine w
out our signa
on both labels.
ware of imitati
For consumpt
indigestion, and
ailments requi
stimulants, O
KENTUCKY T
LOR has
superior.
Sold by all fi
class druggi
grocers, and liq
dealers.

Wright & Tay
Distillers,
Fine Kentuck
Whiskies,
Louisville, Ky

**Hirshfield & **
New Englan
Agents,
31 Doane Stree
Boston.

Instruct your waiter to bring a bottle of

Pfaff's "Monogram" Lager.

If you will do this, it will not be necessary for us to expatiate upon the good qualities of our production.
YOU CAN JUDGE FOR YOURSELF.

H. & J. PFAFF BREWING COMPANY,
Telephone 2608.   16 ARCH STREET, BOSTON.

TRY THE "COLUMBIA BRAND" VIENNA SAUSAGES. SERVED HOT OR COLD AT THESE CONCERTS

They cannot sell you here
Canadian Club Whisky,
Ruinart Champagne,
Royal Liqueur Scotch,
Carstair's Philadelphia Rye,
Fort Hill Bourbon,
Alhambra Sherry,
All of which you will find
of excellent quality;

But you can get

Kaiser Water,

the most refreshing of all table waters,

Chateau d' Arsac Claret,
N. Johnston & Sons' Medoc,
and
California Inglenook Clarets.

SUPPLIED BY

CODMAN & HALL COMPANY,

WINE MERCHANTS,

Opposite New South Station.

WEDNESDAY, MAY 17.

PROGRAMME.

1. MARCH, "Der flotte Reservist" .... Sabathil
2. OVERTURE, "Martha" .... Flotow
3. WALTZ, "Arabian Nights" .... Strauss
4. SELECTION from "Faust" .... Gounod

5. HUNGARIAN MARCH, "Szeghenyi" .... Fahrbach
      (First Time.)
6. QUINTETTE from the "Mastersingers," arranged for String
      Orchestra by . . . . . . G. Sandré
          (First Time.)
   The audience is respectfully requested to preserve silence during the performance of this number.

7. WALTZ, "Barcarolle" .... Waldteufel
8. ENTR'ACTE from "Philemon and Baucis" .... Gounod

9. TWO HUNGARIAN DANCES .... Brahms
10. HYMN TO ST. CECILIA .... Gounod
         Violin Obligato, Mr. K. ONDRICEK.
11. WALTZ from "Puppenfee" .... Bayer
12. MARCH, "Obersteiger" .... Zeller

THE WILSON, AMERICA'S PUREST Mineral Spring Water,

Is used in making our celebrated **Belfast Ginger Ale, Champagne Kola,** Lemon Soda, Club Soda, Vichy, etc. Hotels and Families supplied. Try a sample order of these goods, and be convinced of their superiority, purity, and medicinal qualities. . . . .

All of our beverages bottled at the spring. We ship only in glass, and all bottles and demijohns are sterilized before being filled. . . . .

Wilson Spring and Hotel Co.,
Tel., 3129 Boston. | 45 ARCH STREET.

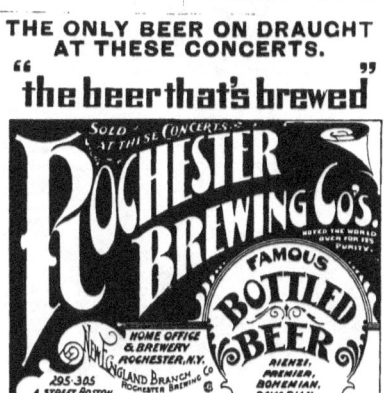

"THE RECOGNIZED FAVORITE OF ALL BEERS."

Schlitz

THE BEER THAT MADE MILWAUKEE FAMOUS.

HIGHEST AWARD FOR PURITY.

Sold at these Concerts. JOS. GAHM & CO., N.E. AGENTS, 125-127 PURCHASE ST.

THE ONLY BEER ON DRAUGHT AT THESE CONCERTS.
"the beer that's brewed"

SOLD AT THESE CONCERTS.

ROCHESTER BREWING CO'S
NOTED THE WORLD OVER FOR ITS PURITY.

FAMOUS BOTTLED BEER

HOME OFFICE & BREWERY ROCHESTER, N.Y.
295-305 A STREET BOSTON
NEW ENGLAND BRANCH ROCHESTER BREWING CO.
Free delivery in city and Suburbs

AIENZI,
PREMIER,
BOHEMIAN,
BAVARIAN,
STANDARD.

THE FALL RIVER LINE

OCCUPYING THE
LONG ISLAND SOUND ROUTE
BETWEEN

Boston and New York

Has the finest quintette of great steamboats that the world has ever seen. The
Priscilla, Puritan, Plymouth, Pilgrim, and Providence

Are the largest, best equipped, safest, and handsomest steamboats ever constructed. This route is one of the most attractive and naturally beautiful traversed by any transportation agency in the world. Trips of the Fall River Line are made throughout the year. Each steamboat has its own orchestra, and the service on each member of the fleet is maintained at the highest possible standard.

Tickets via this route are on sale at all of the principal Ticket Offices in the United States.

From BOSTON. Trains, connecting with steamers at Fall River in 80 minutes, leave Park Square Station, New York, New Haven & Hartford Railroad (Old Colony System), daily at 6 p.m.
From NEW YORK. Steamers leave Pier 19, North River, foot of Warren Street, daily at 5.30 p.m.

S. A. GARDINER, Superintendent, NEW YORK.
GEO. L. CONNOR, Passenger Traffic Manager, NEW HAVEN, CONN.
O. H. TAYLOR, General Passenger Agent, NEW YORK CITY.

HOTEL LANGWOOD,

Middlesex Fells Reservation.

P.O. Address, Melrose, Mass.   Wyoming Station, B. & M. R. R.

Twenty minutes by rail from Boston. Sixty trains daily. Hotel coaches meet trains each way. Four hundred feet above sea level. Beautiful rides, drives, and walks. Golf links, tennis courts, and ball grounds.

OPENS ABOUT MAY 20.

For plans and prices address:

F. W. GASKILL, Manager.

BOSTON OFFICE:
Hemenway Building, 10 Tremont Street, Room 29.

S.S. "Howard." Boston to Norfolk, 522 miles. Norfolk to Baltimore, 200 miles.

1.	2.	3.
Boston	Leave July 9	July 15	August 19
	Arrive July 12	July 31	September 4

S.S. "Toronto." Toronto to Montreal, through the "Thousand Islands" and the "Rapids," 376 miles.

Third Season.

3 Ideal Outings

Personally conducted by
F. R. COMEE, Music Hall, Boston.

No. 1. Ten days. Saratoga-Lake George. 2,130 miles from Buffalo to Duluth, and return on the steamer "North-Land" through the Great Lakes, Erie, Huron, St. Clair, and Superior.

Nos. 2 and 3. Sixteen days. Exactly alike. 700 miles' ocean sail to Norfolk and Baltimore. Over Alleghany Mountains and a day in Chicago. Up Lake Michigan and three days at Mackinac Island. 1,546 miles on steamer "North-West" to Duluth and return to Buffalo through the Great Lakes. Niagara Falls to Toronto. Across Lake Ontario, through the Thousand Islands, and down the St. Lawrence River to Montreal and Boston.

SEND FOR CIRCULARS.

S.S. "Manitou." Chicago to Mackinac Island, across Lake Michigan, 350 miles.

"North-West." Mackinac Island to Duluth and return to Buffalo, 1,555 miles.

Allsopp's

ENGLISH ALE.
"The Red Hand Brand."

Bottled at the brewery, Burton-on-Trent, England, under the personal supervision of the Messrs. Allsopp.

Sold at these concerts.

THURSDAY, MAY 18

PROGRAMME.

1. WERNER MARCH . . . . Zichrer
2. OVERTURE, "Raymond" . . . . Thomas
3. WALTZ, "Faschingskinder" . . . . . Zichrer
   (First Time.)
4. SELECTION, "Carmen" . . . . Bizet
5. BALLET MUSIC, "Queen of Sheba" . . Goldmark
   'Cello Obligato, Mr. KELLER.
6. WALTZ, "Wine, Woman, and Song" . . Strauss
7. TRAUM DER SENNERIN . . . . Labitzky
   Violin Obligati, Messrs. ONDRICEK and HOFFMANN.
   The audience is respectfully requested to preserve silence during the performance of this number.
8. OVERTURE, "Rienzi" . . . . Wagner

9. WALTZ, "Forest Spirits" . . . . . Zach
10. MENUET for String Orchestra . . . Bolzoni
11. LA MOUSMÉ . . . . Ganne
12. MARCH, "Wien, bleibt Wien" . . . Schrammel

The *only* Lithia Water sold at these concerts.

Hygeia Lithia Water

Sparkling and Still.

By its use you will avoid the germs of disease which natural MINERAL WATERS are liable to contain.

For Sale at these concerts and by

S. S. PIERCE CO.

FOR SALE AT THESE CONCERTS.
FAMOUS TANNHAEUSER EXPORT BEER

The finest Light Beer Extant.   Brewery Bottling.   Favorite of Connoisseurs.

Pure,   Palatable,   Perfect.
B. & E. Philadelphia Ale on Draught.
FOR SALE AT THESE CONCERTS.

The purity and keeping quality of the Tannhaeuser Export under all changes of temperature, its uniform excellence being guaranteed, together with its nutritious properties, make it the most pleasant, delicious, and convenient beverage for home consumption.
Put up in corked bottles, and packed in casks of 10 dozen white flint pints, and 10 dozen amber quarts.

Highest Awards wherever exhibited.

The BERGNER & ENGEL BREWING CO.'S N.E. Depot,
508 and 510 Atlantic Avenue, Boston.
Telephone 3805.   SOL. BACHARACH, Manager.

M. Steinert & Sons Co.,

STEINERT HALL BUILDING,

No. 162 Boylston Street, corner Carver, Boston.

STEINWAY & SONS,

HARDMAN, GABLER,
EMERSON, SINGER,

PIANOS.

The Æolian, Aeriol, Orchestrelle, and Pianola,

AND THE

STEINERTONE.

THE ÆOLIAN
AND
THE PIANOLA
FOR SUMMER HOMES.

At this season of the year we receive many orders for these instruments for Summer Residences, and therefore beg to call attention to our extensive assortment now on display, especially suited for this purpose.

The ÆOLIAN meets the requirements of country homes, furnishing, as it does, music suitable for every occasion. It practically takes the place of an orchestra — music for dancing — orchestral concerts, — in short, music of every style and description is always available.

The PIANOLA will appeal to many on account of the very little space it occupies. It will play any kind of a piano, and can also be used upon a rented piano without the slightest injury. For the above reasons it is bound to be very popular for small cottages.

We are glad to be able to announce that we can furnish PIANOLAS with no more than a week's delay, and, at times, the day the order is given.

Persons not familiar with these instruments are cordially invited to call at our warerooms and hear them, or a descriptive catalogue will be mailed free upon application.

M. STEINERT & SONS CO.,
Steinert Hall, 162 Boylston Street, Boston.

ANHEUSER-BUSCH BREWING ASS'N,

ST. LOUIS, MO., U.S.A.

BREWERS OF HIGH=GRADE BEERS EXCLUSIVELY.

Black and Tan.

Michelob.

Muenchener.

Faust.

Pale Lager.

Anheuser Standard.

Served at the Music Hall Concerts.

Also at all first-class hotels, clubs, and bars, and on all Pullman and Wagner cars and ocean and lake steamers.

JACOB WIRTH, Wholesale Dealer, Boston, Mass.

THE MUSIC HALL
Promenade Concerts

BOSTON, TUESDAY, MAY 16, 1899.   SUMMER SEASON. Vol. XIV. No. 8.

SMOKE "LA CELESTINA," THE BEST ALL-HAVANA CIGAR. DANIEL FRANK & CO.

SMOKE THE POPULAR "BARRISTER" CIGARS AT THE POPULAR CONCERTS

THE MUSIC HALL Promenade Concerts
FOURTEENTH SEASON.

C. A. ELLIS, Manager.   F. R. COMEE, Assistant Manager.
Mr. MAX ZACH, Conductor.

TUESDAY, MAY 16.

PROGRAMME.

1. MARCH, "Am I a Wiz?" . . . . . Herbert
2. WALTZ, "Artists' Life" . . . . . Strauss
3. OVERTURE, "Ruy Blas" . . . . Mendelssohn
4. SELECTION, "La Fille de Madame Angot" . Lecocq
5. OVERTURE to "Zampa" . . . . . Herold
6. (a) ENTR'ACTE, "Rosamunde" . . . Schubert
   (b) GAVOTTE from "Mignon" . . . . Thomas
   The audience is respectfully requested to preserve silence during the performance of this number.
7. WALTZ, "Gil Blas" . . . . . . Czibulka
   (First Time.)
8. ENTRÉE TRIOMPHALE DES BOYARDS . Halvorsen
9. OFFENBACHIANA . . . . . . Conrad
10. WALTZ, "Blue Danube" . . . . Strauss
11. POLKA, "Papa-Mama" . . . . . Bayer
12. MARCH from "Puppenfee" . . . . Bayer

ALBUMS OF SONGS,
Containing many popular compositions not published in single form.

IRISH FOLK SONGS, by Charles Wood,	$2.00
RUSSIAN SONGS, by F. Wishaw (2 vols.),	1.00
NINE SONGS, by S. Liddle, . .	1.00
NINE SONGS, by Liza Lehmann, . .	1.00
FIVE SONGS, by Francis Korbay, . .	2.00

Beautifully illustrated by J. S. SARGENT, R.A.

BOOSEY & CO.,
9 East 17th Street,   New York.

YOU CAN
Have your last season's outfit dyed or cleansed and refinished so it will look like new, by our French process. Why discard soiled clothing when it can be overhauled and worn as second best? You can

RELY ON
Our methods of cleansing, and need not hesitate to trust us with articles of the most delicate textures. We dye or cleanse and refinish PROPERLY, *all* materials of household use and clothing of all kinds.

LEWANDO'S
W. L. Crosby, General Manager.
French Cleansers, Fancy Dyers, Fine Launderers.
PRINCIPAL OFFICES:
17 Temple Place, Boston.
479 Fifth Avenue, New York.
Established 70 years.
Largest in America.
Bundles called for and delivered.
Telephones in all offices.

If you are open
to conviction,
to-night

try one 10-cent box of

BETWEEN THE ACTS
Little Cigars

to smoke now—or at any time when you want a short smoke and haven't time for a long one. They are real cigars, but small ones.

They cost so little that you can use them every day as well as not and actually save on your daily cigar expense by substituting them for larger cigars.

FOR SALE HERE.

DRINK
VAN NOSTRAND'S
BOSTON CLUB LAGER
SOLD AT THESE CONCERTS

NORFOLK CABINET
LAGER BEER

A Particularly Fine Lager for Family Use and Clubs.

Bottled in the most careful manner at our own bottling department, and sold by the S. S. Pierce Co. and all other leading grocers in New England.

Other Brands in Bottles:
"Norfolk India Pale Stock Ale."
"Norfolk Extra Golden Ale" (blue label).
"Norfolk Standard Lager."
Our "Cabinet" and "Bismarck Brau" are the most popular refreshments at these concerts.

HABICH & CO.
H. W. HABICH.   Telephone, 56 Roxbury
EDWARD RUHL.   or 1552 Boston.

ESTABROOK & EATON'S MARGUERITE PERFECTOS, 10c. EACH, CONCHAS, 10c., 3 FOR 25c., SOLD AT THE "POPS."

THE ICE-CREAM SERVED AT THESE CONCERTS IS FURNISHED BY WEBER, 25 Temple Place and 33 West Street.

MUSIC HALL PROMENADE PROGRAMME.
PUBLISHED EVERY EVENING DURING THE SUMMER SEASON.

NOTICE TO ADVERTISERS.
The advertising columns in the Programme are controled SOLELY by F. R. Comee, Boston Music Hall Box Office, to whom all communications should be addressed.

The United States Hotel,
SARATOGA SPRINGS, N.Y.

Under a continuous management for 25 years.

Without a peer in its appointments, service, and liberal management.

The largest structure of its kind in the world.

Built entirely of brick.

The Hotel and court cover over seven acres.

For further information, rates, etc., etc., address

GAGE & PERRY,
Proprietors,
UNITED STATES HOTEL,
Saratoga Springs, N.Y.

Colonial Beer...
The Beer that's Brewed in Glass.

* PURE,
CLEAN, PALATABLE.

Order a Bottle.

SOUTHER BREWING CO.,
919 Parker Street,
Roxbury, Mass.

VEUVE CHAFFARD
PURE OLIVE OIL.
IN HONEST BOTTLES.

The Peer of all Cigarettes.
Save the band-label on each box for valuable premiums.

::: ALSO :::

Monopol
High-grade Egyptian Cigarettes.

No. 8A Khedive,
No. 6A Nakina,
No. 9A Egyptian Helles,
No. 70A Princess Lillian

On sale at these concerts and all first-class dealers.

PHILIP KRIM'S
OWN IMPORTATION OF
Rhine Wines,
FOR 30 YEARS AT
163 Shawmut Avenue.
OUR WINES SOLD AT THESE CONCERTS.

HERRICK, COPLEY SQUARE, Telephones 608 and 950 (Back Bay), CHOICE TABLES for Music Hall "Pops."

D. LEIDEN'S SPARKLING MOSELLE,

The only Sparkling Wine sold at these Concerts.

SHINNECOCK

The Perfection of

Scotch Whisky

Sold by
S. S. PIERCE COMPANY.

WEDNESDAY, MAY 17.

PROGRAMME.

1. MARCH, "Der flotte Reservist" . . . Sabathil
2. OVERTURE, "Martha" . . . Flotow
3. WALTZ, "Arabian Nights" . . . Strauss
4. SELECTION from "Faust" . . . Gounod

5. HUNGARIAN MARCH, "Szeghenyi" . . . Fahrbach
   (First Time.)
6. MENUET for String Orchestra . . . Bolzoni
   The audience is respectfully requested to preserve silence during the performance of this number.
7. WALTZ, "Barcarolle" . . . Waldteufel
8. ENTR'ACTE from "Philemon and Baucis" . . . Gounod

9. TWO HUNGARIAN DANCES . . . Brahms
10. HYMN TO ST. CECILIA . . . Gounod
    Violin Obligato, Mr. K. ONDRICEK.
11. WALTZ from "Puppenfee" . . . Bayer
12. MARCH, "Obersteiger" . . . Zeller

Handsomest Dining Hotel in New England.

THE HAYWARD
20 Private Dining-rooms.

Beer and Ale drawn direct from wood in THE DUTCH TAP.

SMITH & KERRISSEY, Proprietors.

"M. S." GINGER ALE.

An epicurean beverage, made with Myles Standish Spring Water and compounded with scrupulous care from the highest grade materials.

To be had at the Promenade Concerts.

L. BOYER'S SONS,
Proprietors,
No. 27 Devonshire St., Boston.

MAIN OFFICE.
No. 90 Wall St., New York.

"AMERICA'S FINEST PRODUCT."

Bartholomay's "APOLLO"
LAGER BEER IN BOTTLES.

Sold at these Concerts.

ALBRECHT & KOELLNER,
SOLE AGENTS,
Telephone, Boston 1751.   295-305 A Street.

Also Agents for the "Crystal Rock" Mineral Water.

PURE BEER

Harvard BREW. CO'S $1000.⁰⁰

PURE BEER

Sold at these Concerts
IN BOTTLES ONLY
20¢ PER BOTTLE.

TABLE LINEN USED AT THESE CONCERTS IS THE L. K. HUSTED LAUNDERING COMPANY, 27 and 29 BROADWAY, CHELSEA, MASS.

Inglenook Vineyard.

The only California Wines sold at these Concerts.

❦❦

THE CODMAN & HALL CO.,
Opposite the South Union Station.

Sole Agents for New England.

IND. COOPE & CO.'S English Ale.

THE SECOND LARGEST BREWERY IN ENGLAND.

Brewers of the finest *light quality* ale. Very highly endorsed by the medical profession. : : : : :

❦❦

THE CODMAN & HALL CO.,
Opposite South Union Station.

Sole Agents for the United States.

DRINK only the PUREST WHISKY

If you want purity and richness flavor, try the only genuine and original

OLD KENTUCKY TAYLOR,

Eight years old, of own distillation and guaranteed pure. Bottled and shipped direct from our warehouses by us. None genuine without our signature on both labels. Beware of imitations. For consumption, indigestion, and all ailments requiring stimulants, OLD KENTUCKY TAYLOR has no superior.

Sold by all first class druggists, grocers, and liquor dealers.

Wright & Taylor
Distillers,
Fine Kentucky Whiskies,
Louisville, Ky.

Hirshfield & Co.
New England Agents,
31 Doane Street
Boston.

Instruct your waiter to bring a bottle of

Pfaff's "Monogram" Lager.

If you will do this, it will not be necessary for us to expatiate upon the good qualities of our production.
YOU CAN JUDGE FOR YOURSELF.

H. & J. PFAFF BREWING COMPANY,
Telephone 2608.   16 ARCH STREET, BOSTON.

TRY THE "COLUMBIA BRAND" VIENNA SAUSAGES. SERVED HOT OR COLD AT THESE CONCERTS.

They cannot sell you here
Canadian Club Whisky,
Ruinart Champagne,
Royal Liqueur Scotch,
Carstair's Philadelphia Rye,
Fort Hill Bourbon,
Alhambra Sherry,
All of which you will find
of excellent quality;

But you can get

Kaiser Water,

the most refreshing of all
table waters,

*Chateau d' Arsac Claret,
N. Johnston & Sons' Medoc,*
and
California Inglenook Clarets.

SUPPLIED BY

CODMAN & HALL COMPANY,

WINE MERCHANTS,

Opposite New South
Station.

THURSDAY, MAY 18.

PROGRAMME.

1. WERNER MARCH . . . . . Zichrer
2. OVERTURE, " Raymond " . . . Thomas
3. WALTZ, " Faschingskinder " . . . Ziehrer
       First Time
4. SELECTION, " Carmen " . . . . Bizet

5. BALLET MUSIC, " Queen of Sheba " . . Goldmark
       Cello Obligato, Mr. KELLER.
6. WALTZ, " Wine, Woman, and Song " . . Strauss
7. TRAUM DER SENNERIN . . . . Labitzky
       Violin Obligati, Messrs. ONDRICEK and HOFFMANN
       The audience is respectfully requested to preserve silence during the performance of this number.
8. OVERTURE, " Rienzi " . . . . Wagner

9. WALTZ, " Forest Spirits " . . . . Zach
10. WEDDING MARCH . . . . . Mendelssohn
11. LA MOUSMÉ . . . . . . Ganne
12. MARCH, " Wien, bleibt Wien " . . . Schrammel

COAL
Best Quality
AT
Lowest Prices

METROPOLITAN COAL COMPANY,
No. 30 Congress Street.

THE WILSON,
AMERICA'S PUREST
Mineral Spring Water,

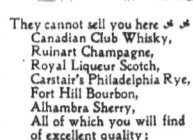

Is used in making our celebrated **Belfast Ginger Ale, Champagne Kola,** Lemon Soda, Club Soda, Vichy, etc. Hotels and Families supplied. Try a sample order of these goods, and be convinced of their superiority, purity, and medicinal qualities. . . . . .

All of our beverages bottled at the spring. . . . We ship only in glass, and all bottles and demijohns are sterilized before being filled. . . . . . .

Wilson Spring and Hotel Co.,
tal., 3129 Boston. | 45 ARCH STREET.

"THE RECOGNIZED FAVORITE OF ALL BEERS."

Schlitz
THE BEER THAT MADE MILWAUKEE FAMOUS.

HIGHEST AWARD FOR PURITY.

Sold at these Concerts. JOS. GAHM & CO., N.E. AGENTS. 125-127 PURCHASE ST.

THE ONLY BEER ON DRAUGHT AT THESE CONCERTS.

"the beer that's brewed"

SOLD AT THESE CONCERTS.

Rochester Brewing Co's
NOTED THE WORLD OVER FOR ITS PURITY.

FAMOUS BOTTLED BEER

HOME OFFICE & BREWERY ROCHESTER, N.Y.

295-305 A STREET BOSTON
ENGLAND BRANCH ROCHESTER BREWING CO
free delivery in city and Suburbs

RIENZI, PREMIER, BOHEMIAN, BAVARIAN, STANDARD.

THE FALL RIVER LINE

OCCUPYING THE
LONG ISLAND SOUND ROUTE
BETWEEN

Boston and New York

Has the finest quintette of great steamboats that the world has ever seen. The

Priscilla, Puritan, Plymouth, Pilgrim, and Providence

Are the largest, best equipped, safest, and handsomest steamboats ever constructed. This route is one of the most attractive and naturally beautiful traversed by any transportation agency in the world. Trips of the Fall River Line are made throughout the year. Each steamboat has its own orchestra, and the service on each member of the fleet is maintained at the highest possible standard.

Tickets via this route are on sale at all of the principal Ticket Offices in the United States.

From BOSTON. Trains, connecting with steamers at Fall River in 80 minutes leave Park Square Station, New York, New Haven & Hartford Railroad (Old Colony System), daily at 6 p.m.
From NEW YORK. Steamers leave Pier 19, North River, foot of Warren Street, daily at 5.30 p.m.

S. A. GARDNER, Superintendent, NEW YORK.
GEO. L. CONNOR, Passenger Traffic Manager, NEW HAVEN, CONN.
O. H. TAYLOR, General Passenger Agent, NEW YORK CITY.

HOTEL LANGWOOD,
Middlesex Fells Reservation.

P.O. Address, Melrose, Mass.   Wyoming Station, B. & M. R.R.

Twenty minutes by rail from Boston. Sixty trains daily. Hotel coaches meet trains each way. Four hundred feet above sea level. Beautiful rides, drives, and walks. Golf links, tennis courts, and ball grounds.

OPENS ABOUT MAY 20.

For plans and prices address:

F. W. GASKILL, Manager.

BOSTON OFFICE:
Hemenway Building, 10 Tremont Street, Room 29.

S.S. "Howard." Boston to Norfolk, 522 miles. Norfolk to Baltimore, 200 miles.

	1.	2.	3.
Boston	Leave	July 8	July 15	August 19
	Arrive	July 12	July 31	September 4

S.S. "Toronto." Toronto to Montreal, through the "Thousand Islands" and the "Rapids," 376 miles.

Third Season.

3 Ideal Outings

Personally conducted by F. R. COMEE, Music Hall, Boston.

No. 1. Ten days. **Saratoga, Lake George,** 2,130 miles from Buffalo to Duluth, and return on the steamer "North-Land" through the Great Lakes, Erie, Huron, St. Clair, and Superior.

Nos. 2 and 3. Sixteen days. Exactly alike. 700 miles' ocean sail to Norfolk and Baltimore. Over Alleghany Mountains and a day in Chicago. Up Lake Michigan and three days at Mackinac Island. 1,346 miles on steamer "North-West" to Duluth and return to Buffalo through the Great Lakes. Niagara Falls to Toronto. Across Lake Ontario, through the Thousand Islands, and down the St. Lawrence River to Montreal and Boston.

SEND FOR CIRCULARS.

S.S. "Manitou." Chicago to Mackinac Island, across Lake Michigan, 350 miles.

"North-West." Mackinac Island to Duluth and return to Buffalo, 1,555 miles.

Allsopp's

ENGLISH ALE.
"The Red Hand Brand."

Bottled at the brewery, Burton-on-Trent, England, under the personal supervision of the Messrs. Allsopp.

Sold at these concerts.

FRIDAY, MAY 19.

PROGRAMME.

1. MARCH, "Fra Bombarda" . . . Czibulka
2. WALTZ, "Doctrinen" . . . E. Strauss
3. OVERTURE, "Oberon" . . . Weber
4. SELECTION from "Traviata" . . . Verdi
5. SUITE I, L'Arlésienne . . . Bizet
   (a) Menuet. (b) Adagietto. (c) Carillon.
6. OVERTURE, "Semiramide" . . . Rossini
7. VALSE CAPRICE, "Honeymoon" . . . Stix
   The audience is respectfully requested to preserve silence during the performance of this number.
8. POLONAISE . . . Tschaikowski
9. PRELUDE to "Le Déluge" . . . Saint-Saens
   Violin Solo, Ma. ONDRICEK.
10. WALTZ, "Vienna Beauties" . . . Ziehrer
11. LA CINQUANTAINE . . . G. Marie
12. MARCH, "Washington Post" . . . Sousa

The *only* Lithia Water sold at these concerts.

Hygeia Lithia Water

Sparkling and Still.

By its use you will avoid the germs of disease which natural MINERAL WATERS are liable to contain.

For Sale at these concerts and by

S. S. PIERCE CO.

The purity and keeping quality of the Tannhaeuser Export under all changes of temperature, its uniform excellence being guaranteed, together with its nutritious properties, make it the most pleasant, delicious, and convenient beverage for home consumption.
Put up in corked bottles, and packed in casks of 10 dozen white flint pints, and 6 dozen amber quarts.

Highest Awards wherever exhibited.

FOR SALE AT THESE CONCERTS.
FAMOUS TANNHAEUSER EXPORT BEER

The finest Light Beer Extant.   Brewery Bottling.   Favorite of Connoisseurs.

Pure,   Palatable,   Perfect.
B. & E. Philadelphia Ale on Draught.
FOR SALE AT THESE CONCERTS.

The BERGNER & ENGEL BREWING CO.'S N.E. Depot,
508 and 510 Atlantic Avenue, Boston.
Telephone 3805.   **SOL. BACHARACH, Manager.**

M. Steinert & Sons Co.,

STEINERT HALL BUILDING,

No. 162 Boylston Street, corner Carver, Boston.

STEINWAY & SONS,

HARDMAN, GABLER,
EMERSON, SINGER,

PIANOS.

The Æolian, Aeriol, Orchestrelle,
and Pianola,

AND THE

STEINERTONE.

THE ÆOLIAN
AND
THE PIANOLA
FOR SUMMER HOMES.

At this season of the year we receive many orders for these instruments for Summer Residences, and therefore beg to call attention to our extensive assortment now on display, especially suited for this purpose.

The ÆOLIAN meets the requirements of country homes, furnishing, as it does, music suitable for every occasion. It practically takes the place of an orchestra — music for dancing — orchestral concerts, — in short, music of every style and description is always available.

The PIANOLA will appeal to many on account of the very little space it occupies. It will play any kind of a piano, and can also be used upon a rented piano without the slightest injury. For the above reasons it is bound to be very popular for small cottages.

We are glad to be able to announce that we can furnish PIANOLAS with no more than a week's delay, and, at times, the day the order is given.

Persons not familiar with these instruments are cordially invited to call at our warerooms and hear them, or a descriptive catalogue will be mailed free upon application.

M. STEINERT & SONS CO.,
Steinert Hall, 162 Boylston Street, Boston.

ANHEUSER-BUSCH BREWING ASS'N,

ST. LOUIS, MO., U.S.A.

BREWERS OF HIGH=GRADE BEERS EXCLUSIVELY.

Black and Tan.

Michelob.

Muenchener.

Faust.

Pale Lager.

Anheuser Standard.

Served at the Music Hall Concerts.

Also at all first-class hotels, clubs, and bars, and on all Pullman and Wagner cars and ocean and lake steamers.

JACOB WIRTH,   Wholesale Dealer,   Boston, Mass.

THE MUSIC HALL
PROMENADE CONCERTS

SMOKE "LA CELESTINA," THE BEST ALL-HAVANA CIGAR. DANIEL FRANK & CO.

SMOKE THE POPULAR "BARRISTER" CIGARS AT THE POPULAR CONCERTS.

PUBLISHED BY
C. A. ELLIS,
MUSIC HALL.

BOSTON, WEDNESDAY, MAY 17, 1899.

SUMMER SEASON.
Vol. XIV. No. 9.

YOU CAN
Have your last season's outfit dyed or cleansed and refinished so it will look like new, by our French process. Why discard soiled clothing when it can be overhauled and worn a second best? You can

RELY ON
Our methods of cleansing, and need not hesitate to trust us with articles of the most delicate textures.
We dye or cleanse and refinish PROPERLY, *all* materials of household use and clothing of all kinds.

LEWANDO'S
W. L. Crosby, General Manager.
French Cleansers, Fancy Dyers,
Fine Launderers
PRINCIPAL OFFICES:
17 Temple Place, Boston.
479 Fifth Avenue, New York.
Established 70 years.
Largest in America.
Bundles called for and delivered.
Telephones in all offices.

Save half your money

do not throw it away in half-smoked cigars! You will find that 50% of your cigar money is thrown away every day if you recall how few cigars you really have time to smoke "up."

BETWEEN THE ACTS
Little Cigars

are pure—clean—all good tobacco, and are in every way a very satisfactory short smoke. While you are listening to the music to-night, try a 10-cent box. The waiter will get them for you as they are for sale here. You will enjoy them!

THE MUSIC HALL: Promenade Concerts

FOURTEENTH SEASON.

C. A. ELLIS, Manager.   F. R. COMEE, Assistant Manager.

Mr. MAX ZACH, Conductor.

WEDNESDAY, MAY 17.

PROGRAMME.

1. MARCH, "Der flotte Reservist" . . . . . . Sabathil
2. OVERTURE, "Martha" . . . . Flotow
3. WALTZ, "Arabian Nights" . . . . Strauss
4. SELECTION from "Faust" . . . . Gounod

5. HUNGARIAN MARCH, "Szeghenyi" . . . . Fahrbach
   (First Time.)
6. MENUET for String Orchestra . . . . . . Bolzoni
   The audience is respectfully requested to preserve silence during the performance of this number.
7. WALTZ, "Barcarolle" . . . . Waldteufel
8. ENTR'ACTE from "Philemon and Baucis" . . . Gounod

9. TWO HUNGARIAN DANCES . . . . Brahms
10. HYMN TO ST. CECILIA . . . . Gounod
    Violin Obligato, Mr. K. ONDRICEK.
11. WALTZ from "Puppenfee" . . . . Bayer
12. MARCH, "Obersteiger" . . . . Zeller

THE TWO MOST POPULAR TWO-STEPS
OF THE SEASON.

THE RUNAWAY GIRL, by Van Baar, ... 60c.
THE CECIL, by Megone, ... 50c.
FOR ORCHESTRA OR PIANO SOLO.

BOOSEY & CO.,
9 EAST 17th STREET,   NEW YORK.

"OH BE JOLLY!"
DRINK VAN NOSTRAND'S
P. B. ALE
SOLD AT THESE CONCERTS

NORFOLK CABINET
LAGER BEER

A Particularly Fine Lager for Family Use and Clubs.
Bottled in the most careful manner at our own bottling department, and sold by the S. S. Pierce Co. and all other leading grocers in New England.

Other Brands in Bottles:
"Norfolk India Pale Stock Ale."
"Norfolk Extra Golden Ale" (blue label).
"Norfolk Standard Lager."
Our "Cabinet" and "Bismarck Brau" are the most popular refreshments at these concerts.

HABICH & CO.

H. W. HARICH, | Telephone, 56 Roxbury
EDWARD RUHL. | or 1350 Boston.

ESTABROOK & EATON'S MARGUERITE PERFECTOS, 10c. EACH
CONCHAS, 10c., 3 FOR 25c., **SOLD AT THE "POPS."**

THE ICE-CREAM SERVED AT THESE CONCERTS IS FURNISHED BY WEBER, 25 Temple Place and 33 West Street.

MUSIC HALL PROMENADE PROGRAMME.

PUBLISHED EVERY EVENING DURING THE SUMMER SEASON.

NOTICE TO ADVERTISERS.

The advertising columns in the Programme are controlled SOLELY by F. R. Comee, Boston Music Hall Box Office, to whom all communications should be addressed.

The United States Hotel,

SARATOGA SPRINGS, N.Y.

Under a continuous management for 25 years.

Without a peer in its appointments, service, and liberal management.

The largest structure of its kind in the world.

Built entirely of brick.

The Hotel and court cover over seven acres.

For further information, rates, etc., etc., address

GAGE & PERRY,
Proprietors,
UNITED STATES HOTEL,
Saratoga Springs, N.Y.

COLONIAL BEER

The Beer that's Brewed in Glass.

Colonial Beer...

PURE, CLEAN, PALATABLE.

Order a Bottle.

SOUTHER BREWING CO.,
919 Parker Street,
Roxbury, Mass.

All The **IMPORTED CIGARS** Sold At These Concerts Are Supplied By The **S. S. PIERCE COMPANY.**

The Peer of all Cigarettes.

Save the band-label on each box for valuable premiums.

::: ALSO :::

Monopol

High-grade Egyptian Cigarettes.

No. 8A Khedive,
No. 6A Nakine,
No. 9A Egyptian Belles,
No. 70A Princess Lillian

On sale at these concerts and all first-class dealers.

OCKENHEIMER BERG, Near Bingen, GERMANY. On the Rhine.

PHILIP KRIM'S OWN IMPORTATION OF **Rhine Wines.** FOR 30 YEARS AT **163 Shawmut Avenue,** OUR WINES SOLD AT THESE CONCERTS.

HERRICK, COPLEY SQUARE, Telephones 608 and 950 (Back Bay), CHOICE TABLES for Music Hall "Pops."

GREAT WESTERN CHAMPAGNE

——————A natural, genuine champagne, of the finest quality produced in America.

Sold by Wine Merchants, Grocers, and Druggists.

THURSDAY, MAY 18.

PROGRAMME.

1. WERNER MARCH . . . . Ziehrer
2. OVERTURE, "Raymond" . . . . . . Thomas
3. WALTZ, "Faschingskinder" . . . . . Ziehrer
   (First Time.)
4. SELECTION, "Carmen" . . . . Bizet
5. BALLET MUSIC, "Queen of Sheba" . Goldmark
   (Cello Obligato, Mr. KELLER.)
6. WALTZ, "Wine, Woman, and Song" . Strauss
7. TRAUM DER SENNERIN . . . . . . Labitzky
   Violin Obligati, Messrs. ONDRICEK and HOFFMANN.
   The audience is respectfully requested to preserve silence during the performance of this number.
8. OVERTURE, "Rienzi" . . . . Wagner
9. WALTZ, "Forest Spirits" . . . . . . Zach
10. WEDDING MARCH . . . . Mendelssohn
11. LA MOUSMÉ . . . . Ganne
12. MARCH, "Wien, bleibt Wien" . . Schrammel

Handsomest Dining Hotel in New England.

THE HAYWARD

20 Private Dining-rooms.

Beer and Ale drawn direct from wood in THE DUTCH TAP.

SMITH & KERRISSEY, Proprietors.

"M. S." GINGER ALE.

An epicurean beverage, made with Myles Standish Spring Water and compounded with scrupulous care from the highest grade materials.

To be had at the Promenade Concerts.

L. BOYER'S SONS,
Proprietors,
No. 27 Devonshire St., Boston.

MAIN OFFICE.
No. 90 Wall St., New York.

"AMERICA'S FINEST PRODUCT."

Bartholomay's "APOLLO"

LAGER BEER IN BOTTLES.

Sold at these Concerts.

ALBRECHT & KOELLNER,
SOLE AGENTS,
Telephone, Boston 1751.   295-305 A Street.

Also Agents for the "Crystal Rock" Mineral Water.

PURE BEER

Harvard BREW. CO'S $1000.00

PURE BEER

Sold at these Concerts.
IN BOTTLES ONLY
20¢ PER BOTTLE.

TABLE LINEN USED AT THESE CONCERTS LAUNDERED BY THE L. K. HUSTED LAUNDERING COMPANY, 27 and 29 BROADWAY, CHELSEA, MASS.

Inglenook Vineyard.

The only California Wines sold at these Concerts.

THE CODMAN & HALL CO.,
Opposite the South Union Station.

Sole Agents for New England.

IND. COOPE & CO.'S English Ale.

THE SECOND LARGEST BREWERY IN ENGLAND.

Brewers of the finest *light quality* ale. Very highly endorsed by the medical profession. : : : : :

THE CODMAN & HALL CO.,
Opposite South Union Station.

Sole Agents for the United States.

DRIN only the

PURE

WHIS

If you want pu and richness flavor, try only genu and origina

OLD KENTUC TAYLOR,

Eight years old, own distillation guaranteed pu Bottled and ship direct from warehouses by None genuine w out our signat on both labels. ware of imitati for consumpti indigestion, and ailments requir stimulants, OL KENTUCKY TA LOR has n superior.

Sold by all fir class druggi grocers, and liqu dealers.

Wright & Tayl Distillers, Fine Kentucky Whiskies, Louisville, Ky.

Hirsfield & Co New England Agents, 31 Doane Street Boston.

Instruct your waiter to bring a bottle of

Pfaff's "Monogram" Lager.

If you will do this, it will not be necessary for us to expatiate upon the good qualities of our production.
YOU CAN JUDGE FOR YOURSELF.

H. & J. PFAFF BREWING COMPANY,
Telephone 2608.   16 ARCH STREET, BOSTON.

TRY THE "COLUMBIA BRAND" VIENNA SAUSAGES. SERVED HOT OR COLD AT THESE CONCERTS.

They cannot sell you here
Canadian Club Whisky,
Ruinart Champagne,
Royal Liqueur Scotch,
Carstair's Philadelphia Rye,
Fort Hill Bourbon,
Alhambra Sherry,
All of which you will find
of excellent quality;

But you can get

Kaiser Water,

the most refreshing of all table waters,

Chateau d'Arsac Claret,
N. Johnston & Sons' Medoc,
and
California Inglenook Clarets.

SUPPLIED BY

CODMAN & HALL COMPANY,

WINE MERCHANTS,

Opposite New South Station.

FRIDAY, MAY 19.

PROGRAMME.

1. MARCH, "Fra Bombarda" . . . . . Czibulka
2. WALTZ, "Doctrinen" . . . . . E. Strauss
3. OVERTURE, "Oberon" . . . . . Weber
4. SELECTION from "Traviata" . . . . . Verdi

5. SUITE I, L'Arlésienne . . . . . Bizet
   (a) Menuet (b) Adagietto (c) Carillon.
6. OVERTURE, "Semiramide" . . . . . Rossini
7. VALSE CAPRICE, "Honeymoon" . . . . . Stix
   The audience is respectfully requested to preserve silence during the performance of this number.
8. POLONAISE . . . . . Tschaikowski

9. PRELUDE to "Le Deluge" . . . . . Saint-Saëns
    Violin Solo, Mr. ONDRICEK.
10. WALTZ, "Vienna Beauties" . . . . . Ziehrer
11. LA CINQUANTAINE . . . . . G. Marie
12. MARCH, "Washington Post" . . . . . Sousa

COAL
Best Quality AT Lowest Prices

METROPOLITAN COAL COMPANY,
No. 30 Congress Street.

THE WILSON, AMERICA'S PUREST
Mineral Spring Water,

Is used in making our celebrated
Belfast Ginger Ale,
Champagne Kola,
Lemon Soda, Club Soda, Vichy, etc. Hotels and Families supplied. Try a sample order of these goods, and be convinced of their superiority, purity, and medicinal qualities.

All of our beverages bottled at the spring. We ship only in glass, and all bottles and demijohns are sterilized before being filled.

Wilson Spring and Hotel Co.,
Tel., 3128 Boston. | 45 ARCH STREET.

"THE RECOGNIZED FAVORITE OF ALL BEERS."

Sold at these Concerts. JOS. GAHM & CO., N.E. AGENTS, 125-127 PURCHASE ST.

THE ONLY BEER ON DRAUGHT AT THESE CONCERTS.
"the beer that's brewed"

THE FALL RIVER LINE

OCCUPYING THE LONG ISLAND SOUND ROUTE BETWEEN

Boston and New York

Has the finest quintette of great steamboats that the world has ever seen. The

Priscilla, Puritan, Plymouth, Pilgrim, and Providence

Are the largest, best equipped, safest, and handsomest steamboats ever constructed. This route is one of the most attractive and naturally beautiful traversed by any transportation agency in the world. Trips of the Fall River Line are made throughout the year.

Each steamboat has its own orchestra, and the service on each member of the fleet is maintained at the highest possible standard.

Tickets via this route are on sale at all of the principal Ticket Offices in the United States.

From BOSTON. Trains, connecting with steamers at Fall River in 80 minutes leave Park Square Station, New York, New Haven & Hartford Railroad (Old Colony System), daily at 6 p.m.

From NEW YORK. Steamers leave Pier 19, North River, foot of Warren Street, daily at 5.30 p.m.

S. A. GARDNER, Superintendent, NEW YORK.
GEO. L. CONNOR, Passenger Traffic Manager, NEW HAVEN, CONN.
O. H. TAYLOR, General Passenger Agent, NEW YORK CITY.

HOTEL LANGWOOD,

Middlesex Fells Reservation.

P.O. Address, Melrose, Mass.   Wyoming Station, B. & M. R.R.

Twenty minutes by rail from Boston. Sixty trains daily. Hotel coaches meet trains each way. Four hundred feet above sea level. Beautiful rides, drives, and walks. Golf links, tennis courts, and ball grounds.

OPENS ABOUT MAY 20.

For plans and prices address:

F. W. GASKILL, Manager.

BOSTON OFFICE:
Hemenway Building, 10 Tremont Street, Room 29.

Third Season.

3 Ideal Outings

Personally conducted by F. R. COMEE, Music Hall, Boston.

S.S. "Howard." Boston to Norfolk, 522 miles. Norfolk to Baltimore, 200 miles.

Boston	1.	2.	3.
Leave	July 2	July 15	August 12
Arrive	July 12	July 31	September 4

S.S. "Toronto." Toronto to Montreal, through the "Thousand Islands" and the "Rapids," 376 miles.

No. 1. Ten days. Saratoga-Lake George. 2,130 miles from Buffalo to Duluth, and return on the steamer "North-Land" through the Great Lakes, Erie, Huron, St. Clair, and Superior.

Nos. 2 and 3. Sixteen days. Exactly alike. 700 miles' ocean sail to Norfolk and Baltimore. Over Alleghany Mountains and a day in Chicago. Up Lake Michigan and three days at Mackinac Island. 1,546 miles on steamer "North-West," to Duluth and return to Buffalo through the Great Lakes. Niagara Falls to Toronto. Across Lake Ontario, through the Thousand Islands, and down the St. Lawrence River to Montreal and Boston.

SEND FOR CIRCULARS.

S.S. "Manitou." Chicago to Mackinac Island, across Lake Michigan, 350 miles.

"North-West." Mackinac Island to Duluth and return to Buffalo, 1,555 miles.

Allsopp's

ENGLISH ALE.
"The Red Hand Brand."

Bottled at the brewery, Burton-on-Trent, England, under the personal supervision of the Messrs. Allsopp.

Sold at these concerts.

SATURDAY, MAY 20.

PROGRAMME.

1. MARCH, "Stars and Stripes" — Sousa
2. OVERTURE, "Mignon" — Thomas
3. WALTZ, "Meerleuchten" — Ziehrer
4. SELECTION, "The Fortune-teller" — Herbert
5. FUNERAL MARCH of a Marionette — Gounod
6. FINALE to Act I., "Lohengrin" — Wagner
7. INTERMEZZO, "Naila" — Delibes
8. OVERTURE, "William Tell" — Rossini
9. SELECTION, "Robin Hood" — De Koven
10. (a) SERENADE — Moszkowski
    (b) MARCH, "Welcome to Dewey" — André
11. WALTZ, "Estudiantina" — Waldteufel
12. MARCH, "A Nigger Fricassee" — Clark
    (First Time.)

The only Lithia Water sold at these concerts.

Hygeia Lithia Water

Sparkling and Still.

By its use you will avoid the germs of disease which natural MINERAL WATERS are liable to contain.

For Sale at these concerts and by

S. S. PIERCE CO.

FOR SALE AT THESE CONCERTS.

FAMOUS TANNHAEUSER EXPORT BEER

The finest Light Beer Extant.   Brewery Bottling.   Favorite of Connoisseurs.

Pure, Palatable, Perfect.

B. & E. Philadelphia Ale on Draught.

FOR SALE AT THESE CONCERTS.

The purity and keeping quality of the Tannhaeuser Export under all changes of temperature, its uniform excellence being guaranteed, together with its nutritious properties, make it the most pleasant, delicious, and convenient beverage for home consumption.
Put up in corked bottles, and packed in casks of 10 dozen white flint pints, and 6 dozen amber quarts.

Highest Awards wherever exhibited.

The BERGNER & ENGEL BREWING CO.'S N.E. Depot,
508 and 510 Atlantic Avenue, Boston.
Telephone 3805.   **SOL. BACHARACH, Manager.**

M. Steinert & Sons Co.,
STEINERT HALL BUILDING,
No. 162 Boylston Street, corner Carver, Boston.

STEINWAY & SONS,
HARDMAN,   GABLER,
EMERSON,   SINGER,
PIANOS.

The Æolian, Aeriol, Orchestrelle, and Pianola,

AND THE
STEINERTONE.

THE ÆOLIAN
AND
THE PIANOLA
FOR SUMMER HOMES.

At this season of the year we receive many orders for these instruments for Summer Residences, and therefore beg to call attention to our extensive assortment now on display, especially suited for this purpose.

The ÆOLIAN meets the requirements of country homes, furnishing, as it does, music suitable for every occasion. It practically takes the place of an orchestra — music for dancing — orchestral concerts, — in short, music of every style and description is always available.

The PIANOLA will appeal to many on account of the very little space it occupies. It will play any kind of a piano, and can also be used upon a rented piano without the slightest injury. For the above reasons it is bound to be very popular for small cottages.

We are glad to be able to announce that we can furnish PIANOLAS with no more than a week's delay, and, at times, the day the order is given.

Persons not familiar with these instruments are cordially invited to call at our warerooms and hear them, or a descriptive catalogue will be mailed free upon application.

M. STEINERT & SONS CO.,
Steinert Hall,   162 Boylston Street,   Boston.

ANHEUSER-BUSCH BREWING ASS'N,
ST. LOUIS, MO., U.S.A.
BREWERS OF HIGH=GRADE BEERS EXCLUSIVELY.

Black and Tan.		Faust.
Michelob.		Pale Lager.
Muenchener.		Anheuser Standard.

Served at the Music Hall Concerts.
Also at all first-class hotels, clubs, and bars, and on all Pullman and Wagner cars and ocean and lake steamers.

JACOB WIRTH,   Wholesale Dealer,   **Boston, Mass.**

THE MUSIC HALL
PROMENADE CONCERTS

PUBLISHED BY C. A. ELLIS, MUSIC HALL.

BOSTON, THURSDAY, MAY 18, 1899.

SUMMER SEASON. Vol. XIV. No. 10.

SMOKE "BARRISTER" CIGARS AT THE POPULAR CONCERTS.

YOU CAN
Have your last season's outfit dyed or cleansed and refinished so it will look like new, by our French process. Why discard soiled clothing when it can be overhauled and worn as second best? You can

RELY ON
Our methods of cleansing, and need not hesitate to trust us with articles of the most delicate textures. We dye or cleanse and refinish PROPERLY, *all* materials of household use and clothing of all kinds.

LEWANDO'S
W. L. Crosby, General Manager.
French Cleansers, Fancy Dyers, Fine Launderers.

PRINCIPAL OFFICES:
17 Temple Place, Boston.
479 Fifth Avenue, New York.
Established 70 years.
Largest in America.
Bundles called for and delivered.
Telephones in all offices.

In no other way
are men as wasteful and extravagant as in cigar smoking—because cigars are thrown away half smoked half the time.

BETWEEN THE ACTS
Little Cigars
are just right for all short smokes. They light right, they burn right, and taste right. Have you ever seen them? At all stores: 10 for 10 cts., or, as they are for sale here, you can try them to-night. Tell the waiter to bring you a 10-cent box of "Between the Acts." They will add to your enjoyment of this concert.

THE MUSIC HALL... Promenade Concerts
FOURTEENTH SEASON.

C. A. ELLIS, Manager.   F. R. COMEE, Assistant Manager.
Mr. MAX ZACH, Conductor.

THURSDAY, MAY 18.

PROGRAMME.

1. WERNER MARCH . . . . . . Ziehrer
2. OVERTURE, "Raymond" . . . . Thomas
3. WALTZ, "Faschingskinder" . . . Ziehrer
   (First Time.)
4. SELECTION, "Carmen" . . . . Bizet
5. BALLET MUSIC, "Queen of Sheba" . . Goldmark
   'Cello Obligato, Mr. KELLER.
6. WALTZ, "Wine, Woman, and Song" . . Strauss
7. TRAUM DER SENNERIN . . . . Labitzky
   Violin Obligati, Messrs. ONDRICEK and HOFFMANN.
   The audience is respectfully requested to preserve silence during the performance of this number.
8. OVERTURE, "Rienzi" . . . . Wagner

9. WALTZ, "Forest Spirits" . . . . Zach
10. WEDDING MARCH . . . . Mendelssohn
11. LA MOUSMÉ . . . . . . Ganne
12. MARCH, "Wien, bleibt Wien" . . Schrammel

Monday, May 22, Soloists' Night.

Now the rage of the LONDON Concerts and Drawing-rooms:

YOU AND I, by Liza Lehmann, ... 60c.
KING CHARLES, by M. V. White, . . . 60c.
LIKE VIOLETS PALE, by F. Allitsen, . . 60c.
WHEN THE WORLD IS FAIR, by F. H. Cowen, 60c.
QUEEN OF MY LIFE, by E. T. Lloyd, . . 60c.

BOOSEY & CO.,
9 East 17th Street,   New York.

A Particularly Fine Lager for Family Use and Clubs.
Bottled in the most careful manner at our own bottling department, and sold by the S. S. Pierce Co. and all other leading grocers in New England.

Other Brands in Bottles:
"Norfolk India Pale Stock Ale."
"Norfolk Extra Golden Ale" (blue label).
"Norfolk Standard Lager."
Our "Cabinet" and "Bismarck Brew" are the most popular refreshments at these concerts.

HABICH & CO.
H. W. HABICH, | Telephone, 56 Roxbury
EDWARD BUHL. | or 1192 Boston.

SMOKE "LA CELESTINA," THE BEST ALL-HAVANA CIGAR. DANIEL FRANK & CO.

ESTABROOK & EATON'S MARGUERITE PERFECTOS, 10c. EACH. CONCHAS, 10c., 3 FOR 25c. SOLD AT THE "POPS."

THE ICE-CREAM SERVED AT THESE CONCERTS IS FURNISHED BY WEBER, 25 Temple Place and 33 West Street.

MUSIC HALL PROMENADE PROGRAMME.

PUBLISHED EVERY EVENING DURING THE SUMMER SEASON.

NOTICE TO ADVERTISERS.

The advertising columns in the Programme are controlled SOLELY by F. R. Comee, Boston Music Hall Box Office, to whom all communications should be addressed.

The United States Hotel,

SARATOGA SPRINGS, N.Y.

Under a continuous management for 25 years.

Without a peer in its appointments, service, and liberal management.

The largest structure of its kind in the world.

Built entirely of brick.

The Hotel and court cover over seven acres.

For further information, rates, etc., etc., address

GAGE & PERRY,
Proprietors,
UNITED STATES HOTEL,
Saratoga Springs, N.Y.

Colonial Beer...

The Beer that's Brewed in Glass.

PURE, CLEAN, PALATABLE.

Order a Bottle.

SOUTHER BREWING CO.,
919 Parker Street,
Roxbury, Mass.

VEUVE CHAFFARD

PURE OLIVE OIL.

IN HONEST BOTTLES.

The Peer of all Cigarettes.

Save the band-label on each box for valuable premiums.

: : : ALSO : : :

Monopol

High-grade Egyptian Cigarettes.

No. 8a Khedive,
No. 9a Nadine,
No. 9a Egyptian Belles,
No. 70a Princess Lillian

On sale at these concerts and all first-class dealers.

OCKENHEIMER BERG, Near Bingen, GERMANY, On the Rhine.

PHILIP KRIM'S

OWN IMPORTATION OF

Rhine Wines,

FOR 30 YEARS

AT

163 Shawmut Avenue.

OUR WINES SOLD AT THESE CONCERTS.

HERRICK, COPLEY SQUARE, Telephones 1608 and 950 (Back Bay), CHOICE TABLES for Music Hall "Pops."

D. LEIDEN'S
SPARKLING
MOSELLE,

The only Sparkling Wine sold at these Concerts.

SHINNECOCK

The Perfection of

Scotch Whisky

Sold by
S. S. PIERCE COMPANY.

FRIDAY, MAY 19.

PROGRAMME.

1. MARCH, "Fra Bombarda" . . . . . Czibulka
2. WALTZ, "Doctrinen" . . . . . . E. Strauss
3. OVERTURE, "Oberon" . . . . . . Weber
4. SELECTION from "Traviata" . . . . Verdi
5. SUITE I., L'Arlésienne . . . . . Bizet
   (a) Menuet. (b) Adagietto. (c) Carillon.
6. OVERTURE, "Semiramide" . . . . Rossini
7. VALSE CAPRICE, "Honeymoon" . . . Stix
   The audience is respectfully requested to preserve silence during the performance of this number.
8. POLONAISE . . . . Tschaikowski
9. PRELUDE to "Le Deluge" . . . . Saint-Saëns
   Violin Solo, MR. ONDRICEK.
10. WALTZ, "Vienna Beauties" . . . . Ziehrer
11. LA CINQUANTAINE . . . . . . G. Marie
12. MARCH, "Washington Post" . . . . Sousa

Handsomest Dining Hotel in New England.

THE HAYWARD

20 Private Dining-rooms.

Beer and Ale drawn direct from wood in THE DUTCH TAP.

SMITH & KERRISSEY, Proprietors.

"M. S."
GINGER ALE.

An epicurean beverage, made with Myles Standish Spring Water and compounded with scrupulous care from the highest grade materials.

To be had at the Promenade Concerts.

L. BOYER'S SONS,
Proprietors,
No. 27 Devonshire St., Boston.

MAIN OFFICE.
No. 90 Wall St., New York.

"AMERICA'S FINEST PRODUCT."

Bartholomay's "APOLLO"

LAGER BEER IN BOTTLES.

Sold at these Concerts.

ALBRECHT & KOELLNER,
SOLE AGENTS,
Telephone, Boston 1751. 295-305 A Street.

Also Agents for the "Crystal Rock" Mineral Water.

PURE BEER

Harvard BREW. CO'S $1000.00

PURE BEER

Sold at these Concerts,
IN BOTTLES ONLY
20¢ PER BOTTLE.

Inglenook Vineyard.

The only California Wines sold at these Concerts.

❦❦

THE CODMAN & HALL CO.,
Opposite the South Union Station.

Sole Agents for New England.

IND. COOPE & CO.'S English Ale.

THE SECOND LARGEST BREWERY IN ENGLAND.

Brewers of the finest *light quality* ale. Very highly endorsed by the medical profession. : : : :

❦❦

THE CODMAN & HALL CO.,
Opposite South Union Station.

Sole Agents for the United States.

DRIN only th

PURE

WHIS

If you want p and richne flavor, try only gen and origin

OLD KENTU TAYLOR

Eight years old own distillation guaranteed p Bottled and shi direct from warehouses by None genuine w out our signa on both labels. ware of imitat For consump indigestion, an ailments requ stimulants, O KENTUCKY L O R has superior.
Sold by all class drugs grocers, and li dealers.

Wright & Tay Distillers, Fine Kentuck Whiskies, Louisville, K

Hirshfield & New Englan Agents, 31 Doane Stre Boston.

Instruct your waiter to bring a bottle of

Pfaff's "Monogram" Lager.

If you will do this, it will not be necessary for us to expatiate upon the good qualities of our production.
YOU CAN JUDGE FOR YOURSELF.

H. & J. PFAFF BREWING COMPANY,
Telephone 2608.   16 ARCH STREET, BOSTON.

TRY THE "COLUMBIA BRAND" VIENNA SAUSAGES. SERVED HOT OR COLD AT THESE CONCERTS.

SATURDAY, MAY 20.

PROGRAMME.

1. MARCH, "Stars and Stripes" — Sousa
2. OVERTURE, "Mignon" — Thomas
3. WALTZ, "Meerleuchten" — Zichrer
4. SELECTION, "The Fortuneteller" — Herbert

5. FUNERAL MARCH of a Marionette — Gounod
6. FINALE to Act I., "Lohengrin" — Wagner
7. INTERMEZZO, "Naila" — Delibes
8. OVERTURE, "William Tell" — Rossini

9. SELECTION, "Robin Hood" — De Koven
10. (a) SERENADE — Moszkowski
    (b) MARCH, "Welcome to Dewey" — Andre
11. WALTZ, "Estudiantina" — Waldteufel
12. MARCH, "A Nigger Frivassee" — Clark
    (First Time.)

They cannot sell you here
Canadian Club Whisky,
Ruinart Champagne,
Royal Liqueur Scotch,
Carstair's Philadelphia Rye,
Fort Hill Bourbon,
Alhambra Sherry,
All of which you will find
of excellent quality ;

But you can get

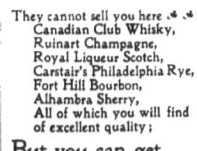

Kaiser Water,

the most refreshing of all table waters,

Chateau d'Arsac Claret,
N. Johnston & Sons' Medoc,
and
California Inglenook Clarets.

SUPPLIED BY

CODMAN & HALL COMPANY,

WINE MERCHANTS,
Opposite New South Station.

COAL

Best Quality
AT
Lowest Prices

METROPOLITAN COAL COMPANY,
No. 30 Congress Street.

THE WILSON,
AMERICA'S PUREST
Mineral Spring Water,

Is used in making our celebrated

Belfast Ginger Ale,
Champagne Kola,

Lemon Soda, Club Soda, Vichy, etc. Hotels and Families supplied. Try a sample order of these goods, and be convinced of their superiority, purity, and medicinal qualities.........

All of our beverages bottled at the spring... We ship only in glass, and all bottles and demijohns are sterilized before being filled........

Wilson Spring and Hotel Co.,
Tel., 3129 Boston. | 45 ARCH STREET.

"THE RECOGNIZED FAVORITE OF ALL BEERS."

Schlitz
THE BEER THAT MADE MILWAUKEE FAMOUS.

HIGHEST AWARD FOR PURITY.

Sold at these Concerts. **JOS. GAHM & CO.,** N.E. AGENTS, 125-127 PURCHASE ST.

THE ONLY BEER ON DRAUGHT AT THESE CONCERTS.
"the beer that's brewed"

Rochester Brewing Co's. FAMOUS BOTTLED BEER

RIENZI, PREMIER, BOHEMIAN, BAVARIAN, STANDARD.

HOME OFFICE & BREWERY ROCHESTER, N.Y.
NEW ENGLAND BRANCH 295-305 A STREET BOSTON
Free delivery in city and Suburbs

THE FALL RIVER LINE

OCCUPYING THE
LONG ISLAND SOUND ROUTE
BETWEEN

Boston and New York

Has the finest quintette of great steamboats
that the world has ever seen. The

Priscilla, Puritan, Plymouth, Pilgrim, and Providence

Are the largest, best equipped, safest, and handsomest steamboats ever constructed. This route is one of the most attractive and naturally beautiful traversed by any transportation agency in the world.

Trips of the Fall River Line are made throughout the year. Each steamboat has its own orchestra, and the service on each member of the fleet is maintained at the highest possible standard.

Tickets via this route are on sale at all of the principal Ticket Offices in the United States.

From BOSTON. Trains, connecting with steamers at Fall River in 80 minutes, leave Park Square Station, New York, New Haven & Hartford Railroad (Old Colony System), daily at 5 p.m.

From NEW YORK. Steamers leave Pier 19, North River, foot of Warren Street, daily at 5.30 p.m.

S. A. GARDNER, GEO. L. CONNOR, O. H. TAYLOR,
Superintendent, Passenger Traffic Manager, General Passenger Agent,
NEW YORK. NEW HAVEN, CONN. NEW YORK CITY.

HOTEL LANGWOOD,

Middlesex Fells Reservation.

P.O. Address, Melrose, Mass. Wyoming Station, B. & M. R.R.

Twenty minutes by rail from Boston. Sixty trains daily. Hotel coaches meet trains each way. Four hundred feet above sea level. Beautiful rides, drives, and walks. Golf links, tennis courts, and ball grounds.

OPENS ABOUT MAY 20.

For plans and prices address:

F. W. GASKILL, Manager.

BOSTON OFFICE:
Hemenway Building, 10 Tremont Street, Room 29.

Third Season.

3 Ideal Outings

Personally conducted by
F. R. COMEE, Music
Hall, Boston.

S.S. "Howard." Boston to Norfolk, 522 miles. Norfolk to Baltimore, 200 miles.

Boston	1.	2.	3.
Leave	July 1	July 15	August 19
Arrive	July 12	July 31	September 4

S.S. "Toronto." Toronto to Montreal, through the "Thousand Islands" and the "Rapids," 376 miles.

No. 1. Ten days. Saratoga, Lake George, 2,136 miles from Buffalo to Duluth, and return on the steamer "North-Land" through the Great Lakes, Erie, Huron, St. Clair, and Superior.

Nos. 2 and 3. Sixteen days. Exactly alike. 700 miles' ocean sail to Norfolk and Baltimore. Over Alleghany Mountains and a day in Chicago. Up Lake Michigan and three days at Mackinac Island. 1,546 miles on steamer "North-West" to Duluth and return to Buffalo through the Great Lakes. Niagara Falls to Toronto. Across Lake Ontario, through the Thousand Islands, and down the St. Lawrence River to Montreal and Boston.

SEND FOR CIRCULARS.

S.S. "Manitou." Chicago to Mackinac Island, across Lake Michigan, 350 miles.

"North-West." Mackinac Island to Duluth and return to Buffalo, 1,555 miles.

Allsopp's

ENGLISH ALE.
"The Red Hand Brand."

Bottled at the brewery, Burton-on-Trent, England, under the personal supervision of the Messrs. Allsopp.

Sold at these concerts.

MONDAY, MAY 22.
SOLOISTS' NIGHT.

PROGRAMME.

1. RADETZKY MARCH . . . . Strauss
2. WALTZ, "Violets" . . . . . . Waldteufel
3. OVERTURE, "Phèdre" . . . . . Massenet
4. FLUTE SOLO, "Air Varie, Tremolo" . . Depresermann
   M. A. MAQUARRE.
5. OVERTURE, "Strawberry Leaves" . Miss Tippett
6. VIOLIN SOLO . . . .
   Mr. K. ONDRICEK.
7. INVITATION TO DANCE . . . . . Weber
8. RIDE OF THE WALKYRIES . . . . Wagner

---

9. MARCH from "Strawberry Leaves" . Miss Tippett
10. WALTZ, "Gross Wien" . . . . . Strauss
11. POLKA, "Love-letter" . . . . . Ziehrer
    (First Time.)
12. ORIENTAL MARCH . . . . Zach

The *only* Lithia Water sold at these concerts.

Hygeia Lithia Water

Sparkling and Still.

By its use you will avoid the germs of disease which natural MINERAL WATERS are liable to contain.

For Sale at these concerts and by

S. S. PIERCE CO.

The purity and keeping quality of the Tannhaeuser Export under all changes of temperature, its uniform excellence being guaranteed, together with its nutritious properties, make it the most pleasant, delicious, and convenient beverage for home consumption.
Put up in corked bottles, and packed in casks of 10 dozen white flint pints, and 6 dozen amber quarts.

Highest Awards wherever exhibited.

FOR SALE AT THESE CONCERTS.
FAMOUS TANNHAEUSER EXPORT BEER

The finest Light Beer Extant. Brewery Bottling. Favorite of Connoisseurs.

Pure, Palatable, Perfect.

B. & E. Philadelphia Ale on Draught.
FOR SALE AT THESE CONCERTS.

The BERGNER & ENGEL BREWING CO.'S N.E. Depot,
508 and 510 Atlantic Avenue, Boston.
Telephone 3805.   **SOL. BACHARACH, Manager.**

M. Steinert & Sons Co.,

STEINERT HALL BUILDING,

No. 162 Boylston Street, corner Carver, Boston.

STEINWAY & SONS,

HARDMAN,	GABLER,
EMERSON,	SINGER,

PIANOS.

The Æolian, Aeriol, Orchestrelle, and Pianola.

THE ÆOLIAN
AND
THE PIANOLA
FOR SUMMER HOMES.

At this season of the year we receive many orders for these instruments for Summer Residences, and therefore beg to call attention to our extensive assortment now on display, especially suited for this purpose.

The ÆOLIAN meets the requirements of country homes, furnishing, as it does, music suitable for every occasion. It practically takes the place of an orchestra — music for dancing — orchestral concerts, — in short, music of every style and description is always available.

The PIANOLA will appeal to many on account of the very little space it occupies. It will play any kind of a piano, and can also be used upon a rented piano without the slightest injury. For the above reasons it is bound to be very popular for small cottages.

We are glad to be able to announce that we can furnish PIANOLAS with no more than a week's delay, and, at times, the day the order is given.

Persons not familiar with these instruments are cordially invited to call at our warerooms and hear them, or a descriptive catalogue will be mailed free upon application.

M. STEINERT & SONS CO.,
Steinert Hall, 162 Boylston Street, Boston.

ANHEUSER-BUSCH BREWING ASS'N,

ST. LOUIS, MO., U.S.A.

BREWERS OF HIGH=GRADE BEERS EXCLUSIVELY.

Black and Tan.	Faust.
Michelob.	Pale Lager.
Muenchener.	Anheuser Standard.

Served at the Music Hall Concerts.

Also at all first-class hotels, clubs, and bars, and on all Pullman and Wagner cars and ocean and lake steamers.

JACOB WIRTH,	**Wholesale Dealer,**	**Boston, Mass.**

THE MUSIC HALL
PROMENADE CONCERTS

PUBLISHED BY
C. A. ELLIS,
MUSIC HALL.

BOSTON, FRIDAY, MAY 19, 1899.

SUMMER SEASON.
Vol. XIV. No. 11.

THE MUSIC HALL... **Promenade Concerts**

FOURTEENTH SEASON.

C. A. ELLIS, Manager.   F. R. COMEE, Assistant Manager.

Mr. MAX ZACH, Conductor.

FRIDAY, MAY 19.

PROGRAMME.

1. MARCH, "Fra Bombarda" . . . . . Czibulka
2. WALTZ, "Doctrinen" . . . . . E. Strauss
3. OVERTURE, "Oberon" . . . . . Weber
4. SELECTION from "Traviata" . . . . Verdi

5. SELECTION from "Mikado" . . . . . Sullivan
6. OVERTURE, "Semiramide" . . . . . Rossini
7. VALSE CAPRICE, "Honeymoon" . . . Stix

The audience is respectfully requested to preserve silence during the performance of this number.

8. POLONAISE . . . . . . Tschaikowski
9. PRELUDE to "Le Déluge" . . . . Saint-Saëns
    Violin Solo, Mr. ONDRICEK.
10. WALTZ, "Vienna Beauties" . . . . Ziehrer
11. LA CINQUANTAINE . . . . . G. Marie
12. MARCH, "Washington Post" . . . . Sousa

Monday, May 22, Soloists' Night.

HERE ARE A FEW NAMES FROM OUR LIST OF COMPOSERS:

ENGLISH.— Stephen Adams, F. H. Cowen, S. Liddle, C. V. Stanford, A. C. Mackenzie, R. H. Walthew, H. R. Shelley, Goring Thomas, Frances Allitsen, Maude V. White, Edward German, Mary Carmichael, Liza Lehmann, etc.

FRENCH.— C. Chaminade, Jane Vieu, L. Denza, P. Delmet, Bemberg, Guy d'Hardelot, De Leva, F. P. Tosti, etc.

ITALIAN.— F. P. Tosti, P. Mascagni, G. Puccini, G. Verdi, Don Lorenzo Perosi, etc.

THE MOST REPRESENTATIVE PUBLISHING HOUSE IN AMERICA.

BOOSEY & CO., 9 East 17th Street, New York.

ESTABROOK & EATON'S MARGUERITE PERFECTOS, 10c. EACH CONCHAS, 10c., 3 FOR 25c., SOLD AT THE "POPS."

THE ICE-CREAM SERVED AT THESE CONCERTS IS FURNISHED BY WEBER, 25 Temple Place and 33 West Street.

MUSIC HALL PROMENADE PROGRAMME.

PUBLISHED EVERY EVENING DURING THE SUMMER SEASON.

NOTICE TO ADVERTISERS.

The advertising columns in the Programme are controlled SOLELY by F. R. Comee, Boston Music Hall Box Office, to whom all communications should be addressed.

The United States Hotel,

SARATOGA SPRINGS, N.Y.

Under a continuous management for 25 years.

Without a peer in its appointments, service, and liberal management.

The largest structure of its kind in the world.

Built entirely of brick.

The Hotel and court cover over seven acres.

For further information, rates, etc., etc., address

GAGE & PERRY,
Proprietors,
UNITED STATES HOTEL,
Saratoga Springs, N.Y.

Colonial Beer...

The Beer that's Brewed in Glass.

PURE, CLEAN, PALATABLE.

Order a Bottle.

SOUTHER BREWING CO.,
919 Parker Street,
Roxbury, Mass.

All The **IMPORTED CIGARS** Sold At These Concerts Are Supplied By The **S. S. PIERCE COMPANY.**

The Peer of all Cigarettes.

Save the band-label on each box for valuable premiums.

::: ALSO :::

Monopol

High-grade Egyptian Cigarettes.

No. 8A Khedive,
No. 9A Nadine,
No. 9A Egyptian Belles,
No. 70A Princess Lillian

On sale at these concerts and all first-class dealers.

OCKENHEIMER BERG, Near Bingen, GERMANY, On the Rhine.

PHILIP KRIM'S OWN IMPORTATION OF **Rhine Wines.** FOR 30 YEARS AT **163 Shawmut Avenue.** OUR WINES SOLD AT THESE CONCERTS.

HERRICK, COPLEY SQUARE, Telephones 608 and 950 (Back Bay), CHOICE TABLES for Music Hall "Pops."

GREAT WESTERN CHAMPAGNE

———A natural, genuine champagne, of the finest quality produced in America.

Sold by Wine Merchants, Grocers, and Druggists.

SATURDAY, MAY 20.

PROGRAMME.

1. MARCH, "Stars and Stripes" — Sousa
2. OVERTURE, "Mignon" — Thomas
3. WALTZ, "Meerleuchten" — Ziehrer
4. SELECTION, "The Fortune-teller" — Herbert

5. FUNERAL MARCH of a Marionette — Gounod
6. FINALE to Act I., "Lohengrin" — Wagner
7. INTERMEZZO, "Naila" — Delibes
8. OVERTURE, "William Tell" — Rossini

9. SELECTION, "Robin Hood" — De Koven
10. (a) SERENADE — Moszkowski
    (b) MARCH, "Welcome to Dewey" — André
11. WALTZ, "Estudiantina" — Waldteufel
12. MARCH, "A Nigger Fricassee" — Clark
    (First Time.)

Handsomest Dining Hotel in New England.

THE HAYWARD

20 Private Dining-rooms.

Beer and Ale drawn direct from wood in THE DUTCH TAP.

SMITH & KERRISSEY, Proprietors.

"M. S." GINGER ALE.

An epicurean beverage, made with Myles Standish Spring Water and compounded with scrupulous care from the highest grade materials.

To be had at the Promenade Concerts.

L. BOYER'S SONS,
Proprietors,
No. 27 Devonshire St., Boston.

MAIN OFFICE.
No. 90 Wall St., New York.

"AMERICA'S FINEST PRODUCT."

Bartholomay's "APOLLO"

LAGER BEER IN BOTTLES.

Sold at these Concerts.

ALBRECHT & KOELLNER,
SOLE AGENTS,
Telephone, Boston 1751.   295-305 A Street.

Also Agents for the "Crystal Rock" Mineral Water.

PURE BEER

$1000.00

PURE BEER

Sold at these Concerts,
IN BOTTLES ONLY
20¢ PER BOTTLE.

TABLE LINEN USED AT THESE CONCERTS LAUNDERED BY THE L. K. HUSTED LAUNDERING COMPANY. 27 and 29 BROADWAY, CHELSEA, MASS.

Inglenook Vineyard.

The only California Wines sold at these Concerts.

THE CODMAN & HALL CO.,
Opposite the South Union Station.

Sole Agents for New England.

IND. COOPE & CO.'S English Ale.

THE SECOND LARGEST BREWERY IN ENGLAND.

Brewers of the finest *light* quality ale. Very highly endorsed by the medical profession. : : : : :

THE CODMAN & HALL CO.,
Opposite South Union Station.

Sole Agents for the United States.

Instruct your waiter to bring a bottle of

Pfaff's "Monogram" Lager.

If you will do this, it will not be necessary for us to expatiate upon the good qualities of our production.
YOU CAN JUDGE FOR YOURSELF.

H. & J. PFAFF BREWING COMPANY,
Telephone 2608.   16 ARCH STREET, BOSTON.

DRINK only the PURE WHISKE...

If you want pure and richness flavor, try only genuine and original

OLD KENTUCK TAYLOR,

Eight years old, own distillation guaranteed pure Bottled and shipped direct from warehouses by None genuine without our signature on both labels. Beware of imitations For consumption indigestion, and ailments requiring stimulants, OLD KENTUCKY TA YLOR has no superior.

Sold by all first class druggists grocers and liquor dealers.

Wright & Taylor
Distillers,
Fine Kentucky Whiskies,
Louisville, Ky.

Hirshfield & Co
New England Agents,
31 Doane Street,
Boston.

TRY THE "COLUMBIA BRAND" VIENNA SAUSAGES. SERVED HOT OR COLD AT THESE CONCERTS.

They cannot sell you here
Canadian Club Whisky,
Ruinart Champagne,
Royal Liqueur Scotch,
Carstair's Philadelphia Rye,
Fort Hill Bourbon,
Alhambra Sherry,
All of which you will find
of excellent quality;

But you can get

Kaiser Water,

the most refreshing of all table waters,

*Chateau d'Arsac Claret,
N. Johnston & Sons' Medoc,*
and
California Inglenook Clarets.

SUPPLIED BY

CODMAN & HALL COMPANY,

WINE MERCHANTS,

Opposite New South Station.

MONDAY, MAY 22.

SOLOISTS' NIGHT.

PROGRAMME.

1. RADETZKY MARCH . . . Strauss
2. WALTZ, "Violets" . . . Waldteufel
3. OVERTURE, "Phèdre" . . . Massenet
4. FLUTE SOLO, "Air Varié, Tremolo" . Demessermann
   M. A. MAQUARRE.
5. OVERTURE, "Strawberry Leaves" . Miss Tippett
6. VIOLIN SOLO, (a) Andante . . . De Beriot
   (b) Spanish Dance . . Sarasate
   M. K. ONDRICEK.
7. INVITATION TO DANCE . . . Weber
8. RIDE OF THE WALKYRIES . . . Wagner
9. MARCH from "Strawberry Leaves" . Miss Tippett
10. WALTZ, "Gross Wien" . . . Strauss
11. POLKA, "Love letter" . . . Ziehrer
    (First Time)
12. ORIENTAL MARCH . . . Zach

COAL

Best Quality
AT
Lowest Prices

METROPOLITAN COAL COMPANY,
No. 30 Congress Street.

THE WILSON,
AMERICA'S PUREST
Mineral Spring Water,

Is used in making our celebrated **Belfast Ginger Ale, Champagne Kola,** Lemon Soda, Club Soda, Vichy, etc. Hotels and Families supplied. Try a sample order of these goods, and be convinced of their superiority, purity, and medicinal qualities. . . . .

All of our beverages bottled at the spring. We ship only in glass, and all bottles and demijohns are sterilized before being filled . . . .

Wilson Spring and Hotel Co.,
Tel., 3129 Boston. | 45 ARCH STREET.

"THE RECOGNIZED FAVORITE OF ALL BEERS."

Schlitz
THE BEER THAT MADE MILWAUKEE FAMOUS.
HIGHEST AWARD FOR PURITY.

Sold at these Concerts. JOS. GAHM & CO., N.E. AGENTS, 125-127 PURCHASE ST.

THE ONLY BEER ON DRAUGHT AT THESE CONCERTS.
"the beer that's brewed"

Rochester Brewing Co's.
FAMOUS BOTTLED BEER
HOME OFFICE & BREWERY ROCHESTER, N.Y.
295-305 A STREET BOSTON
NEW ENGLAND BRANCH
ROCHESTER BREWING CO.
Free delivery in city and Suburbs

AGENTS:
PREMIER,
BOHEMIAN,
BAVARIAN,
STANDARD.

THE FALL RIVER LINE

OCCUPYING THE
LONG ISLAND SOUND ROUTE
BETWEEN

Boston and New York

Has the finest quintette of great steamboats that the world has ever seen. The
Priscilla, Puritan, Plymouth, Pilgrim, and Providence

Are the largest, best equipped, safest, and handsomest steamboats ever constructed. This route is one of the most attractive and naturally beautiful traversed by any transportation agency in the world. Trips of the Fall River Line are made throughout the year.

Each steamboat has its own orchestra, and the service on each member of the fleet is maintained at the highest possible standard.

Tickets via this route are on sale at all of the principal Ticket Offices in the United States.

From BOSTON. Trains, connecting with steamers at Fall River in 80 minutes leave Park Square Station, New York, New Haven & Hartford Railroad (Old Colony System), daily at 6 p.m.

From NEW YORK. Steamers leave Pier 19, North River, foot of Warren Street, daily at 5.30 p.m.

S. A. GARDNER, Superintendent, NEW YORK.
GEO. L. CONNOR, Passenger Traffic Manager, NEW HAVEN, CONN.
O. H. TAYLOR, General Passenger Agent, NEW YORK CITY.

HOTEL LANGWOOD,

Middlesex Fells Reservation.

P.O. Address, Melrose, Mass.   Wyoming Station, B. & M. R.R.

Twenty minutes by rail from Boston. Sixty trains daily. Hotel coaches meet trains each way. Four hundred feet above sea level. Beautiful rides, drives, and walks. Golf links, tennis courts, and ball grounds.

OPENS ABOUT MAY 20.

For plans and prices address:

F. W. GASKILL, Manager.

BOSTON OFFICE:
Hemenway Building, 10 Tremont Street, Room 29.

S.S. "Howard." Boston to Norfolk, 522 miles. Norfolk to Baltimore, 200 miles.

	1.	2.	3.
Boston	Leave July 2	July 15	August 19
	Arrive July 12	July 31	September 4

S.S. "Toronto." Toronto to Montreal, through the "Thousand Islands" and the "Rapids," 376 miles.

Third Season.

3 Ideal Outings

Personally conducted by F. R. COMEE, Music Hall, Boston.

No. 1. Ten days. **Saratoga, Lake George,** 2,130 miles from Buffalo to Duluth, and return on the steamer "North-Land" through the Great Lakes, Erie, Huron, St. Clair, and Superior.

Nos. 2 and 3. Sixteen days. Exactly alike. 700 miles' ocean sail to **Norfolk** and **Baltimore.** Over Alleghany Mountains and a day in **Chicago.** Up Lake Michigan and three days at **Mackinac Island.** 1,546 miles on steamer "North-West" to Duluth and return to Buffalo through the Great Lakes. Niagara Falls to Toronto. Across Lake Ontario, through the Thousand Islands, and down the St. Lawrence River to **Montreal** and **Boston.**

SEND FOR CIRCULARS.

S.S. "Manitou." Chicago to Mackinac Island, across Lake Michigan, 350 miles.

"North-West." Mackinac Island to Duluth and return to Buffalo, 1,555 miles.

Allsopp's

ENGLISH ALE.
"The Red Hand Brand."

Bottled at the brewery, Burton-on-Trent, England, under the personal supervision of the Messrs. Allsopp.

Sold at these concerts.

TUESDAY, MAY 23.

PROGRAMME.

1. MARCH, "Hoch Habsburg" . . . . Kral
2. WALTZ, "Nachtschwärmer" . . . . Zichrer
3. OVERTURE, "Benvenuto Cellini" . . . . . Berlioz
4. SELECTION from "The Wizard of the Nile" . Herbert
5. WALTZ, "Vienna Bonbons" . . . . Strauss
   (First Time)
6. NOCTURNE . . . . Marshall
   The audience is respectfully requested to preserve silence during the performance of this number.
7. PROLOGUE to "Pagliacci" . . . . Leoncavallo
8. SLAVONIC DANCE . . . . Dvorak
9. SELECTION, "Cavalleria Rusticana" . . . Mascagni
10. WALTZ, "Amour et Printemps" . . . . . . Waldteufel
11. GALOP, "Kosackenritt" . . . . Millöcker
12. MARCH, "Donna Juanita" . . . . Suppe

The *only* Lithia Water sold at these concerts.

Hygeia Lithia Water

Sparkling and Still.

By its use you will avoid the germs of disease which natural MINERAL WATERS are liable to contain.

For Sale at these concerts and by

S. S. PIERCE CO.

The purity and keeping quality of the Tannhaeuser Export under all changes of temperature, its uniform excellence being guaranteed, together with its nutritious properties, make it the most pleasant, delicious, and convenient beverage for home consumption.
Put up in corked bottles, and packed in casks of 10 dozen white flint pints, and 6 dozen amber quarts.
Highest Awards wherever exhibited.

FOR SALE AT THESE CONCERTS.
FAMOUS TANNHAEUSER EXPORT BEER
The finest Light Beer Extant.   Brewery Bottling.   Favorite of Connoisseurs.

Pure,   Palatable,   Perfect.

B. & E. Philadelphia Ale on Draught.
FOR SALE AT THESE CONCERTS.

The BERGNER & ENGEL BREWING CO.'S N.E. Depot,
508 and 510 Atlantic Avenue, Boston.
Telephone 3805.   SOL. BACHARACH, Manager.

M. Steinert & Sons Co.,

STEINERT HALL BUILDING,

No. 162 Boylston Street, corner Carver, Boston.

STEINWAY & SONS,

HARDMAN,   GABLER,
EMERSON,   SINGER,

PIANOS.

The Æolian, Aeriol, Orchestrelle, and Pianola.

THE ÆOLIAN
AND
THE PIANOLA
FOR SUMMER HOMES.

At this season of the year we receive many orders for these instruments for Summer Residences, and therefore beg to call attention to our extensive assortment now on display, especially suited for this purpose.

The ÆOLIAN meets the requirements of country homes, furnishing, as it does, music suitable for every occasion. It practically takes the place of an orchestra — music for dancing — orchestral concerts, — in short, music of every style and description is always available.

The PIANOLA will appeal to many on account of the very little space it occupies. It will play any kind of a piano, and can also be used upon a rented piano without the slightest injury. For the above reasons it is bound to be very popular for small cottages.

We are glad to be able to announce that we can furnish PIANOLAS with no more than a week's delay, and, at times, the day the order is given.

Persons not familiar with these instruments are cordially invited to call at our warerooms and hear them, or a descriptive catalogue will be mailed free upon application.

M. STEINERT & SONS CO.,
Steinert Hall,   162 Boylston Street,   Boston.

ANHEUSER-BUSCH BREWING ASS'N,

ST. LOUIS, MO., U.S.A.

BREWERS OF HIGH-GRADE BEERS EXCLUSIVELY.

Black and Tan.   Faust.

Michelob.   Pale Lager.

Muenchener.   Anheuser Standard.

Served at the Music Hall Concerts.

Also at all first-class hotels, clubs, and bars, and on all Pullman and Wagner cars and ocean and lake steamers.

JACOB WIRTH,   Wholesale Dealer,   **Boston, Mass.**

THE MUSIC HALL
Promenade Concerts

C. A. ELLIS, *Publisher* — MUSIC HALL

BOSTON, SATURDAY, MAY 20, 1899.

SUMMER SEASON. Vol. XIV. No. 12.

Left margin: SMOKE THE POPULAR "BARRISTER" CIGARS AT THE POPULAR CONCERTS.

Right margin: SMOKE "LA CELESTINA," THE BEST ALL-HAVANA CIGAR. DANIEL FRANK & CO.

YOU CAN
Have your last season's outfit dyed or cleansed and refinished so it will look like new, by our French process. Why discard soiled clothing when it can be overhauled and worn as second best? You can

RELY ON
Our methods of cleansing, and need not hesitate to trust us with articles of the most delicate textures.
We dye or cleanse and refinish PROPERLY, *all* materials of household use and clothing of all kinds.

LEWANDO'S
W. L. Crosby, General Manager.
French Cleansers, Fancy Dyers, Fine Launderers.
PRINCIPAL OFFICES:
17 Temple Place, Boston.
479 Fifth Avenue, New York.
Established 70 years.
Largest in America.
Bundles called for and delivered.
Telephones in all offices.

If you are open to conviction, to-night
try one 10-cent box of

BETWEEN THE ACTS
Little Cigars

to smoke now — or at any time when you want a short smoke and haven't time for a long one. They are real cigars, but small ones.

They cost so little that you can use them every day as well as not and actually save on your daily cigar expense by substituting them for larger cigars.

FOR SALE HERE.

THE MUSIC HALL ... Promenade Concerts
FOURTEENTH SEASON.

C. A. ELLIS, Manager.   F. R. COMEE, Assistant Manager.
Mr. MAX ZACH, Conductor.

SATURDAY, MAY 20.

PROGRAMME.

1. MARCH, "Stars and Stripes" . . . . . . Sousa
2. OVERTURE, "Mignon" . . . . Thomas
3. WALTZ, "Meerleuchten" . . . . Zichrer
4. SELECTION, "The Fortune-teller" . . . Herbert

5. FUNERAL MARCH of a Marionette . . . Gounod
6. FINALE to Act I., "Lohengrin" . . . . Wagner
7. INTERMEZZO, "Naila" . . . . Delibes
8. OVERTURE, "William Tell" . . . . . . Rossini

9. SELECTION, "Robin Hood" . . . . . . De Koven
10. (*a*) SERENADE . . . . Moszkowski
    (*b*) MARCH, "Welcome to Dewey" . . . André
11. WALTZ, "Estudiantina" . . . . Waldteufel
12. MARCH, "A Nigger Fricassee" . . . . Clark
    (First Time.)

Monday, May 22, Soloists' Night.

ALBUMS OF SONGS,
Containing many popular compositions not published in single form.

IRISH FOLK SONGS, by Charles Wood,	$2.00
RUSSIAN SONGS, by F. Wishaw (2 vols.),	1.00
NINE SONGS, by S. Liddle,	1.00
NINE SONGS, by Liza Lehmann,	1.00
FIVE SONGS, by Francis Korbay,	2.00

Beautifully illustrated by J. S. SARGENT, R.A.

BOOSEY & CO.,
9 East 17th Street,   New York.

LAGER BEER

A Particularly Fine Lager for Family Use and Clubs.
Bottled in the most careful manner at our own bottling department, and sold by the S. S. Pierce Co. and all other leading grocers in New England.

Other Brands in Bottles:
"Norfolk India Pale Stock Ale."
"Norfolk Extra Golden Ale" (blue labels).
"Norfolk Standard Lager."
Our "Cabinet" and "Bismarck Brau" are the most popular refreshments at these concerts.

HABICH & CO.
H. W. HABICH,   Telephone, 56 Roxbury
EDWARD RUHL.   or 1132 Boston.

ESTABROOK & EATON'S MARGUERITE   PERFECTOS, 10c. EACH, CONCHAS, 10c., 3 FOR 25c.   SOLD AT THE "POPS."

THE ICE-CREAM SERVED AT THESE CONCERTS IS FURNISHED BY WEBER, 25 Temple Place and 33 West Street.

MUSIC HALL PROMENADE PROGRAMME.
PUBLISHED EVERY EVENING DURING THE SUMMER SEASON.

NOTICE TO ADVERTISERS.
The advertising columns in the Programme are controlled SOLELY by F. R. Comee, Boston Music Hall Box Office, to whom all communications should be addressed.

The United States Hotel,
SARATOGA SPRINGS, N.Y.

Under a continuous management for 25 years.

Without a peer in its appointments, service, and liberal management.

The largest structure of its kind in the world.

Built entirely of brick.

The Hotel and court cover over seven acres.

For further information, rates, etc., address

GAGE & PERRY,
Proprietors,
UNITED STATES HOTEL,
Saratoga Springs, N.Y.

Colonial Beer...
The Beer that's Brewed in Glass.

PURE, CLEAN, PALATABLE.

Order a Bottle.

SOUTHER BREWING CO.,
919 Parker Street,
Roxbury, Mass.

VEUVE CHAFFARD

PURE OLIVE OIL.

IN HONEST BOTTLES.

The Peer of all Cigarettes.
Save the band-label on each box for valuable premiums.

::: ALSO :::

Monopol
High-grade Egyptian Cigarettes.

No. 8a Khedive,
No. 6½ Nadino,
No. 9a Egyptian Belles,
No. 70a Princess Lillian

On sale at these concerts and all first-class dealers.

OCKENHEIMER BERG,
Near Bingen, GERMANY. On the Rhine.

PHILIP KRIM'S
OWN IMPORTATION OF
Rhine Wines.
FOR 30 YEARS AT
163 Shawmut Avenue.

OUR WINES SOLD AT THESE CONCERTS.

HERRICK, COPLEY SQUARE, Telephones 608 and 950 (Back Bay), CHOICE TABLES for Music Hall "Pops."

D. LEIDEN'S
SPARKLING
MOSELLE,

The only Sparkling Wine sold at these Concerts.

SHINNECOCK

The Perfection of

Scotch Whisky

Sold by
S. S. PIERCE COMPANY.

MONDAY, MAY 22.
SOLOISTS' NIGHT.

PROGRAMME.

1. RADETZKY MARCH . . . . . Strauss
2. WALTZ, "Violets" . . . . Waldteufel
3. OVERTURE, "Phèdre" . . . . Massenet
4. FLUTE SOLO, "Air Varie, Tremolo" . Demessemann
   M. A. MAQUARRE.
5. OVERTURE, "Strawberry Leaves" . Constance Tippett
6. VIOLIN SOLO, (a) Andante . . De Beriot
   (b) Spanish Dance . . Sarasate
   Mr. K. ONDRICEK.
7. INVITATION TO DANCE . . . Weber
8. RIDE OF THE WALKYRIES . . Wagner

9. MARCH from "Strawberry Leaves" . Constance Tippett
10. WALTZ, "Gross Wien" . . . . Strauss
11. POLKA, "Love letter" . . . . Ziehrer
    (First Time.)
12. ORIENTAL MARCH . . . . Zach

Handsomest Dining Hotel in New England.

THE HAYWARD

20 Private Dining-rooms.

Beer and Ale drawn direct from wood in THE DUTCH TAP.

SMITH & KERRISSEY, Proprietors.

"M. S."
GINGER ALE.

An epicurean beverage, made with Myles Standish Spring Water and compounded with scrupulous care from the highest grade materials.

To be had at the Promenade Concerts.

L. BOYER'S SONS,
Proprietors,
No. 27 Devonshire St., Boston.

MAIN OFFICE.
No. 90 Wall St., New York.

"AMERICA'S FINEST PRODUCT."

Bartholomay's "APOLLO"

LAGER BEER IN BOTTLES.

Sold at these Concerts.

ALBRECHT & KOELLNER,
SOLE AGENTS,
Telephone, Boston 1751.   295-305 A Street.

Also Agents for the "Crystal Rock" Mineral Water.

PURE BEER

Harvard BREW. CO'S $1000.⁰⁰

PURE BEER

Sold at these Concerts
IN BOTTLES ONLY
20¢ PER BOTTLE.

Inglenook Vineyard.

The only California Wines sold at these Concerts.

❧❧

THE CODMAN & HALL CO.,

Opposite the South Union Station.

Sole Agents for New England.

IND. COOPE & CO.'S English Ale.

THE SECOND LARGEST BREWERY IN ENGLAND.

Brewers of the finest *light quality* ale. Very highly endorsed by the medical profession. : : : : :

❧❧

THE CODMAN & HALL CO.,

Opposite South Union Station.

Sole Agents for the United States.

DRIN
only th

PURE

WHIS

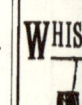

If you want pe
and richnes
flavor, try
only a en u
and origin

**OLD KENTU
TAYLOR,**

Eight years old,
own distillation
guaranteed pu
Bottled and ship
direct from
warehouses by
None genuine w
out our signa
on both labels.
ware of imitati
For consumpt
indigestion and
ailments requi
stimulants no
KENTUCKY T
LOR has
superior.
Sold by all fi
class druggi
grocers, and liq
dealers.

Wright & Tayl
Distillers,
Fine Kentuck
Whiskies,
Louisville, Ky

Hirshfield & C
New Englan
Agents,
31 Doane Stree
Boston.

Instruct your waiter to bring a bottle of **Pfaff's "Monogram" Lager.**

If you will do this, it will not be necessary for us to expatiate upon the good qualities of our production.
YOU CAN JUDGE FOR YOURSELF.

H. & J. PFAFF BREWING COMPANY,

Telephone 2608.   16 ARCH STREET, BOSTON.

TRY THE "COLUMBIA BRAND" VIENNA SAUSAGES. SERVED HOT OR COLD AT THESE CONCERTS.

They cannot sell you here
Canadian Club Whisky,
Ruinart Champagne,
Royal Liqueur Scotch,
Carstair's Philadelphia Rye,
Fort Hill Bourbon,
Alhambra Sherry,
All of which you will find
of excellent quality;

But you can get

Kaiser Water,

the most refreshing of all
table waters,

Chateau d'Arsac Claret,
N. Johnston & Sons' Medoc,
and
California Inglenook Clarets.

SUPPLIED BY

CODMAN & HALL COMPANY,

WINE MERCHANTS,
Opposite New South
Station.

TUESDAY, MAY 23.

PROGRAMME.

1. MARCH, " Hoch Habsburg " . . . . . Kral
2. WALTZ, " Nachtschwarmer " . . . . Ziehrer
3. OVERTURE, " Benvenuto Cellini " . . . Berlioz
4. SELECTION from " The Wizard of the Nile " . Herbert

5. WALTZ, " Vienna Bonbons " . . . . Strauss
(First Time.)
6. NOCTURNE . . . . Marshall
The audience is respectfully requested to preserve silence during the performance of this number.
7. PROLOGUE to " Pagliacci " . . . Leoncavallo
8. SLAVONIC DANCE . . . . . . Dvorak

9. SELECTION, " Cavalleria Rusticana " . . Mascagni
10. WALTZ, " Amour et Printemps " . . . Waldteufel
11. GALOP, " Kosackenritt " . . . . Millöcker
12. MARCH, " Donna Juanita " . . . . . Suppé

COAL
Best Quality
AT
Lowest Prices

METROPOLITAN COAL COMPANY,
No. 30 Congress Street.

THE WILSON,
AMERICA'S PUREST
Mineral Spring Water,

Is used in making our celebrated
**Belfast Ginger Ale,
Champagne Kola,**
Lemon Soda, Club Soda, Vichy, etc. Hotels and Families supplied. Try a sample order of these goods, and be convinced of their superiority, purity, and medicinal qualities...

All of our beverages bottled at the spring. We ship only in glass, and all bottles and demijohns are sterilized before being filled...

Wilson Spring and Hotel Co.,
Tel., 3129 Boston. | 45 ARCH STREET.

"THE RECOGNIZED FAVORITE OF ALL BEERS."

Sold at these Concerts. JOS. GAHM & CO., N.E. AGENTS, 125-127 PURCHASE ST.

THE ONLY BEER ON DRAUGHT AT THESE CONCERTS.
"the beer that's brewed"

Free delivery in city and Suburbs

THE FALL RIVER LINE

OCCUPYING THE
LONG ISLAND SOUND ROUTE
BETWEEN

Boston and New York

Has the finest quintette of great steamboats that the world has ever seen. The

Priscilla, Puritan, Plymouth, Pilgrim, and Providence

Are the largest, best equipped, safest, and handsomest steamboats ever constructed. This route is one of the most attractive and naturally beautiful traversed by any transportation agency in the world. Trips of the Fall River Line are made throughout the year.

Each steamboat has its own orchestra, and the service on each member of the fleet is maintained at the highest possible standard.

Tickets via this route are on sale at all of the principal Ticket Offices in the United States.

From BOSTON. Trains, connecting with steamers at Fall River in 80 minutes, leave Park Square Station, New York, New Haven & Hartford Railroad (Old Colony System), daily at 5 p.m.

From NEW YORK. Steamers leave Pier 19, North River, foot of Warren Street, daily at 5 30 p m

B. A. GARDNER,
Superintendent,
NEW YORK.

GEO. L. CONNOR,
Passenger Traffic Manager,
NEW HAVEN, CONN.

O. H. TAYLOR,
General Passenger Agent,
NEW YORK CITY.

HOTEL LANGWOOD,

Middlesex Fells Reservation.

P.O. Address, Melrose, Mass.   Wyoming Station, B. & M. R.R.

Twenty minutes by rail from Boston. Sixty trains daily. Hotel coaches meet trains each way. Four hundred feet above sea level. Beautiful rides, drives, and walks. Golf links, tennis courts, and ball grounds.

OPENS ABOUT MAY 20.

For plans and prices address :

F. W. GASKILL, Manager.

BOSTON OFFICE :
Hemenway Building, 10 Tremont Street, Room 29.

Third Season.

3 Ideal Outings

Personally conducted by
F. R. COMEE, Music
Hall, Boston.

S.S. "Howard." Boston to Norfolk, 522 miles. Norfolk to Baltimore, 200 miles.

Boston	1.	2.	3.
Leave	July 2	July 15	August 18
Arrive	July 12	July 31	September 4

S.S. "Toronto." Toronto to Montreal, through the "Thousand Islands" and the "Rapids," 376 miles.

No. 1. Ten days. Saratoga, Lake George, 2,130 miles from Buffalo to Duluth, and return on the steamer "North-Land" through the Great Lakes, Erie, Huron, St. Clair, and Superior.

Nos. 2 and 3. Sixteen days. Exactly alike. 700 miles' ocean sail to Norfolk and Baltimore. Over Alleghany Mountains and a day in Chicago. Up Lake Michigan and three days at Mackinac Island. 1,546 miles on steamer "North-West" to Duluth and return to Buffalo through the Great Lakes. Niagara Falls to Toronto. Across Lake Ontario, through the Thousand Islands, and down the St. Lawrence River to Montreal and Boston.

SEND FOR CIRCULARS.

S.S. "Manitou." Chicago to Mackinac Island, across Lake Michigan, 350 miles.

"North-West." Mackinac Island to Duluth and return to Buffalo, 1,555 miles.

Allsopp's

ENGLISH ALE.
"The Red Hand Brand."

Bottled at the brewery, Burton-on-Trent, England, under the personal supervision of the Messrs. Allsopp.

Sold at these concerts.

WEDNESDAY, MAY 24.

PROGRAMME.

1. MARCH, "King Cotton" — Sousa
2. OVERTURE, "Pique Dame" — Suppé
3. WALTZ, "Die Schönbrunner" — Lanner
4. POTPOURRI, "Grande Duchesse" — Offenbach

5. WALTZ, "Kaiser" — Strauss
6. LIEBESGESTÄNDNISS — Keller
   The audience is respectfully requested to preserve silence during the performance of this number.
   (First Time.)
7. THE DARKIES' DREAM — Langey
8. FESTIVAL MARCH — Converse
   (First Time.)

9. SELECTIONS FROM THE OPERAS OF — Meyerbeer
10. WALTZ, "Grubenlichter" — Zeller
11. POLKA MAZOURKA, "Die Libelle" — Josef Strauss
12. SZECHENYI MARCH — Fahrbach

The *only* Lithia Water sold at these concerts.

Hygeia Lithia Water

Sparkling and Still.

By its use you will avoid the germs of disease which natural MINERAL WATERS are liable to contain.

For Sale at these concerts and by

S. S. PIERCE CO.

The purity and keeping quality of the Tannhaeuser Export under all changes of temperature, its uniform excellence being guaranteed, together with its nutritious properties, make it the most pleasant, delicious, and convenient beverage for home consumption. Put up in corked bottles, and packed in casks of 10 dozen white flint pints, and 6 dozen amber quarts.

Highest Awards wherever exhibited.

FOR SALE AT THESE CONCERTS.

FAMOUS TANNHAEUSER EXPORT BEER

The finest Light Beer Extant.   Brewery Bottling.   Favorite of Connoisseurs.

Pure,   Palatable,   Perfect.

B. & E. Philadelphia Ale on Draught.

FOR SALE AT THESE CONCERTS.

The BERGNER & ENGEL BREWING CO.'S N.E. Depot,

508 and 510 Atlantic Avenue, Boston.

Telephone 3805.   SOL. BACHARACH, Manager.

M. Steinert & Sons Co.,
STEINERT HALL BUILDING,
No. 162 Boylston Street, corner Carver, Boston.

STEINWAY & SONS,
HARDMAN,   GABLER,
EMERSON,   SINGER,
PIANOS.

The Æolian, Aeriol, Orchestrelle, and Pianola.

THE ÆOLIAN
AND
THE PIANOLA
FOR SUMMER HOMES.

At this season of the year we receive many orders for these instruments for Summer Residences, and therefore beg to call attention to our extensive assortment now on display, especially suited for this purpose.

The ÆOLIAN meets the requirements of country homes, furnishing, as it does, music suitable for every occasion. It practically takes the place of an orchestra — music for dancing — orchestral concerts, — in short, music of every style and description is always available.

The PIANOLA will appeal to many on account of the very little space it occupies. It will play any kind of a piano, and can also be used upon a rented piano without the slightest injury. For the above reasons it is bound to be very popular for small cottages.

We are glad to be able to announce that we can furnish PIANOLAS with no more than a week's delay, and, at times, the day the order is given.

Persons not familiar with these instruments are cordially invited to call at our warerooms and hear them, or a descriptive catalogue will be mailed free upon application.

M. STEINERT & SONS CO.,
Steinert Hall,   162 Boylston Street,   Boston.

ANHEUSER-BUSCH BREWING ASS'N,
ST. LOUIS, MO., U.S.A,

BREWERS OF HIGH=GRADE BEERS EXCLUSIVELY.

Black and Tan.   Faust.

Michelob.   Pale Lager.

Muenchener.   Anheuser Standard.

Served at the Music Hall Concerts.
Also at all first-class hotels, clubs, and bars, and on all Pullman and Wagner cars and ocean and lake steamers.

JACOB WIRTH,   **Wholesale Dealer,**   **Boston, Mass.**

THE MUSIC HALL
PROMENADE CONCERTS

SMOKE THE POPULAR "BARRISTER" CIGARS AT THE POPULAR CONCERTS.

SMOKE "LA CELESTINA," THE BEST ALL-HAVANA CIGAR. DANIEL FRANK & CO.

BOSTON, MONDAY, MAY 22, 1899.

SUMMER SEASON.
Vol. XIV. No. 13.

YOU CAN
Have your last season's outfit dyed or cleansed and refinished so it will look like new, by our French process. Why discard soiled clothing when it can be overhauled and worn as second best? You can

RELY ON
Our methods of cleansing, and need not hesitate to trust us with articles of the most delicate textures.
We dye or cleanse and refinish PROPERLY, *all* materials of household use and clothing of all kinds.

LEWANDO'S
W. L. Crosby, General Manager.
French Cleansers, Fancy Dyers, Fine Launderers.
PRINCIPAL OFFICES:
17 Temple Place, Boston.
479 Fifth Avenue, New York.
Established 70 years.
Largest in America.
Bundles called for and delivered.
Telephones in all offices.

Save half your money
do not throw it away in half-smoked cigars! You will find that 50% of your cigar money is thrown away every day if you recall how few cigars you really have time to smoke "up."

BETWEEN THE ACTS Little Cigars
are pure—clean—all good tobacco, and are in every way a very satisfactory short smoke. While you are listening to the music to-night, try a 10-cent box. The waiter will get them for you as they are for sale here. You will enjoy them!

THE MUSIC HALL... Promenade Concerts
FOURTEENTH SEASON.

C. A. ELLIS, Manager.   F. R. COMEE, Assistant Manager.
Mr. MAX ZACH, Conductor.

MONDAY, MAY 22.
SOLOISTS' NIGHT.

PROGRAMME.

1. RADETZKY MARCH . . . . Strauss
2. WALTZ, "Violets" . . . . Waldteufel
3. OVERTURE, "Phèdre" . . . . . . Massenet
4. FLUTE SOLO, "Air Varié, Tremolo" . . Demessermann
    M. A. MAQUARRE.
5. OVERTURE, "Strawberry Leaves" . . Constance Tippett
6. VIOLIN SOLO, (*a*) Andante . . . . De Bériot
    (*b*) Spanish Dance . . . . Sarasate
    Ms. K. ONDRICEK.
7. INVITATION TO DANCE . . . . . Weber
8. RIDE OF THE WALKYRIES . . . . Wagner
9. MARCH from "Strawberry Leaves" . . Constance Tippett
10. WALTZ, "Gross Wien" . . . . . Strauss
11. POLKA, "Love-letter" . . . . . Ziehrer
    (First Time.)
12. ORIENTAL MARCH . . . . Zach

THE TWO
MOST POPULAR TWO-STEPS
OF THE SEASON.

THE RUNAWAY GIRL, by Van Baar, ... 60c.
THE CECIL, by Megone, ... 50c.
FOR ORCHESTRA OR PIANO SOLO.

BOOSEY & CO.,
9 EAST 17th STREET,   NEW YORK.

"OH BE JOLLY"
DRINK VAN NOSTRAND'S
P. B. ALE
SOLD AT THESE CONCERTS

NORFOLK CABINET

LAGER BEER
A Particularly Fine Lager for Family Use and Clubs.
Bottled in the most careful manner at our own bottling department, and sold by the S. S. Pierce Co. and all other leading grocers in New England.
Other Brands in Bottles:
"Norfolk India Pale Stock Ale."
"Norfolk Extra Golden Ale" (blue label).
"Norfolk Standard Lager."
Our "Cabinet" and "Bismarck Brau" are the most popular refreshments at these concerts.
HABICH & CO.
H. W. HABICH.   Telephone, 56 Roxbury
EDWARD RUHL.   or 1152 Boston.

ESTABROOK & EATON'S MARGUERITE PERFECTOS, 10c. EACH, CONCHAS, 10c., 3 FOR 25c., SOLD AT THE "POPS."

THE ICE-CREAM SERVED AT THESE CONCERTS IS FURNISHED BY WEBER, 25 Temple Place and 33 West Street.

MUSIC HALL PROMENADE PROGRAMME.

PUBLISHED EVERY EVENING DURING THE SUMMER SEASON.

NOTICE TO ADVERTISERS.

The advertising columns in the Programme are controlled SOLELY by P. R. Comee, Boston Music Hall Box Office, to whom all communications should be addressed.

The United States Hotel,

SARATOGA SPRINGS, N.Y.

Under a continuous management for 25 years.

Without a peer in its appointments, service, and liberal management.

The largest structure of its kind in the world.

Built entirely of brick.

The Hotel and court cover over seven acres.

For further information, rates, etc., etc., address

GAGE & PERRY,
Proprietors,
UNITED STATES HOTEL,
Saratoga Springs, N.Y.

COLONIAL BEER

The Beer that's Brewed in Glass.

Colonial Beer...

PURE, CLEAN, PALATABLE.

Order a Bottle.

SOUTHER BREWING CO.,
919 Parker Street,
Roxbury, Mass.

All The
IMPORTED CIGARS

Sold At These Concerts Are Supplied By The
S. S. PIERCE COMPANY.

The Peer of all Cigarettes.

Save the band-label on each box for valuable premiums.

::: ALSO :::

Monopol

High-grade Egyptian Cigarettes.

No. 8A Khedive,
No. 6A Nadine,
No. 9A Egyptian Belles,
No. 78A Princess Lillian

On sale at these concerts and all first-class dealers.

OCKENHEIMER BERG,
Near Bingen, GERMANY. On the Rhine.

PHILIP KRIM'S
OWN IMPORTATION OF
Rhine Wines.
FOR 30 YEARS AT
163 Shawmut Avenue.
OUR WINES SOLD AT THESE CONCERTS.

HERRICK, COPLEY SQUARE, Telephones 608 and 950 (Back Bay), CHOICE TABLES for Music Hall "Pops."

GREAT WESTERN CHAMPAGNE

——A natural, genuine champagne, of the finest quality produced in America.

Sold by Wine Merchants, Grocers, and Druggists.

TUESDAY, MAY 23.

PROGRAMME.

1. MARCH, "Hoch Habsburg" . . . . . Kral
2. WALTZ, "Nachtschwärmer" . . . . Ziehrer
3. OVERTURE, "Benvenuto Cellini" . . . Berlioz
4. SELECTION from "The Wizard of the Nile" . Herbert

5. WALTZ, "Vienna Bonbons" . . . . Strauss
   (First Time.)
6. NOCTURNE . . . . Marshall
   The audience is respectfully requested to preserve silence during the performance of this number.
7. PROLOGUE to "Pagliacci" . . . . Leoncavallo
8. SLAVONIC DANCE . . . . Dvorak

9. SELECTION, "Cavalleria Rusticana" . . Mascagni
10. WALTZ, "Amour et Printemps" . . . Waldteufel
11. GALOP, "Kosackenritt" . . . . . Millöcker
12. MARCH, "Donna Juanita" . . . . . Suppé

THE HAYWARD,
16 and 22 Hayward Place.
LADIES' AND GENTS' CAFÉ.   Open until 1 a.m.

SCIARRETTA'S NEAPOLITAN TRIO give concerts daily from 6 P.M. until 1 A.M.
Signor SALVATORE SCIARRETTI, Lyric Tenor, is highly endorsed by Vice-President Garret A. Hobart, Chauncey M. Depew, Eugene Ysaye, Raoul Pugno, Jean Gerardy, and many other prominent people.
SMITH & KERRISSEY, Proprietors.

AN HISTORIC RESORT.

The loveliest place on the New England coast to spend a short vacation or the whole season is the

MYLES STANDISH HOTEL,
at SOUTH DUXBURY, MASS.

Everything that money and intelligence can do has been done to make this hotel better, if possible, than it was last season.
The greatest pains will be taken to have the table service absolutely excellent. Of the house itself and its surroundings too much cannot be said. It is a resort of nice people, who come year after year, gaining strength, vitality, and pleasure.
Send for our 1899 booklet.

L. BOYER'S SONS, Proprietors,
27 Devonshire Street, Boston, Mass.,
Or ALFRED S. AMER, Manager,
90 Wall Street, New York
(Until June 1).
Myles Standish Hotel,
South Duxbury, Mass.

"AMERICA'S FINEST PRODUCT."

Bartholomay's "APOLLO"

LAGER BEER IN BOTTLES.

Sold at these Concerts.

ALBRECHT & KOELLNER,
SOLE AGENTS,
Telephone, Boston 1751.   295-305 A Street.

Also Agents for the "Crystal Rock" Mineral Water.

PURE BEER

BREW. CO'S $1000.00

PURE BEER

Sold at these Concerts,
IN BOTTLES ONLY
20¢ PER BOTTLE.

TABLE LINEN USED AT THESE CONCERTS THE L. K. HUSTED LAUNDERING COMPANY. 27 and 29 BROADWAY, CHELSEA, MASS.

Inglenook Vineyard.

The only California Wines sold at these Concerts.

❧❧

THE CODMAN & HALL CO.,
Opposite the South Union Station.

Sole Agents for New England.

IND. COOPE & CO.'S English Ale.

THE SECOND LARGEST BREWERY IN ENGLAND.

Brewers of the finest *light quality* ale. Very highly endorsed by the medical profession. : : : : :

❧❧

THE CODMAN & HALL CO.,
Opposite South Union Station.

Sole Agents for the United States.

DRIN only th
PURE
WHIS

If you want Tay and richne flavor, try only gen and origin

OLD KENTU TAYLOR,

Eight years old own distillation guaranteed p Bottled and shi direct from warehouses by None genuine out our sign on both labels. ware of imitat For consump indigestion, an ailments requi stimulants, O KENTUCKY T LOR has superior.
Sold by all f class drugg grocers, and li dealers.

Wright & Tay Distillers, Fine Kentuck Whiskies, Louisville, Ky

Hirsbfield & New Englan Agents, 31 Doane Stre Boston.

Instruct your waiter to bring a bottle of

Pfaff's "Monogram" Lager.

If you will do this, it will not be necessary for us to expatiate upon the good qualities of our production.
YOU CAN JUDGE FOR YOURSELF.

H. & J. PFAFF BREWING COMPANY,
Telephone 2608.   16 ARCH STREET, BOSTON.

TRY THE "COLUMBIA BRAND" VIENNA SAUSAGES. SERVED HOT OR COLD AT THESE CONCERTS.

They cannot sell you here
Canadian Club Whisky,
Ruinart Champagne,
Royal Liqueur Scotch,
Carstair's Philadelphia Rye,
Fort Hill Bourbon,
Alhambra Sherry,
All of which you will find
of excellent quality;

But you can get

Kaiser Water,

the most refreshing of all table waters,

Chateau d' Arsac Claret,
N. Johnston & Sons' Medoc,
and
California Inglenook Clarets.

SUPPLIED BY

CODMAN & HALL COMPANY,

WINE MERCHANTS,
Opposite New South Station.

WEDNESDAY, MAY 24.

PROGRAMME.

1. MARCH, "King Cotton" . . . . . Sousa
2. OVERTURE, "Pique Dame" . . . . Suppé
3. WALTZ, "Die Schönbrunner" . . . Lanner
4. POTPOURRI, "Grande Duchesse" . . Offenbach
5. WALTZ, "Kaiser" . . . . . . Strauss
6. LIEBESGESTÄNDNISS . . . . . Keller
   The audience is respectfully requested to preserve silence during the performance of this number.
   (First Time.)
7. THE DARKIES' DREAM . . . . Langey
8. FESTIVAL MARCH . . . . . Converse
   (First Time.)
9. SELECTIONS FROM THE OPERAS OF . Meyerbeer
10. WALTZ, "Grubenlichter" . . . . Zeller
11. POLKA MAZOURKA, "Die Libelle" . Josef Strauss
12. SZECHENYI MARCH . . . . . Fahrbach

COAL Best Quality AT Lowest Prices

METROPOLITAN COAL COMPANY,
No. 30 Congress Street.

THE WILSON, AMERICA'S PUREST

Mineral Spring Water,

Is used in making our celebrated **Belfast Ginger Ale, Champagne Kola,**
Lemon Soda, Club Soda, Vichy, etc. Hotels and Families supplied. Try a sample order of these goods, and be convinced of their superiority, purity, and medicinal qualities. . . . . . .

All of our beverages bottled at the spring. We ship only in glass, and all bottles and demijohns are sterilized before being filled. . . . . . .

Wilson Spring and Hotel Co.,
Tel., 3129 Boston. | 45 ARCH STREET.

"THE RECOGNIZED FAVORITE OF ALL BEERS."

THE ONLY BEER ON DRAUGHT AT THESE CONCERTS.
"the beer that's brewed"

Schlitz
THE BEER THAT MADE MILWAUKEE FAMOUS.
HIGHEST AWARD FOR PURITY.
Sold at these Concerts. JOS. GAHM & CO., N.E. AGENTS, 125-127 PURCHASE ST.

Rochester Brewing Co's. FAMOUS BOTTLED BEER
HOME OFFICE & BREWERY ROCHESTER, N.Y.
NEW ENGLAND BRANCH
295-305 A STREET BOSTON
Free delivery in city and Suburbs
AGENTS: PREMIER, BOHEMIAN, BAVARIAN, STANDARD.

THE FALL RIVER LINE

OCCUPYING THE
LONG ISLAND SOUND ROUTE
BETWEEN

Boston and New York

Has the finest quintette of great steamboats that the world has ever seen. The

Priscilla, Puritan, Plymouth, Pilgrim, and Providence

Are the largest, best equipped, safest, and handsomest steamboats ever constructed. This route is one of the most attractive and naturally beautiful traversed by any transportation agency in the world.

Trips of the Fall River Line are made throughout the year. Each steamboat has its own orchestra, and the service on each member of the fleet is maintained at the highest possible standard.

Tickets via this route are on sale at all of the principal Ticket Offices in the United States.

From BOSTON. Trains, connecting with steamers at Fall River in 80 minutes, leave Park Square Station, New York, New Haven & Hartford Railroad (Old Colony System), daily at 6 p.m.

From NEW YORK. Steamers leave Pier 19, North River, foot of Warren Street, daily at 5.30 p.m.

S. A. GARDNER, Superintendent, NEW YORK.
GEO. L. CONNOR, Passenger Traffic Manager, NEW HAVEN, CONN.
O. H. TAYLOR, General Passenger Agent, NEW YORK CITY.

PRESIDENT McKINLEY wrote a friend, . . . "Last summer I took a trip from Cleveland to Duluth on the 'North-West,' and never did I have a more enjoyable vacation. The scenery is superb and the vessel a veritable floating palace." . . .

HOTEL LANGWOOD,

Middlesex Fells Reservation.

P.O. Address, Melrose, Mass.   Wyoming Station, B. & M. R.R.

Twenty minutes by rail from Boston. Sixty trains daily. Hotel coaches meet trains each way. Four hundred feet above sea level. Beautiful rides, drives, and walks. Golf links, tennis courts, and ball grounds.

OPENS ABOUT MAY 20.

For plans and prices address:

F. W. GASKILL, Manager.

BOSTON OFFICE:
Hemenway Building, 10 Tremont Street, Room 29.

THIRD SEASON.

3 Ideal Outings

Personally conducted by
F. R. COMEE,
Music Hall, Boston.

| Boston | 1. Leave July 2 Arrive July 12 | 2. July 15 July 31 | 3. August 19 September 4 |

No. 1. Ten days. **Saratoga, Lake George,** 2,130 miles from **Buffalo** to **Duluth,** and return on the steamer "North-Land" through the **Great Lakes, Erie, Huron, St. Clair,** and **Superior.**

Nos. 2 and 3. Sixteen days. Exactly alike. 700 miles' ocean sail to **Norfolk** and **Baltimore.** Over **Alleghany Mountains** and a day in **Chicago.** Up **Lake Michigan** and three days at **Mackinac Island.** 1,546 miles on steamer "North-West" to **Duluth** and return to **Buffalo** through the **Great Lakes, Niagara Falls** to **Toronto.** Across **Lake Ontario,** through the **Thousand Islands,** and down the **St. Lawrence River** to **Montreal** and **Boston.**

SEND FOR CIRCULARS.

Allsopp's

ENGLISH ALE.
"The Red Hand Brand."

Bottled at the brewery, Burton-on-Trent, England, under the personal supervision of the Messrs. Allsopp.

Sold at these concerts.

THURSDAY, MAY 25.

PROGRAMME.

1. MARCH, " Hands across the Sea " . . . . . . Sousa
   (First Time.)
2. WALTZ, " Rosen aus dem Süden " . . . . . . Strauss
3. OVERTURE, " Le Roi l'a dit " . . . . . . Delibes
4. SELECTION, " The Belle of New York " . . . Kerker
5. INTRODUCTION to Act III., " Lohengrin " . . Wagner
6. NOCTURNE in F . . . . Chopin-Glazounow
   The audience is respectfully requested to preserve silence during the performance of this number.
7. WALTZ, " Pomona " . . . . Waldteufel
8. MARCH from " Tannhäuser " . . . . . . Wagner
9. OVERTURE, " Banditenstreiche " . . . . . . Suppé
10. LARGO, ... Händel
    Violin Obligato, Mr. ONDRICEK.
11. GAVOTTE, " Amaryllis " . . . . Ghys
12. TIMBUCTOO MARCH . . . . Ramadell
    (First Time.)

The *only* Lithia Water sold at these concerts.

Hygeia Lithia Water

Sparkling and Still.

By its use you will avoid the germs of disease which natural MINERAL WATERS are liable to contain.

For Sale at these concerts and by

S. S. PIERCE CO.

The purity and keeping quality of the Tannhaeuser Export under all changes of temperature, its uniform excellence being guaranteed, together with its nutritious properties, make it the most pleasant, delicious, and convenient beverage for home consumption.
Put up in corked bottles, and packed in casks of 10 dozen white-flint pints, and 6 dozen amber quarts.

Highest Awards wherever exhibited.

FOR SALE AT THESE CONCERTS.

FAMOUS TANNHAEUSER EXPORT BEER

The finest Light Beer Extant. Brewery Bottling. Favorite of Connoisseurs.

Pure,   Palatable,   Perfect.

B. & E. Philadelphia Ale on Draught.
FOR SALE AT THESE CONCERTS.

The BERGNER & ENGEL BREWING CO.'S N.E. Depot,
508 and 510 Atlantic Avenue, Boston.
Telephone 3805.   SOL. BACHARACH, Manager.

M. Steinert & Sons Co.,

STEINERT HALL BUILDING,

No. 162 Boylston Street, corner Carver, Boston.

STEINWAY & SONS,

HARDMAN,   GABLER,
EMERSON,   SINGER,

PIANOS.

The Æolian, Aeriol, Orchestrelle,

and Pianola.

THE ÆOLIAN
AND
THE PIANOLA
FOR SUMMER HOMES.

At this season of the year we receive many orders for these instruments for Summer Residences, and therefore beg to call attention to our extensive assortment now on display, especially suited for this purpose.

The ÆOLIAN meets the requirements of country homes, furnishing, as it does, music suitable for every occasion. It practically takes the place of an orchestra — music for dancing — orchestral concerts, — in short, music of every style and description is always available.

The PIANOLA will appeal to many on account of the very little space it occupies. It will play any kind of a piano, and can also be used upon a rented piano without the slightest injury. For the above reasons it is bound to be very popular for small cottages.

We are glad to be able to announce that we can furnish PIANOLAS with no more than a week's delay, and, at times, the day the order is given.

Persons not familiar with these instruments are cordially invited to call at our warerooms and hear them, or a descriptive catalogue will be mailed free upon application.

M. STEINERT & SONS CO.,
Steinert Hall,   162 Boylston Street,   Boston.

ANHEUSER-BUSCH BREWING ASS'N,
ST. LOUIS, MO., U.S.A.
BREWERS OF HIGH=GRADE BEERS EXCLUSIVELY.

Black and Tan.   Faust.

Michelob.   Pale Lager.

Muenchener.   Anheuser Standard.

Served at the Music Hall Concerts.

Also at all first-class hotels, clubs, and bars, and on all Pullman and Wagner cars and ocean and lake steamers.

JACOB WIRTH,   **Wholesale Dealer,**   **Boston, Mass.**

THE MUSIC HALL
PROMENADE CONCERTS

C. A. ELLIS, PUBLISHED BY MUSIC HALL.

BOSTON, TUESDAY, MAY 23, 1899.

SUMMER SEASON. Vol. XIV. No. 14.

THE MUSIC HALL... Promenade Concerts
FOURTEENTH SEASON.

C. A. ELLIS, Manager.   F. R. COMEE, Assistant Manager.
Mr. MAX ZACH, Conductor.

TUESDAY, MAY 23.

PROGRAMME.

1. MARCH, "Hoch Habsburg" . . . . . Kral
2. WALTZ, "Nachtschwärmer" . . . Ziehrer
3. OVERTURE, "Benvenuto Cellini" . . Berlioz
4. SELECTION from "The Wizard of the Nile" . Herbert

5. WALTZ, "Vienna Bonbons" . . . Strauss
   (First Time.)
6. NOCTURNE . . . . Marshall
   The audience is respectfully requested to preserve silence during the performance of this number.
7. PROLOGUE to " Pagliacci " . . . Leoncavallo
8. SLAVONIC DANCE . . . . . Dvorak

9. SELECTION, "Cavalleria Rusticana" . . Mascagni
10. WALTZ, "Amour et Printemps" . . Waldteufel
11. GALOP, "Kosackenritt" . . . . Millöcker
12. MARCH, "Donna Juanita" . . . . Suppé

Monday, May 29, Bicycle Night.
Tuesday, May 30, Patriotic Night.
Wednesday, May 31, Wagner Night.
Saturday, June 3, Conductor Zach's Farewell Appearance.

Now the rage of the LONDON Concerts and Drawing-rooms:

YOU AND I, by Liza Lehmann, . . . 60c.
KING CHARLES, by M. V. White, . . 60c.
LIKE VIOLETS PALE, by F. Allitsen, . . 60c.
WHEN THE WORLD IS FAIR, by F. H. Cowen, 60c.
QUEEN OF MY LIFE, by E. T. Lloyd, . 60c.

BOOSEY & CO.,
9 East 17th Street,   New York.

THE ICE-CREAM SERVED AT THESE CONCERTS IS FURNISHED BY WEBER, 25 Temple Place and 33 West Street.

MUSIC HALL PROMENADE PROGRAMME.
PUBLISHED EVERY EVENING DURING THE SUMMER SEASON.

NOTICE TO ADVERTISERS.
The advertising columns in the Programme are controlled SOLELY by F. R. Comee, Boston Music Hall Box Office, to whom all communications should be addressed.

The United States Hotel,
SARATOGA SPRINGS, N.Y.

Under a continuous management for 25 years.

Without a peer in its appointments, service, and liberal management.

The largest structure of its kind in the world.

Built entirely of brick.

The Hotel and court cover over seven acres.

For further information, rates, etc., etc., address

GAGE & PERRY,
Proprietors,
UNITED STATES HOTEL,
Saratoga Springs, N.Y.

Colonial Beer...
The Beer that's Brewed in Glass.

PURE, CLEAN, PALATABLE.

Order a Bottle.

SOUTHER BREWING CO.,
919 Parker Street,
Roxbury, Mass.

VEUVE CHAFFARD

PURE OLIVE OIL.
IN HONEST BOTTLES.

The Peer of all Cigarettes.
Save the band-label on each box for valuable premiums.

!!! ALSO !!!

Monopol
High-grade Egyptian Cigarettes.

No. 2A Khedive,
No. 66A Nadine,
No. 9A Egyptian Belles,
No. 70A Princess Lillian

On sale at these concerts and all first-class dealers.

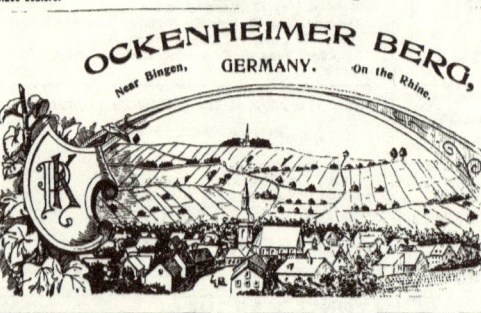

OCKENHEIMER BERG,
Near Bingen, GERMANY. On the Rhine.

PHILIP KRIM'S
OWN IMPORTATION OF
Rhine Wines,
FOR 30 YEARS AT
163 Shawmut Avenue.

OUR WINES SOLD AT THESE CONCERTS.

HERRICK, COPLEY SQUARE, Telephones 608 and 950 (Back Bay), CHOICE TABLES for Music Hall "Pops."

D. LEIDEN'S
SPARKLING
MOSELLE,

The only
Sparkling Wine
sold at these
Concerts.

SHINNECOCK

The
Perfection
of

Scotch
Whisky

Sold by
S. S. PIERCE COMPANY.

WEDNESDAY, MAY 24.
PROGRAMME.

1. MARCH, "King Cotton" . . . . . Sousa
2. OVERTURE, "Pique Dame" . . . . Suppé
3. WALTZ, "Die Schönbrunner" . . . Lanner
4. POTPOURRI, "Grande Duchesse" . . Offenbach
  — — —
5. WALTZ, "Kaiser" . . . . Strauss
6. LIEBESGESTÄNDNISS . . . . . . Keller
   The audience is respectfully requested to preserve silence during the performance of this number.
   (First Time.)
7. THE DARKIES' DREAM . . . . . Langey
8. FESTIVAL MARCH . . . . Converse
   (First Time.)
9. SELECTIONS FROM THE OPERAS OF . Meyerbeer
10. WALTZ, "Grubenlichter" . . . . Zeller
11. POLKA MAZOURKA, "Die Libelle" . Josef Strauss
12. SZECHENYI MARCH . . . . . . Fahrbach

THE HAYWARD,
16 and 22 Hayward Place.
LADIES' AND GENTS' CAFÉ.   Open until 1 a.m.

SCIARRETTA'S NEAPOLITAN TRIO give concerts daily from 6 P.M. until 1 A.M.
Signor SALVATORE SCIARRETTI, Lyric Tenor,
Is highly endorsed by Vice-President Garrett A. Hobart, Chauncey M. Depew, Eugene Ysaÿe, Raoul Pugno, Jean Gerardy, and many other prominent people.
SMITH & KERRISSEY, Proprietors.

AN
HISTORIC
RESORT.

The loveliest place on the New England coast to spend a short vacation or the whole season is the

MYLES STANDISH HOTEL,
at SOUTH DUXBURY, MASS.

Everything that money and intelligence can do has been done to make this hotel better, if possible, than it was last season.
The greatest pains will be taken to have the table service absolutely excellent. Of the house itself and its surroundings too much cannot be said. It is a resort of nice people, who come year after year, gaining strength, vitality, and pleasure.
Send for our 1899 booklet.

L. BOYER'S SONS, Proprietors,
27 Devonshire Street, Boston, Mass.,
Or ALFRED S. AMER, Manager,
90 Wall Street, New York
(Until June 1).
Myles Standish Hotel,
South Duxbury, Mass.

"AMERICA'S FINEST PRODUCT."

Bartholomay's "APOLLO"
LAGER BEER IN BOTTLES.

Sold at these Concerts.

ALBRECHT & KOELLNER,
SOLE AGENTS,
Telephone, Boston 1751.   295-305 A Street.

Also Agents for the "Crystal Rock" Mineral Water.

PURE BEER
Harvard
BREW. CO'S $1000.00
PURE BEER
Sold at these Concerts
IN BOTTLES ONLY
20¢ PER BOTTLE.

Inglenook Vineyard.

The only California Wines sold at these Concerts.

THE CODMAN & HALL CO.,
Opposite the South Union Station.

Sole Agents for New England.

IND. COOPE & CO.'S English Ale.

THE SECOND LARGEST BREWERY IN ENGLAND.

Brewers of the finest *light quality* ale. Very highly endorsed by the medical profession. : : : : :

THE CODMAN & HALL CO.,
Opposite South Union Station.

Sole Agents for the United States.

DRINK only the **PUREST WHISKY**

If you want purity and richness of flavor, try our only genuine and original

OLD KENTUCKY TAYLOR,

Eight years old, our own distillation and guaranteed pure. Bottled and shipped direct from our warehouses by us. None genuine without our signature on both labels. Beware of imitations. For consumption indigestion, and all ailments requiring stimulants OLD KENTUCKY TAYLOR has no superior. Sold by all first-class druggists, grocers, and liquor dealers.

Wright & Taylor
Distillers,
Fine Kentucky Whiskies,
Louisville, Ky.

Hirshfield & Co.,
New England Agents,
31 Doane Street,
Boston.

Instruct your waiter to bring a bottle of **Pfaff's "Monogram" Lager.**

If you will do this, it will not be necessary for us to expatiate upon the good qualities of our production.
YOU CAN JUDGE FOR YOURSELF.

H. & J. PFAFF BREWING COMPANY,
Telephone 2608.   16 ARCH STREET, BOSTON.

TRY THE "COLUMBIA BRAND" VIENNA SAUSAGES. SERVED HOT OR COLD AT THESE CONCERTS.

They cannot sell you here
Canadian Club Whisky,
Ruinart Champagne,
Royal Liqueur Scotch,
Carstair's Philadelphia Rye,
Fort Hill Bourbon,
Alhambra Sherry,
All of which you will find
of excellent quality;

But you can get

Kaiser Water,

the most refreshing of all
table waters.

*Chateau d'Arsac Claret,
N. Johnston & Sons' Medoc,*
and
California Inglenook Clarets.

SUPPLIED BY

CODMAN & HALL COMPANY,

WINE MERCHANTS,
Opposite New South Station.

THURSDAY, MAY 25.

PROGRAMME.

1. MARCH, "Hands across the Sea" . . . Sousa
   (First Time.)
2. WALTZ, "Rosen aus dem Süden" . . . Strauss
3. OVERTURE, "Le Roi l'a dit" . . . Delibes
4. SELECTION, "The Belle of New York" . . . Kerker
5. INTRODUCTION to Act III, "Lohengrin" . . . Wagner
6. BOSNIAN SONG AND KOLO (National Dance) . . . Komzak
   The audience is respectfully requested to preserve silence during the performance of this number.
7. WALTZ, "Pomone" . . . Waldteufel
8. MARCH from "Tannhäuser" . . . Wagner
   Violin Obligato, Mr. ONDRICEK.
9. OVERTURE, "Banditenstreiche" . . . Suppé
10. LARGO . . . Händel
11. GAVOTTE, "Amaryllis" . . . Ghys
12. TIMBUCTOO MARCH . . . Ramsdell
    (First Time.)

COAL

**Best Quality
AT
Lowest Prices**

**METROPOLITAN COAL COMPANY,
No. 30 Congress Street.**

THE WILSON, AMERICA'S PUREST

**Mineral
Spring
Water,**

Is used
in making
our celebrated

**Belfast
Ginger Ale,
Champagne
Kola,**

Lemon Soda, Club Soda,
Vichy, etc. Hotels and Families supplied. Try a sample order of these goods, and be convinced of their superiority, purity, and medicinal qualities.

All of our beverages bottled at the spring. We ship only in glass, and all bottles and demijohns are sterilized before being filled.

Wilson Spring and Hotel Co.,
Tel., 3129 Boston. | 45 ARCH STREET.

"THE RECOGNIZED FAVORITE OF ALL BEERS."

Schlitz

THE BEER THAT MADE MILWAUKEE FAMOUS.

HIGHEST AWARD FOR PURITY.

Sold at these Concerts. JOS. GAHM & CO., N.E. AGENTS, 125-127 PURCHASE ST.

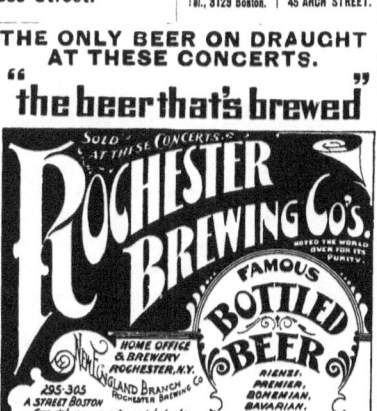

THE ONLY BEER ON DRAUGHT AT THESE CONCERTS.

"the beer that's brewed"

SOLD AT THESE CONCERTS

Rochester Brewing Co's.
NOTED THE WORLD OVER FOR ITS PURITY.

FAMOUS BOTTLED BEER

HOME OFFICE & BREWERY ROCHESTER, N.Y.
295-305 A STREET BOSTON
NEW ENGLAND BRANCH ROCHESTER BREWING CO.
Free delivery in city and Suburbs

RIENSI.
PREMIER.
BOHEMIAN.
BAVARIAN.
STANDARD.

THE FALL RIVER LINE

OCCUPYING THE
LONG ISLAND SOUND ROUTE,
BETWEEN

Boston and New York

Has the finest quintette of great steamboats that the world has ever seen. The

Priscilla, Puritan, Plymouth, Pilgrim, and Providence

Are the largest, best equipped, safest, and handsomest steamboats ever constructed. This route is one of the most attractive and naturally beautiful traversed by any transportation agency in the world. Trips of the Fall River Line are made throughout the year.

Each steamboat has its own orchestra, and the service on each member of the fleet is maintained at the highest possible standard.

Tickets via this route are on sale at all of the principal Ticket Offices in the United States.

From BOSTON. Trains, connecting with steamers at Fall River in 80 minutes, leave Park Square Station, New York, New Haven & Hartford Railroad (Old Colony System), daily at 6 p.m.

From NEW YORK. Steamers leave Pier 19, North River, foot of Warren Street, daily at 5.30 p.m.

S. A. GARDNER, GEO. L. CONNOR, O. H. TAYLOR,
Superintendent, Passenger Traffic Manager, General Passenger Agent,
NEW YORK. NEW HAVEN, CONN. NEW YORK CITY.

HOTEL LANGWOOD,

Middlesex Fells Reservation.

P.O. Address, Melrose, Mass.   Wyoming Station, B. & M. R.R.

Twenty minutes by rail from Boston. Sixty trains daily. Hotel coaches meet trains each way. Four hundred feet above sea level. Beautiful rides, drives, and walks. Golf links, tennis courts, and ball grounds.

OPENS ABOUT MAY 20.

For plans and prices address :

F. W. GASKILL, Manager.

BOSTON OFFICE :
Hemenway Building, 10 Tremont Street, Room 29.

THIRD SEASON.

Three Ideal Outings,

Personally conducted by F. R. COMEE, Music Hall, Boston.

	1.	2.	3.
BOSTON Leave	July 2	July 15	August 19
Arrive	July 12	July 31	September 4

No. 1. Ten days. **Saratoga. Lake George.** 2,130 miles from **Buffalo** to **Duluth**, and return on the steamer "**North-Land**" through the **Great Lakes, Erie, Huron, St. Clair,** and **Superior.**

Nos. 2 and 3. Sixteen days. Exactly alike. 700 miles' ocean sail to **Norfolk** and **Baltimore**. Over **Alleghany Mountains** and a day in **Chicago.** Up **Lake Michigan** and three days at **Mackinac Island.** 1,546 miles on steamer "**North-West**" to **Duluth** and return to **Buffalo** through the **Great Lakes**. **Niagara Falls** to **Toronto**. Across **Lake Ontario**, through the **Thousand Islands**, and down the **St. Lawrence River** to **Montreal** and **Boston**.

SEND FOR CIRCULARS.

Allsopp's

ENGLISH ALE.
"The Red Hand Brand."

Bottled at the brewery, Burton-on-Trent, England, under the personal supervision of the Messrs. Allsopp.

Sold at these concerts.

FRIDAY, MAY 26.

PROGRAMME.

1. MARCH, "The Charlatan" . . . . . Sousa
2. OVERTURE, "Orpheus aux Enfers" . . Offenbach
3. WALTZ, "Myrthenblüthen" . . . . Strauss
4. PRELUDE to "Lohengrin" . . . . . Wagner

5. HUNGARIAN MARCH . . . . . . Berlioz
6. OVERTURE, "Semiramide" . . . . Rossini
7. EN RÊVE . . . . Gabriel-Marie
   The audience is respectfully requested to preserve silence during the performance of this number.
8. GALOP CHROMATIQUE . . . . . . Liszt

9. MILITARY MARCH . . . . Zach
   (First Time.)
10. HYMN TO ST. CECILIA . . . . . Gounod
    Violin Solo, Mr. ONDRICEK.
11. WALTZ, "Cagliostro" . . . . . . Strauss
12. MARCH from "The Serenade" . . . Herbert

The *only* Lithia Water sold at these concerts.

Hygeia Lithia Water

Sparkling and Still.

By its use you will avoid the germs of disease which natural MINERAL WATERS are liable to contain.

For Sale at these concerts and by

S. S. PIERCE CO.

The purity and keeping quality of the Tannhaeuser Export under all changes of temperature, its uniform excellence being guaranteed, together with its nutritious properties, make it the most pleasant, delicious, and convenient beverage for home consumption.

Put up in corked bottles, and packed in casks of 10 dozen white flint pints, and 6 dozen amber quarts.

Highest Awards wherever exhibited.

FOR SALE AT THESE CONCERTS.

FAMOUS TANNHAEUSER EXPORT BEER

The finest Light Beer Extant. Brewery Bottling. Favorite of Connoisseurs.

Pure, Palatable, Perfect.

B. & E. Philadelphia Ale on Draught.
FOR SALE AT THESE CONCERTS.

The BERGNER & ENGEL BREWING CO.'S N.E. Depot,
508 and 510 Atlantic Avenue, Boston.
Telephone 3805.   **SOL. BACHARACH, Manager.**

M. Steinert & Sons Co.,	THE ÆOLIAN
STEINERT HALL BUILDING,	AND
No. 162 Boylston Street, corner Carver, Boston.	THE PIANOLA
	FOR SUMMER HOMES.

M. Steinert & Sons Co.,
STEINERT HALL BUILDING,
No. 162 Boylston Street, corner Carver, Boston.

STEINWAY & SONS,

HARDMAN,   GABLER,
EMERSON,   SINGER,

PIANOS.

The Æolian, Aeriol, Orchestrelle, and Pianola.

THE ÆOLIAN
AND
THE PIANOLA
FOR SUMMER HOMES.

At this season of the year we receive many orders for these instruments for Summer Residences, and therefore beg to call attention to our extensive assortment now on display, especially suited for this purpose.

The ÆOLIAN meets the requirements of country homes, furnishing, as it does, music suitable for every occasion. It practically takes the place of an orchestra — music for dancing — orchestral concerts, — in short, music of every style and description is always available.

The PIANOLA will appeal to many on account of the very little space it occupies. It will play any kind of a piano, and can also be used upon a rented piano without the slightest injury. For the above reasons it is bound to be very popular for small cottages.

We are glad to be able to announce that we can furnish PIANOLAS with no more than a week's delay, and, at times, the day the order is given.

Persons not familiar with these instruments are cordially invited to call at our warerooms and hear them, or a descriptive catalogue will be mailed free upon application.

M. STEINERT & SONS CO.,
Steinert Hall,   162 Boylston Street,   Boston.

ANHEUSER-BUSCH BREWING ASS'N,

ST. LOUIS, MO., U.S.A.

BREWERS OF HIGH=GRADE BEERS EXCLUSIVELY.

Black and Tan.

Michelob.

Muenchener.

Faust.

Pale Lager.

Anheuser Standard.

Served at the Music Hall Concerts.

Also at all first-class hotels, clubs, and bars, and on all Pullman and Wagner cars and ocean and lake steamers.

JACOB WIRTH,   Wholesale Dealer,   **Boston, Mass.**

THE MUSIC HALL
PROMENADE CONCERTS

SMOKE THE POPULAR "BARRISTER" CIGARS AT THE POPULAR CONCERTS.

SMOKE "LA CELESTINA," THE BEST ALL-HAVANA CIGAR. DANIEL FRANK & CO.

PUBLISHED BY
C. A. ELLIS, MUSIC HALL.

BOSTON, WEDNESDAY, MAY 24, 1899.

SUMMER SEASON.
Vol. XIV. No. 15.

YOU CAN
Have your last season's outfit dyed or cleansed and refinished so it will look like new, by our French process. Why discard soiled clothing when it can be overhauled and worn as second best? You can

RELY ON
Our methods of cleansing, and need not hesitate to trust us with articles of the most delicate textures.
We dye or cleanse and refinish PROPERLY, *all* materials for household use and clothing of all kinds.

LEWANDO'S
W. L. Crosby, General Manager.
French Cleansers, Fancy Dyers, Fine Launderers.
PRINCIPAL OFFICES:
17 Temple Place, Boston.
479 Fifth Avenue, New York.
Established 70 years.
Largest in America.
Bundles called for and delivered.
Telephones in all offices.

Knowledge differs from Experience.
You may know "all about"

BETWEEN THE ACTS
Little Cigars

but have you ever tried them yourself? Do you know how desirable they really are—how good they are—how economical they are—how convenient they are—how satisfactory they are? You can know—once for all—by having the waiter bring you a 10-cent box of ten—to smoke now—to-night—while you are enjoying this concert. They are for sale here.

THE MUSIC HALL :: Promenade Concerts
FOURTEENTH SEASON.

C. A. ELLIS, Manager. F. R. COMEE, Assistant Manager.

Mr. MAX ZACH, Conductor.

WEDNESDAY, MAY 24.

PROGRAMME.

1. MARCH, "King Cotton" . . . . . Sousa
2. OVERTURE, "Pique Dame" . . . . Suppé
3. WALTZ, "Die Schönbrunner" . . . Lanner
4. POTPOURRI, "Grande Duchesse" . . Offenbach

5. WALTZ, "Kaiser" . . . . . . Strauss
6. LIEBESGESTÄNDNISS . . . . . Keller
   The audience is respectfully requested to preserve silence during the performance of this number.
   (First Time.)
7. THE DARKIES' DREAM . . . . Langey
8. FESTIVAL MARCH . . . . . Converse
   (First Time.)
9. SELECTIONS FROM THE OPERAS OF . Meyerbeer
10. WALTZ, "Grubenlichter" . . . . Zeller
11. POLKA MAZOURKA, "Die Libelle" . Josef Strauss
12. SZECHENYI MARCH . . . . Fahrbach

Monday, May 29, Bicycle Night.
Tuesday, May 30, Patriotic Night.
Wednesday, May 31, Wagner Night.
Saturday, June 3, Conductor Zach's Farewell Appearance.

HERE ARE A FEW NAMES FROM OUR LIST OF COMPOSERS:

ENGLISH.— Stephen Adams, F. H. Cowen, S. Liddle, C. V. Stanford, A. C. Mackenzie, R. H. Walthew, H. R. Shelley, Goring Thomas, Frances Allitsen, Maude V. White, Edward German, Mary Carmichael, Liza Lehmann, etc.
FRENCH.— C. Chaminade, Jane Vieu, L. Denza, P. Delmet, Hemberg, Guy d'Hardelot, De Leva, F. P. Tosti, etc.
ITALIAN.— F. P. Tosti, P. Mascagni, G. Puccini, G. Verdi, Don Lorenzo Perosi, etc.

THE MOST REPRESENTATIVE PUBLISHING HOUSE IN AMERICA.

BOOSEY & CO., 9 East 17th Street, New York.

BEST BEER BREWED

DRINK VAN NOSTRAND'S
P. B. ALE
SOLD AT THESE CONCERTS

NORFOLK CABINET LAGER BEER

A Particularly Fine Lager for Family Use and Clubs.
Bottled in the most careful manner at our own bottling department, and sold by the S. S. Pierce Co. and all other leading grocers in New England.
Other Brands in Bottles:
"Norfolk India Pale Stock Ale."
"Norfolk Extra Golden Ale" (blue label).
"Norfolk Standard Lager."
Our "Cabinet" and "Bismarck Brew" are the most popular refreshments at these concerts.

HABICH & CO.
H. W. HABICH. | Telephone, 86 Roxbury
EDWARD RUHL. | or 1152 Boston.

ESTABROOK & EATON'S MARGUERITE PERFECTOS, 10c. EACH. CONCHAS, 10c., 3 FOR 25c. SOLD AT THE "POPS."

THE ICE-CREAM SERVED AT THESE CONCERTS IS FURNISHED BY WEBER, 25 Temple Place and 33 West Street.

MUSIC HALL PROMENADE PROGRAMME.
PUBLISHED EVERY EVENING DURING THE SUMMER SEASON.

NOTICE TO ADVERTISERS.
The advertising columns in the Programme are controlled SOLELY by F. R. Comee, Boston Music Hall Box Office, to whom all communications should be addressed.

The United States Hotel,

SARATOGA SPRINGS, N.Y.

Under a continuous management for 25 years.

Without a peer in its appointments, service, and liberal management.

The largest structure of its kind in the world.

Built entirely of brick.

The Hotel and court cover over seven acres.

For further information, rates, etc., etc., address

GAGE & PERRY,
Proprietors,
UNITED STATES HOTEL,
Saratoga Springs, N.Y.

Colonial Beer...
The Beer that's Brewed in Glass.

PURE, CLEAN, PALATABLE.

Order a Bottle.

SOUTHER BREWING CO.,
919 Parker Street,
Roxbury, Mass.

All The
IMPORTED CIGARS

Sold At These Concerts Are Supplied By The

S. S. PIERCE COMPANY.

The Peer of all Cigarettes.
Save the band-label on each box for valuable premiums.

::: ALSO :::

Monopol

High-grade Egyptian Cigarettes.

No. 8a Khedive,
No. 6½ Nadine,
No. 9a Egyptian Belles,
No. 70a Princess Lillian

On sale at these concerts and all first-class dealers.

OCKENHEIMER BERG,
Near Bingen, GERMANY. on the Rhine.

PHILIP KRIM'S
OWN IMPORTATION OF
Rhine Wines,
FOR 30 YEARS AT
163 Shawmut Avenue.

OUR WINES SOLD AT THESE CONCERTS.

HERRICK, COPLEY SQUARE, Telephones 608 and 950 (Back Bay), CHOICE TABLES for Music Hall "Pops."

GREAT WESTERN CHAMPAGNE

——A natural, genuine champagne, of the finest quality produced in America.

Sold by Wine Merchants, Grocers, and Druggists.

THURSDAY, MAY 25.

PROGRAMME.

1. MARCH, "Hands across the Sea" . . . Sousa
   (First Time.)
2. WALTZ, "Rosen aus dem Süden" . . . Strauss
3. OVERTURE, "Le Roi l'a dit" . . . D. libes
4. SELECTION, "The Belle of New York" . . Kerker
5. INTRODUCTION to Act III., "Lohengrin" . . Wagner
6. BOSNIAN SONG AND KOLO (National Dance) . . Komzak
   The audience is respectfully requested to preserve silence during the performance of this number.
7. WALTZ, "Pomone" . . . Waldteufel
8. MARCH from "Tannhauser" . . . Wagner
9. OVERTURE, "Banditenstreiche" . . . Suppé
10. LARGO, ... Händel
    Violin Obligato, MR. ONDRICEK.
11. GAVOTTE, "Amaryllis" . . . Ghys
12. TIMBUCTOO MARCH . . . . . Ramadel
    (First Time.)

THE HAYWARD,
16 and 22 Hayward Place.
LADIES' AND GENTS' CAFÉ.   Open until 1 a.m.

SCIARRETTA'S NEAPOLITAN TRIO give concerts daily from 6 P.M. until 1 A.M.
Signor SALVATORE SCIARRETTI, Lyric Tenor, is highly endorsed by Vice-President Garrett A. Hobart, Chauncey M. Depew, Eugene Ysaye, Raoul Pugno, Jean Gerardy, and many other prominent people.
SMITH & KERRISSEY, Proprietors.

AN HISTORIC RESORT.

The loveliest place on the New England coast to spend a short vacation or the whole season is the

MYLES STANDISH HOTEL,

at SOUTH DUXBURY, MASS.

Everything that money and intelligence can do has been done to make this hotel better, if possible, than it was last season.
The greatest pains will be taken to have the table service absolutely excellent. Of the house itself and its surroundings too much cannot be said. It is a resort of nice people, who come year after year, gaining strength, vitality, and pleasure.
Send for our 1899 booklet.

L. BOYER'S SONS, Proprietors,
27 Devonshire Street, Boston, Mass.,
Or ALFRED S. AMER, Manager,
90 Wall Street, New York
(Until June 1).
Myles Standish Hotel,
South Duxbury, Mass.

"AMERICA'S FINEST PRODUCT."

Bartholomay's "APOLLO"

LAGER BEER IN BOTTLES.

Sold at these Concerts.

ALBRECHT & KOELLNER,
SOLE AGENTS,
Telephone, Boston 1751.   295-305 A Street.

Also Agents for the "Crystal Rock" Mineral Water.

PURE BEER

BREW. CO'S $1000.⁰⁰

PURE BEER

Sold at these Concerts,
IN BOTTLES ONLY
20¢ PER BOTTLE.

Inglenook Vineyard.

The only California Wines sold at these Concerts.

THE CODMAN & HALL CO.,
Opposite the South Union Station.

<u>Sole Agents for New England.</u>

IND. COOPE & CO.'S English Ale.

THE SECOND LARGEST BREWERY IN ENGLAND.

Brewers of the finest *light quality* ale. Very highly endorsed by the medical profession. : : : :

THE CODMAN & HALL CO.,
Opposite South Union Station.

<u>Sole Agents for the United States.</u>

Instruct your waiter to bring a bottle of **Pfaff's "Monogram" Lager.**

If you will do this, it will not be necessary for us to expatiate upon the good qualities of our production.
YOU CAN JUDGE FOR YOURSELF.

H. & J. PFAFF BREWING COMPANY,
Telephone 2608.   16 ARCH STREET, BOSTON.

TRY THE "COLUMBIA BRAND" VIENNA SAUSAGES. SERVED HOT OR COLD AT THESE CONCERTS.

They cannot sell you here
  Canadian Club Whisky,
  Ruinart Champagne,
  Royal Liqueur Scotch,
  Carstair's Philadelphia Rye,
  Fort Hill Bourbon,
  Alhambra Sherry,
All of which you will find
of excellent quality;

But you can get

Kaiser Water,

the most refreshing of all
table waters,

Chateau d'Arsac Claret,
N. Johnston & Sons' Medoc,
  and
California Inglenook Clarets.

SUPPLIED BY

CODMAN & HALL
  COMPANY,
    WINE MERCHANTS,
Opposite New South
    Station.

FRIDAY, MAY 26.

PROGRAMME.

1. MARCH, "The Charlatan" . . . . Sousa
2. OVERTURE, "Orpheus aux Enfers" . . . . . Offenbach
3. WALTZ, "Myrthenblüthen" . . . . Strauss
4. PRELUDE to "Lohengrin" . . . . Wagner

5. HUNGARIAN MARCH . . . . Berlioz
6. OVERTURE, "Semiramide" . . . . Rossini
7. EN RÊVE . . . . Gabriel-Marie
    The audience is respectfully requested to preserve silence during the performance of
    this number.
8. GALOP CHROMATIQUE . . . . Liszt

9. MILITARY MARCH . . . . Zach
      (First Time.)
10. HYMN TO ST. CECILIA . . . . Gounod
      Violin Solo, Mr. ONDRICEK.
11. WALTZ, "Cagliostro" . . . . Strauss
12. MARCH from "The Serenade" . . . . . . Herbert

COAL Best Quality AT Lowest Prices

METROPOLITAN COAL COMPANY,
No. 30 Congress Street.

THE WILSON, AMERICA'S PUREST

Mineral Spring Water,

Is used
in making
our celebrated

Belfast
Ginger Ale,
Champagne
    Kola,

Lemon Soda, Club Soda,
Vichy, etc. Hotels and Families supplied. Try a sample order of these
goods, and be convinced
of their superiority,
purity, and medicinal
qualities...

All
of our
beverages
bottled at
the spring....
We ship only in
glass, and all bottles and demijohns
are sterilized before
being filled....

Wilson Spring and Hotel Co.,
Tel., 3129 Boston. | 45 ARCH STREET.

"THE RECOGNIZED
FAVORITE OF ALL BEERS."

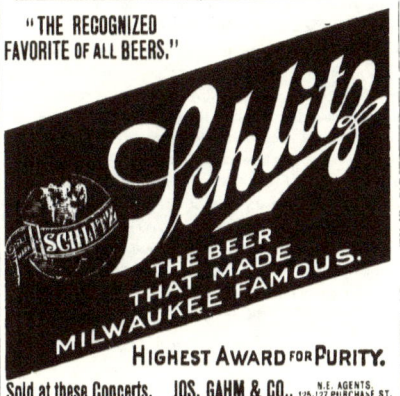

Sold at these Concerts. JOS. GAHM & CO., N.E. AGENTS, 125-127 PURCHASE ST.

THE ONLY BEER ON DRAUGHT
AT THESE CONCERTS.
"the beer that's brewed"

THE FALL RIVER LINE

OCCUPYING THE LONG ISLAND SOUND ROUTE BETWEEN

Boston and New York

Has the finest quintette of great steamboats that the world has ever seen. The

Priscilla, Puritan, Plymouth, Pilgrim, and Providence

Are the largest, best equipped, safest, and handsomest steamboats ever constructed. This route is one of the most attractive and naturally beautiful traversed by any transportation agency in the world.

Trips of the Fall River Line are made throughout the year.

Each steamboat has its own orchestra, and the service on each member of the fleet is maintained at the highest possible standard.

Tickets via this route are on sale at all of the principal Ticket Offices in the United States.

From BOSTON. Trains, connecting with steamers at Fall River in 80 minutes, leave Park Square Station, New York, New Haven & Hartford Railroad (Old Colony System), daily at 6 p.m.

From NEW YORK. Steamers leave Pier 19, North River, foot of Warren Street, daily at 5.30 p.m.

S. A. GARDNER, Superintendent, New York.
GEO. L. CONNOR, Passenger Traffic Manager, New Haven, Conn.
O. H. TAYLOR, General Passenger Agent, New York City.

HOTEL LANGWOOD,
Middlesex Fells Reservation.

P.O. Address, Melrose, Mass.   Wyoming Station, B. & M. R.R.

Twenty minutes by rail from Boston. Sixty trains daily. Hotel coaches meet trains each way. Four hundred feet above sea level. Beautiful rides, drives, and walks. Golf links, tennis courts, and ball grounds.

OPENS ABOUT MAY 20.

For plans and prices address:

F. W. GASKILL, Manager.

BOSTON OFFICE:
Hemenway Building, 10 Tremont Street, Room 29.

THIRD SEASON.

3 Ideal Outings

Personally conducted by
F. R. COMEE,
Music Hall,
Boston.

Boston	1.	2.	3.
Leave	July 2	July 15	August 19
Arrive	July 12	July 31	September 4

No. 1. Ten days. **Saratoga, Lake George,** 2,130 miles from **Buffalo** to **Duluth,** and return on the steamer "North-Land" through the **Great Lakes, Erie, Huron, St. Clair, and Superior.**

Nos. 2 and 3. Sixteen days. Exactly alike. 700 miles' ocean sail to **Norfolk** and **Baltimore.** Over **Alleghany Mountains** and a day in **Chicago.** Up Lake **Michigan** and three days at **Mackinac Island.** 1,546 miles on steamer "North-West" to **Duluth** and return to Buffalo through the **Great Lakes, Niagara Falls** to **Toronto.** Across Lake **Ontario,** through the **Thousand Islands,** and down the St. **Lawrence River** to **Montreal** and **Boston.**

No country in the world can duplicate the journey of 1,065 miles in one steamer on fresh water from **Buffalo** to **Duluth** through the Great Northern Lakes. These "Ideal Outings" are not cheap trips, as they are too extensive, trip No. 1 covering 3,000 miles, Nos. 2 and 3, which are exactly alike, covering 4,000 miles, and with only one night in a sleeping-car. There need be no fear of seasickness, as frequent experience has proved the Great Lakes to be unusually smooth in July and August. We travel first-class in every way. The parties are strictly limited, as it is impossible to secure equally good accommodations for a large number. The fatigue of too steady travel is avoided by from one to three days' rest at Old Point Comfort, Chicago, Mackinac Island, Duluth, Niagara Falls, Saratoga, etc. The average temperature through the Great Lakes in midsummer is 60°. No tourist who has made the journey has yet expressed disappointment: on the contrary, all are amazed at its extent and beauty.

SEND FOR CIRCULARS.

Allsopp's

ENGLISH ALE.
"The Red Hand Brand."

Bottled at the brewery, Burton-on-Trent, England, under the personal supervision of the Messrs. Allsopp.

Sold at these concerts.

SATURDAY, MAY 27.

PROGRAMME.

1. MARCH, "Up the Street" . . . Morse
2. OVERTURE, "Light Cavalry" . . . Suppé
3. WALTZ, "Jolly Fellows" . . . Vollstedt
4. SELECTION, "The Serenade" . . . Herbert
5. TWO HUNGARIAN DANCES . . . Brahms
6. NARCISSUS . . . Nevin
7. OVERTURE, "Flying Dutchman" . . . Wagner
8. MARCH, "Hands across the Sea" . . . Sousa
9. INTERMEZZO from "Cavalleria Rusticana" . . . Mascagni
10. OVERTURE to "Zampa" . . . Herold
11. AT A GEORGIA CAMP-MEETING . . . Mills
12. MARCH, "Runaway Girl" . . . Ch. v. Baar

The *only* Lithia Water sold at these concerts.

Hygeia Lithia Water

Sparkling and Still.

By its use you will avoid the germs of disease which natural MINERAL WATERS are liable to contain.

For Sale at these concerts and by

S. S. PIERCE CO.

The purity and keeping quality of the Tannhaeuser Export under all changes of temperature, its uniform excellence being guaranteed, together with its nutritious properties, make it the most pleasant, delicious, and convenient beverage for home consumption.
Put up in corked bottles, and packed in casks of 10 dozen white flint pints, and 6 dozen amber quarts.
Highest Awards wherever exhibited.

FOR SALE AT THESE CONCERTS.
FAMOUS TANNHAEUSER EXPORT BEER
The finest Light Beer Extant. Brewery Bottling. Favorite of Connoisseurs.

Pure,   Palatable,   Perfect.
B. & E. Philadelphia Ale on Draught.
FOR SALE AT THESE CONCERTS.

The BERGNER & ENGEL BREWING CO.'S N.E. Depot,
508 and 510 Atlantic Avenue, Boston.
Telephone 3805.   SOL. BACHARACH, Manager.

M. Steinert & Sons Co.,

STEINERT HALL BUILDING,

No. 162 Boylston Street, corner Carver, Boston.

STEINWAY & SONS,

HARDMAN,   GABLER,
EMERSON,   SINGER,

PIANOS.

The Æolian, Aeriol, Orchestrelle, and Pianola.

THE ÆOLIAN
AND
THE PIANOLA
FOR SUMMER HOMES.

At this season of the year we receive many orders for these instruments for Summer Residences, and therefore beg to call attention to our extensive assortment now on display, especially suited for this purpose.

The ÆOLIAN meets the requirements of country homes, furnishing, as it does, music suitable for every occasion. It practically takes the place of an orchestra — music for dancing — orchestral concerts,— in short, music of every style and description is always available.

The PIANOLA will appeal to many on account of the very little space it occupies. It will play any kind of a piano, and can also be used upon a rented piano without the slightest injury. For the above reasons it is bound to be very popular for small cottages.

We are glad to be able to announce that we can furnish PIANOLAS with no more than a week's delay, and, at times, the day the order is given.

Persons not familiar with these instruments are cordially invited to call at our warerooms and hear them, or a descriptive catalogue will be mailed free upon application.

M. STEINERT & SONS CO.,
Steinert Hall,   162 Boylston Street,   Boston.

ANHEUSER-BUSCH BREWING ASS'N,

ST. LOUIS, MO., U.S.A.

BREWERS OF HIGH=GRADE BEERS EXCLUSIVELY.

Black and Tan.	Faust.
Michelob.	Pale Lager.
Muenchener.	Anheuser Standard.

Served at the Music Hall Concerts.

Also at all first-class hotels, clubs, and bars, and on all Pullman and Wagner cars and ocean and lake steamers.

JACOB WIRTH,   Wholesale Dealer,   Boston, Mass.

THE MUSIC HALL
PROMENADE CONCERTS

BOSTON, THURSDAY, MAY 25, 1899.

SUMMER SEASON. Vol. XIV. No. 16.

PUBLISHED BY C. A. ELLIS, MUSIC HALL.

THE MUSIC HALL Promenade Concerts
FOURTEENTH SEASON.

C. A. ELLIS, Manager.   F. R. COMEE, Assistant Manager.

Mr. MAX ZACH, Conductor.

THURSDAY, MAY 25.
PROGRAMME.

1. MARCH, " Hands across the Sea " . . . . Sousa
    (First Time.)
2. WALTZ, " Rosen aus dem Süden " . . . Strauss
3. OVERTURE, " Le Roi l'a dit " . . . . Delibes
4. SELECTION, " The Belle of New York " . . Kerker
5. INTRODUCTION to Act III., " Lohengrin " . . Wagner
6. BOSNIAN SONG AND KOLO (National Dance) . . Komzak
    The audience is respectfully requested to preserve silence during the performance of this number.
7. WALTZ, " Pomone " . . . . . Waldteufel
8. MARCH from " Tannhäuser " . . . . Wagner
9. OVERTURE, " Banditenstreiche " . . . Suppé
10. LARGO, ... Händel
    Violin Obligato, MR. ONDRICEK.
11. GAVOTTE, " Amaryllis " . . . . . Ghys
12. TIMBUCTOO MARCH . . . . . Ramsdell
    (First Time.)

Monday, May 29, Bicycle Night.
Tuesday, May 30, Patriotic Night.
Wednesday, May 31, Wagner Night.
Saturday, June 3, Conductor Zach's Farewell Appearance.

ALBUMS OF SONGS,
Containing many popular compositions not published in single form.

IRISH FOLK SONGS, by Charles Wood,	$2.00
RUSSIAN SONGS, by F. Wishaw (2 vols.),	1.00
NINE SONGS, by S. Liddle,	1.00
NINE SONGS, by Liza Lehmann,	1.00
FIVE SONGS, by Francis Korbay,	2.00

Beautifully Illustrated by J. S. SARGENT, R.A.

BOOSEY & CO.,
9 East 17th Street,   New York.

YOU CAN
Have your last season's outfit dyed or cleansed and refinished so it will look like new, by our French process. Why discard soiled clothing when it can be overhauled and worn as second best? You can

RELY ON

Our methods of cleansing, and need not hesitate to trust us with articles of the most delicate textures.
We dye or cleanse and refinish PROPERLY, *all* materials of household use and clothing of all kinds.

LEWANDO'S
W. L. Crosby, General Manager.
French Cleansers, Fancy Dyers, Fine Launderers.
PRINCIPAL OFFICES:
17 Temple Place, Boston.
479 Fifth Avenue, New York.
Established 70 years.
Largest in America.
Bundles called for and delivered.
Telephones in all offices.

If you are open to conviction, to-night
try one 10-cent box of

BETWEEN THE ACTS
Little Cigars

to smoke now—or at any time when you want a short smoke, and haven't time for a long one. They are real cigars, but small ones.
They cost so little that you can use them every day as well as not and actually save on your daily cigar expense by substituting them for larger cigars.

FOR SALE HERE.

DRINK VAN NOSTRAND'S BOSTON CLUB LAGER
SOLD AT THESE CONCERTS

NORFOLK CABINET LAGER BEER

A Particularly Fine Lager for Family Use and Clubs.
Bottled in the most careful manner at our own bottling department, and sold by the S. S. Pierce Co. and all other leading grocers in New England.

Other Brands in Bottles :
" Norfolk India Pale Stock ale."
" Norfolk Extra Golden Ale " (blue label).
" Norfolk Standard Lager."
Our " Cabinet " and " Bismarck Brau " are the most popular refreshments at these concerts.

HABICH & CO.
H. W. HABICH. | Telephone, 56 Roxbury
EDWARD BUHL. | or 1152 Boston.

SMOKE "LA CELESTINA," THE BEST ALL-HAVANA CIGAR. DANIEL FRANK & CO.

SMOKE THE POPULAR "BARRISTER" CIGARS AT THE POPULAR CONCERTS.

ESTABROOK & EATON'S MARGUERITE PERFECTOS, 10c. EACH. CONCHAS, 10c., 3 FOR 25c. **SOLD AT THE "POPS."**

THE ICE-CREAM SERVED AT THESE CONCERTS IS FURNISHED BY WEBER, 25 Temple Place and 33 West Street.

MUSIC HALL PROMENADE PROGRAMME.
PUBLISHED EVERY EVENING DURING THE SUMMER SEASON.

NOTICE TO ADVERTISERS.
The advertising columns in the Programme are controlled SOLELY by F. R. Comee, Boston Music Hall Box Office, to whom all communications should be addressed.

The United States Hotel,
SARATOGA SPRINGS, N.Y.

Under a continuous management for 25 years.

Without a peer in its appointments, service, and liberal management.

The largest structure of its kind in the world.

Built entirely of brick.

The Hotel and court cover over seven acres.

For further information, rates, etc., etc., address

GAGE & PERRY,
Proprietors,
UNITED STATES HOTEL,
Saratoga Springs, N.Y.

Colonial Beer...
The Beer that's Brewed in Glass.

PURE, CLEAN, PALATABLE.

Order a Bottle.

SOUTHER BREWING CO.,
919 Parker Street,
Roxbury, Mass.

VEUVE CHAFFARD

PURE OLIVE OIL.
IN HONEST BOTTLES.

The Peer of all Cigarettes.
Save the band-label on each box for valuable premiums.

::: ALSO :::

Monopol

High-grade Egyptian Cigarettes.

No. 8A Khedive,
No. 6A Nadine,
No. 9A Egyptian Belles.
No. 70A Princess Lillian

On sale at these concerts and all first-class dealers.

PHILIP KRIM'S
OWN IMPORTATION OF
Rhine Wines.
FOR 30 YEARS AT
163 Shawmut Avenue.

OUR WINES SOLD AT THESE CONCERTS.

HERRICK, COPLEY SQUARE, Telephones 608 and 950 (Back Bay), CHOICE TABLES for Music Hall "Pops."

D. LEIDEN'S SPARKLING MOSELLE,

The only Sparkling Wine sold at these Concerts.

FRIDAY, MAY 26.

PROGRAMME.

1. MARCH, "The Charlatan" . . . . Sousa
2. OVERTURE, "Orpheus aux Enfers" . . Offenbach
3. WALTZ, "Myrthenblüthen" . . . Strauss
4. PRELUDE to "Lohengrin" . . . Wagner

5. HUNGARIAN MARCH . . . . Berlioz
6. OVERTURE, "Semiramide" . . . Rossini
7. EN RÊVE . . . . . . Gabriel-Marie
   The audience is respectfully requested to preserve silence during the performance of this number.
8. GALOP CHROMATIQUE . . . . Liszt

9. MILITARY MARCH . . . . . Zach
   (First Time.)
10. HYMN TO ST. CECILIA . . . Gounod
    Violin Solo, Mr. ONDRICEK.
11. WALTZ, "Cagliostro" . . . . Strauss
12. MARCH from "The Serenade" . . . Herbert

AN HISTORIC RESORT.

The loveliest place on the New England coast to spend a short vacation or the whole season is the

MYLES STANDISH HOTEL,

at SOUTH DUXBURY, MASS.

Everything that money and intelligence can do has been done to make this hotel better, if possible, than it was last season.
The greatest pains will be taken to have the table service absolutely excellent. Of the house itself and its surroundings too much cannot be said. It is a resort of nice people, who come year after year, gaining strength, vitality, and pleasure.
Send for our 1899 booklet.

L. BOYER'S SONS, Proprietors,
27 Devonshire Street, Boston, Mass.,
Or ALFRED S. AMER, Manager,
90 Wall Street, New York
(Until June 1).
Myles Standish Hotel,
South Duxbury, Mass.

SHINNECOCK

The Perfection of Scotch Whisky

Sold by
S. S. PIERCE COMPANY.

THE HAYWARD,
16 and 22 Hayward Place.
LADIES' AND GENTS' CAFÉ. Open until 1 a.m.

SCIARRETTA'S NEAPOLITAN TRIO give concerts daily from 6 P.M. until 1 A.M.
Signor SALVATORE SCIARRETTI, Lyric Tenor,
is highly endorsed by Vice-President Garrett A. Hobart, Chauncey M. Depew, Eugene Ysaye, Raoul Pugno, Jean Gerardy, and many other prominent people.
SMITH & KERRISSEY, Proprietors.

"AMERICA'S FINEST PRODUCT."

Bartholomay's "APOLLO"

LAGER BEER IN BOTTLES.

Sold at these Concerts.

ALBRECHT & KOELLNER,
SOLE AGENTS,
Telephone, Boston 1751.   295-305 A Street.

Also Agents for the "Crystal Rock" Mineral Water.

PURE BEER

$1000.00

PURE BEER

Sold at these Concerts
IN BOTTLES ONLY
20¢ PER BOTTLE.

Inglenook Vineyard.

The only California Wines sold at these Concerts.

❧❧

THE CODMAN & HALL CO.,
Opposite the South Union Station.

Sole Agents for New England.

IND. COOPE & CO.'S English Ale.

THE SECOND LARGEST BREWERY IN ENGLAND.

Brewers of the finest *light quality* ale. Very highly endorsed by the medical profession. : : : : :

❧❧

THE CODMAN & HALL CO.,
Opposite South Union Station.

Sole Agents for the United States.

Instruct your waiter to bring a bottle of

Pfaff's "Monogram" Lager.

If you will do this, it will not be necessary for us to expatiate upon the good qualities of our production.
YOU CAN JUDGE FOR YOURSELF.

H. & J. PFAFF BREWING COMPANY,
Telephone 2608.   16 ARCH STREET, BOSTON.

TRY THE "COLUMBIA BRAND" VIENNA SAUSAGES. SERVED HOT OR COLD AT THESE CONCERTS.

SATURDAY, MAY 27.

PROGRAMME.

1. MARCH, "Up the Street" . . . . Morse
2. OVERTURE, "Light Cavalry" . . . . Suppé
3. WALTZ, "Jolly Fellows" . . . . Vollstedt
4. SELECTION, "The Serenade" . . . . Herbert
5. TWO HUNGARIAN DANCES . . . . Brahms
6. NARCISSUS . . . . Nevin
7. OVERTURE, "Flying Dutchman" . . . . Wagner
8. MARCH, "Hands across the Sea" . . . . . . Sousa
9. INTERMEZZO from "Cavalleria Rusticana" . . Mascagni
10. OVERTURE to "Zampa" . . . . Hérold
11. AT A GEORGIA CAMP-MEETING . . . . Mills
12. MARCH, "Runaway Girl" . . . . Ch. v. Baar

They cannot sell you here
Canadian Club Whisky,
Ruinart Champagne,
Royal Liqueur Scotch,
Carstair's Philadelphia Rye,
Fort Hill Bourbon,
Alhambra Sherry,
All of which you will find
of excellent quality;

But you can get

Kaiser Water,

the most refreshing of all table waters,

Chateau d' Arsac Claret,
N. Johnston & Sons' Medoc,
and
California Inglenook Clarets.

SUPPLIED BY

CODMAN & HALL COMPANY,

WINE MERCHANTS,
Opposite New South Station.

COAL Best Quality AT Lowest Prices

METROPOLITAN COAL COMPANY,
No. 30 Congress Street.

THE WILSON, AMERICA'S PUREST Mineral Spring Water,

Is used in making our celebrated **Belfast Ginger Ale, Champagne Kola,** Lemon Soda, Club Soda, Vichy, etc. Hotels and Families supplied. Try a sample order of these goods, and be convinced of their superiority, purity, and medicinal qualities. . . . .

All of our beverages bottled at the spring. We ship only in glass, and all bottles and demijohns are sterilized before being filled. . . . . . .

Wilson Spring and Hotel Co.,
Tel., 3129 Boston. | 45 ARCH STREET.

"THE RECOGNIZED FAVORITE OF ALL BEERS."

Schlitz

THE BEER THAT MADE MILWAUKEE FAMOUS.

HIGHEST AWARD FOR PURITY.

Sold at these Concerts. JOS. GAHM & CO., N.E. AGENTS, 175-127 PURCHASE ST.

THE ONLY BEER ON DRAUGHT AT THESE CONCERTS.
"the beer that's brewed"

THE FALL RIVER LINE

OCCUPYING THE
LONG ISLAND SOUND ROUTE
BETWEEN

Boston and New York

Has the finest quintette of great steamboats
that the world has ever seen. The

Priscilla, Puritan, Plymouth, Pilgrim, and Providence

Are the largest, best equipped, safest, and handsomest steamboats ever constructed. This route is one of the most attractive and naturally beautiful traversed by any transportation agency in the world. Trips of the Fall River Line are made throughout the year.

Each steamboat has its own orchestra, and the service on each member of the fleet is maintained at the highest possible standard.

Tickets via this route are on sale at all of the principal Ticket Offices in the United States.

From BOSTON. Trains, connecting with steamers at Fall River in 80 minutes, leave Park Square Station, New York, New Haven & Hartford Railroad (Old Colony System), daily at 6 p.m.

From NEW YORK. Steamers leave Pier 19, North River, foot of Warren Street, daily at 5.30 p.m.

S. A. GARDNER,   GEO. L. CONNOR,   O. H. TAYLOR,
Superintendent,   Passenger Traffic Manager,   General Passenger Agent,
NEW YORK.   NEW HAVEN, CONN.   NEW YORK CITY.

HOTEL LANGWOOD,

Middlesex Fells Reservation.

P.O. Address, Melrose, Mass.   Wyoming Station, B. & M. R.R.

Twenty minutes by rail from Boston. Sixty trains daily. Hotel coaches meet trains each way. Four hundred feet above sea level. Beautiful rides, drives, and walks. Golf links, tennis courts, and ball grounds.

OPENS ABOUT MAY 20.

For plans and prices address:

F. W. GASKILL, Manager.

BOSTON OFFICE:
Hemenway Building, 10 Tremont Street, Room 29.

THIRD SEASON.

3 Ideal Outings

Personally conducted by
F. R. COMEE,
Music Hall,
Boston.

	1.	2.	3.
Boston Leave	July 2	July 15	August 19
Arrive	July 12	July 31	September 4

No. 1. Ten days. **Saratoga, Lake George,** 2,130 miles from **Buffalo to Duluth,** and return on the steamer "North-Land" through the **Great Lakes, Erie, Huron, St. Clair, and Superior.**

Nos. 2 and 3. Sixteen days. Exactly alike. 700 miles' ocean sail to **Norfolk and Baltimore.** Over **Alleghany Mountains** and a day in **Chicago.** Up Lake Michigan and three days at **Mackinac Island.** 1,546 miles on steamer "North-West" to **Duluth** and return to **Buffalo** through the **Great Lakes, Niagara Falls to Toronto.** Across Lake **Ontario,** through the **Thousand Islands,** and down the **St. Lawrence River** to **Montreal and Boston.**

No country in the world can duplicate the journey of **1,065 miles in one steamer on fresh water** from **Buffalo** to **Duluth** through the Great Northern Lakes. These "Ideal Outings" are not cheap trips, as they are too extensive, trip No. 1 covering 3,000 miles, Nos. 2 and 3, which are exactly alike, covering 4,000 miles, and with only one night in a sleeping-car. There need be no fear of seasickness, as frequent experience has proved the Great Lakes to be unusually smooth in July and August. We travel first-class in every way. The parties are strictly limited, as it is impossible to secure equally good accommodations for a large number. The fatigue of too steady travel is avoided by from one to three days' rest at Old Point Comfort, Chicago, Mackinac Island, Duluth, Niagara Falls, Saratoga, etc. The average temperature through the Great Lakes in midsummer is 60°. No tourist who has made the journey has yet expressed disappointment: on the contrary, all are amazed at its extent and beauty.

SEND FOR CIRCULARS.

Allsopp's

ENGLISH ALE.
"The Red Hand Brand."

Bottled at the brewery, Burton-on-Trent, England, under the personal supervision of the Messrs. Allsopp.

Sold at these concerts.

MONDAY, MAY 29.
BICYCLE NIGHT.

PROGRAMME.

1.	BRIDE-ELECT MARCH	Sousa
2.	INTERMEZZO, "Naila"	Delibes
3.	CARMEN SELECTION	Bizet
4.	YOUR REQUEST	
5.	CORONATION MARCH	Meyerbeer
6.	LUSTIGE BRÜDER (Jolly Fellows) WALTZ	Vollstedt
7.	ENTRÉE TRIOMPHALE DES BOYARDS	Halvorsen
8.	NOCTURNE	Marshall
	(b) Last Movement of Suite, "Peer Gynt"	Grieg
9.	IL TROVATORE SELECTION	Verdi
10.	CRUBENLICHTER WALTZ	Zeller
11.	HUNTER'S YARN POLKA	Komzak
12.	THE STARS AND STRIPES FOREVER	Sousa

The *only* Lithia Water sold at these concerts.

Hygeia Lithia Water

Sparkling and Still.

By its use you will avoid the germs of disease which natural MINERAL WATERS are liable to contain.

For Sale at these concerts and by

S. S. PIERCE CO.

FOR SALE AT THESE CONCERTS.
FAMOUS TANNHAEUSER EXPORT BEER

The finest Light Beer Extant.   Brewery Bottling.   Favorite of Connoisseurs.

Pure,   Palatable,   Perfect.

B. & E. Philadelphia Ale on Draught.
FOR SALE AT THESE CONCERTS.

The purity and keeping quality of the Tannhaeuser Export under all changes of temperature, its uniform excellence being guaranteed, together with its nutritious properties, make it the most pleasant, delicious, and convenient beverage for home consumption.

Put up in corked bottles, and packed in casks of 10 dozen white flint pints, and 6 dozen amber quarts.

Highest Awards wherever exhibited.

The BERGNER & ENGEL BREWING CO.'S N.E. Depot,
508 and 510 Atlantic Avenue, Boston.
Telephone 3805.   SOL. BACHARACH, Manager.

M. Steinert & Sons Co.,

STEINERT HALL BUILDING,

No. 162 Boylston Street, corner Carver, Boston.

STEINWAY & SONS,

| HARDMAN, | GABLER, |
| EMERSON, | SINGER, |

PIANOS.

The Æolian, Aeriol, Orchestrelle, and Pianola.

THE ÆOLIAN
AND
THE PIANOLA
FOR SUMMER HOMES.

At this season of the year we receive many orders for these instruments for Summer Residences, and therefore beg to call attention to our extensive assortment now on display, especially suited for this purpose.

The ÆOLIAN meets the requirements of country homes, furnishing, as it does, music suitable for every occasion. It practically takes the place of an orchestra — music for dancing — orchestral concerts, — in short, music of every style and description is always available.

The PIANOLA will appeal to many on account of the very little space it occupies. It will play any kind of a piano, and can also be used upon a rented piano without the slightest injury. For the above reasons it is bound to be very popular for small cottages.

We are glad to be able to announce that we can furnish PIANOLAS with no more than a week's delay, and, at times, the day the order is given.

Persons not familiar with these instruments are cordially invited to call at our warerooms and hear them, or a descriptive catalogue will be mailed free upon application.

M. STEINERT & SONS CO.,
Steinert Hall, 162 Boylston Street, Boston.

ANHEUSER-BUSCH BREWING ASS'N,

ST. LOUIS, MO., U.S.A.

BREWERS OF HIGH-GRADE BEERS EXCLUSIVELY.

Black and Tan.	Faust.
Michelob.	Pale Lager.
Muenchener.	Anheuser Standard.

Served at the Music Hall Concerts.

Also at all first-class hotels, clubs, and bars, and on all Pullman and Wagner cars and ocean and lake steamers.

JACOB WIRTH,   Wholesale Dealer,   **Boston, Mass.**

THE MUSIC HALL
PROMENADE CONCERTS

PUBLISHED BY
C. A. ELLIS,
MUSIC HALL.

BOSTON, FRIDAY, MAY 26, 1899.

SUMMER SEASON.
Vol. XIV. No. 17.

SMOKE "LA CELESTINA," THE BEST ALL-HAVANA CIGAR. DANIEL FRANK & CO.

SMOKE THE POPULAR "BARRISTER" CIGARS AT THE POPULAR CONCERTS.

YOU CAN
Have your last season's outfit dyed or cleansed and refinished so it will look like new, by our French process. Why discard soiled clothing when it can be overhauled and worn as second best? You can

RELY ON
Our methods of cleansing, and need not hesitate to trust us with articles of the most delicate textures.
We dye or cleanse and refinish PROPERLY, *all* materials of household use and clothing of all kinds.

LEWANDO'S
W. L. Crosby, General Manager.
French Cleansers, Fancy Dyers, Fine Launderers.
PRINCIPAL OFFICES:
17 Temple Place, Boston.
479 Fifth Avenue, New York.
Established 70 years.
Largest in America.
Bundles called for and delivered.
Telephones in all offices.

Save half your money
do not throw it away in half-smoked cigars! You will find that 50% of your cigar money is thrown away every day if you recall how few cigars you really have time to smoke "up."

BETWEEN THE ACTS
Little Cigars
are pure—clean—all good tobacco, and are in every way a very satisfactory short smoke. While you are listening to the music to-night, try a 10-cent box. The waiter will get them for you as they are for sale here. You will enjoy them!

THE MUSIC HALL :: Promenade Concerts
FOURTEENTH SEASON.

C. A. ELLIS, Manager.   F. R. COMEE, Assistant Manager.

Mr. MAX ZACH, Conductor.

FRIDAY, MAY 26.
PROGRAMME.

1. MARCH, "The Charlatan" . . . . . . Sousa
2. OVERTURE, "Orpheus aux Enfers" . . . Offenbach
3. WALTZ, "Myrthenblüthen" . . . . . Strauss
4. PRELUDE to "Lohengrin" . . . . . Wagner

5. HUNGARIAN MARCH . . . . . . Berlioz
6. OVERTURE, "Semiramide" . . . . . Rossini
7. EN RÊVE . . . . Gabriel-Marie
   The audience is respectfully requested to preserve silence during the performance of this number.
8. GALOP CHROMATIQUE . . . . . . Liszt

9. MILITARY MARCH . . . . Zach
   (First Time.)
10. HYMN TO ST. CECILIA . . . . . Gounod
    Violin Solo, Mr. ONDRICEK.
11. WALTZ, "Cagliostro" . . . . . . Strauss
12. MARCH from "The Serenade" . . . . Herbert

Monday, May 29, Bicycle Night.
Tuesday, May 30, Patriotic Night.
Wednesday, May 31, Wagner Night.
Saturday, June 3, Conductor Zach's Farewell Appearance.

SPECIAL NOTICE.—Owing to a long-standing engagement of Music Hall, there will be no concert on the evening of Thursday, June 1.

THE TWO MOST POPULAR TWO-STEPS
OF THE SEASON.

THE RUNAWAY GIRL, by Van Baar, ... 60c.
THE CECIL, by Megone, ... 50c.
FOR ORCHESTRA OR PIANO SOLO.

BOOSEY & CO.,
9 EAST 17th STREET,   NEW YORK.

BEST BEER BREWED

OH BE JOLLY!
DRINK VAN NOSTRAND'S
P. B. ALE
SOLD AT THESE CONCERTS

NORFOLK CABINET
LAGER BEER

A Particularly Fine Lager for Family Use and Clubs.
Bottled in the most careful manner at our own bottling department, and sold by the S. S. Pierce Co. and all other leading grocers in New England.

Other Brands in Bottles:
"Norfolk India Pale Stock Ale."
"Norfolk Extra Golden Ale" (blue label).
"Norfolk Standard Lager."
Our "Cabinet" and "Bismarck Brau" are the most popular refreshments at these concerts.

HABICH & CO.

H. W. HABICH,   Telephone, 56 Roxbury
EDWARD BUHL.   or 1152 Boston.

ESTABROOK & EATON'S MARGUERITE PERFECTOS, 10c. EACH. CONCHAS, 10c., 3 FOR 25c., SOLD AT THE "POPS."

THE ICE-CREAM SERVED AT THESE CONCERTS IS FURNISHED BY WEBER, 25 Temple Place and 33 West Street.

MUSIC HALL PROMENADE PROGRAMME.
PUBLISHED EVERY EVENING DURING THE SUMMER SEASON.

NOTICE TO ADVERTISERS.
The advertising columns in the Programme are controlled SOLELY by F. R. Comee, Boston Music Hall Box Office, to whom all communications should be addressed.

The United States Hotel,
SARATOGA SPRINGS, N.Y.

Under a continuous management for 25 years.

Without a peer in its appointments, service, and liberal management.

The largest structure of its kind in the world.

Built entirely of brick.

The Hotel and court cover over seven acres.

For further information, rates, etc., etc., address

GAGE & PERRY,
Proprietors,
UNITED STATES HOTEL,
Saratoga Springs, N.Y.

Colonial Beer
The Beer that's Brewed in Glass.
Colonial Beer...
PURE, CLEAN, PALATABLE.
Order a Bottle.
SOUTHER BREWING CO.,
919 Parker Street,
Roxbury, Mass.

VEUVE CHAFFARD
PURE OLIVE OIL.
IN HONEST BOTTLES.

The Peer of all Cigarettes.
Save the band-label on each box for valuable premiums.
::: ALSO :::
Monopol
High-grade Egyptian Cigarettes.
No. 8a Khedive,
No. 9a Nadine,
No. 9a Egyptian Belles.
No. 10a Princess Lillian
On sale at these concerts and all first-class dealers.

OCKENHEIMER BERG,
Near Bingen, GERMANY. On the Rhine.

PHILIP KRIM'S
OWN IMPORTATION OF
Rhine Wines,
FOR 30 YEARS
AT
163 Shawmut Avenue.
OUR WINES SOLD AT THESE CONCERTS.

HERRICK, COPLEY SQUARE, Telephones 608 and 950 (Back Bay), CHOICE TABLES for Music Hall "Pops."

D. LEIDEN'S SPARKLING MOSELLE,

The only Sparkling Wine sold at these Concerts.

SHINNECOCK

The Perfection of

Scotch Whisky

Sold by
S. S. PIERCE COMPANY.

FRIDAY, MAY 26.

PROGRAMME.

1. MARCH, "The Charlatan" . . . . Sousa
2. OVERTURE, "Orpheus aux Enfers" . Offenbach
3. WALTZ, "Myrthenblüthen" . . . Strauss
4. PRELUDE to "Lohengrin" . . . Wagner

5. HUNGARIAN MARCH . . . . . Berlioz
6. OVERTURE, "Semiramide" . . . Rossini
7. EN RÊVE . . . . . . Gabriel-Marie
   The audience is respectfully requested to preserve silence during the performance of this number.
8. GALOP CHROMATIQUE . . . . Li-at

9. MILITARY MARCH . . . . . Zach
   (First Time.)
10. HYMN TO ST. CECILIA . . . . Gounod
    Violin Solo, MR. ONDRICEK.
11. WALTZ, "Cagliostro" . . . . Strauss
12. MARCH from "The Serenade" . . Herbert

THE HAYWARD,
16 and 22 Hayward Place.
LADIES' AND GENTS' CAFÉ. Open until 1 a.m.

SCIARRETTA'S NEAPOLITAN TRIO give concerts daily from 6 P.M. until 1 A.M.
Signor SALVATORE SCIARRETTI, Lyric Tenor,
is highly endorsed by Vice-President Garret A. Hobart, Chauncey M. Depew, Eugene Ysaye, Raoul Pugno, Jean Gerardy, and many other prominent people.

SMITH & KERRISSEY, Proprietors.

AN HISTORIC RESORT.

The loveliest place on the New England coast to spend a short vacation or the whole season is the

MYLES STANDISH HOTEL,
at SOUTH DUXBURY, MASS.

Everything that money and intelligence can do has been done to make this hotel better, if possible, than it was last season.
The greatest pains will be taken to have the table service absolutely excellent. Of the house itself and its surroundings too much cannot be said. It is a resort of nice people, who come year after year, gaining strength, vitality, and pleasure.
Send for our 1899 booklet.

L. BOYER'S SONS, Proprietors,
27 Devonshire Street, Boston, Mass.,
Or ALFRED S. AMER, Manager,
90 Wall Street, New York
(Until June 1).
Myles Standish Hotel,
South Duxbury, Mass.

"AMERICA'S FINEST PRODUCT."

Bartholomay's "APOLLO"
LAGER BEER IN BOTTLES.

Sold at these Concerts.

ALBRECHT & KOELLNER,
SOLE AGENTS,
Telephone, Boston 1751. 295-305 A Street.

Also Agents for the "Crystal Rock" Mineral Water.

PURE BEER
Harvard BREW. CO'S
$1000.00
PURE BEER
Sold at these Concerts
IN BOTTLES ONLY
20¢ PER BOTTLE.

Inglenook Vineyard.

The only California Wines sold at these Concerts.

THE CODMAN & HALL CO.,
Opposite the South Union Station.

Sole Agents for New England.

IND. COOPE & CO.'S English Ale.

THE SECOND LARGEST BREWERY IN ENGLAND.

Brewers of the finest *light quality* ale. Very highly endorsed by the medical profession. : : : : :

THE CODMAN & HALL CO.,
Opposite South Union Station.

Sole Agents for the United States.

DRIN
only the

PURE
WHIS

If you want pu and richness flavor, try only genu and origina

OLD KENTUC TAYLOR,

Eight years old, own distillation guaranteed pu Bottled and ship direct from warehouses by None genuine wi out our signate on both labels. ware of imitatio For consumptio indigestion, and ailments requiri stimulants, OL KENTUCKY TA LOR has n superior.

Sold by all the class druggis grocers, and liqu dealers

Wright & Taylo
Distillers,
Fine Kentucky Whiskies,
Louisville, Ky.

Hirshfield & Co
New England Agents,
31 Doane Street Boston.

Instruct your waiter to bring a bottle of

Pfaff's "Monogram" Lager.

If you will do this, it will not be necessary for us to expatiate upon the good qualities of our production.
YOU CAN JUDGE FOR YOURSELF.

H. & J. PFAFF BREWING COMPANY,
Telephone 2608.   16 ARCH STREET, BOSTON.

TRY THE "COLUMBIA BRAND" VIENNA SAUSAGES. SERVED HOT OR COLD AT THESE CONCERTS.

They cannot sell you here
Canadian Club Whisky,
Ruinart Champagne,
Royal Liqueur Scotch,
Carstair's Philadelphia Rye,
Fort Hill Bourbon,
Alhambra Sherry,
All of which you will find
of excellent quality;

But you can get

Kaiser Water,

the most refreshing of all
table waters,

Chateau d'Arsac Claret,
N. Johnston & Sons' Medoc,
and
California Inglenook Clarets.

SUPPLIED BY

CODMAN & HALL COMPANY,

WINE MERCHANTS,

Opposite New South Station.

SATURDAY, MAY 27.

PROGRAMME.

1. MARCH, "Up the Street" . . . . Morse
2. OVERTURE, "Light Cavalry" . . . . . Suppé
3. WALTZ, "Jolly Fellows" . . . . Vollstedt
4. SELECTION, "The Serenade" . . . . . Herbert
5. TWO HUNGARIAN DANCES . . . . . Brahms
6. NARCISSUS . . . . Nevin
7. OVERTURE, "Flying Dutchman" . . . Wagner
8. MARCH, "Hands across the Sea" . . . Sousa
9. INTERMEZZO from "Cavalleria Rusticana" . . Mascagni
10. OVERTURE to "Zampa" . . . . Hérold
11. AT A GEORGIA CAMP-MEETING . . . Mills
12. MARCH, "Runaway Girl" . . . . . . Ch. v. Baar

COAL
Best Quality
AT
Lowest Prices

METROPOLITAN COAL COMPANY,
No. 30 Congress Street.

THE WILSON,
AMERICA'S PUREST
Mineral Spring Water,

Is used in making our celebrated
Belfast Ginger Ale,
Champagne Kola,
Lemon Soda, Club Soda, Vichy, etc. Hotels and Families supplied. Try a sample order of these goods, and be convinced of their superiority, purity, and medicinal qualities.

All of our beverages bottled at the spring. We ship only in glass, and all bottles and demijohns are sterilized before being filled.

Wilson Spring and Hotel Co.,
Tel., 3129 Boston. | 45 ARCH STREET.

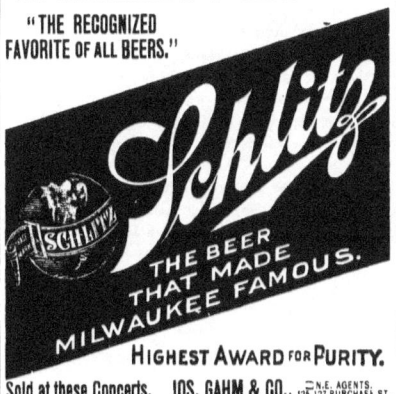

THE FALL RIVER LINE

OCCUPYING THE LONG ISLAND SOUND ROUTE BETWEEN

Boston and New York

Has the finest quintette of great steamboats that the world has ever seen. The

Priscilla, Puritan, Plymouth, Pilgrim, and Providence

Are the largest, best equipped, safest, and handsomest steamboats ever constructed. This route is one of the most attractive and naturally beautiful traversed by any transportation agency in the world. Trips of the Fall River Line are made throughout the year.

Each steamboat has its own orchestra, and the service on each member of the fleet is maintained at the highest possible standard.

Tickets via this route are on sale at all of the principal Ticket Offices in the United States.

From BOSTON. Trains, connecting with steamers at Fall River in 80 minutes, leave Park Square Station, New York, New Haven & Hartford Railroad (Old Colony System), daily at 6 p.m.

From NEW YORK. Steamers leave Pier 19, North River, foot of Warren Street, daily at 5.30 p.m.

S. A. GARDNER, Superintendent, NEW YORK.
GEO. L. CONNOR, Passenger Traffic Manager, NEW HAVEN, CONN.
O. H. TAYLOR, General Passenger Agent, NEW YORK CITY.

HOTEL LANGWOOD,

Middlesex Fells Reservation.

P.O. Address, Melrose, Mass.   Wyoming Station, B. & M. R.R.

Twenty minutes by rail from Boston. Sixty trains daily. Hotel coaches meet trains each way. Four hundred feet above sea level. Beautiful rides, drives, and walks. Golf links, tennis courts, and ball grounds.

OPENS ABOUT MAY 20.

For plans and prices address:

F. W. GASKILL, Manager.

BOSTON OFFICE:
Hemenway Building, 10 Tremont Street, Room 29.

THIRD SEASON.

3 Ideal Outings

Personally conducted by F. R. COMEE, Music Hall, Boston.

Boston	1.	2.	3.
Leave	July 2	July 15	August 19
Arrive	July 12	July 31	September 4

No. 1. Ten days. **Saratoga, Lake George,** 2,130 miles from **Buffalo to Duluth,** and return on the steamer "North-Land" through the **Great Lakes, Erie, Huron, St. Clair,** and **Superior.**

Nos. 2 and 3. Sixteen days. Exactly alike. 700 miles' ocean sail to **Norfolk and Baltimore.** Over **Alleghany Mountains** and a day in **Chicago.** Up **Lake Michigan** and three days at **Mackinac Island.** 1,546 miles on steamer "North-West" to **Duluth** and return to **Buffalo** through the **Great Lakes, Niagara Falls** to **Toronto.** Across **Lake Ontario,** through the **Thousand Islands,** and down the **St. Lawrence River** to **Montreal** and **Boston.**

No country in the world can duplicate the journey of 1,065 miles in one steamer on fresh water from Buffalo to Duluth through the Great Northern Lakes. These "Ideal Outings" are not cheap trips, as they are too extensive, trip No. 1 covering 3,000 miles, Nos. 2 and 3, which are exactly alike, covering 4,000 miles, and with only one night in a sleeping-car. There need be no fear of seasickness, as frequent experience has proved the Great Lakes to be unusually smooth in July and August. We travel first-class in every way. The parties are strictly limited, as it is impossible to secure equally good accommodations for a large number. The fatigue of too steady travel is avoided by from one to three days' rest at Old Point Comfort, Chicago, Mackinac Island, Duluth, Niagara Falls, Saratoga, etc. The average temperature through the Great Lakes in midsummer is 60°. No tourist who has made the journey has yet expressed disappointment: on the contrary, all are amazed at its extent and beauty.

SEND FOR CIRCULARS.

Allsopp's

ENGLISH ALE.
"The Red Hand Brand."

Bottled at the brewery, Burton-on-Trent, England, under the personal supervision of the Messrs. Allsopp.

Sold at these concerts.

MONDAY, MAY 29.
BICYCLE NIGHT.

PROGRAMME.

1. **B**RIDE-ELECT MARCH . . . . . Sousa
2. **I**NTERMEZZO, " Naila" . . . . . Delibes
3. **C**ARMEN SELECTION . . . . . Bizet
4. **Y**OUR REQUEST
5. **C**ORONATION MARCH . . . . . Meyerbeer
6. **L**USTIGE BRÜDER (Jolly Fellows) WALTZ . Vollstedt
7. **E**NTRÉE TRIOMPHALE DES BOYARDS . Halvorsen
8. **N**OCTURNE . . . . Marshall
   (*b*) Last Movement of Suite, "Peer Gynt" . Grieg
9. **I**L TROVATORE SELECTION . . . Verdi
10. **G**RUBENLICHTER WALTZ . . . . Zeller
11. **H**UNTER'S YARN POLKA . . . . Komzak
12. **T**HE STARS AND STRIPES FOREVER . Sousa

The *only* Lithia Water sold at these concerts.

Hygeia Lithia Water

Sparkling and Still.

By its use you will avoid the germs of disease which natural MINERAL WATERS are liable to contain.

For Sale at these concerts and by

S. S. PIERCE Co.

The purity and keeping quality of the Tannhaeuser Export under all changes of temperature, its uniform excellence being guaranteed, together with its nutritious properties, make it the most pleasant, delicious, and convenient beverage for home consumption.
Put up in corked bottles, and packed in casks of 10 dozen white flint pints, and 6 dozen amber quarts.

Highest Awards wherever exhibited.

FOR SALE AT THESE CONCERTS.
FAMOUS TANNHAEUSER EXPORT BEER
The finest Light Beer Extant.   Brewery Bottling.   Favorite of Connoisseurs.

Pure,   Palatable,   Perfect.
B. & E. Philadelphia Ale on Draught.
FOR SALE AT THESE CONCERTS.

The BERGNER & ENGEL BREWING CO.'S N.E. Depot,
508 and 510 Atlantic Avenue, Boston.
Telephone 3805.   SOL. BACHARACH, Manager.

M. Steinert & Sons Co.,

STEINERT HALL BUILDING,

No. 162 Boylston Street, corner Carver, Boston.

STEINWAY & SONS,

HARDMAN,   GABLER,
EMERSON,   SINGER,

PIANOS.

The Æolian, Aeriol, Orchestrelle, and Pianola.

THE ÆOLIAN
AND
THE PIANOLA
FOR SUMMER HOMES.

At this season of the year we receive many orders for these instruments for Summer Residences, and therefore beg to call attention to our extensive assortment now on display, especially suited for this purpose.

The ÆOLIAN meets the requirements of country homes, furnishing, as it does, music suitable for every occasion. It practically takes the place of an orchestra — music for dancing — orchestral concerts, — in short, music of every style and description is always available.

The PIANOLA will appeal to many on account of the very little space it occupies. It will play any kind of a piano, and can also be used upon a rented piano without the slightest injury. For the above reasons it is bound to be very popular for small cottages.

We are glad to be able to announce that we can furnish PIANOLAS with no more than a week's delay, and, at times, the day the order is given.

Persons not familiar with these instruments are cordially invited to call at our warerooms and hear them, or a descriptive catalogue will be mailed free upon application.

M. STEINERT & SONS CO.,
Steinert Hall,   162 Boylston Street,   Boston.

ANHEUSER-BUSCH BREWING ASS'N,
ST. LOUIS, MO., U.S.A.

BREWERS OF HIGH-GRADE BEERS EXCLUSIVELY.

Black and Tan.	Faust.
Michelob.	Pale Lager.
Muenchener.	Anheuser Standard.

Served at the Music Hall Concerts.

Also at all first-class hotels, clubs, and bars, and on all Pullman and Wagner cars and ocean and lake steamers.

JACOB WIRTH,   **Wholesale Dealer,**   **Boston, Mass.**

THE MUSIC HALL
PROMENADE CONCERTS

PUBLISHED BY
C. A. ELLIS,
MUSIC HALL.

BOSTON, SATURDAY, MAY 27, 1899.

SUMMER SEASON.
Vol. XIV. No. 18.

SMOKE "LA CELESTINA," THE BEST ALL-HAVANA CIGAR. DANIEL FRANK & CO.

SMOKE THE POPULAR "BARRISTER" CIGARS AT THE POPULAR CONCERTS

YOU CAN
Have your last season's outfit dyed or cleansed and refinished so it will look like new, by our French process. Why discard soiled clothing when it can be overhauled and worn as second best? You can

RELY ON
Our methods of cleansing, and need not hesitate to trust us with articles of the most delicate textures.
We dye or cleanse and refinish PROPERLY, *all* materials of household use and clothing of all kinds.

LEWANDO'S
W. L. Crosby, General Manager.
French Cleansers, Fancy Dyers, Fine Launderers.
PRINCIPAL OFFICES:
17 Temple Place, Boston.
479 Fifth Avenue, New York.
Established 70 years.
Largest in America.
Bundles called for and delivered.
Telephones in all offices.

In no other way
are men as wasteful and extravagant as in cigar smoking — because cigars are thrown away half smoked half the time.

BETWEEN THE ACTS
Little Cigars
are just right for all short smokes. They light right, they burn right, and taste right. Have you ever seen them? At all stores; 10 for 10 cts., or, as they are for sale here, you can try them to-night. Tell the waiter to bring you a 10-cent box of "Between the Acts." They will add to your enjoyment of this concert.

THE MUSIC HALL... Promenade Concerts
FOURTEENTH SEASON.
C. A. ELLIS, Manager. F. R. COMEE, Assistant Manager.
Mr. MAX ZACH, Conductor.

SATURDAY, MAY 27.

PROGRAMME.

1. MARCH, "Up the Street" . . . . . Morse
2. OVERTURE, "Light Cavalry" . . . Suppé
3. WALTZ, "Jolly Fellows" . . . . . Vollstedt
4. SELECTION, "The Serenade" . . . Herbert
5. TWO HUNGARIAN DANCES . . . Brahms
6. NARCISSUS . . . . Nevin
7. OVERTURE, "Flying Dutchman" . Wagner
8. MARCH, "Hands across the Sea" . Sousa
9. INTERMEZZO from "Cavalleria Rusticana" . . Mascagni
10. OVERTURE to "Zampa" . . . . . Hérold
11. AT A GEORGIA CAMP-MEETING . Mills
12. MARCH, "Runaway Girl" . . . . Ch. v. Baar

Monday, May 29, Bicycle Night.
Tuesday, May 30, Patriotic Night.
Wednesday, May 31, Wagner Night.
Saturday, June 3, Conductor Zach's Farewell Appearance.
Tuesday, June 6, Technology Night.

SPECIAL NOTICE. — Owing to a long-standing engagement of Music Hall, there will be no concert on the evening of Thursday, June 1.

Now the rage of the LONDON Concerts and Drawing-rooms:

YOU AND I, by Liza Lehmann, ... 60c.
KING CHARLES, by M. V. White, . . . 60c.
LIKE VIOLETS PALE, by F. Allitsen, . . 60c.
WHEN THE WORLD IS FAIR, by F. H. Cowen, 60c.
QUEEN OF MY LIFE, by E. T. Lloyd, . . 60c.

BOOSEY & CO.,
9 East 17th Street, New York.

DRINK
VAN NOSTRAND'S
BOSTON CLUB LAGER
SOLD AT THESE CONCERTS

NORFOLK CABINET
LAGER BEER
A Particularly Fine Lager for Family Use and Clubs.
Bottled in the most careful manner at our own bottling department, and sold by the S. S. Pierce Co. and all other leading grocers in New England.
Other Brands in Bottles:
"Norfolk India Pale Stock Ale."
"Norfolk Extra Golden Ale" (blue label).
"Norfolk Standard Lager."
Our "Cabinet" and "Bismarck Braeu" are the most popular refreshments at these concerts.
HABICH & CO.
H. W. HABICH. Telephone, 56 Roxbury
EDWARD RUHL. or 1152 Boston.

ESTABROOK & EATON'S MARGUERITE PERFECTOS, 10c. EACH. **SOLD AT THE "POPS."**
CONCHAS, 10c. 3 FOR 25c.

THE ICE-CREAM SERVED AT THESE CONCERTS IS FURNISHED BY WEBER, 25 Temple Place and 33 West Street.

MUSIC HALL PROMENADE PROGRAMME.

PUBLISHED EVERY EVENING DURING THE SUMMER SEASON.

NOTICE TO ADVERTISERS.

The advertising columns in the Programme are controlled SOLELY by F. R. Comee, Boston Music Hall Box Office, to whom all communications should be addressed.

The United States Hotel,

SARATOGA SPRINGS, N.Y.

Under a continuous management for 25 years.

Without a peer in its appointments, service, and liberal management.

The largest structure of its kind in the world.

Built entirely of brick.

The Hotel and court cover over seven acres.

For further information, rates, etc., etc., address

GAGE & PERRY,
Proprietors,
UNITED STATES HOTEL,
Saratoga Springs, N.Y.

Colonial Beer...

The Beer that's Brewed in Glass.

PURE, CLEAN, PALATABLE.

Order a Bottle.

SOUTHER BREWING CO.,
919 Parker Street,
Roxbury, Mass.

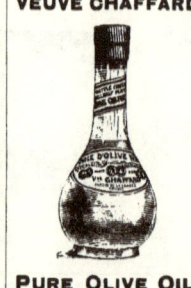

VEUVE CHAFFARD

PURE OLIVE OIL.

IN HONEST BOTTLES.

The Peer of all Cigarettes.

Save the band-label on each box for valuable premiums.

::: ALSO :::

Monopol

High-grade Egyptian Cigarettes.

No. 8A Khedive,
No. 8¼ Nadine,
No. 9A Egyptian Belles,
No. 70A Princess Lillian

On sale at these concerts and all first-class dealers.

OCKENHEIMER BERG,
Near Bingen, GERMANY. On the Rhine.

PHILIP KRIM'S OWN IMPORTATION OF **Rhine Wines.**

FOR 30 YEARS AT

163 Shawmut Avenue.

OUR WINES SOLD AT THESE CONCERTS.

HERRICK, COPLEY SQUARE, Telephones 608 and 950 (Back Bay), CHOICE TABLES for Music Hall "Pops."

D. LEIDEN'S
SPARKLING
MOSELLE,

The only
Sparkling Wine
sold at these
Concerts.

SHINNECOCK

The
Perfection
of

Scotch

Whisky

Sold by
S. S. PIERCE COMPANY.

MONDAY, MAY 29.

BICYCLE NIGHT.

PROGRAMME.

1. BRIDE-ELECT MARCH . . . . . . Sousa
2. INTERMEZZO, "Naila" . . . . . . Delibes
3. CARMEN SELECTION . . . . . . Bizet
4. YOUR REQUEST .
5. CORONATION MARCH . . . . . . Meyerbeer
6. LUSTIGE BRÜDER (Jolly Fellows) WALTZ . Vollstedt
7. ENTRÉE TRIOMPHALE DES BOYARDS . Halvorsen
8. NOCTURNE . . . . Marshall
   (A) Last Movement of Suite, " Peer Gynt" Grieg
9. IL TROVATORE SELECTION . . . Verdi
10. GRUBENLICHTER WALTZ . . . . Zeller
11. HUNTER'S YARN POLKA . . . . Komzak
12. THE STARS AND STRIPES FOREVER . . Sousa

THE HAYWARD,
16 and 22 Hayward Place.
LADIES' AND GENTS' CAFÉ. Open until 1 a.m.

SCIARRETTA'S NEAPOLITAN TRIO give concerts daily
from 6 P.M. until 1 A.M.
Signor SALVATORE SCIARRETTI, Lyric Tenor,
is highly endorsed by Vice-President Garrett A. Hobart, Chauncey M. Depew,
Eugene Ysaye, Raoul Pugno, Jean Gerardy, and many other prominent people.
SMITH & KERRISSEY, Proprietors.

AN
HISTORIC
RESORT.

The loveliest place on the New
England coast to spend a short
vacation or the whole season is the

MYLES STANDISH HOTEL,
at SOUTH DUXBURY, MASS.

Everything that money and intelligence can do has been done to make this hotel better, if possible, than it was last season.
The greatest pains will be taken to have the table service absolutely excellent. Of the house itself and its surroundings too much cannot be said. It is a resort of nice people, who come year after year, gaining strength, vitality, and pleasure.
Send for our 1899 booklet.

L. BOYER'S SONS, Proprietors,
27 Devonshire Street, Boston, Mass.,
Or ALFRED S. AMER, Manager,
90 Wall Street, New York
(Until June 1).
Myles Standish Hotel,
South Duxbury, Mass.

"AMERICA'S FINEST PRODUCT."

Bartholomay's "APOLLO"

LAGER BEER IN BOTTLES.

Sold at these Concerts.

ALBRECHT & KOELLNER,
SOLE AGENTS,
Telephone, Boston 1751. 295-305 A Street.

Also Agents for the "Crystal Rock" Mineral Water.

PURE BEER

Harvard
BREW. CO'S $1000.⁰⁰

PURE BEER

Sold at these Concerts,
IN BOTTLES ONLY
20¢ PER BOTTLE.

TABLE LINEN USED AT THESE CONCERTS IS LAUNDERED BY THE L. K. HUSTED LAUNDERING COMPANY, 27 and 29 BROADWAY, CHELSEA, MASS.

Inglenook Vineyard.

The only California Wines sold at these Concerts.

※ ※

THE CODMAN & HALL CO.,
Opposite the South Union Station.

Sole Agents for *New England*.

IND. COOPE & CO.'S English Ale.

THE SECOND LARGEST BREWERY IN ENGLAND.

Brewers of the finest *light quality* ale. Very highly endorsed by the medical profession. : : : : :

※ ※

THE CODMAN & HALL CO.,
Opposite South Union Station.

Sole Agents for the United States.

DRI only th
PUR
WHIS

If you want and richn flavor, try only gen and origin

OLD KENT TAYLOR

Eight years old own distillati guaranteed p Bottled and shi direct from warehouses b None genuine out our sign on both labels ware of imitat For consump indigestion, an ailments requ stimulants, O KENTUCKY T LOR fives superior.
Sold by all class drug grocers, and li dealers.

Wright & Tay
Distillers,
Fine Kentuck Whiskies,
Louisville, K

Hirshfield &
New Englan Agents,
31 Doane Stre Boston.

Instruct your waiter to bring a bottle of

Pfaff's "Monogram" Lager.

If you will do this, it will not be necessary for us to expatiate upon the good qualities of our production.
YOU CAN JUDGE FOR YOURSELF.

H. & J. PFAFF BREWING COMPANY,
Telephone 2608.   16 ARCH STREET, BOSTON.

TRY THE "COLUMBIA BRAND" VIENNA SAUSAGES. SERVED HOT OR COLD AT THESE CONCERTS.

They cannot sell you here
Canadian Club Whisky,
Ruinart Champagne,
Royal Liqueur Scotch,
Carstair's Philadelphia Rye,
Fort Hill Bourbon,
Alhambra Sherry,
All of which you will find
of excellent quality;

But you can get

Kaiser Water,

the most refreshing of all
table waters,

Chateau d'Arsac Claret,
N. Johnston & Sons' Medoc,
and
California Inglenook Clarets.

SUPPLIED BY
CODMAN & HALL COMPANY,
WINE MERCHANTS,
Opposite New South Station.

TUESDAY, MAY 30.
PATRIOTIC NIGHT.

PROGRAMME.

1. MARCH, "The Stars and Stripes Forever" . . Sousa
2. WALTZ, "Près de Toi" . . . Waldteufel
3. OVERTURE, "Jubel" . . . Weber
4. SELECTION, "Robin Hood" . . . De Koven

5. AMERICAN FANTASY . . . Herbert
6. WALTZ CAPRICE, "Honeymoon" . . . Stix
7. WHISTLING RUFUS . . . Mills
8. OVERTURE, "William Tell" . . . Rossini

9. MARCH from "The Runaway Girl" . . C. von Haar
10. OVERTURE, "Tabasco" . . . Chadwick
11. IN THE MILL (for String Orchestra) . . . Gillet
12. MARCH from "The Serenade" . . . Herbert

COAL
Best Quality
AT
Lowest Prices

METROPOLITAN COAL COMPANY,
No. 30 Congress Street.

THE WILSON,
AMERICA'S PUREST
Mineral Spring Water,

Is used in making our celebrated
Belfast Ginger Ale, Champagne Kola, Lemon Soda, Club Soda, Vichy, etc. Hotels and Families supplied. Try a sample order of these goods, and be convinced of their superiority, purity, and medicinal qualities.

All of our beverages bottled at the spring. We ship only in glass, and all bottles and demijohns are sterilized before being filled.

Wilson Spring and Hotel Co.,
Tel., 3129 Boston. | 45 ARCH STREET.

"THE RECOGNIZED FAVORITE OF ALL BEERS."

Schlitz
THE BEER THAT MADE MILWAUKEE FAMOUS.
HIGHEST AWARD FOR PURITY.
Sold at these Concerts. JOS. GAHM & CO., N.E. AGENTS, 175-127 PURCHASE ST.

THE ONLY BEER ON DRAUGHT AT THESE CONCERTS.
"the beer that's brewed"

ROCHESTER BREWING CO'S
FAMOUS BOTTLED BEER
HOME OFFICE & BREWERY ROCHESTER, N.Y.
295-305 A STREET BOSTON
NEW ENGLAND BRANCH
Free delivery in city and Suburbs
RIENZI, PREMIER, BOHEMIAN, BAVARIAN, STANDARD.

THE FALL RIVER LINE
OCCUPYING THE LONG ISLAND SOUND ROUTE BETWEEN
Boston and New York

Has the finest quintette of great steamboats that the world has ever seen. The

Priscilla, Puritan, Plymouth, Pilgrim, and Providence

Are the largest, best equipped, safest, and handsomest steamboats ever constructed. This route is one of the most attractive and naturally beautiful traversed by any transportation agency in the world. Trips of the Fall River Line are made throughout the year.

Each steamboat has its own orchestra, and the service on each member of the fleet is maintained at the highest possible standard.

Tickets via this route are on sale at all of the principal Ticket Offices in the United States.

From BOSTON. Trains, connecting with steamers at Fall River in 80 minutes, leave Park Square Station, New York, New Haven & Hartford Railroad (Old Colony System), daily at 6 p.m.

From NEW YORK. Steamers leave Pier 19, North River, foot of Warren Street, daily at 5.30 p m.

S. A. GARDINER, Superintendent, NEW YORK.
GEO. L. CONNOR, Passenger Traffic Manager, NEW HAVEN, CONN.
O. H. TAYLOR, General Passenger Agent, NEW YORK CITY.

HOTEL LANGWOOD,
Middlesex Fells Reservation.

P.O. Address, Melrose, Mass. — Wyoming Station, B. & M. R.R.

Twenty minutes by rail from Boston. Sixty trains daily. Hotel coaches meet trains each way. Four hundred feet above sea level. Beautiful rides, drives, and walks. Golf links, tennis courts, and ball grounds.

OPENS ABOUT MAY 20.

For plans and prices address:

F. W. GASKILL, Manager.

BOSTON OFFICE:
Hemenway Building, 10 Tremont Street, Room 29.

---

3 Ideal Outings

THIRD SEASON.

Personally conducted by
F. R. COMEE,
Music Hall,
Boston.

	1.	2.	3.
Boston Leave	July 3	July 16	August 19
Arrive	July 12	July 31	September 4

No. 1. Ten days. **Saratoga, Lake George**, 2,130 miles from **Buffalo** to **Duluth**, and return on the steamer "North-Land" through the **Great Lakes, Erie, Huron, St. Clair,** and **Superior**.

Nos. 2 and 3. Sixteen days. Exactly alike. 700 miles' ocean sail to **Norfolk** and **Baltimore**. Over **Alleghany Mountains** and a day in **Chicago**. Up **Lake Michigan** and three days at **Mackinac Island**. 1,546 miles on steamer "North-West" to **Duluth** and return to **Buffalo** through the **Great Lakes, Niagara Falls** to **Toronto**. Across Lake **Ontario**, through the **Thousand Islands**, and down the **St. Lawrence River** to **Montreal** and **Boston**.

SEND FOR CIRCULARS.

The ocean sail of 722 miles from Boston to Baltimore via the inside route is both restful and charming in either July or August. The day at Old Point Comfort and Fortress Monroe is an agreeable change. The ride in an observation car over the Alleghany Mountains affords scenery not surpassed in Europe. The Auditorium Hotel in Chicago and the drives in either Lincoln or South Park give a delightful impression of the city. Then follows the splendid sail the entire length of Lake Michigan on the superb steamer "Manitou," first-class and "up to date" in every detail, 350 miles in twenty-four hours, stopping at Charlevoix and Harbor View. We reach Mackinac at noon, and now for two halcyon days at the Grand Hotel, with a glorious view overlooking the lake. A fascinating shore drive of twelve miles or a nine-mile inland drive. Excellent fishing. An excellent orchestra playing morning, evening, during meals, and at the Saturday night hop. Details from Mackinac on in later issue.

Allsopp's

ENGLISH ALE.
"The Red Hand Brand."

Bottled at the brewery, Burton-on-Trent, England, under the personal supervision of the Messrs. Allsopp.

Sold at these concerts.

WEDNESDAY, MAY 31.
WAGNER NIGHT.

PROGRAMME.

1. MARCH, " Under the Double Eagle " . . F. Wagner
2. CHORUS OF THE SAILORS, from " Flying Dutchman," R. Wagner
3. WALTZ, " Vienna Bonbons " Strauss
4. OVERTURE, " Tannhäuser " R. Wagner
5. PRELUDE to Act III., " Lohengrin " . R. Wagner
6. ALBUMBLATT . . . . R. Wagner
   The audience is respectfully requested to preserve silence during the performance of this number.
7. PRELUDE to Act I., " Lohengrin " . R. Wagner
8. FIRE-CHARM R. Wagner
9. PRIZE-SONG from " The Mastersingers " . R. Wagner
   Trombone Solo, Mr. C. HAMPE.
10. OVERTURE to " Rienzi " . R. Wagner
11. WALTZ, " Morgenblatter " . Strauss
12. MARCH, " Vienna Dude " . F. Wagner

The *only* Lithia Water sold at these concerts.

Hygeia Lithia Water

Sparkling and Still.

By its use you will avoid the germs of disease which natural MINERAL WATERS are liable to contain.

For Sale at these concerts and by

S. S. PIERCE CO.

The purity and keeping quality of the Tannhaeuser Export under all changes of temperature, its uniform excellence being guaranteed, together with its nutritious properties, make it the most pleasant, delicious, and convenient beverage for home consumption.
Put up in corked bottles, and packed in casks of 10 dozen white flint pints, and 6 dozen amber quarts.
Highest Awards wherever exhibited.

FOR SALE AT THESE CONCERTS.
FAMOUS TANNHAEUSER EXPORT BEER
The finest Light Beer Extant.   Brewery Bottling.   Favorite of Connoisseurs.

Pure,   Palatable,   Perfect.
B. & E. Philadelphia Ale on Draught.
FOR SALE AT THESE CONCERTS.

The BERGNER & ENGEL BREWING CO.'S N.E. Depot,
508 and 510 Atlantic Avenue, Boston.
Telephone 3805.   SOL. BACHARACH, Manager.

M. Steinert & Sons Co.,

STEINERT HALL BUILDING,

No. 162 Boylston Street, corner Carver, Boston.

STEINWAY & SONS,

HARDMAN,   GABLER,
EMERSON,   SINGER,

PIANOS.

The Æolian, Aeriol, Orchestrelle,

and Pianola.

THE ÆOLIAN
AND
THE PIANOLA
FOR SUMMER HOMES.

At this season of the year we receive many orders for these instruments for Summer Residences, and therefore beg to call attention to our extensive assortment now on display, especially suited for this purpose.

The ÆOLIAN meets the requirements of country homes, furnishing, as it does, music suitable for every occasion. It practically takes the place of an orchestra — music for dancing — orchestral concerts, — in short, music of every style and description is always available.

The PIANOLA will appeal to many on account of the very little space it occupies. It will play any kind of a piano, and can also be used upon a rented piano without the slightest injury. For the above reasons it is bound to be very popular for small cottages.

We are glad to be able to announce that we can furnish PIANOLAS with no more than a week's delay, and, at times, the day the order is given.

Persons not familiar with these instruments are cordially invited to call at our warerooms and hear them, or a descriptive catalogue will be mailed free upon application.

M. STEINERT & SONS CO.,
Steinert Hall,   162 Boylston Street,   Boston.

ANHEUSER-BUSCH BREWING ASS'N,

ST. LOUIS, MO., U.S.A.

BREWERS OF HIGH=GRADE BEERS EXCLUSIVELY.

Black and Tan.   Faust.

Michelob.   Pale Lager.

Muenchener.   Anheuser Standard.

Served at the Music Hall Concerts.

Also at all first-class hotels, clubs, and bars, and on all Pullman and Wagner cars and ocean and lake steamers.

JACOB WIRTH,   **Wholesale Dealer,**   **Boston, Mass.**

SMOKE THE POPULAR "BARRISTER" CIGARS AT THE POPULAR CONCERTS.

SMOKE "LA CELESTINA," THE BEST ALL-HAVANA CIGAR. DANIEL FRANK & CO.

THE MUSIC HALL
PROMENADE CONCERTS

PUBLISHED BY
C. A. ELLIS,
MUSIC HALL.

BOSTON, MONDAY, MAY 29, 1899.

SUMMER SEASON.
Vol. XIV. No. 19.

YOU CAN
Have your last season's outfit dyed or cleansed and refinished so it will look like new, by our French process. Why discard soiled clothing when it can be overhauled and worn as second best? You can

RELY ON
Our methods of cleansing, and need not hesitate to trust us with articles of the most delicate textures.
We dye or cleanse and refinish PROPERLY, *all* materials of household use and clothing of all kinds.

LEWANDO'S
W. L. Crosby, General Manager.
French Cleansers, Fancy Dyers,
Fine Launderers.
PRINCIPAL OFFICES:
17 Temple Place, Boston.
479 Fifth Avenue, New York.
Established 70 years.
Largest in America.
Bundles called for and delivered.
Telephones in all offices.

Knowledge
Experience.
differs from

You may know "all about"

BETWEEN THE ACTS
Little Cigars

but have you ever tried them yourself? Do you know how desirable they really are—how good they are—how economical they are—how convenient they are—how satisfactory they are? You can know—once for all—by having the waiter bring you a 10-cent box of ten—to smoke now—to-night—while you are enjoying this concert. They are for sale here.

THE MUSIC HALL... Promenade Concerts
FOURTEENTH SEASON.

C. A. ELLIS, Manager.   F. R. COMEE, Assistant Manager.
Mr. MAX ZACH, Conductor.

MONDAY, MAY 29.
BICYCLE NIGHT.

PROGRAMME.

1. BRIDE-ELECT MARCH . . . . Sousa
2. INTERMEZZO, "Naila" . . . . Delibes
3. CARMEN SELECTION . . . . Bizet
4. YOUR REQUEST
5. CORONATION MARCH . . . . Meyerbeer
6. LUSTIGE BRÜDER (Jolly Fellows) WALTZ . . Vollstedt
7. ENTRÉE TRIOMPHALE DES BOYARDS . . . Halvorsen
8. NOCTURNE . . . . Marshall
    (*b*) Last Movement of Suite, "Peer Gynt" . Grieg
    The audience is respectfully requested to preserve silence during the performance of this number.
9. IL TROVATORE SELECTION . . . . Verdi
10. GRUBENLICHTER WALTZ . . . . Zeller
11. HUNTER'S YARN POLKA . . . . Komzak
12. THE STARS AND STRIPES FOREVER . . . Sousa

Tuesday, May 30, Patriotic Night.
Wednesday, May 31, Wagner Night.
Saturday, June 3, Conductor Zach's Farewell Appearance.
Tuesday, June 6, Technology Night.

SPECIAL NOTICE.—Owing to a long-standing engagement of Music Hall, there will be no concert on the evening of Thursday, June 1.

HERE ARE A FEW NAMES FROM OUR LIST OF COMPOSERS:

ENGLISH.— Stephen Adams, F. H. Cowen, S. Liddle, C. V. Stanford, A. C. Mackenzie, R. H. Walthew, H. R. Shelley, Goring Thomas, Frances Allitsen, Maude V. White, Edward German, Mary Carmichael, Liza Lehmann, etc.

FRENCH.— C. Chaminade, Jane Vieu, L. Denza, P. Delmet, Bemberg, Guy d'Hardelot, De Leva, F. P. Tosti, etc.

ITALIAN.— F. P. Tosti, P. Mascagni, G. Puccini, G. Verdi, Don Lorenzo Perosi, etc.

THE MOST REPRESENTATIVE PUBLISHING HOUSE IN AMERICA.

BOOSEY & CO., 9 East 17th Street, New York.

A Particularly Fine Lager for Family Use and Clubs.

Bottled in the most careful manner at our own bottling department, and sold by the N. S. Pierce Co. and all other leading grocers in New England.

Other Brands in Bottles:
"Norfolk India Pale Stock Ale."
"Norfolk Extra Golden Ale" (blue label).
"Norfolk Standard Lager."
Our "Cabinet" and "Bismarck Brau" are the most popular refreshments at these concerts.

HABICH & CO.

H. W. HABICH, | Telephones, 56 Roxbury
EDWARD RUHL. | or 1152 Boston.

ESTABROOK & EATON'S MARGUERITE PERFECTOS, 10c. EACH. CONCHAS, 10c., 5 FOR 25c., SOLD AT THE "POPS."

THE ICE-CREAM SERVED AT THESE CONCERTS IS FURNISHED BY WEBER, 25 Temple Place and 33 West Street.

MUSIC HALL PROMENADE PROGRAMME.
PUBLISHED EVERY EVENING DURING THE SUMMER SEASON.

NOTICE TO ADVERTISERS.
The advertising columns in the Programme are controlled SOLELY by F. R. Comee, Boston Music Hall Box Office, to whom all communications should be addressed.

The United States Hotel,
SARATOGA SPRINGS, N.Y.

Under a continuous management for 25 years.

Without a peer in its appointments, service, and liberal management.

The largest structure of its kind in the world.

Built entirely of brick.

The Hotel and court cover over seven acres.

For further information, rates, etc., etc., address

GAGE & PERRY,
Proprietors,
UNITED STATES HOTEL,
Saratoga Springs, N.Y.

Colonial Beer...
The Beer that's Brewed in Glass.

PURE, CLEAN, PALATABLE.

Order a Bottle.

SOUTHER BREWING CO.,
919 Parker Street,
Roxbury, Mass.

All The
IMPORTED CIGARS
Sold At These Concerts Are Supplied By The
S. S. PIERCE COMPANY.

The Peer of all Cigarettes.
Save the band-label on each box for valuable premiums.

!!! ALSO !!!

Monopol
High-grade Egyptian Cigarettes.

No. 8A Khedive,
No. 9A Nadine,
No. 70A Princess Lillian.

On sale at these concerts and all first-class dealers.

OCKENHEIMER BERG,
Near Bingen, GERMANY. On the Rhine.

PHILIP KRIM'S
OWN IMPORTATION OF
Rhine Wines.
FOR 30 YEARS AT
163 Shawmut Avenue.
OUR WINES SOLD AT THESE CONCERTS.

HERRICK, COPLEY SQUARE, Telephones 608 and 950 (Back Bay), CHOICE TABLES for Music Hall "Pops."

GREAT WESTERN CHAMPAGNE

―――― A natural, genuine champagne, of the finest quality produced in America.

Sold by Wine Merchants, Grocers, and Druggists.

TUESDAY, MAY 30.
PATRIOTIC NIGHT.
PROGRAMME.

1. MARCH, "The Stars and Stripes Forever" . Sousa
2. WALTZ, " Près de Toi " . Waldteufel
3. OVERTURE, " Jubel " . Weber
4. SELECTION, " Robin Hood " De Koven

5. AMERICAN FANTASY . Herbert
6. WALTZ CAPRICE, " Honeymoon " . Six
7. WHISTLING RUFUS Mills
8. OVERTURE, " William Tell " Rossini

9. MARCH from " The Runaway Girl " . C. von Baar
10. OVERTURE, " Tabasco " . Chadwick
11. IN THE MILL (for String Orchestra) . Gillet
12. MARCH from " The Serenade " . Herbert

THE HAYWARD,
16 and 22 Hayward Place.
LADIES' AND GENTS' CAFÉ.   Open until 1 a.m.

SCIARRETTA'S NEAPOLITAN TRIO give concerts daily from 6 P.M. until 1 A.M.
Signor **SALVATORE SCIARRETTI**, Lyric Tenor,
Is highly endorsed by Vice-President Garret A. Hobart, Chauncey M. Depew, Eugene Ysaye, Raoul Pugno, Jean Gerardy, and many other prominent people.
SMITH & KERRISSEY, Proprietors.

AN HISTORIC RESORT.

The loveliest place on the New England coast to spend a short vacation or the whole season is the

MYLES STANDISH HOTEL,
at SOUTH DUXBURY, MASS.

Everything that money and intelligence can do has been done to make this hotel better, if possible, than it was last season.
The greatest pains will be taken to have the table service absolutely excellent. Of the house itself and its surroundings too much cannot be said. It is a resort of nice people, who come year after year, gaining strength, vitality, and pleasure.
Send for our 1899 booklet.

L. BOYER'S SONS, Proprietors,
27 Devonshire Street, Boston, Mass.,

Or ALFRED S. AMER, Manager,
90 Wall Street, New York
(Until June 1).
Myles Standish Hotel,
South Duxbury, Mass.

"AMERICA'S FINEST PRODUCT."
Bartholomay's "APOLLO"
LAGER BEER IN BOTTLES.

Sold at these Concerts.

ALBRECHT & KOELLNER,
SOLE AGENTS,
Telephone, Boston 1751.   295-305 A Street.

Also Agents for the "Crystal Rock" Mineral Water.

PURE BEER

BREW. CO'S $1000.⁰⁰
PURE BEER
Sold at these Concerts,
IN BOTTLES ONLY
20¢ PER BOTTLE.

TABLE LINEN USED AT THESE CONCERTS AND LAUNDERED BY THE L. K. HUSTED LAUNDERING COMPANY, 27 and 29 BROADWAY, CHELSEA, MASS.

Inglenook Vineyard.

The only California Wines sold at these Concerts.

❧❧

THE CODMAN & HALL CO.,
Opposite the South Union Station.

Sole Agents for New England.

IND. COOPE & CO.'S English Ale.

THE SECOND LARGEST BREWERY IN ENGLAND.

Brewers of the finest *light quality* ale. Very highly endorsed by the medical profession. : : : : :

❧❧

THE CODMAN & HALL CO.,
Opposite South Union Station.

Sole Agents for the United States.

DRIN
only th
PURE
WHIS

If you want p
and richn
flavor, try
only gen
and origin

OLD KENT
TAYLOR,

Eight years old
own distillatio
guaranteed p
Bottled and shi
direct from
warehouses by
None genuine
out our sign
on both labels.
ware of imitat
For consump
indigestion, an
ailments requ
stimulants, O
KENTUCKY T
L O R has
superior.
Sold by all
class drugs
grocers, and li
dealers.

Wright & Tay
Distillers,
Fine Kentuck
Whiskies.
Louisville, K

Hirshfield &
New Englan
Agents,
31 Doane Stre
Boston.

Instruct your waiter to bring a bottle of **Pfaff's "Monogram" Lager.**

If you will do this, it will not be necessary for us to expatiate upon the good qualities of our production.
YOU CAN JUDGE FOR YOURSELF.

H. & J. PFAFF BREWING COMPANY,
Telephone 2608.   16 ARCH STREET, BOSTON.

TRY THE "COLUMBIA BRAND" VIENNA SAUSAGES. SERVED HOT OR COLD AT THESE CONCERTS.

They cannot sell you here
Canadian Club Whisky,
Ruinart Champagne,
Royal Liqueur Scotch,
Carstair's Philadelphia Rye,
Fort Hill Bourbon,
Alhambra Sherry,
All of which you will find
of excellent quality;

But you can get

Kaiser Water,

the most refreshing of all
table waters,

Chateau d'Arsac Claret,
N. Johnston & Sons' Medoc,
and
California Inglenook Clarets.

SUPPLIED BY

CODMAN & HALL COMPANY,

WINE MERCHANTS,

Opposite New South Station.

WEDNESDAY, MAY 31.

WAGNER NIGHT.

PROGRAMME.

1. MARCH, "Under the Double Eagle" . . . F. Wagner
2. CHORUS OF THE SAILORS, from "Flying Dutchman," R. Wagner
3. WALTZ, "Vienna Bonbons" . . . Strauss
4. OVERTURE, "Tannhauser" . . . R. Wagner

5. PRELUDE to Act III., "Lohengrin" . . . R. Wagner
6. ALBUMBLATT . . . R. Wagner
   The audience is respectfully requested to preserve silence during the performance of this number.
7. PRELUDE to Act I., "Lohengrin" . . . R. Wagner
8. FIRE-CHARM . . . R. Wagner

9. PRIZE-SONG from "The Mastersingers" . . . R. Wagner
   Trombone Solo, Mr. C. HAMPE.
10. OVERTURE to "Rienzi" . . . R. Wagner
11. WALTZ, "Morgenblatter" . . . Strauss
12. MARCH, "Vienna Dude" . . . F. Wagner

COAL Best Quality AT Lowest Prices

METROPOLITAN COAL COMPANY,
No. 30 Congress Street.

WILSON BELFAST GINGER ALE and **Champagne Kola** are sold at these concerts.

DRINK WILSON CHAMPAGNE KOLA.

It produces energy, activity, and force. Its medical virtues are endorsed by physicians.

The **Wilson** is acknowledged to be America's purest spring water. Bottled only in glass at the spring, North Raymond, Me.

In making our BELFAST GINGERALE we use only the purest ginger.

Beware of Imitations.

Drink the **Wilson** and you are sure of the best.

Wilson Spring and Hotel Co.,
45 Arch Street.
Telephone 3129, Boston. Boston, Mass.

THE ONLY BEER ON DRAUGHT AT THESE CONCERTS.

"the beer that's brewed"

ROCHESTER BREWING CO'S FAMOUS BOTTLED BEER

HOME OFFICE & BREWERY ROCHESTER, N.Y.
295-305 A STREET BOSTON
NEW ENGLAND BRANCH ROCHESTER BREWING CO
Free delivery in city and Suburbs

RIENSI, PREMIER, BOHEMIAN, BAVARIAN, STANDARD.

THE FALL RIVER LINE

OCCUPYING THE
LONG ISLAND SOUND ROUTE
BETWEEN

Boston and New York

Has the finest quintette of great steamboats that the world has ever seen. The

Priscilla, Puritan, Plymouth, Pilgrim, and Providence

Are the largest, best equipped, safest, and handsomest steamboats ever constructed. This route is one of the most attractive and naturally beautiful traversed by any transportation agency in the world.

Trips of the Fall River Line are made throughout the year. Each steamboat has its own orchestra, and the service on each member of the fleet is maintained at the highest possible standard.

Tickets via this route are on sale at all of the principal Ticket Offices in the United States.

From BOSTON, Trains, connecting with steamers at Fall River in 80 minutes leave Park Square Station, New York, New Haven & Hartford Railroad (Old Colony System), daily at 6 p.m.

From NEW YORK, Steamers leave Pier 19, North River, foot of Warren Street, daily at 5.30 p.m.

S. A. GARDNER, Superintendent, NEW YORK.
GEO. L. CONNOR, Passenger Traffic Manager, NEW HAVEN, CONN.
O. H. TAYLOR, General Passenger Agent, NEW YORK CITY.

HOTEL LANGWOOD

Middlesex Fells Reservation.

P.O. Address, Melrose, Mass.   Wyoming Station, B. & M. R.R.

Twenty minutes by rail from Boston. Sixty trains daily. Hotel coaches meet trains each way. Four hundred feet above sea level. Beautiful rides, drives, and walks. Golf links, tennis courts, and ball grounds.

OPENS ABOUT MAY 20.

For plans and prices address:

F. W. GASKILL, Manager.

BOSTON OFFICE:
Hemenway Building, 10 Tremont Street, Room 29.

---

3 Ideal Outings

THIRD SEASON.

Personally conducted by
F. R. COMEE,
Music Hall,
Boston.

Boston	1.	2.	3.
Leave	July 2	July 15	August 19
Arrive	July 12	July 31	September 4

No. 1. Ten days. **Saratoga, Lake George,** 2,130 miles from **Buffalo to Duluth,** and return on the steamer "**North-Land**" through the **Great Lakes, Erie, Huron, St. Clair, and Superior.**

Nos. 2 and 3. Sixteen days. Exactly alike. 700 miles' ocean sail to **Norfolk** and **Baltimore.** Over **Alleghany Mountains** and a day in **Chicago.** Up Lake **Michigan** and three days at **Mackinac Island.** 1,546 miles on steamer "**North-West**" to **Duluth** and return to **Buffalo** through the **Great Lakes, Niagara Falls** to **Toronto.** Across **Lake Ontario,** through the **Thousand Islands,** and down the **St. Lawrence River** to **Montreal** and **Boston.**

The ocean sail of 722 miles from Boston to Baltimore via the inside route is both restful and charming in either July or August. The day at Old Point Comfort and Fortress Monroe is an agreeable change. The ride in an observation car over the Alleghany Mountains affords scenery not surpassed in Europe. The Auditorium Hotel in Chicago and the drives in either Lincoln or South Park give a delightful impression of the city. Then follows the splendid sail the entire length of Lake Michigan on the superb steamer "Manitou," first-class and "up to date" in every detail, 350 miles in twenty-four hours, stopping at Charlevoix and Harbor View. We reach Mackinac at noon, and now for two halcyon days at the Grand Hotel, with a glorious view overlooking the lake. A fascinating shore drive of twelve miles or a nine-mile inland drive. Excellent fishing. An excellent orchestra playing morning, evening, during meals, and at the Saturday night hop. Details from Mackinac on in later issue.

SEND FOR CIRCULARS.

Allsopp's

ENGLISH ALE.
"The Red Hand Brand."

Bottled at the brewery, Burton-on-Trent, England, under the personal supervision of the Messrs. Allsopp.

Sold at these concerts.

FRIDAY, JUNE 2.

PROGRAMME.

1. MARCH, "Der flotte Reservist" . . . Sabathil
2. OVERTURE, "Fra Diavolo" . . . Auber
3. WALTZ, "New Vienna" . . . Strauss
4. SELECTION, "Aida" . . . Verdi

5. RHAPSODY in F . . . Liszt
6. (a) REVERIE } for String Orchestra . . . Macquarre
   (b) THE INDIAN }
   (First Time.)
   The audience is respectfully requested to preserve silence during the performance of this number.
7. WALTZ, "Snowballs" . . . Zichrer
8. MARCHE JOYEUSE . . . Chabrier

9. WALTZ, "Harlequin's Voyage" . . . Zach
10. TRÄUMEREI . . . Schumann
11. POLKA, "Tyrolean" . . . Zeller
12. MARCH, "Obersteiger" . . . Zeller

The *only* Lithia Water sold at these concerts.

Hygeia Lithia Water

Sparkling and Still.

By its use you will avoid the germs of disease which natural MINERAL WATERS are liable to contain.

For Sale at these concerts and by

S. S. PIERCE CO.

FOR SALE AT THESE CONCERTS.

FAMOUS TANNHAEUSER EXPORT BEER

The finest Light Beer Extant.   Brewery Bottling.   Favorite of Connoisseurs.

Pure,   Palatable,   Perfect.

B. & E. Philadelphia Ale on Draught.

FOR SALE AT THESE CONCERTS.

The purity and keeping quality of the Tannhaeuser Export under all changes of temperature, its uniform excellence being guaranteed, together with its nutritious properties, make it the most pleasant, delicious, and convenient beverage for home consumption.
Put up in corked bottles, and packed in casks of 10 dozen white flint pints, and 6 dozen amber quarts.

Highest Awards wherever exhibited.

The BERGNER & ENGEL BREWING CO.'S N.E. Depot,
508 and 510 Atlantic Avenue, Boston.
Telephone 3805.   SOL. BACHARACH, Manager.

M. Steinert & Sons Co.,

STEINERT HALL BUILDING,

No. 162 Boylston Street, corner Carver, Boston.

STEINWAY & SONS,

HARDMAN,   GABLER,
EMERSON,   SINGER,

PIANOS.

The Æolian, Aeriol, Orchestrelle,

and Pianola.

THE ÆOLIAN
AND
THE PIANOLA
FOR SUMMER HOMES.

At this season of the year we receive many orders for these instruments for Summer Residences, and therefore beg to call attention to our extensive assortment now on display, especially suited for this purpose.

The ÆOLIAN meets the requirements of country homes, furnishing, as it does, music suitable for every occasion. It practically takes the place of an orchestra — music for dancing — orchestral concerts, — in short, music of every style and description is always available.

The PIANOLA will appeal to many on account of the very little space it occupies. It will play any kind of a piano, and can also be used upon a rented piano without the slightest injury. For the above reasons it is bound to be very popular for small cottages.

We are glad to be able to announce that we can furnish PIANOLAS with no more than a week's delay, and, at times, the day the order is given.

Persons not familiar with these instruments are cordially invited to call at our warerooms and hear them, or a descriptive catalogue will be mailed free upon application.

M. STEINERT & SONS CO.,
Steinert Hall,   162 Boylston Street,   Boston.

ANHEUSER-BUSCH BREWING ASS'N,

ST. LOUIS, MO., U.S.A.

BREWERS OF HIGH=GRADE BEERS EXCLUSIVELY.

Black and Tan.

Michelob.

Muenchener.

Faust.

Pale Lager.

Anheuser Standard.

Served at the Music Hall Concerts.

Also at all first-class hotels, clubs, and bars, and on all Pullman and Wagner cars and ocean and lake steamers.

JACOB WIRTH,   Wholesale Dealer,   **Boston, Mass.**

THE MUSIC HALL
Promenade Concerts

PUBLISHED BY
C. A. ELLIS,
MUSIC HALL.

BOSTON, TUESDAY, MAY 30, 1899.

SUMMER SEASON.
Vol. XIV. No. 20.

YOU CAN
Have your last season's outfit dyed or cleaned and refinished so it will look like new, by our French process. Why discard soiled clothing when it can be overhauled and worn as second best? You can

RELY ON
Our methods of cleansing and need not hesitate to trust us with articles of the most delicate textures.
We dye or cleanse and refinish PROPERLY, *all* materials of household use and clothing of all kinds.

LEWANDO'S
W. L. Crosby, General Manager.
French Cleansers, Fancy Dyers,
Fine Launderers.

PRINCIPAL OFFICES:
17 Temple Place, Boston.
479 Fifth Avenue, New York.
Established 70 years.
Largest in America.
Bundles called for and delivered.
Telephones in all offices.

THE MUSIC HALL... **Promenade Concerts**
FOURTEENTH SEASON.

C. A. ELLIS, Manager.   F. R. COMEE, Assistant Manager.

Mr. MAX ZACH, Conductor.

TUESDAY, MAY 30.
PATRIOTIC NIGHT.

PROGRAMME.

1. MARCH, "The Stars and Stripes Forever" . . Sousa
2. WALTZ, "Près de Toi" . . . . . Waldteufel
3. OVERTURE, "Jubel" . . . . . Weber
4. SELECTION, "Robin Hood" . . . . De Koven
5. AMERICAN FANTASY . . . . Herbert
6. WALTZ CAPRICE, "Honeymoon" . . . Stix
7. WHISTLING RUFUS . . . . Mills
8. OVERTURE, "William Tell" . . . Rossini
9. MARCH from "The Runaway Girl" . . C. von Baar
10. OVERTURE, "Tabasco" . . . . Chadwick
11. IN THE MILL (for String Orchestra) . . . Gillet
12. MARCH from "The Serenade" . . . Herbert

Wednesday, May 31, Wagner Night.
Saturday, June 3, Conductor Zach's Farewell Appearance.
Tuesday, June 6, Technology Night.

SPECIAL NOTICE.—Owing to a long-standing engagement of Music Hall, there will be no concert on the evening of Thursday, June 1.

ALBUMS OF SONGS,
Containing many popular compositions not published in single form.

IRISH FOLK SONGS, by Charles Wood, . . $2.00
RUSSIAN SONGS, by F. Wishaw (2 vols.), . . 1.00
NINE SONGS, by S. Liddle, ... 1.00
NINE SONGS, by Liza Lehmann, . . . 1.00
FIVE SONGS, by Francis Korbay, ... 2.00

Beautifully illustrated by J. S. SARGENT, R.A.

BOOSEY & CO.,
9 East 17th Street,   New York.

If you are open
to conviction,
to-night

try one 10-cent box of

BETWEEN THE ACTS
Little Cigars

to smoke now—or at any time when you want a short smoke and haven't time for a long one. They are real cigars, but small ones.

They cost so little that you can use them every day as well as not and actually save on your daily cigar expense by substituting them for larger cigars.

FOR SALE HERE.

DRINK
VAN NOSTRAND'S
BOSTON CLUB LAGER
SOLD AT THESE CONCERTS

NORFOLK CABINET
LAGER BEER

A Particularly Fine Lager for Family Use and Clubs.

Bottled in the most careful manner at our own bottling departments, and sold by the S. S. Pierce Co. and all other leading grocers in New England.

Other Brands in Bottles:
"Norfolk India Pale Stock Ale."
"Norfolk Extra Golden Ale" (blue label).
"Norfolk Standard Lager."
Our "Cabinet" and "Bismarck Brau" are the most popular refreshments at these concerts.

HABICH & CO.
H. W. HABICH, | Telephone, 56 Roxbury
EDWARD BUHL. | or 1182 Boston.

ESTABROOK & EATON'S MARGUERITE PERFECTOS, 10c. EACH. CONCHAS, 10c., 3 FOR 25c. **SOLD AT THE "POPS."**

THE ICE-CREAM SERVED AT THESE CONCERTS IS FURNISHED BY **WEBER,** 25 Temple Place and 33 West Street.

MUSIC HALL PROMENADE PROGRAMME.

PUBLISHED EVERY EVENING DURING THE SUMMER SEASON.

NOTICE TO ADVERTISERS.

The advertising columns in the Programme are controlled SOLELY by F. R. Comee, Boston Music Hall Box Office, to whom all communications should be addressed.

The United States Hotel,

SARATOGA SPRINGS, N.Y.

Under a continuous management for 25 years.

Without a peer in its appointments, service, and liberal management.

The largest structure of its kind in the world.

Built entirely of brick.

The Hotel and court cover over seven acres.

For further information, rates, etc., etc., address

GAGE & PERRY,
Proprietors,
UNITED STATES HOTEL,
Saratoga Springs, N.Y.

COLONIAL BEER

The Beer that's Brewed in Glass.

Colonial Beer...

PURE, CLEAN, PALATABLE.

Order a Bottle.

SOUTHER BREWING CO.,
919 Parker Street,
Roxbury, Mass.

VEUVE CHAFFARD

PURE OLIVE OIL.

IN HONEST BOTTLES.

The Peer of all Cigarettes.

Save the band-label on each box for valuable premiums.

::: ALSO :::

Monopol.

High-grade Egyptian Cigarettes.

No. 8A Khedive,
No. 66A Nadine,
No. 9A Egyptian Belles,
No. 75A Princess Lillian

On sale at these concerts and all first-class dealers.

OCKENHEIMER BERG, Near Bingen, GERMANY. On the Rhine.

PHILIP KRIM'S
OWN
IMPORTATION
OF
Rhine Wines,
FOR 30 YEARS
AT
163 Shawmut Avenue,
OUR WINES
SOLD AT
THESE
CONCERTS.

HERRICK, COPLEY SQUARE, Telephones 608 and 950 (Back Bay), CHOICE TABLES for Music Hall "Pops."

D. LEIDEN'S SPARKLING MOSELLE,

The only Sparkling Wine sold at these Concerts.

SHINNECOCK

The Perfection of Scotch Whisky

Sold by
S. S. PIERCE COMPANY.

WEDNESDAY, MAY 31.
WAGNER NIGHT.

PROGRAMME.

1. MARCH, "Un'et the Double Eagle" . . . . F. Wagner
2. CHORUS OF THE SAILORS, from "Flying Dutchman," R. Wagner
3. WALTZ, "Vienna Bonbons" . . . . . Strauss
4. OVERTURE, "Tannhäuser" . . . . R. Wagner
5. PRELUDE to Act III., "Lohengrin". . . . R. Wagner
6. ALBUMBLATT . . . . R. Wagner
   The audience is respectfully requested to preserve silence during the performance of this number.
7. PRELUDE to Act I, "Lohengrin" . . . R. Wagner
8. FIRE-CHARM . . . . R. Wagner
9. PRIZE-SONG from "The Mastersingers" . . R. Wagner
    Trombone Solo, Mr. C. HAMPE.
10. OVERTURE to "Rienzi" . . . . . R. Wagner
11. WALTZ, "Morgenblätter" . . . . . Strauss
12. MARCH, "Vienna Dude" . . . . . F. Wagner

THE HAYWARD,
16 and 22 Hayward Place.
LADIES' AND GENTS' CAFÉ. Open until 1 a.m.

SCIARRETTA'S NEAPOLITAN TRIO give concerts daily
from 6 P.M. until 1 A.M.

Signor SALVATORE SCIARRETTI, Lyric Tenor,
Is highly endorsed by Vice-President Garrett A. Hobart, Chauncey M. Depew,
Eugene Ysaye, Raoul Pugno, Jean Gerardy, and many other prominent people.

SMITH & KERRISSEY, Proprietors.

AN HISTORIC RESORT.

The loveliest place on the New England coast to spend a short vacation or the whole season is the

MYLES STANDISH HOTEL,
at SOUTH DUXBURY, MASS.

Everything that money and intelligence can do has been done to make this hotel better, if possible, than it was last season.

The greatest pains will be taken to have the table service absolutely excellent. Of the house itself and its surroundings too much cannot be said. It is a resort of nice people, who come year after year, gaining strength, vitality, and pleasure.
Send for our 1899 booklet.

L. BOYER'S SONS, Proprietors,
27 Devonshire Street, Boston, Mass.,

Or ALFRED S. AMER, Manager,
90 Wall Street, New York
(Until June 1).
Myles Standish Hotel,
South Duxbury, Mass.

"AMERICA'S FINEST PRODUCT."

Bartholomay's "APOLLO"
LAGER BEER IN BOTTLES.

Sold at these Concerts.

ALBRECHT & KOELLNER,
SOLE AGENTS,
Telephone, Boston 1751.   295-305 A Street.

Also Agents for the "Crystal Rock" Mineral Water.

PURE BEER
Harvard BREW. CO'S $1000.00
PURE BEER
Sold at these Concerts
IN BOTTLES ONLY
20¢ PER BOTTLE.

Inglenook Vineyard.

The only California Wines sold at these Concerts.

THE CODMAN & HALL CO.,
Opposite the South Union Station.

Sole Agents for New England.

IND. COOPE & CO.'S English Ale.

THE SECOND LARGEST BREWERY IN ENGLAND.

Brewers of the finest *light quality* ale. Very highly endorsed by the medical profession. : : : : :

THE CODMAN & HALL CO.,
Opposite South Union Station.

Sole Agents for the United States.

Instruct your waiter to bring a bottle of

Pfaff's "Monogram" Lager.

If you will do this, it will not be necessary for us to expatiate upon the good qualities of our production.
YOU CAN JUDGE FOR YOURSELF.

H. & J. PFAFF BREWING COMPANY,
Telephone 2608. 16 ARCH STREET, BOSTON.

DRINK only the PUREST WHISKY

If you want purity and richness of flavor try the only genuine and original

OLD KENTUCKY TAYLOR,

Eight years old, own distillation, guaranteed pure. Bottled and shipped direct from warehouses by us. None genuine without our signature on both labels. Beware of imitations. For consumption, indigestion, and all ailments requiring stimulants, OLD KENTUCKY TAYLOR has no superior.

Sold by all first class druggists, grocers, and liquor dealers.

Wright & Taylor
Distillers,
Fine Kentucky Whiskies,
Louisville, Ky.

Hirshfield & Co.
New England Agents,
31 Doane Street,
Boston.

TABLE LINEN USED AT THESE CONCERTS LAUNDERED BY THE L. K. HUSTED LAUNDERING COMPANY. 27 and 29 BROADWAY, CHELSEA, MASS.

IBIA BRAND" VIENNA SAUSAGES. SERVED HOT OR COLD AT THESE CONCERTS.

FRIDAY, JUNE 2.

PROGRAMME.

1. MARCH, "Der flotte Reservist" . . . . Sabathil
2. OVERTURE, " Fra Diavolo " . . . . . . Auber
3. WALTZ, " New Vienna " . . . . Strauss
4. SELECTION, " Aida " . . . . Verdi

5. RHAPSODY in F . . . . Liszt
6. (a) REVERIE } for String Orchestra . . Maquarre
   (b) THE INDIAN }
   (First Time.)
   The audience is respectfully requested to preserve silence during the performance of this number.
7. WALTZ, " Snowballs " . . . . Ziehrer
8. MARCHE JOYEUSE . . . . Chabrier

9. WALTZ, " Harlequin's Voyage" . . . . Zach
10. TRÄUMEREI . . . . Schumann
11. POLKA, " Tyrolean " . . . . Zeller
12. MARCH, " Obersteiger " . . . . . . Zeller

COAL
Best Quality AT Lowest Prices

METROPOLITAN COAL COMPANY,
No. 30 Congress Street.

WILSON BELFAST GINGER ALE
and
Champagne Kola
are sold at these concerts.

DRINK WILSON CHAMPAGNE KOLA.

It produces energy, activity, and force. Its medical virtues are endorsed by physicians.

The **Wilson** is acknowledged to be America's purest spring water.
Bottled only in glass at the spring, North Raymond, Me.

In making our **BELFAST GIN-GER ALE** we use only the purest ginger.

Beware of imitations.

Drink the **Wilson** and you are sure of the best.

Wilson Spring and Hotel Co.,
46 Arch Street.
Telephone 3129, Boston. Boston, Mass.

THE ONLY BEER ON DRAUGHT AT THESE CONCERTS.
" the beer that's brewed "

SOLD AT THESE CONCERTS

ROCHESTER BREWING CO'S
NOTED THE WORLD OVER FOR ITS PURITY

FAMOUS **BOTTLED BEER**

HOME OFFICE & BREWERY ROCHESTER, N.Y.
NEW ENGLAND BRANCH 295-305 A STREET BOSTON ROCHESTER BREWING CO.
Free delivery in city and Suburbs

AGENTS: PREMIER, BOHEMIAN, BAVARIAN, STANDARD.

Schlitz BEER MADE [MILWAUKEE] FAMOUS
[HIGHEST] AWARD FOR PURITY.
GAHM & CO., N.E. AGENTS, 125-127 PURCHASE ST.

THE FALL RIVER LINE

OCCUPYING THE
LONG ISLAND SOUND ROUTE
BETWEEN

Boston and New York

Has the finest quintette of great steamboats that the world has ever seen. The

Priscilla, Puritan, Plymouth, Pilgrim, and Providence

Are the largest, best equipped, safest, and handsomest steamboats ever constructed. This route is one of the most attractive and naturally beautiful traversed by any transportation agency in the world.

Trips of the Fall River Line are made throughout the year.

Each steamboat has its own orchestra, and the service on each member of the fleet is maintained at the highest possible standard.

Tickets via this route are on sale at all of the principal Ticket Offices in the United States.

From BOSTON. Trains connecting with steamers at Fall River in 80 minutes, leave Park Square Station, New York, New Haven & Hartford Railroad (Old Colony System), daily at 6 p.m.

From NEW YORK. Steamers leave Pier 19, North River, foot of Warren Street, daily at 5.30 p.m.

S. A. GARDNER,   GEO. L. CONNOR,   O. H. TAYLOR,
Superintendent,   Passenger Traffic Manager,   General Passenger Agent,
NEW YORK.   NEW HAVEN, CONN.   NEW YORK CITY.

HOTEL LANGWOOD,

Middlesex Fells Reservation.

P.O. Address, Melrose, Mass.   Wyoming Station, B. & M. R.R.

Twenty minutes by rail from Boston. Sixty trains daily. Hotel coaches meet trains each way. Four hundred feet above sea level. Beautiful rides, drives, and walks. Golf links, tennis courts, and ball grounds.

OPENS ABOUT MAY 20.

For plans and prices address:

F. W. GASKILL, Manager.

BOSTON OFFICE:
Hemenway Building, 10 Tremont Street, Room 29.

---

3 Ideal Outings

THIRD SEASON.

Personally conducted by
F. R. COMEE,
Music Hall,
Boston.

	1.	2.	3.
Boston	Leave July 3	July 15	August 19
	Arrive July 12	July 31	September 4

No. 1. Ten days. **Saratoga, Lake George,** 2,130 miles from **Buffalo** to **Duluth,** and return on the steamer "North-Land" through the **Great Lakes, Erie, Huron, St. Clair,** and **Superior.**

Nos. 2 and 3. Sixteen days. Exactly alike. 700 miles' ocean sail to **Norfolk** and **Baltimore.** Over **Alleghany Mountains** and a day in **Chicago.** Up Lake Michigan and three days at **Mackinac Island.** 1,546 miles on steamer "North-West" to **Duluth** and return to **Buffalo** through the **Great Lakes, Niagara Falls** to **Toronto.** Across **Lake Ontario,** through the **Thousand Islands,** and down the **St. Lawrence River** to **Montreal** and **Boston.**

The ocean sail of 722 miles from Boston to Baltimore via the inside route is both restful and charming in either July or August. The day at Old Point Comfort and Fortress Monroe is an agreeable change. The ride in an observation car over the Alleghany Mountains affords scenery not surpassed in Europe. The Auditorium Hotel in Chicago and the drives in either Lincoln or South Park give a delightful impression of the city. Then follows the splendid sail the entire length of Lake Michigan on the superb steamer "Manitou," first-class and "up to date" in every detail, 350 miles in twenty-four hours, stopping at Charlevoix and Harbor View. We reach Mackinac at noon, and now for two halcyon days at the Grand Hotel, with a glorious view overlooking the lake. A fascinating shore drive of twelve miles or a nine-mile inland drive. Excellent fishing. An excellent orchestra playing morning, evening, during meals, and at the Saturday night hop. Details from Mackinac on in later issue.

SEND FOR CIRCULARS.

Allsopp's

ENGLISH ALE.

"The Red Hand Brand."

Bottled at the brewery, Burton-on-Trent, England, under the personal supervision of the Messrs. Allsopp.

Sold at these concerts.

SATURDAY, JUNE 3.

FAREWELL APPEARANCE OF CONDUCTOR ZACH.

PROGRAMME.

1. MARCH, "Princess Ninetta" . . . Strauss
2. OVERTURE, "Meistersinger" . . . Wagner
3. WALTZ, "Vienna Blood" . . . Strauss
4. HORN QUARTET
5. WALTZ, "Harlequin's Wedding" . . . Zach
   (First Time.)
6. SOLO for Violoncello . . .
   Mr. JOSEF KELLER.
7. OVERTURE, "1812" . . . Tschaikowski
8. MILITARY MARCH . . . Zach
9. MENUET . . . Bolzoni
   The audience is respectfully requested to preserve silence during the performance of this number.
10. WALTZ, "Blue Danube" . . . Strauss
11. MARCH, "Hoch Habsburg" . . . Kral

The *only* Lithia Water sold at these concerts.

Hygeia Lithia Water

Sparkling and Still.

By its use you will avoid the germs of disease which natural MINERAL WATERS are liable to contain.

For Sale at these concerts and by

S. S. PIERCE CO.

The purity and keeping quality of the Tannhaeuser Export under all changes of temperature, its uniform excellence being guaranteed, together with its nutritious properties, make it the most pleasant, delicious, and convenient beverage for home consumption.

Put up in corked bottles, and packed in casks of 10 dozen white flint pints, and 6 dozen amber quarts.

Highest Awards wherever exhibited.

FOR SALE AT THESE CONCERTS.

FAMOUS TANHAEUSER EXPORT BEER

The finest Light Beer Extant. Brewery Bottling. Favorite of Connoisseurs.

Pure,   Palatable,   Perfect.

B. & E. Philadelphia Ale on Draught.

FOR SALE AT THESE CONCERTS.

The BERGNER & ENGEL BREWING CO.'S N.E. Depot,

508 and 510 Atlantic Avenue, Boston.

Telephone 3805.   SOL. BACHARACH, Manager.

M. Steinert & Sons Co.,

STEINERT HALL BUILDING,

No. 162 Boylston Street, corner Carver, Boston.

STEINWAY & SONS,

HARDMAN, GABLER,
EMERSON, SINGER,

PIANOS.

The Æolian, Aeriol, Orchestrelle, and Pianola.

THE ÆOLIAN
AND
THE PIANOLA
FOR SUMMER HOMES.

At this season of the year we receive many orders for these instruments for Summer Residences, and therefore beg to call attention to our extensive assortment now on display, especially suited for this purpose.

The ÆOLIAN meets the requirements of country homes, furnishing, as it does, music suitable for every occasion. It practically takes the place of an orchestra — music for dancing — orchestral concerts,— in short, music of every style and description is always available.

The PIANOLA will appeal to many on account of the very little space it occupies. It will play any kind of a piano, and can also be used upon a rented piano without the slightest injury. For the above reasons it is bound to be very popular for small cottages.

We are glad to be able to announce that we can furnish PIANOLAS with no more than a week's delay, and, at times, the day the order is given.

Persons not familiar with these instruments are cordially invited to call at our warerooms and hear them, or a descriptive catalogue will be mailed free upon application.

M. STEINERT & SONS CO.,
Steinert Hall, 162 Boylston Street, Boston.

ANHEUSER-BUSCH BREWING ASS'N,

ST. LOUIS, MO., U.S.A.

BREWERS OF HIGH=GRADE BEERS EXCLUSIVELY.

Black and Tan. Faust.
Michelob. Pale Lager.
Muenchener. Anheuser Standard.

Served at the Music Hall Concerts.

Also at all first-class hotels, clubs, and bars, and on all Pullman and Wagner cars and ocean and lake steamers.

JACOB WIRTH,   Wholesale Dealer,   Boston, Mass.

THE MUSIC HALL
PROMENADE CONCERTS

SMOKE "LA CELESTINA," THE BEST ALL-HAVANA CIGAR. DANIEL FRANK & CO.

SMOKE THE POPULAR "BARRISTER" CIGARS AT THE POPULAR CONCERTS.

PUBLISHED BY
C. A. ELLIS,
MUSIC HALL.

BOSTON, WEDNESDAY, MAY 31, 1899.

SUMMER SEASON.
Vol. XIV. No. 21.

YOU CAN
Have your last season's outfit dyed or cleansed and refinished so it will look like new, by our French process. Why discard soiled clothing when it can be overhauled and worn as second best? You are

RELY ON
Our methods of cleansing, and need not hesitate to trust us with articles of the most delicate textures.
We dye or cleanse and refinish PROPERLY, all materials of household use and clothing of all kinds.

LEWANDO'S
W. L. Crosby, General Manager.
French Cleansers, Fancy Dyers, Fine Launderers.
PRINCIPAL OFFICES:
17 Temple Place, Boston.
470 Fifth Avenue, New York.
Established 70 years.
Largest in America.
Bundles called for and delivered.
Telephones in all offices.

THE MUSIC HALL Promenade Concerts
FOURTEENTH SEASON.

C. A. ELLIS, Manager.   F. R. COMEE, Assistant Manager.
Mr. MAX ZACH, Conductor.

WEDNESDAY, MAY 31.
WAGNER NIGHT.

PROGRAMME.

1. MARCH, "Under the Double Eagle" . . . . . . F. Wagner
2. CHORUS OF THE SAILORS, from "Flying Dutchman," R. Wagner
3. WALTZ, "Vienna Bonbons" . . . . Strauss
4. OVERTURE, "Tannhäuser" . . . . R. Wagner
5. PRELUDE to Act III., "Lohengrin" . . . . . R. Wagner
6. ALBUMBLATT . . . . R. Wagner
   The audience is respectfully requested to preserve silence during the performance of this number.
7. PRELUDE to Act I, "Lohengrin" . . . . . R. Wagner
8. FIRE-CHARM . . . . R. Wagner
9. PRIZE-SONG from "The Mastersingers" . . . R. Wagner
   Trombone Solo, Mr. C. HAMPE.
10. OVERTURE to "Rienzi" . . . . R. Wagner
11. WALTZ, "Morgenblätter" . . . . Strauss
12. MARCH, "Vienna Dude" . . . . F. Wagner

Saturday, June 3, Conductor Zach's Farewell Appearance.
Tuesday, June 6, Technology Night.

SPECIAL NOTICE.—Owing to a long-standing engagement of Music Hall, there will be no concert on the evening of Thursday, June 1.

THE TWO MOST POPULAR TWO-STEPS
OF THE SEASON.

THE RUNAWAY GIRL, by Van Baar, ... 60c.
THE CECIL, by Megone, ... 50c.
FOR ORCHESTRA OR PIANO SOLO.

BOOSEY & CO.,
9 EAST 17th STREET,   NEW YORK.

LAGER BEER
A Particularly Fine Lager for Family Use and Clubs.
Bottled in the most careful manner at our own bottling department, and sold by the S. S. Pierce Co. and all other leading grocers in New England.

Other Brands in Bottles:
"Norfolk India Pale Stock Ale."
"Norfolk Extra Golden Ale" (blue label).
"Norfolk Standard Lager."
Our "Cabinet" and "Bismarck Brau" are the most popular refreshments at these concerts.

HABICH & CO.

H. W. HABICH,   Telephone, 51 Roxbury
EDWARD KUHL.   or 1152 Boston.

Save half your money
do not throw it away in half-smoked cigars! You will find that 50% of your cigar money is thrown away every day if you recall how few cigars you really have time to smoke "up."

BETWEEN THE ACTS
Little Cigars
are pure—clean—all good tobacco, and are in every way a very satisfactory short smoke. While you are listening to the music to-night, try a 10-cent box. The waiter will get them for you as they are for sale here. You will enjoy them!

ESTABROOK & EATON'S MARGUERITE PERFECTOS, 10c. EACH. CONCHAS, 10c., 3 FOR 25c. **SOLD AT THE "POPS."**

THE ICE-CREAM SERVED AT THESE CONCERTS IS FURNISHED BY **WEBER,** 25 Temple Place and 33 West Street.

MUSIC HALL PROMENADE PROGRAMME.
PUBLISHED EVERY EVENING DURING THE SUMMER SEASON.

NOTICE TO ADVERTISERS.

The advertising columns in the Programme are controlled SOLELY by F. R. Comee, Boston Music Hall Box Office, to whom all communications should be addressed.

The United States Hotel,

SARATOGA SPRINGS, N.Y.

Under a continuous management for 25 years.

Without a peer in its appointments, service, and liberal management.

The largest structure of its kind in the world.

Built entirely of brick.

The Hotel and court cover over seven acres.

For further information, rates, etc., etc., address

GAGE & PERRY,
Proprietors,
UNITED STATES HOTEL,
Saratoga Springs, N.Y.

Colonial Beer...

The Beer that's Brewed in Glass.

PURE, CLEAN, PALATABLE.

Order a Bottle.

SOUTHER BREWING CO.,
919 Parker Street,
Roxbury, Mass.

All The **IMPORTED CIGARS**

Sold At These Concerts Are Supplied By The **S. S. PIERCE COMPANY.**

The Peer of all Cigarettes.

Save the band-label on each box for valuable premiums.

::: ALSO :::

Monopol

High-grade Egyptian Cigarettes.

No. 8A Khedive,
No. 9A Egyptian Belles,
No. 9A Nadine,
No. 70A Princess Lillian

On sale at these concerts and all first-class dealers.

OCKENHEIMER BERG, Near Bingen, GERMANY. On the Rhine.

PHILIP KRIM'S OWN IMPORTATION OF **Rhine Wines,** FOR 30 YEARS AT **163 Shawmut Avenue.**

OUR WINES SOLD AT THESE CONCERTS.

HERRICK, COPLEY SQUARE, Telephones 608 and 950 (Back Bay), CHOICE TABLES for Music Hall "Pops."

GREAT WESTERN
CHAMPAGNE

——————A natural, genuine champagne, of the finest quality produced in America.

Sold by Wine Merchants, Grocers, and Druggists.

FRIDAY, JUNE 2.

PROGRAMME.

1. MARCH, "Der flotte Reservist" . . . Sabathil
2. OVERTURE, "Fra Diavolo" . . . Auber
3. WALTZ, "New Vienna" . . . Strauss
4. SELECTION, "Aïda" . . . Verdi

5. BALLET MUSIC, "Queen of Sheba" . . . Goldmark
   'Cello Obligato, Mr. J. KELLER.
6. WALTZ, "Snowballs" . . . Ziehrer
7. (a) REVERIE } for String Orchestra . Maquarre
   (b) THE INDIAN } (First Time.)
   The audience is respectfully requested to preserve silence during the performance of this number.
8. RHAPSODY in F . . . Liszt

9. WALTZ, "Harlequin's Voyage" . . . Zach
10. TRÄUMEREI . . . Schumann
11. POLKA, "Tyrolean" . . . Zeller
12. MARCH, "Obersteiger" . . . Zeller

THE HAYWARD,
16 and 22 Hayward Place.
LADIES' AND GENTS' CAFÉ.   Open until 1 a.m.

SCIARRETTA'S NEAPOLITAN TRIO give concerts daily from 6 P.M. until 1 A.M.
Signor SALVATORE SCIARRETTI, Lyric Tenor,
Is highly endorsed by Vice-President Garrett A. Hobart, Chauncey M. Depew, Eugene Ysaye, Raoul Pugno, Jean Gerardy, and many other prominent people.
SMITH & KERRISSEY, Proprietors.

AN HISTORIC RESORT.

The loveliest place on the New England coast to spend a short vacation or the whole season is the

MYLES STANDISH HOTEL,
at SOUTH DUXBURY, MASS.

Everything that money and intelligence can do has been done to make this hotel better, if possible, than it was last season.
The greatest pains will be taken to have the table service absolutely excellent. Of the house itself and its surroundings too much cannot be said. It is a resort of nice people, who come year after year, gaining strength, vitality, and pleasure.
Send for our 1899 booklet.

L. BOYER'S SONS, Proprietors,
27 Devonshire Street, Boston, Mass.,
Or ALFRED S. AMER, Manager,
90 Wall Street, New York
(Until June 1).
Myles Standish Hotel,
South Duxbury, Mass.

."AMERICA'S FINEST PRODUCT."

Bartholomay's "APOLLO"
LAGER BEER IN BOTTLES.

Sold at these Concerts.

ALBRECHT & KOELLNER,
SOLE AGENTS,
Telephone, Boston 1751.   295-305 A Street.

Also Agents for the "Crystal Rock" Mineral Water.

PURE BEER

BREW. CO'S $1000.⁰⁰

PURE BEER
Sold at these Concerts,
IN BOTTLES ONLY
20¢ PER BOTTLE.

TABLE LINEN USED AT THESE CONCERTS LAUNDERED BY THE L. K. HUSTED LAUNDERING COMPANY, 27 and 29 BROADWAY, CHELSEA, MASS.

Inglenook Vineyard.

The only California Wines sold at these Concerts.

❧❧

THE CODMAN & HALL CO.,
Opposite the South Union Station.

Sole Agents for New England.

IND. COOPE & CO.'S English Ale.

THE SECOND LARGEST BREWERY IN ENGLAND.

Brewers of the finest *light quality* ale. Very highly endorsed by the medical profession. : : : : :

❧❧

THE CODMAN & HALL CO.,
Opposite South Union Station.

Sole Agents for the United States.

DRIN only th

PURE

WHIS

If you want p and richne flavor, try only genu and origin

OLD KENTU TAYLOR,

Eight years old own distillatio guaranteed p Bottled and shi direct from warehouses by None genuine out our sign on both labels ware of imitati For consump indigestion, an ailments requi stimulants, O KENTUCKY T L O R has superior.

Sold by all f class drugg grocers, and h dealers.

Wright & Tay Distillers, Fine Kentuc Whiskies, Louisville, Ky

Hirshfield & New Englan Agents, 31 Doane Stree Boston.

Instruct your waiter to bring a bottle of

Pfaff's "Monogram" Lager.

If you will do this, it will not be necessary for us to expatiate upon the good qualities of our production.
YOU CAN JUDGE FOR YOURSELF.

H. & J. PFAFF BREWING COMPANY,
Telephone 2608.   16 ARCH STREET, BOSTON.

TRY THE "COLUMBIA BRAND" VIENNA SAUSAGES. SERVED HOT OR COLD AT THESE CONCERTS.

SATURDAY, JUNE 3.

FAREWELL APPEARANCE OF CONDUCTOR ZACH.

PROGRAMME.

1. MARCH, "Princess Ninetta" . . . . . Strauss
2. OVERTURE, "Meistersinger" . . . . . Wagner
3. WALTZ, "Vienna Blood" . . . . . Strauss
4. HORN QUARTET
5. WALTZ, "Harlequin's Wedding" . . . Zach
   (First Time.)
6. SOLO for Violoncello
   Mr. JOSEF KELLER
7. OVERTURE, "1812" . . . . . Tschaikowski
8. MILITARY MARCH . . . . . Zach
9. MENUET . . . . . Bolzoni
   The audience is respectfully requested to preserve silence during the performance of this number.
10. WALTZ, "Blue Danube" . . . . . Strauss
11. MARCH, "Hoch Habsburg" . . . . . Kral

They cannot sell you here
Canadian Club Whisky,
Ruinart Champagne,
Royal Liqueur Scotch,
Carstair's Philadelphia Rye,
Fort Hill Bourbon,
Alhambra Sherry,
All of which you will find of excellent quality;

But you can get

Kaiser Water,

the most refreshing of all table waters,

Chateau d'Arsac Claret,
N. Johnston & Sons' Medoc,
and
California Inglenook Clarets.

SUPPLIED BY

CODMAN & HALL COMPANY,

WINE MERCHANTS,

Opposite New South Station.

WILSON BELFAST GINGER ALE

and Champagne Kola are sold at these concerts.

DRINK WILSON CHAMPAGNE KOLA.

It produces energy, activity, and force. Its medical virtues are endorsed by physicians.

The **Wilson** is acknowledged to be America's purest spring water. Bottled only in glass at the spring. North Raymond, Me.

In making our BELFAST GINGERALE we use only the purest ginger.

Beware of imitations.

Drink the **Wilson** and you are sure of the best.

Wilson Spring and Hotel Co.,
45 Arch Street.
Telephone 3129, Boston. Boston, Mass.

COAL — Best Quality AT Lowest Prices

METROPOLITAN COAL COMPANY, No. 30 Congress Street.

THE FALL RIVER LINE

OCCUPYING THE
LONG ISLAND SOUND ROUTE
BETWEEN

Boston and New York

Has the finest quintette of great steamboats that the world has ever seen. The

Priscilla, Puritan, Plymouth, Pilgrim, and Providence

Are the largest, best equipped, safest, and handsomest steamboats ever constructed. This route is one of the most attractive and naturally beautiful traversed by any transportation agency in the world.

Trips of the Fall River Line are made throughout the year.

Each steamboat has its own orchestra, and the service on each member of the fleet is maintained at the highest possible standard.

Tickets via this route are on sale at all of the principal Ticket Offices in the United States.

From BOSTON. Trains, connecting with steamers at Fall River in 80 minutes, leave Park Square Station, New York, New Haven & Hartford Railroad (Old Colony System), daily at 6 p.m.

From NEW YORK. Steamers leave Pier 19, North River, foot of Warren Street, daily at 5.30 p m.

S. A. GARDNER,   GEO. L. CONNOR,   O. H. TAYLOR,
Superintendent,   Passenger Traffic Manager,   General Passenger Agent,
NEW YORK.   NEW HAVEN, CONN.   NEW YORK CITY.

HOTEL LANGWOOD,

Middlesex Fells Reservation.

P.O. Address, Melrose, Mass.   Wyoming Station, B. & M. R.R.

Twenty minutes by rail from Boston. Sixty trains daily. Hotel coaches meet trains each way. Four hundred feet above sea level. Beautiful rides, drives, and walks. Golf links, tennis courts, and ball grounds.

OPENS ABOUT MAY 20.

For plans and prices address :

F. W. GASKILL, Manager.

BOSTON OFFICE:
Hemenway Building, 10 Tremont Street, Room 29.

S.S. "Howard." Boston to Norfolk, 522 miles. Norfolk to Baltimore, 200 miles.

	1.	2.	3.
Boston	Leave July 2	July 15	August 19
	Arrive July 12	July 25	September 4

S.S. "Toronto." Toronto to Montreal, through the "Thousand Islands" and the "Rapids," 376 miles.

Third Season.

3 Ideal Outings

Personally conducted by
F. R. COMEE, Music Hall, Boston.

No. 1. Ten days. Saratoga, Lake George. 2,150 miles from Buffalo to Duluth, and return on the steamer "North-Land" through the Great Lakes, Erie, Huron, St. Clair, and Superior.

Nos. 2 and 3. Sixteen days. Exactly alike. 700 miles' ocean sail to Norfolk and Baltimore. Over Alleghany Mountains and a day in Chicago. Up Lake Michigan and three days at Mackinac Island. 1,546 miles on steamer "North-West" to Duluth and return to Buffalo through the Great Lakes. Niagara Falls to Toronto. Across Lake Ontario, through the Thousand Islands, and down the St. Lawrence River to Montreal and Boston.

SEND FOR CIRCULARS.

S.S. "Manitou." Chicago to Mackinac Island, across Lake Michigan, 350 miles.

"North-West." Mackinac Island to Duluth and return to Buffalo, 1,555 miles.

Allsopp's

ENGLISH ALE.

"The Red Hand Brand."

Bottled at the brewery, Burton-on-Trent, England, under the personal supervision of the Messrs. Allsopp.

Sold at these concerts.

MONDAY, JUNE 5.

FIRST APPEARANCE OF CONDUCTOR
GUSTAV STRUBE.

PROGRAMME.

1. MARCH, "U. S. Volunteers" . . . Strube
(First Time.)
2. OVERTURE, "Merry Wives of Windsor" . . Nicolai
3. WALTZ, "In's Centrum" . . Strauss
4. WAR MARCH from "Rienzi" . . . Wagner
(First Time.)

---

5. OVERTURE, "Oberon" . . . Weber
6. PROCESSION OF THE WOMEN, from "Lohengrin" . Wagner
7. MAZOURKA . . . . . Chopin
(First Time.)
8. SELECTION, "Trovatore" . . . Verdi

---

9. GROSSMUTTERCHEN . . . . . Langer
Solo Violin, Mr. ONDRICEK.
The audience is respectfully requested to preserve silence during the performance of this number.
10. OVERTURE, "Light Cavalry" . . Suppé
11. WALTZ, "Morgenblätter" . . . Strauss
12. MARCH, "Up the Street" . . . Morse

The *only* Lithia Water sold at these concerts.

Hygeia Lithia Water

Sparkling and Still.

By its use you will avoid the germs of disease which natural MINERAL WATERS are liable to contain.

For Sale at these concerts and by

S. S. PIERCE CO.

The purity and keeping quality of the Tannhaeuser Export under all changes of temperature, its uniform excellence being guaranteed, together with its nutritious properties, make it the most pleasant, delicious, and convenient beverage for home consumption.
Put up in corked bottles, and packed in casks of 10 dozen white flint pints, and 6 dozen amber quarts.

Highest Awards wherever exhibited.

FOR SALE AT THESE CONCERTS.

FAMOUS TANNHAEUSER EXPORT BEER

The finest Light Beer Extant.   Brewery Bottling.   Favorite of Connoisseurs.

Pure,   Palatable,   Perfect.

B. & E. Philadelphia Ale on Draught.

FOR SALE AT THESE CONCERTS.

The BERGNER & ENGEL BREWING CO.'S N.E. Depot,

508 and 510 Atlantic Avenue, Boston.

Telephone 3805.   **SOL. BACHARACH, Manager.**

M. Steinert & Sons Co.,

STEINERT HALL BUILDING,

No. 162 Boylston Street, corner Carver, Boston.

STEINWAY & SONS,

HARDMAN,   GABLER,
EMERSON,   SINGER,

PIANOS.

The Æolian, Aeriol, Orchestrelle, and Pianola.

THE ÆOLIAN
AND
THE PIANOLA
FOR SUMMER HOMES.

At this season of the year we receive many orders for these instruments for Summer Residences, and therefore beg to call attention to our extensive assortment now on display, especially suited for this purpose.

The ÆOLIAN meets the requirements of country homes, furnishing, as it does, music suitable for every occasion. It practically takes the place of an orchestra — music for dancing — orchestral concerts, — in short, music of every style and description is always available.

The PIANOLA will appeal to many on account of the very little space it occupies. It will play any kind of a piano, and can also be used upon a rented piano without the slightest injury. For the above reasons it is bound to be very popular for small cottages.

We are glad to be able to announce that we can furnish PIANOLAS with no more than a week's delay, and, at times, the day the order is given.

Persons not familiar with these instruments are cordially invited to call at our warerooms and hear them, or a descriptive catalogue will be mailed free upon application.

M. STEINERT & SONS CO.,
Steinert Hall,   162 Boylston Street,   Boston.

ANHEUSER-BUSCH BREWING ASS'N,

ST. LOUIS, MO., U.S.A.

BREWERS OF HIGH=GRADE BEERS EXCLUSIVELY.

Black and Tan.	Faust.
Michelob.	Pale Lager.
Muenchener.	Anheuser Standard.

Served at the Music Hall Concerts.

Also at all first-class hotels, clubs, and bars, and on all Pullman and Wagner cars and ocean and lake steamers.

JACOB WIRTH,   Wholesale Dealer,   Boston, Mass.

THE MUSIC HALL
PROMENADE CONCERTS

SMOKE THE POPULAR "BARRISTER" CIGARS AT THE POPULAR CONCERTS.

SMOKE "LA CELESTINA," THE BEST ALL-HAVANA CIGAR. DANIEL FRANK & CO.

PUBLISHED BY
C. A. ELLIS,
MUSIC HALL.

BOSTON, FRIDAY, JUNE 2, 1899.

SUMMER SEASON.
Vol. XIV. No. 22.

YOU CAN
Have your last season's outfit dyed or cleansed and refinished so it will look like new, by our French process. Why discard soiled clothing when it can be overhauled and worn as second best? You can

RELY ON
Our methods of cleansing, and need not hesitate to trust us with articles of the most delicate textures.
We dye or cleanse and refinish PROPERLY, *all* materials for household use and clothing of all kinds.

LEWANDO'S
W. L. Crosby, General Manager.
French Cleansers, Fancy Dyers, Fine Launderers.
PRINCIPAL OFFICES:
17 Temple Place, Boston.
479 Fifth Avenue, New York.
Established 70 years.
Largest in America.
Bundles called for and delivered.
Telephones in all offices.

In no other way
are men as wasteful and extravagant as in cigar smoking—because cigars are thrown away half smoked half the time.

BETWEEN THE ACTS
Little Cigars
are just right for all short smokes. They light right, they burn right, and taste right. Have you ever seen them? At all stores: 10 for 10 cts., or, as they are for sale here, you can try them to-night. Tell the waiter to bring you a 10-cent box of "Between the Acts." They will add to your enjoyment of this concert.

THE MUSIC HALL
Promenade Concerts
FOURTEENTH SEASON.

C. A. ELLIS, Manager. F. R. COMEE, Assistant Manager.
Mr. MAX ZACH, Conductor.

FRIDAY, JUNE 2.
PROGRAMME.

1. MARCH, "Der flotte Reservist"		Sabathil
2. OVERTURE, "Fra Diavolo"		Auber
3. WALTZ, "New Vienna"		Strauss
4. SELECTION, "Aïda"		Verdi
5. BALLET MUSIC, "Queen of Sheba"		Goldmark
'Cello Obligato, Mr. J. KELLER.		
6. WALTZ, "Snowballs"		Ziehrer
7. (a) REVERIE } for String Orchestra		Maquarre
(b) THE INDIAN } (First Time.)		

The audience is respectfully requested to preserve silence during the performance of this number.

8. RHAPSODY in F		Liszt
9. WALTZ, "Harlequin's Voyage"		Zach
10. TRÄUMEREI		Schumann
11. POLKA, "Tyrolean"		Zeller
12. MARCH, "Obersteiger"		Zeller

Saturday, June 3, Conductor Zach's Farewell Appearance.
Tuesday, June 6, Technology Night.

Now the rage of the LONDON Concerts and Drawing-rooms:

YOU AND I, by Liza Lehmann,	60c.
KING CHARLES, by M. V. White,	60c.
LIKE VIOLETS PALE, by F. Allitsen,	60c.
WHEN THE WORLD IS FAIR, by F. H. Cowen,	60c.
QUEEN OF MY LIFE, by E. T. Lloyd,	60c.

BOOSEY & CO.,
9 East 17th Street,   New York.

DRINK
VAN NOSTRAND'S
BOSTON
CLUB
LAGER
SOLD AT THESE CONCERTS

NORFOLK CABINET
LAGER BEER
A Particularly Fine Lager for Family Use and Clubs.
Bottled in the most careful manner at our own bottling department, and sold by the S. S. Pierce Co. and all other leading grocers in New England.

Other Brands in Bottles:
"Norfolk India Pale Stock Ale"
"Norfolk Extra Golden Ale" (blue label).
"Norfolk Standard Lager"
Our "Cabinet" and "Bismarck Brau" are the most popular refreshments at these concerts.

HABICH & CO.
H. W. HABICH,   Telephone, 56 Roxbury
EDWARD RUHL.   or 1182 Boston.

ESTABROOK & EATON'S MARGUERITE PERFECTOS, 10c. EACH.
CONCHAS, 10c., 3 FOR 25c., SOLD AT THE "POPS."

THE ICE-CREAM SERVED AT THESE CONCERTS IS FURNISHED BY **WEBER,** 25 Temple Place and 33 West Street.

MUSIC HALL PROMENADE PROGRAMME.

PUBLISHED EVERY EVENING DURING THE SUMMER SEASON.

NOTICE TO ADVERTISERS.

The advertising columns in the Programme are controlled SOLELY by F. R. Comee, Boston Music Hall Box Office, to whom all communications should be addressed.

The United States Hotel,

SARATOGA SPRINGS, N.Y.

Under a continuous management for 25 years.

Without a peer in its appointments, service, and liberal management.

The largest structure of its kind in the world.

Built entirely of brick.

The Hotel and court cover over seven acres.

For further information, rates, etc., etc., address

GAGE & PERRY,
Proprietors,
UNITED STATES HOTEL,
Saratoga Springs, N.Y.

Colonial Beer...

The Beer that's Brewed in Glass.

PURE, CLEAN, PALATABLE.

Order a Bottle.

SOUTHER BREWING CO.,
919 Parker Street,
Roxbury, Mass.

VEUVE CHAFFARD

PURE OLIVE OIL.

IN HONEST BOTTLES.

The Peer of all Cigarettes.

Save the band-label on each box for valuable premiums.

::: ALSO :::

Monopol

High-grade Egyptian Cigarettes.

No. 8A Khedive,
No. 9A Nadine,
No. 9A Egyptian Belles,
No. 10A Princess Lillian

On sale at these concerts and all first-class dealers.

OCKENHEIMER BERG,
Near Bingen, GERMANY, On the Rhine.

PHILIP KRIM'S
OWN IMPORTATION OF
Rhine Wines.
FOR 30 YEARS AT
163 Shawmut Avenue.
OUR WINES SOLD AT THESE CONCERTS.

HERRICK, COPLEY SQUARE, Telephones 608 and 950 (Back Bay), CHOICE TABLES for Music Hall "Pops."

D. LEIDEN'S
SPARKLING
MOSELLE,

The only Sparkling Wine sold at these Concerts.

SHINNECOCK

The Perfection of Scotch Whisky

Sold by
S. S. PIERCE COMPANY.

SATURDAY, JUNE 3.
FAREWELL APPEARANCE OF CONDUCTOR ZACH.

PROGRAMME.

1. MARCH, " Princess Ninetta " . . . Strauss
2. OVERTURE, " Meistersinger " . . . Wagner
3. WALTZ, " Vienna Blood " . . . Strauss
4. HORN QUARTET
5. WALTZ, " Harlequin's Wedding " . . . Zach
   (First Time.)
6. SOLO for Violoncello . . .
   Mr. JOSEF KELLER.
7. OVERTURE, " 1812 " . . . Tschaikowski
8. MILITARY MARCH . . . Zach
9. MENUET . . . Bolzoni
   The audience is respectfully requested to preserve silence during the performance of this number.
10. WALTZ, " Blue Danube " . . . Strauss
11. MARCH, " Hoch Habsburg " . . . Kral

THE HAYWARD,
16 and 22 Hayward Place.
LADIES' AND GENTS' CAFE. Open until 1 a.m.

SCIARRETTA'S NEAPOLITAN TRIO give concerts daily from 6 P.M. until 1 A.M.

Signor SALVATORE SCIARRETTI, Lyric Tenor, is highly endorsed by Vice-President Garrett A. Hobart, Chauncey M. Depew, Eugene Ysaye, Raoul Pugno, Jean Gerardy, and many other prominent people.

SMITH & KERRISSEY, Proprietors.

AN
HISTORIC
RESORT.

The loveliest place on the New England coast to spend a short vacation or the whole season is the

MYLES STANDISH HOTEL,
at SOUTH DUXBURY, MASS.

Everything that money and intelligence can do has been done to make this hotel better, if possible, than it was last season.
The greatest pains will be taken to have the table service absolutely excellent. Of the house itself and its surroundings too much cannot be said. It is a resort of nice people, who come year after year, gaining strength, vitality, and pleasure.
Send for our 1899 booklet.

L. BOYER'S SONS, Proprietors,
27 Devonshire Street, Boston, Mass.,

Or ALFRED S. AMER, Manager,
90 Wall Street, New York
(Until June 1).
Myles Standish Hotel,
South Duxbury, Mass.

"AMERICA'S FINEST PRODUCT."

Bartholomay's "APOLLO"
LAGER BEER IN BOTTLES.

Sold at these Concerts.

ALBRECHT & KOELLNER,
SOLE AGENTS,
Telephone, Boston 1751.   295-305 A Street.

Also Agents for the " Crystal Rock " Mineral Water.

PURE BEER
Harvard
BREW. CO'S $1000.00
PURE BEER
Sold at these Concerts,
IN BOTTLES ONLY
20¢ PER BOTTLE.

TABLE LINEN USED AT THESE CONCERTS THE L. K. HUSTED LAUNDERING COMPANY, 27 and 29 BROADWAY, CHELSEA, MASS.
LAUNDERED BY

Inglenook Vineyard.

The only California Wines sold at these Concerts.

❧ ❧

THE CODMAN & HALL CO.,
Opposite the South Union Station.

Sole Agents for New England.

IND. COOPE & CO.'S English Ale.

THE SECOND LARGEST BREWERY IN ENGLAND.

Brewers of the finest *light quality* ale. Very highly endorsed by the medical profession. : : : :

❧ ❧

THE CODMAN & HALL CO.,
Opposite South Union Station.

Sole Agents for the United States.

DRIN
only th
PURE
+
WHIS

If you want p
and richne
flavor, try
only gen
and origin

OLD KENTU
TAYLOR,

Eight years old
own distillation
guaranteed p
Bottled and shi
direct from
warehouses by
None genuine w
out our signa
on both labels.
ware of imitati
For consum
indigestion, an
ailments requi
stimulants, O
KENTUCKY T
LOR has
superior.
Sold by all f
class drugg
grocers, and li
dealers.

Wright & Tay
Distillers,
Fine Kentuck
Whiskies,
Louisville, Ky

Hirshfield &
New England
Agents,
31 Doane Stree
Boston.

Instruct your waiter to bring a bottle of

Pfaff's "Monogram" Lager.

If you will do this, it will not be necessary for us to expatiate upon the good qualities of our production.
YOU CAN JUDGE FOR YOURSELF.

H. & J. PFAFF BREWING COMPANY,
Telephone 2608.   16 ARCH STREET, BOSTON.

TRY THE "COLUMBIA BRAND" VIENNA SAUSAGES. SERVED HOT OR COLD AT THESE CONCERTS.

They cannot sell you here
Canadian Club Whisky,
Ruinart Champagne,
Royal Liqueur Scotch,
Carstair's Philadelphia Rye,
Fort Hill Bourbon,
Alhambra Sherry,
All of which you will find
of excellent quality;

But you can get

Kaiser Water,

the most refreshing of all table waters,

Chateau d' Arsac Claret,
N. Johnston & Sons' Medoc,
and
California Inglenook Clarets.

SUPPLIED BY

CODMAN & HALL COMPANY,

WINE MERCHANTS,

Opposite New South Station.

MONDAY, JUNE 5.
FIRST APPEARANCE OF CONDUCTOR
GUSTAV STRUBE.

PROGRAMME.

1. MARCH, " U. S. Volunteers " . . . Strube
   (First Time)
2. OVERTURE, " Merry Wives of Windsor " . Nicolai
3. WALTZ, " In's Centrum " . . . Strauss
4. WAR MARCH from " Rienzi " . . . Wagner
   (First Time)
5. OVERTURE, " Oberon " . . . Weber
6. PROCESSION OF THE WOMEN, from " Lohengrin " . Wagner
7. MAZOURKA . . . Chopin
   (First Time)
8. SELECTION, " Trovatore " . . . Verdi
9. GROSSMÜTTERCHEN . . . Langer
   Solo Violin, Mr. ONDRICEK.
   The audience is respectfully requested to preserve silence during the performance of this number.
10. OVERTURE, " Light Cavalry " . . . Suppé
11. WALTZ, " Morgenblätter " . . . Strauss
12. MARCH, " Up the Street " . . . Morse

COAL
Best Quality
AT
Lowest Prices

METROPOLITAN COAL COMPANY,
No. 30 Congress Street.

WILSON BELFAST GINGER ALE
and
Champagne Kola

are sold at these concerts.

DRINK
WILSON
CHAMPAGNE
KOLA.

It produces energy, activity, and force. Its medical virtues are endorsed by physicians.

The **Wilson** is acknowledged to be America's purest spring water. Bottled only in glass at the spring, North Raymond, Me.

In making our BELFAST GINGER ALE we use only the purest ginger.

Beware of imitations.

Drink the **Wilson** and you are sure of the best.

Wilson Spring
and Hotel Co.,
45 Arch Street.
Telephone 3129, Boston. Boston, Mass.

"THE RECOGNIZED FAVORITE OF ALL BEERS."

Schlitz
THE BEER THAT MADE MILWAUKEE FAMOUS.
HIGHEST AWARD FOR PURITY.
Sold at these Concerts. JOS. GAHM & CO., N.E. AGENTS, 175-127 PURCHASE ST.

THE ONLY BEER ON DRAUGHT AT THESE CONCERTS.
"the beer that's brewed"
SOLD AT THESE CONCERTS
ROCHESTER BREWING CO'S
NOTED THE WORLD OVER FOR ITS PURITY.
FAMOUS BOTTLED BEER
HOME OFFICE & BREWERY ROCHESTER, N.Y.
NEW ENGLAND BRANCH, 295-305 A STREET BOSTON
ROCHESTER BREWING CO
Free delivery in city and Suburbs
RIENZI, PREMIER, BOHEMIAN, BAVARIAN, STANDARD.

THE FALL RIVER LINE

OCCUPYING THE
LONG ISLAND SOUND ROUTE
BETWEEN

Boston and New York

Has the finest quintette of great steamboats that the world has ever seen. The

Priscilla, Puritan, Plymouth, Pilgrim, and Providence

Are the largest, best equipped, safest, and handsomest steamboats ever constructed. This route is one of the most attractive and naturally beautiful traversed by any transportation agency in the world. Trips of the Fall River Line are made throughout the year. Each steamboat has its own orchestra, and the service on each member of the fleet is maintained at the highest possible standard.

Tickets via this route are on sale at all of the principal Ticket Offices in the United States.

From BOSTON. Trains, connecting with steamers at Fall River in 80 minutes, leave Park Square Station, New York, New Haven & Hartford Railroad (Old Colony System), daily at 6 p.m.
From NEW YORK. Steamers leave Pier 19, North River, foot of Warren Street, daily at 5.30 p.m.

S. A. GARDNER, GEO. L. CONNOR, O. H. TAYLOR,
Superintendent, Passenger Traffic Manager, General Passenger Agent,
NEW YORK. NEW HAVEN, CONN. NEW YORK CITY.

HOTEL LANGWOOD,

Middlesex Fells Reservation.

P.O. Address, Melrose, Mass.   Wyoming Station, B. & M. R.R.

Twenty minutes by rail from Boston. Sixty trains daily. Hotel coaches meet trains each way. Four hundred feet above sea level. Beautiful rides, drives, and walks. Golf links, tennis courts, and ball grounds.

OPENS ABOUT MAY 20.

For plans and prices address:

F. W. GASKILL, Manager.

BOSTON OFFICE:
Hemenway Building, 10 Tremont Street, Room 29.

S.S. "Howard." Boston to Norfolk, 522 miles. Norfolk to Baltimore, 200 miles.

	1.	2.	3.
Boston	Leave July 2	July 18	August 19
	Arrive July 13	July 31	September 4

S.S. "Toronto." Toronto to Montreal, through the "Thousand Islands" and the "Rapids," 376 miles.

Third Season.

3 Ideal Outings

Personally conducted by F. R. COMEE, Music Hall, Boston.

No. 1. Ten days. Saratoga-Lake George. 2,150 miles from Buffalo to Duluth, and return on the steamer "North-Land" through the Great Lakes, Erie, Huron, St. Clair, and Superior.

Nos. 2 and 3. Sixteen days. Exactly alike. 700 miles' ocean sail to Norfolk and Baltimore. Over Alleghany Mountains and a day in Chicago. Up Lake Michigan and three days at Mackinac Island. 1,546 miles on steamer "North-West" to Duluth and return to Buffalo through the Great Lakes. Niagara Falls to Toronto. Across Lake Ontario, through the Thousand Islands, and down the St. Lawrence River to Montreal and Boston.

SEND FOR CIRCULARS.

S.S. "Manitou." Chicago to Mackinac Island, across Lake Michigan, 350 miles.

"North-West." Mackinac Island to Duluth and return to Buffalo, 1,555 miles.

Allsopp's

ENGLISH ALE.
"The Red Hand Brand."

Bottled at the brewery, Burton-on-Trent, England, under the personal supervision of the Messrs. Allsopp.

Sold at these concerts.

TUESDAY, JUNE 6.
TECHNOLOGY NIGHT.

PROGRAMME.

1. MARCH, "El Capitan" — Sousa
2. ARTIST'S LIFE, Waltz — Strauss
3. SUITE, "Peer Gynt" — Grieg
4. SELECTION, "The Fortune-teller" — Herbert

5. INVITATION TO DANCE — Weber
6. NARCISSUS — Nevin
7. SELECTION, "The Belle of New York" — Kerker
8. TWO SLAVONIC DANCES — Dvorak

9. TECHNOLOGY MINSTRELS, Selection
10. ESPANA — Waldteufel
11. COLLEGE OVERTURE — Moses
12. HUSARENRITT — Spindler

The *only* Lithia Water sold at these concerts.

Hygeia Lithia Water

Sparkling and Still.

By its use you will avoid the germs of disease which natural MINERAL WATERS are liable to contain.

For Sale at these concerts and by

S. S. PIERCE CO.

FOR SALE AT THESE CONCERTS.

FAMOUS TANNHAEUSER EXPORT BEER

The finest Light Beer Extant.   Brewery Bottling.   Favorite of Connoisseurs.

Pure,   Palatable,   Perfect.

B. & E. Philadelphia Ale on Draught.

FOR SALE AT THESE CONCERTS.

The purity and keeping quality of the Tannhaeuser Export under all changes of temperature, its uniform excellence being guaranteed, together with its nutritious properties, make it the most pleasant, delicious, and convenient beverage for home consumption.
Put up in corked bottles, and packed in casks of 10 dozen white flint pints, and 6 dozen amber quarts.

Highest Awards wherever exhibited.

The BERGNER & ENGEL BREWING CO.'S N.E. Depot,
508 and 510 Atlantic Avenue, Boston.
Telephone 3805.   SOL. BACHARACH, Manager.

M. Steinert & Sons Co.,

STEINERT HALL BUILDING,

No. 162 Boylston Street, corner Carver, Boston.

STEINWAY & SONS,

HARDMAN,　　　　　　GABLER,
EMERSON,　　　　　　　SINGER,

PIANOS.

The Æolian, Aeriol, Orchestrelle,

and Pianola.

THE ÆOLIAN
AND
THE PIANOLA
FOR SUMMER HOMES.

At this season of the year we receive many orders for these instruments for Summer Residences, and therefore beg to call attention to our extensive assortment now on display, especially suited for this purpose.

The ÆOLIAN meets the requirements of country homes, furnishing, as it does, music suitable for every occasion. It practically takes the place of an orchestra — music for dancing — orchestral concerts, — in short, music of every style and description is always available.

The PIANOLA will appeal to many on account of the very little space it occupies. It will play any kind of a piano, and can also be used upon a rented piano without the slightest injury. For the above reasons it is bound to be very popular for small cottages.

We are glad to be able to announce that we can furnish PIANOLAS with no more than a week's delay, and, at times, the day the order is given.

Persons not familiar with these instruments are cordially invited to call at our warerooms and hear them, or a descriptive catalogue will be mailed free upon application.

M. STEINERT & SONS CO.,
Steinert Hall,　162 Boylston Street,　Boston.

ANHEUSER-BUSCH BREWING ASS'N,
ST. LOUIS, MO., U.S.A.
BREWERS OF HIGH=GRADE BEERS EXCLUSIVELY.

Black and Tan.　　　　　　　　　　　　Faust.

Michelob.　　　　　　　　　　　　　　Pale Lager.

Muenchener.　　　　　　　　　　　　　Anheuser Standard.

Served at the Music Hall Concerts.

Also at all first-class hotels, clubs, and bars, and on all Pullman and Wagner cars and ocean and lake steamers.

JACOB WIRTH,　　　　Wholesale Dealer,　　　　**Boston, Mass.**

THE MUSIC HALL
PROMENADE CONCERTS

PUBLISHED BY
C. A. ELLIS,
MUSIC HALL.

BOSTON, MONDAY, JUNE 5, 1899.

SUMMER SEASON.
Vol. XIV. No. 24.

SMOKE "LA CELESTINA," THE BEST ALL-HAVANA CIGAR. DANIEL FRANK & CO.

SMOKE THE POPULAR "BARRISTER" CIGARS AT THE POPULAR CONCERTS

YOU CAN
Have your last season's outfit dyed or cleansed and refinished so it will look like new, by our French process. Why discard soiled clothing when it can be overhauled and worn as second best? You can

RELY ON
Our methods of cleansing, and need not hesitate to trust us with articles of the most delicate textures.
We dye or cleanse and refinish PROPERLY, *all* materials of household use and clothing of all kinds.

LEWANDO'S
W. L. Crosby, General Manager.
French Cleansers, Fancy Dyers,
Fine Launderers.

PRINCIPAL OFFICES:
17 Temple Place, Boston.
479 Fifth Avenue, New York.
Established 70 years.
Largest in America.
Bundles called for and delivered.
Telephones in all offices.

If you are open
to conviction,
to-night
try one 10-cent box of

BETWEEN THE ACTS
Little Cigars

to smoke now—or at any time when you want a short smoke and haven't time for a long one. They are real cigars, but small ones.
They cost so little that you can use them every day as well as not and actually save on your daily cigar expense by substituting them for larger cigars.

FOR SALE HERE.

THE
MUSIC :: **Promenade Concerts**
HALL ::
FOURTEENTH SEASON.

C. A. ELLIS, Manager.   F. R. COMEE, Assistant Manager.

Mr. MAX ZACH, Conductor.

MONDAY, JUNE 5.
FIRST APPEARANCE OF CONDUCTOR
GUSTAV STRUBE.

PROGRAMME.

1.	MARCH, "U. S. Volunteers" (First Time.)	Strube
2.	OVERTURE, "Merry Wives of Windsor"	Nicolai
3.	WALTZ, "In's Centrum"	Strauss
4.	WAR MARCH from "Rienzi" (First Time.)	Wagner
5.	OVERTURE, "Oberon"	Weber
6.	PROCESSION OF THE WOMEN, from "Lohengrin"	Wagner
7.	MAZOURKA (First Time.)	Chopin
8.	SELECTION, "Trovatore"	Verdi
9.	GROSSMÜTTERCHEN Solo Violin, Mr. ONDRICEK.	Langer

The audience is respectfully requested to preserve silence during the performance of this number.

10.	OVERTURE, "Light Cavalry"	Suppé
11.	WALTZ, "Morgenblätter"	Strauss
12.	MARCH, "Up the Street"	Morse

Tuesday, June 6, Technology Night.

To secure satisfactory service, patrons are URGED by the Management to report PROMPTLY any inattention. Complaints made so late that patrons cannot recall either the number of the table or the waiter are obviously useless.

ALBUMS OF SONGS,
Containing many popular compositions not published in single form.

IRISH FOLK SONGS, by Charles Wood,	$2.00
RUSSIAN SONGS, by F. Wishaw (2 vols.),	1.00
NINE SONGS, by S. Liddle,	1.00
NINE SONGS, by Liza Lehmann,	1.00
FIVE SONGS, by Francis Korbay,	2.00

Beautifully illustrated by J. S. SARGENT, R.A.

BOOSEY & CO.,
9 East 17th Street,   New York.

DRINK
**VAN NOSTRAND'S
BOSTON
CLUB
LAGER**
SOLD AT THESE CONCERTS.

**NORFOLK
CABINET**

LAGER BEER
A Particularly Fine Lager for Family Use and Clubs.

Bottled in the most careful manner at our own bottling department, and sold by the S. S. Pierre Co. and all other leading grocers in New England.

Other Brands in Bottles:
"Norfolk India Pale Stock Ale."
"Norfolk Extra Golden Ale" (blue labels.)
"Norfolk Standard Lager."
Our "Cabinet" and "Bismarck Brew" are the most popular refreshments at these concerts.

HABICH & CO.
H. W. HABICH,   Telephone, 56 Roxbury
EDWARD RUHL.   or 1152 Boston.

ESTABROOK & EATON'S MARGUERITE PERFECTOS, 10c. EACH. CONCHAS, 10c. 3 FOR 25c. **SOLD AT THE "POPS."**

THE ICE-CREAM SERVED AT THESE CONCERTS IS FURNISHED BY WEBER, 25 Temple Place and 33 West Street.

MUSIC HALL PROMENADE PROGRAMME.

PUBLISHED EVERY EVENING DURING THE SUMMER SEASON.

NOTICE TO ADVERTISERS.

The advertising columns in the Programme are controlled SOLELY by F. R. Comee, Boston Music Hall Box Office, to whom all communications should be addressed.

The United States Hotel,

SARATOGA SPRINGS, N.Y.

Under a continuous management for 25 years.

Without a peer in its appointments, service, and liberal management.

The largest structure of its kind in the world.

Built entirely of brick.

The Hotel and court cover over seven acres.

For further information, rates, etc., etc., address

GAGE & PERRY,
Proprietors,
UNITED STATES HOTEL,
Saratoga Springs, N.Y.

The Beer that's Brewed in Glass.

Colonial Beer...

PURE, CLEAN, PALATABLE.

Order a Bottle.

SOUTHER BREWING CO.,
919 Parker Street,
Roxbury, Mass.

VEUVE CHAFFARD

PURE OLIVE OIL.

IN HONEST BOTTLES.

The Peer of all Cigarettes.

Save the band-label on each box for valuable premiums.

::: ALSO :::

Monopol

High-grade Egyptian Cigarettes.

No. 8A Khedive,
No. 6A Nadine,
No. 9A Egyptian Belles,
No. 70A Princess Lillian

On sale at these concerts and all first-class dealers.

OCKENHEIMER BERG,
Near Bingen, GERMANY. On the Rhine.

PHILIP KRIM'S

OWN IMPORTATION OF

Rhine Wines,

FOR 30 YEARS

AT

163 Shawmut Avenue.

OUR WINES SOLD AT THESE CONCERTS.

HERRICK, COPLEY SQUARE, Telephones 608 and 950 (Back Bay), CHOICE TABLES for Music Hall ' Pops."

D. LEIDEN'S SPARKLING MOSELLE,:

The only Sparkling Wine sold at these Concerts.

SHINNECOCK

The Perfection of

Scotch Whisky

Sold by
S. S. PIERCE COMPANY.

TUESDAY, JUNE 6.
TECHNOLOGY NIGHT.

PROGRAMME.

1. MARCH, "El Capitan" . . . . Sousa
2. ARTIST'S LIFE, Waltz . . . . Strauss
3. SUITE, "Peer Gynt" . . . . Grieg
4. SELECTION, "The Fortune-teller" . . . Herbert

5. INVITATION TO DANCE . . . . Weber
6. NARCISSUS . . . . Nevin
7. SELECTION, "The Belle of New York" . Kerker
8. TWO SLAVONIC DANCES . . . . Dvorak

9. TECHNOLOGY MINSTRELS, Selection
10. ESPAÑA . . . . Waldteufel
11. COLLEGE OVERTURE . . . . Moses
12. HUSARENRITT . . . . Spindler

THE HAYWARD,
16 and 22 Hayward Place.
LADIES' AND GENTS' CAFE.   Open until 1 a.m.

SCIARRETTA'S NEAPOLITAN TRIO give concerts daily from 6 P.M. until 1 A.M.
Signor SALVATORE SCIARRETTI, Lyric Tenor, is highly endorsed by Vice-President Garrett A. Hobart, Chauncey M. Depew, Eugène Ysaÿe, Raoul Pugno, Jean Gerardy, and many other prominent people.

SMITH & KERRISSEY, Proprietors.

AN HISTORIC RESORT.

The loveliest place on the New England coast to spend a short vacation or the whole season is the

MYLES STANDISH HOTEL,
at SOUTH DUXBURY, MASS.

Everything that money and intelligence can do has been done to make this hotel better, if possible, than it was last season.
The greatest pains will be taken to have the table service absolutely excellent. Of the house itself and its surroundings too much cannot be said. It is a resort of nice people, who come year after year, gaining strength, vitality, and pleasure.
Send for our 1899 booklet.

L. BOYER'S SONS, Proprietors,
27 Devonshire Street, Boston, Mass.,
Or ALFRED S. AMER, Manager,
90 Wall Street, New York
(Until June 1).
Myles Standish Hotel,
South Duxbury, Mass.

"AMERICA'S FINEST PRODUCT."

Bartholomay's "APOLLO"

LAGER BEER IN BOTTLES.

Sold at these Concerts.

ALBRECHT & KOELLNER,
SOLE AGENTS,
Telephone, Boston 1751.   295-305 A Street.

Also Agents for the "Crystal Rock" Mineral Water.

PURE BEER

Harvard

BREW. CO'S $1000.00

PURE BEER

Sold at these Concerts
IN BOTTLES ONLY

20¢ PER BOTTLE.

Inglenook Vineyard.

The only California Wines sold at these Concerts.

THE CODMAN & HALL CO.,
Opposite the South Union Station.

Sole Agents for New England.

IND. COOPE & CO.'S English Ale.

THE SECOND LARGEST BREWERY IN ENGLAND.

Brewers of the finest *light quality* ale. Very highly endorsed by the medical profession. : : : : :

THE CODMAN & HALL CO.,
Opposite South Union Station.

Sole Agents for the United States.

DRINK only the PURE WHISKEY

If you want purity and richness of flavor, try only genuine and original

OLD KENTUCKY TAYLOR,

Eight years old, of own distillation, guaranteed pure. Bottled and shipped direct from warehouses by None genuine without our signature on both labels. Beware of imitations. For consumption, indigestion, and ailments requiring stimulants OLD KENTUCKY TAYLOR has no superior.

Sold by all first class druggists, grocers, and liquor dealers.

Wright & Taylor,
Distillers,
Fine Kentucky Whiskies,
Louisville, Ky.

Hirshfield & Co.
New England Agents,
31 Doane Street,
Boston.

Instruct your waiter to bring a bottle of **Pfaff's "Monogram" Lager.**

If you will do this, it will not be necessary for us to expatiate upon the good qualities of our production.
YOU CAN JUDGE FOR YOURSELF.

H. & J. PFAFF BREWING COMPANY,
Telephone 2608.   16 ARCH STREET, BOSTON.

TRY THE "COLUMBIA BRAND" VIENNA SAUSAGES. SERVED HOT OR COLD AT THESE CONCERTS.

They cannot sell you here
Canadian Club Whisky,
Ruinart Champagne,
Royal Liqueur Scotch,
Carstair's Philadelphia Rye,
Fort Hill Bourbon,
Alhambra Sherry,
All of which you will find
of excellent quality;

But you can get

Kaiser Water,

the most refreshing of all table waters,

Chateau d'Arsac Claret,
N. Johnston & Sons' Médoc,
and
California Inglenook Clarets.

SUPPLIED BY

CODMAN & HALL COMPANY,

WINE MERCHANTS,

Opposite New South Station.

WEDNESDAY, JUNE 7.

PROGRAMME.

1. TEUFELSMARSCH . . . . Suppé
2. OVERTURE, "Raymond" . . . . Thomas
3. WALTZ, "Legends from the Vienna Woods." Strauss
4. SELECTION, "Robin Hood." . . . De Koven
5. OVERTURE, "Zampa." . . . . . Herold
6. PRELUDE, Act V., "Manfred." . . Reinecke
   (First Time.)
   The audience is respectfully requested to preserve silence during the performance of this number.
7. TWO HUNGARIAN DANCES . . . Brahms
8. SUITE ALGERIENNE . . . . . Saint-Saëns
9. OVERTURE, "Marriage of Figaro" . . Mozart
10. SELECTION, "Cavalleria Rusticana" . Mascagni
11. POLKA, "The Mill in the Forest." . . Eilenberg
12. MARCH, "Hoch Habsburg." . . . Kral

COAL

Best Quality

AT

Lowest Prices

METROPOLITAN COAL COMPANY,

No. 30 Congress Street.

WILSON BELFAST GINGER ALE

and

Champagne Kola

are sold at these concerts.

DRINK WILSON CHAMPAGNE KOLA.

It produces energy, activity, and force. Its medical virtues are endorsed by physicians.

The **Wilson** is acknowledged to be America's purest spring water. Bottled only in glass at the spring, North Raymond, Me.

In making our BELFAST GINGERALE we use only the purest ginger.

Beware of imitations.

Drink the **Wilson** and you are sure of the best.

Wilson Spring and Hotel Co.,

45 Arch Street,

Telephone 3129, Boston. Boston, Mass.

THE FALL RIVER LINE

OCCUPYING THE
LONG ISLAND SOUND ROUTE
BETWEEN

Boston and New York

Has the finest quintette of great steamboats that the world has ever seen. The

Priscilla, Puritan, Plymouth, Pilgrim, and Providence

Are the largest, best equipped, safest, and handsomest steamboats ever constructed. This route is one of the most attractive and naturally beautiful traversed by any transportation agency in the world.

Trips of the Fall River Line are made throughout the year. Each steamboat has its own orchestra, and the service on each member of the fleet is maintained at the highest possible standard.

Tickets via this route are on sale at all of the principal Ticket Offices in the United States.

From BOSTON. Trains, connecting with steamers at Fall River in 80 minutes leave Park Square Station, New York, New Haven & Hartford Railroad (Old Colony System), daily at 6 p.m.

From NEW YORK. Steamers leave Pier 19, North River, foot of Warren Street, daily at 5.30 p.m.

S. A. GARDNER, Superintendent, NEW YORK.
GEO. L. CONNOR, Passenger Traffic Manager, NEW HAVEN, CONN.
O. H. TAYLOR, General Passenger Agent, NEW YORK CITY.

HOTEL LANGWOOD,

Middlesex Fells Reservation.

P.O. Address, Melrose, Mass.   Wyoming Station, B. & M. R.R.

Twenty minutes by rail from Boston. Sixty trains daily. Hotel coaches meet trains each way. Four hundred feet above sea level. Beautiful rides, drives, and walks. Golf links, tennis courts, and ball grounds.

OPENS ABOUT MAY 20.

For plans and prices address:

F. W. GASKILL, Manager.

BOSTON OFFICE:
Hemenway Building, 10 Tremont Street, Room 29.

Third Season.

3 Ideal Outings

Personally conducted by
F. R. COMEE, Music Hall, Boston.

S.S. "Howard." Boston to Norfolk, 522 miles. Norfolk to Baltimore, 200 miles.

	1.	2.	3.
Boston	Leave	July 2	July 15	August 19
	Arrive	July 12	July 31	September 4

S.S. "Toronto." Toronto to Montreal, through the "Thousand Islands" and the "Rapids," 376 miles.

No. 1. Ten days. Saratoga, Lake George, 2,130 miles from Buffalo to Duluth and return on the steamer "North-Land" through the Great Lakes, Erie, Huron, St. Clair, and Superior.

Nos. 2 and 3. Sixteen days. Exactly alike. 700 miles' ocean sail to Norfolk and Baltimore. Over Alleghany Mountains and a day in Chicago. Up Lake Michigan and three days at Mackinac Island. 1,546 miles on steamer "North-West" to Duluth and return to Buffalo through the Great Lakes. Niagara Falls to Toronto. Across Lake Ontario, through the Thousand Islands, and down the St. Lawrence River to Montreal and Boston.

SEND FOR CIRCULARS.

S.S. "Manitou." Chicago to Mackinac Island, across Lake Michigan, 350 miles.

"North-West." Mackinac Island to Duluth and return to Buffalo, 1,555 miles.

Allsopp's

ENGLISH ALE.
"The Red Hand Brand."

Bottled at the brewery, Burton-on-Trent, England, under the personal supervision of the Messrs. Allsopp.

Sold at these concerts.

THURSDAY, JUNE 8.

PROGRAMME.

1. MARCH, "Hobson's Choice" .... Strube
2. OVERTURE, "Semiramide" .... Rossini
3. WALTZ, "Schöner Mai" .... Strauss
4. SELECTION, "Aïda" .... Verdi
5. OVERTURE, "A Night in Granada" .... Kreutzer
   (First Time)
6. (a) EVENING SONG .... Schumann
   (b) MARCH from "The Ruins of Athens" .... Beethoven
   The audience is respectfully requested to preserve silence during the performance of this number.
7. MELODY .... Rubinstein
8. HUNGARIAN RHAPSODY No. 2 .... Liszt
9. OVERTURE, "Orpheus" .... Offenbach
10. POLKA, "Sängerlust" .... Strauss
11. WALTZ, "Grubenlichter" .... Zeller
12. MARCH, "Boccaccio" .... Suppé

The *only* Lithia Water sold at these concerts.

Hygeia Lithia Water

Sparkling and Still.

By its use you will avoid the germs of disease which natural MINERAL WATERS are liable to contain.

For Sale at these concerts and by

S. S. PIERCE CO.

The purity and keeping quality of the Tannhaeuser Export under all changes of temperature, its uniform excellence being guaranteed, together with its nutritious properties, make it the most pleasant, delicious, and convenient beverage for home consumption.
Put up in corked bottles, and packed in casks of 10 dozen white flint pints, and 6 dozen amber quarts.

Highest Awards wherever exhibited.

FOR SALE AT THESE CONCERTS.

FAMOUS TANNHAEUSER EXPORT BEER

The finest Light Beer Extant. Brewery Bottling. Favorite of Connoisseurs.

Pure,   Palatable,   Perfect.

B. & E. Philadelphia Ale on Draught.
FOR SALE AT THESE CONCERTS.

The BERGNER & ENGEL BREWING CO.'S N.E. Depot,
508 and 510 Atlantic Avenue, Boston.
Telephone 3805.   SOL. BACHARACH, Manager.

M. Steinert & Sons Co.,

STEINERT HALL BUILDING,

No. 162 Boylston Street, corner Carver, Boston.

STEINWAY & SONS,

HARDMAN,   GABLER,
EMERSON,   SINGER,

PIANOS.

The Æolian, Aeriol, Orchestrelle, and Pianola.

THE ÆOLIAN
AND
THE PIANOLA
FOR SUMMER HOMES.

At this season of the year we receive many orders for these instruments for Summer Residences, and therefore beg to call attention to our extensive assortment now on display, especially suited for this purpose.

The ÆOLIAN meets the requirements of country homes, furnishing, as it does, music suitable for every occasion. It practically takes the place of an orchestra — music for dancing — orchestral concerts, — in short, music of every style and description is always available.

The PIANOLA will appeal to many on account of the very little space it occupies. It will play any kind of a piano, and can also be used upon a rented piano without the slightest injury. For the above reasons it is bound to be very popular for small cottages.

We are glad to be able to announce that we can furnish PIANOLAS with no more than a week's delay, and, at times, the day the order is given.

Persons not familiar with these instruments are cordially invited to call at our warerooms and hear them, or a descriptive catalogue will be mailed free upon application.

M. STEINERT & SONS CO.,
Steinert Hall,   162 Boylston Street,   Boston.

ANHEUSER-BUSCH BREWING ASS'N,

ST. LOUIS, MO., U.S.A.

BREWERS OF HIGH-GRADE BEERS EXCLUSIVELY.

Black and Tan.

Michelob.

Muenchener.

Faust.

Pale Lager.

Anheuser Standard.

Served at the Music Hall Concerts.

Also at all first-class hotels, clubs, and bars, and on all Pullman and Wagner cars and ocean and lake steamers.

JACOB WIRTH,   **Wholesale Dealer,**   **Boston, Mass.**

THE MUSIC HALL
PROMENADE CONCERTS

SMOKE "LA CELESTINA," THE BEST ALL-HAVANA CIGAR. DANIEL FRANK & CO.

SMOKE THE POPULAR "BARRISTER" CIGARS AT THE POPULAR CONCERTS

PUBLISHED BY
C. A. ELLIS,
MUSIC HALL.

BOSTON, TUESDAY, JUNE 6, 1899.

SUMMER SEASON.
Vol. XIV. No. 25.

YOU CAN

Have your last season's outfit dyed or cleansed and refinished so it will look like new, by our French process. Why discard soiled clothing when it can be overhauled and worn as second best? You can

RELY ON

Our methods of cleansing, and need not hesitate to trust us with articles of the most delicate textures.

We dye or cleanse and refinish PROPERLY, all materials of household use and clothing of all kinds.

LEWANDO'S

W. L. Crosby, General Manager.
French Cleansers, Fancy Dyers, Fine Launderers.

PRINCIPAL OFFICES:
17 Temple Place, Boston.
407 Fifth Avenue, New York
Established 70 years.
Largest in America.
Bundles called for and delivered
Telephones in all offices.

THE
MUSIC
HALL

Promenade Concerts

FOURTEENTH SEASON.

C. A. ELLIS, Manager. F. R. COMEE, Assistant Manager.

Mr. GUSTAV STRUBE, Conductor.

TUESDAY, JUNE 6.

TECHNOLOGY NIGHT.

PROGRAMME.

1. MARCH, "El Capitan" . . . . Sousa
2. ARTIST'S LIFE, Waltz . . . . Strauss
3. SUITE, " Peer Gynt " . . . . Grieg
4. SELECTION, "The Fortune-teller" . . Herbert
5. INVITATION TO DANCE . . . . Weber
6. NARCISSUS . . . . Nevin
7. SELECTION, "The Belle of New York" . Kerker
8. TWO SLAVONIC DANCES . . . . . . Dvorak
9. TANNHAUSER OVERTURE . . . . . . Wagner
10. ESPANA . . . . Waldteufel
11. COLLEGE OVERTURE . . . . Moses
12. HUSARENRITT . . . . Spindler

Friday, June 9, Light Opera Night.
Monday, June 12, Wagner Night.

To secure satisfactory service, patrons are URGED by the Management to report PROMPTLY any inattention. Complaints made so late that patrons cannot recall either the number of the table or the waiter are obviously useless.

THE TWO
MOST POPULAR TWO-STEPS
OF THE SEASON.

THE RUNAWAY GIRL, by Van Baar, ... 60c.
THE CECIL, by Megone, ... 50c.

FOR ORCHESTRA OR PIANO SOLO.

BOOSEY & CO.,
9 EAST 17th STREET,   NEW YORK.

A Particularly Fine Lager for Family Use and Clubs.

Bottled in the most careful manner at our own bottling department, and sold by the S. S. Pierce Co. and all other leading grocers in New England.

Other Brands in Bottles:
"Norfolk India Pale Stock Ale"
"Norfolk Extra Golden Ale" (blue label),
"Norfolk Standard Lager"

Our "Cabinet" and "Bismarck Braeu" are the most popular refreshments at these concerts.

HABICH & CO.

H. W. HABICH, Telephone, 56 Roxbury
EDWARD BUHL. or 1152 Boston.

Save half
your money

do not throw it away in half-smoked cigars! You will find that 50% of your cigar money is thrown away every day if you recall how few cigars you really have time to smoke "up."

BETWEEN
THE ACTS
Little Cigars

are pure—clean—all good tobacco, and are in every way a very satisfactory short smoke. While you are listening to the music to-night, try a 10-cent box. The waiter will get them for you as they are for sale here. You will enjoy them!

ESTABROOK & EATON'S MARGUERITE PERFECTOS, 10c. EACH, CONCHAS, 10c., 3 FOR 25c., SOLD AT THE "POPS."

THE ICE-CREAM SERVED AT THESE CONCERTS IS FURNISHED BY **WEBER**, 25 Temple Place and 33 West Street.

MUSIC HALL PROMENADE PROGRAMME.

PUBLISHED EVERY EVENING DURING THE SUMMER SEASON.

NOTICE TO ADVERTISERS.

The advertising columns in the Programme are controlled SOLELY by F. R. Comee, Boston Music Hall Box Office, to whom all communications should be addressed.

The United States Hotel,

SARATOGA SPRINGS, N.Y.

Under a continuous management for 25 years.

Without a peer in its appointments, service, and liberal management.

The largest structure of its kind in the world.

Built entirely of brick.

The Hotel and court cover over seven acres.

For further information, rates, etc., address

GAGE & PERRY,
Proprietors,
UNITED STATES HOTEL,
Saratoga Springs, N.Y.

Colonial Beer...

The Beer that's Brewed in Glass.

PURE, CLEAN, PALATABLE.

Order a Bottle.

SOUTHER BREWING CO.,
919 Parker Street,
Roxbury, Mass.

All The IMPORTED CIGARS

Sold At These Concerts Are Supplied By The

S. S. PIERCE COMPANY.

The Peer of all Cigarettes.

Save the band-label on each box for valuable premiums.

ALSO

Monopol

High-grade Egyptian Cigarettes

No. 55 Khedive.
No. 105 Nadine.
No. 95 Egyptian Belles
No. 704 Princess Lillian

On sale at these concerts and all first-class dealers.

OCKENHEIMER BERG, Near Bingen. **GERMANY.** On the Rhine.

PHILIP KRIM'S OWN IMPORTATION OF **Rhine Wines,** FOR 30 YEARS AT **163 Shawmut Avenue.**

OUR WINES SOLD AT THESE CONCERTS.

HERRICK, COPLEY SQUARE, Telephones 608 and 950 (Back Bay), CHOICE TABLES for Music Hall 'Pops."

GREAT WESTERN
CHAMPAGNE

———— A natural, genuine champagne, of the finest quality produced in America.

Sold by Wine Merchants, Grocers and Druggists

WEDNESDAY, JUNE 7.

PROGRAMME.

1. TEUFELSMARSCH . . . . Suppe
2. OVERTURE, "Raymond" . . . . Thomas
3. WALTZ, "Legends from the Vienna Woods" . Strauss
4. SELECTION, "Robin Hood" . . . . . . De Koven

5. OVERTURE, "Zampa" . . . . Herold
6. PRELUDE, Act V., "Manfred" . . . . . Reinecke
   (First Time)
   The audience is respectfully requested to preserve silence during the performance of this number.
7. TWO HUNGARIAN DANCES . . . . Brahms
8. SUITE ALGERIENNE . . . . Saint-Saens

9. OVERTURE, "Marriage of Figaro" . . . . Mozart
10. SELECTION, "Cavalleria Rusticana" . . . Mascagni
11. POLKA, "The Mill in the Forest" . . . . Eilenberg
12. MARCH, "Hoch Habsburg" . . . . Kral

THE HAYWARD,
16 and 22 Hayward Place.
LADIES' AND GENTS' CAFE.   Open until 1 a.m.

SCIARRETTA'S NEAPOLITAN TRIO give concerts daily from 6 P.M. until 1 A.M.
Signor SALVATORE SCIARRETTI, Lyric Tenor,
Is highly endorsed by Vice-President Garrett A. Hobart, Chauncey M. Depew, Eugene V'saye, Raoul Pugno, Juan Gerardy, and many other prominent people.

SMITH & KERRISSEY, Proprietors.

AN HISTORIC RESORT.

The loveliest place on the New England coast to spend a short vacation or the whole season is the

MYLES STANDISH HOTEL,
at SOUTH DUXBURY, MASS.

Everything that money and intelligence can do has been done to make this hotel better, if possible, than it was last season.
The greatest pains will be taken to have the table service absolutely excellent. Of the house itself and its surroundings too much cannot be said. It is a resort of nice people, who come year after year, gaining strength, vitality, and pleasure.
Send for our 1899 booklet.

L. BOYER'S SONS, Proprietors,
27 Devonshire Street, Boston, Mass.,
Or ALFRED S. AMER, Manager,
93 Wall Street, New York
(Until June 1).
Myles Standish Hotel,
South Duxbury, Mass.

"AMERICA'S FINEST PRODUCT."
Bartholomay's "APOLLO"
LAGER BEER IN BOTTLES.

Sold at these Concerts.

ALBRECHT & KOELLNER,
SOLE AGENTS,
Telephone, Boston 1751.   295-305 A Street.

Also Agents for the "Crystal Rock" Mineral Water.

PURE BEER
Harvard BREW. CO'S $1000.⁰⁰
PURE BEER
Sold at these Concerts
IN BOTTLES ONLY
20¢ PER BOTTLE.

Inglenook Vineyard.

The only California Wines sold at these Concerts.

❧❧

THE CODMAN & HALL CO.,
Opposite the South Union Station.

Sole Agents for New England.

IND. COOPE & CO.'S English Ale.

THE SECOND LARGEST BREWERY IN ENGLAND.

Brewers of the finest *light quality* ale. Very highly endorsed by the medical profession. : : : :

❧❧

THE CODMAN & HALL CO.,
Opposite South Union Station.

Sole Agents for the United States.

Instruct your waiter to bring a bottle of **Pfaff's "Monogram" Lager.**

If you will do this, it will not be necessary for us to expatiate upon the good qualities of our production.
YOU CAN JUDGE FOR YOURSELF.

H. & J. PFAFF BREWING COMPANY,
Telephone 2608.   16 ARCH STREET, BOSTON.

TRY THE "COLUMBIA BRAND" VIENNA SAUSAGES. SERVED HOT OR COLD AT THESE CONCERTS.

They cannot sell you here
Canadian Club Whisky,
Ruinart Champagne,
Royal Liqueur Scotch,
Carstair's Philadelphia Rye,
Fort Hill Bourbon,
Alhambra Sherry,
All of which you will find
of excellent quality;

But you can get

Kaiser Water,

the most refreshing of all table waters,

*Chateau d'Arsac Claret,
N. Johnston & Sons' Medoc,*
and
California Inglenook Clarets.

SUPPLIED BY

CODMAN & HALL COMPANY,

WINE MERCHANTS,

Opposite New South Station.

THURSDAY, JUNE 8.

PROGRAMME.

1. MARCH, "Hobson's Choice" . . . . . . Strube
2. OVERTURE, "Semiramide" . . . . . . Rossini
3. WALTZ, "Schöner Mai" . . . . . . Strauss
4. SELECTION, "Aïda" . . . . . . Verdi
5. OVERTURE, "A Night in Granada" . . . . . . Kreutzer
   (First Time)
6. (a) EVENING SONG . . . . . . Schumann
   (b) MARCH from "The Ruins of Athens" . . . . . . Beethoven
   The audience is respectfully requested to preserve silence during the performance of this number.
7. MELODY . . . . . . Rubinstein
8. HUNGARIAN RHAPSODY No. 2 . . . . . . Liszt
9. OVERTURE, "Orpheus" . . . . . . Offenbach
10. POLKA, "Sängerlust" . . . . . . Strauss
11. WALTZ, "Glühwürmchen" . . . . . . Zeller
12. MARCH, "Boccaccio" . . . . . . Suppé

COAL   Best Quality AT Lowest Prices

METROPOLITAN COAL COMPANY,

No. 30 Congress Street.

WILSON BELFAST GINGER ALE

and Champagne Kola are sold at these concerts.

DRINK
WILSON CHAMPAGNE KOLA.

It produces energy, activity, and force. Its medical virtues are endorsed by physicians.

The **Wilson** is acknowledged to be America's purest spring water. Bottled only in glass at the spring, North Raymond, Me.

In making our BELFAST GIN-GER ALE we use only the purest ginger.

Beware of imitations.

Drink the Wilson and you are sure of the best.

Wilson Spring and Hotel Co.,

45 Arch Street,
Telephone 3129, Boston.   Boston, Mass.

"THE RECOGNIZED FAVORITE OF ALL BEERS."

THE ONLY BEER ON DRAUGHT AT THESE CONCERTS.

"the beer that's brewed"

Sold at these Concerts.   JOS. GAHM & CO., N.E. AGENTS, 175-127 PURCHASE ST.

THE FALL RIVER LINE

OCCUPYING THE
LONG ISLAND SOUND ROUTE
BETWEEN

Boston and New York

Has the finest quintette of great steamboats that the world has ever seen. The

Priscilla, Puritan, Plymouth, Pilgrim, and Providence

Are the largest, best equipped, safest, and handsomest steamboats ever constructed. This route is one of the most attractive and naturally beautiful traversed by any transportation agency in the world. Trips of the Fall River Line are made throughout the year.

Each steamboat has its own orchestra, and the service on each member of the fleet is maintained at the highest possible standard.

Tickets via this route are on sale at all of the principal Ticket Offices in the United States.

From BOSTON. Trains, connecting with steamers at Fall River in 80 minutes, leave Park Square Station, New York, New Haven & Hartford Railroad (Old Colony System), daily at 6 p.m.

From NEW YORK. Steamers leave Pier 19, North River, foot of Warren Street, daily at 5.30 p.m.

S. A. GARDNER, Superintendent, NEW YORK.
GEO. L. CONNOR, Passenger Traffic Manager, NEW HAVEN, CONN.
O. H. TAYLOR, General Passenger Agent, NEW YORK CITY.

HOTEL LANGWOOD,

Middlesex Fells Reservation.

P.O. Address, Melrose, Mass.   Wyoming Station, P. & M. R.R.

Twenty minutes by rail from Boston. Sixty trains daily. Hotel coaches meet trains each way. Four hundred feet above sea level. Beautiful rides, drives, and walks. Golf links, tennis courts, and ball grounds.

OPENS ABOUT MAY 20.

For plans and prices address:

F. W. GASKILL, Manager.

BOSTON OFFICE:
Hemenway Building, 10 Tremont Street, Room 29.

Third Season.

3 Ideal Outings

Personally conducted by F. R. COMEE, Music Hall, Boston.

S.S. "Howard." Boston to Norfolk, 522 miles. Norfolk to Baltimore, 200 miles.

	1.	2.	3.
Boston	Leave July 2	July 13	August 19
	Arrive July 12	July 31	September 4

S.S. "Toronto." Toronto to Montreal, through the "Thousand Islands" and the "Rapids," 376 miles.

No. 1. Ten days. Saratoga, Lake George, 2,130 miles from Buffalo to Duluth, and return on the steamer "North-Land" through the Great Lakes, Erie, Huron, St. Clair, and Superior.

Nos. 2 and 3. Sixteen days. Exactly alike, 700 miles' ocean sail to Norfolk and Baltimore. Over Alleghany Mountains and a day in Chicago. Up Lake Michigan and three days at Mackinac Island. 1,186 miles on steamer "North-West" to Duluth and return to Buffalo through the Great Lakes. Niagara Falls to Toronto. Across Lake Ontario, through the Thousand Islands, and down the St. Lawrence River to Montreal and Boston.

SEND FOR CIRCULARS.

S.S. "Manitou." Chicago to Mackinac Island, across Lake Michigan, 350 miles.

"North-West." Mackinac Island to Duluth and return to Buffalo, 1,555 miles.

Allsopp's

ENGLISH ALE.
"The Red Hand Brand."

Bottled at the brewery, Burton-on-Trent, England, under the personal supervision of the Messrs. Allsopp.

Sold at these concerts.

FRIDAY, JUNE 9.
LIGHT OPERA NIGHT.

PROGRAMME.

1. MARCH, "Am I a Wiz?" — Herbert
2. SELECTION, "The Runaway Girl" — Ch. von Baar
3. WALTZ from "Die Fledermaus" — Strauss
4. OVERTURE, "Sphinx" — Thompson
5. SELECTION, "La Fille de Madame Angot" — Lecocq
6. WALTZ AND PIZZICATO from Ballet Music, "Sylvia" — Delibes
7. CAVATINA — Raff
8. OVERTURE, "Tabasco" — Chadwick
9. SELECTION, "The Belle of New York" — Kerker
10. WALTZ, "Vienna Blood" — Strauss
11. ENTRÉE TRIOMPHALE DES BOYARDS — Halvorsen
12. BOCCACCIO MARCH — Suppé

The *only* Lithia Water sold at these concerts.

Hygeia Lithia Water

Sparkling and Still.

By its use you will avoid the germs of disease which natural MINERAL WATERS are liable to contain.

For Sale at these concerts and by

S. S. PIERCE CO.

The purity and keeping quality of the Tannhaeuser Export under all changes of temperature, its uniform excellence being guaranteed, together with its nutritious properties, make it the most pleasant, delicious, and convenient beverage for home consumption.
Put up in corked bottles, and packed in casks of 10 dozen white flint pints, and 6 dozen amber quarts.

Highest Awards wherever exhibited.

FOR SALE AT THESE CONCERTS.
FAMOUS TANNHAEUSER EXPORT BEER

The finest Light Beer Extant.   Brewery Bottling.   Favorite of Connoisseurs.

Pure,   Palatable,   Perfect.

B. & E. Philadelphia Ale on Draught.
FOR SALE AT THESE CONCERTS.

The BERGNER & ENGEL BREWING CO.'S N.E. Depot,
508 and 510 Atlantic Avenue, Boston.
Telephone 3805.   SOL. BACHARACH, Manager.

M. Steinert & Sons Co.,

STEINERT HALL BUILDING,

No. 162 Boylston Street, corner Carver, Boston.

STEINWAY & SONS,

HARDMAN, GABLER,
EMERSON, SINGER,

PIANOS.

The Æolian, Aeriol, Orchestrelle, and Pianola.

THE ÆOLIAN
AND
THE PIANOLA
FOR SUMMER HOMES.

At this season of the year we receive many orders for these instruments for Summer Residences, and therefore beg to call attention to our extensive assortment now on display, especially suited for this purpose.

The ÆOLIAN meets the requirements of country homes, furnishing, as it does, music suitable for every occasion. It practically takes the place of an orchestra — music for dancing – orchestral concerts. — In short, music of every style and description is always available.

The PIANOLA will appeal to many on account of the very little space it occupies. It will play any kind of a piano, and can also be used upon a rented piano without the slightest injury. For the above reasons it is bound to be very popular for small cottages.

We are glad to be able to announce that we can furnish PIANOLAS with no more than a week's delay, and, at times, the day the order is given.

Persons not familiar with these instruments are cordially invited to call at our warerooms and hear them, or a descriptive catalogue will be mailed free upon application.

M. STEINERT & SONS CO.,
Steinert Hall, 162 Boylston Street, Boston.

ANHEUSER-BUSCH BREWING ASS'N,

ST. LOUIS, MO., U.S.A.

BREWERS OF HIGH=GRADE BEERS EXCLUSIVELY.

Black and Tan. Faust.
Michelob. Pale Lager.
Muenchener. Anheuser Standard.

Served at the Music Hall Concerts.

Also at all first-class hotels, clubs, and bars, and on all Pullman and Wagner cars and ocean and lake steamers.

JACOB WIRTH,   Wholesale Dealer,   Boston, Mass.

SMOKE THE POPULAR "BARRISTER" CIGARS AT THE POPULAR CONCERTS.

SMOKE "LA CELESTINA," THE BEST ALL-HAVANA CIGAR. DANIEL FRANK & CO.

THE MUSIC HALL — PROMENADE CONCERTS

BOSTON, WEDNESDAY, JUNE 7, 1899.

SUMMER SEASON. Vol. XIV. No. 26.

THE MUSIC HALL... Promenade Concerts
FOURTEENTH SEASON.

C. A. ELLIS, Manager.   F. R. COMEE, Assistant Manager.

Mr. GUSTAV STRUBE, Conductor.

WEDNESDAY, JUNE 7.

PROGRAMME.

1. TEUFELSMARSCH . . . . Suppé
2. OVERTURE, "Raymond" . . . . Thomas
3. WALTZ, "Legends from the Vienna Woods" . . Strauss
4. SELECTION, "Robin Hood" . . . . . De Koven

5. OVERTURE, "Zampa" . . . . Hérold
6. PRELUDE, Act V., "Manfred" . . . . . Reinecke
   (First Time)
   The audience is respectfully requested to preserve silence during the performance of this number.

7. TWO HUNGARIAN DANCES . . . . . . Brahms
8. SUITE ALGÉRIENNE . . . . Saint-Saëns

9. OVERTURE, "Marriage of Figaro" . . . . Mozart
10. SELECTION, "Cavalleria Rusticana" . . . Mascagni
11. POLKA, "The Mill in the Forest" . . . . Eilenberg
12. MARCH, "Hoch Habsburg" . . . . . . Kral

Friday, June 9, Light Opera Night.
Monday, June 12, Wagner Night.

To secure satisfactory service, patrons are URGED by the Management to report PROMPTLY any inattention. Complaints made so late that patrons cannot recall either the number of the table or the waiter are obviously useless.

Now the rage of the LONDON Concerts and Drawing-rooms:

YOU AND I, by Liza Lehmann,	60c.
KING CHARLES, by M. V. White,	60c.
LIKE VIOLETS PALE, by F. Allitsen,	60c.
WHEN THE WORLD IS FAIR, by F. H. Cowen,	60c.
QUEEN OF MY LIFE, by E. T. Lloyd,	60c.

BOOSEY & CO.,
9 East 17th Street,   New York.

YOU CAN
Have your last season's outfit dyed or cleansed and refinished so it will look like new, by our French process. Why discard soiled clothing when it can be overhauled and worn as second best? You can

RELY ON
Our methods of cleansing, and need not hesitate to trust us with articles of the most delicate textures.
We dye or cleanse and refinish PROPERLY, *all* materials of household use and clothing of all kinds.

LEWANDO'S
W. L. Crosby, General Manager.
French Cleansers, Fancy Dyers, Fine Launderers.

PRINCIPAL OFFICES:
17 Temple Place, Boston.
479 Fifth Avenue, New York.
Established 70 years.
Largest in America.
Bundles called for and delivered.
Telephones in all offices.

In no other way
are men as wasteful and extravagant as in cigar smoking — because cigars are thrown away half smoked half the time.

BETWEEN THE ACTS
Little Cigars
are just right for all short smokes. They light right, they burn right, and taste right. Have you ever seen them? At all stores: 10 for 10 cts., or, as they are for sale here, you can try them to-night. Tell the waiter to bring you a 10-cent box of "Between the Acts." They will add to your enjoyment of this concert.

A Particularly Fine Lager for Family Use and Clubs.
Bottled in the most careful manner at our own bottling department, and sold by the S. S. Pierce Co. and all other leading grocers in New England.

Other Brands in Bottles:
"Norfolk India Pale Stock Ale."
"Norfolk Extra Golden Ale" (blue label).
"Norfolk Standard Lager."
Our "Cabinet" and "Bismarck Brau" are the most popular refreshments at these concerts.

HABICH & CO.

H. W. HABICH,   Telephone, 56 Roxbury
EDWARD BUHL.   or 1151 Boston.

ESTABROOK & EATON'S MARGUERITE PERFECTOS, 10c. EACH CONCHAS, 10c., 3 FOR 25c. SOLD AT THE "POPS."

THE ICE-CREAM SERVED AT THESE CONCERTS IS FURNISHED BY WEBER, 25 Temple Place and 33 West Street.

MUSIC HALL PROMENADE PROGRAMME.
PUBLISHED EVERY EVENING DURING THE SUMMER SEASON.

NOTICE TO ADVERTISERS.
The advertising columns in the Programme are controlled SOLELY by F. R. Comee, Boston Music Hall Box Office, to whom all communications should be addressed.

The United States Hotel,

SARATOGA SPRINGS, N.Y.

Under a continuous management for 25 years.

Without a peer in its appointments, service, and liberal management.

The largest structure of its kind in the world.

Built entirely of brick.

The Hotel and court cover over seven acres.

For further information, rates, etc., etc., address

GAGE & PERRY,
Proprietors,
UNITED STATES HOTEL,
Saratoga Springs, N.Y.

Colonial Beer...

The Beer that's Brewed in Glass.

PURE, CLEAN, PALATABLE.

Order a Bottle.

SOUTHER BREWING CO.,
919 Parker Street,
Roxbury, Mass.

VEUVE CHAFFARD

PURE OLIVE OIL.

IN HONEST BOTTLES.

The Peer of all Cigarettes.
Save the band-label on each box for valuable premiums.

::: ALSO :::

Monopol

High-grade Egyptian Cigarettes.

No. 88 Khedive,
No. 68 Nadine,
No. 98 Egyptian Belles,
No. 208 Princess Lillian

On sale at these concerts and all first-class dealers.

OCKENHEIMER BERG, Near Bingen, GERMANY, on the Rhine.

PHILIP KRIM'S OWN IMPORTATION OF **Rhine Wines,** FOR 30 YEARS AT **163 Shawmut Avenue.** OUR WINES SOLD AT THESE CONCERTS.

HERRICK, COPLEY SQUARE, Telephones 608 and 950 (Back Bay), CHOICE TABLES for Music Hall "Pops."

THURSDAY, JUNE 8.

PROGRAMME.

1. MARCH, "Hobson's Choice" . . . . . Straube
2. OVERTURE, "Semiramide" . . . . . Rossini
3. WALTZ, "Schö er Mai" . . . . . Strauss
4. SELECTION, "Aïda" . . . . . Verdi

5. OVERTURE, "A Night in Granada" . . . Kreutzer
   (First Time.)
6. (a) EVENING SONG . . . . . Schumann
   (b) MARCH from "The Ruins of Athens" . . Beethoven
   The audience is respectfully requested to preserve silence during the performance of this number.
7. MELODY . . . . Rubinstein
8. HUNGARIAN RHAPSODY No. 2 . . . . Liszt

9. OVERTURE, "Orpheus" . . . . . Offenbach
10. POLKA, "Sängerlust" . . . . . Strauss
11. WALTZ, "Grubenlichter" . . . . . Zeller
12. MARCH, "Boccaccio" . . . . . Suppé

D. LEIDEN'S
SPARKLING
MOSELLE,

The only Sparkling Wine sold at these Concerts.

SHINNECOCK

The Perfection of

Scotch Whisky

Sold by
S. S. PIERCE COMPANY.

THE HAYWARD,
16 and 22 Hayward Place.
LADIES' AND GENTS' CAFÉ.   Open until 1 a.m.

SCIARRETTA'S NEAPOLITAN TRIO give concerts daily from 6 P.M. until 1 A.M.
Signor SALVATORE SCIARRETTI, Lyric Tenor,
is highly endorsed by Vice-President Garrett A. Hobart, Chauncey M. Depew, Eugene Ysaye, Raoul Pugno, Jean Gerardy, and many other prominent people.
SMITH & KERRISSEY, Proprietors.

AN HISTORIC RESORT.

The loveliest place on the New England coast to spend a short vacation or the whole season is the

MYLES STANDISH HOTEL,
at SOUTH DUXBURY, MASS.

Everything that money and intelligence can do has been done to make this hotel better, if possible, than it was last season.

The greatest pains will be taken to have the table service absolutely excellent. Of the house itself and its surroundings too much cannot be said. It is a resort of nice people, who come year after year, gaining strength, vitality, and pleasure.
Send for our 1899 booklet.

L. BOYER'S SONS, Proprietors,
27 Devonshire Street, Boston, Mass.,
Or ALFRED S. AMER, Manager,
90 Wall Street, New York
(Until June 1).

Myles Standish Hotel,
South Duxbury, Mass.

"AMERICA'S FINEST PRODUCT."

Bartholomay's "APOLLO"

LAGER BEER IN BOTTLES.

Sold at these Concerts.

ALBRECHT & KOELLNER,
SOLE AGENTS,
Telephone, Boston 1751.   295-305 A Street.

Also Agents for the "Crystal Rock" Mineral Water.

PURE BEER
Harvard
BREW. CO'S $1000.00
PURE BEER
Sold at these Concerts,
IN BOTTLES ONLY
20¢ PER BOTTLE.

TABLE LINEN USED AT THESE CONCERTS LAUNDERED BY THE L. K. HUSTED LAUNDERING COMPANY, 27 and 29 BROADWAY, CHELSEA, MASS.

Inglenook Vineyard.

The only California Wines sold at these Concerts.

❧❧

THE CODMAN & HALL CO.,
Opposite the South Union Station.

Sole Agents for New England.

IND. COOPE & CO.'S English Ale.

THE SECOND LARGEST BREWERY IN ENGLAND.

Brewers of the finest *light quality* ale. Very highly endorsed by the medical profession. : : : : :

❧❧

THE CODMAN & HALL CO.,
Opposite South Union Station.

Sole Agents for the United States.

DRINK only the

PURE

WHIS

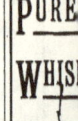

If you want p and richne flavor, try only gen and origin

OLD KENTU TAYLOR,

Eight years old own distillation guaranteed p Bottled and shi direct from warehouses by None genuine w out our signa on both labels. ware of imitat For consump indigestion, an ailments requ stimulants. O KENTUCKY T LOR has superior.
Sold by all class drugs grocers, and li dealers.

Wright & Tay Distillers, Fine Kentuc Whiskies, Louisville, K

Hirshfield & New Englan Agents, 31 Doane Stre Boston.

Instruct your waiter to bring a bottle of

Pfaff's "Monogram" Lager.

If you will do this, it will not be necessary for us to expatiate upon the good qualities of our production.
YOU CAN JUDGE FOR YOURSELF.

H. & J. PFAFF BREWING COMPANY,
Telephone 2608.   16 ARCH STREET, BOSTON.

TRY THE "COLUMBIA BRAND" VIENNA SAUSAGES. SERVED HOT OR COLD AT THESE CONCERTS.

They cannot sell you here
Canadian Club Whisky,
Ruinart Champagne,
Royal Liqueur Scotch,
Carstair's Philadelphia Rye,
Fort Hill Bourbon,
Alhambra Sherry,
All of which you will find of excellent quality;

But you can get

Kaiser Water,

the most refreshing of all table waters,

Chateau d'Arsac Claret,
N. Johnston & Sons' Medoc,
and
California Inglenook Clarets.

SUPPLIED BY

CODMAN & HALL COMPANY,

WINE MERCHANTS,

Opposite New South Station.

FRIDAY, JUNE 9.

LIGHT OPERA NIGHT.

PROGRAMME.

1. MARCH, "Am I a Wiz?" — Herbert
2. SELECTION, "The Runaway Girl" — Ch. von Baar
3. WALTZ from "Die Fledermaus" — Strauss
4. OVERTURE, "Sphinx" — Thompson
5. SELECTION, "La Fille de Madame Angot" — Lecocq
6. WALTZ AND PIZZICATO from Ballet Music, "Sylvia" — Delibes
7. CAVATINA — Raff
8. OVERTURE, "Tabasco" — Chadwick
9. SELECTION, "The Belle of New York" — Kerker
10. WALTZ, "Vienna Blood" — Strauss
11. ENTRÉE TRIOMPHALE DES BOYARDS — Halvorsen
12. BOCCACCIO MARCH — Suppé

COAL

Best Quality
AT
Lowest Prices

METROPOLITAN COAL COMPANY,
No. 30 Congress Street.

WILSON BELFAST GINGER ALE
and
Champagne Kola

are sold at these concerts.

DRINK
WILSON CHAMPAGNE KOLA.

It produces energy, activity, and force. Its medical virtues are endorsed by physicians.

The **Wilson** is acknowledged to be America's purest spring water.
Bottled only in glass at the spring.
North Raymond, Me.

In making our BELFAST GINGER ALE we use only the purest ginger.

Beware of imitations.

Drink the **Wilson** and you are sure of the best.

Wilson Spring and Hotel Co.,
45 Arch Street.
Telephone 3129, Boston. Boston, Mass.

"THE RECOGNIZED FAVORITE OF ALL BEERS."

Schlitz
THE BEER THAT MADE MILWAUKEE FAMOUS.
HIGHEST AWARD FOR PURITY.
Sold at these Concerts. JOS. GAHM & CO., N.E. AGENTS, 175-177 PURCHASE ST.

THE ONLY BEER ON DRAUGHT AT THESE CONCERTS.
"the beer that's brewed"
SOLD AT THESE CONCERTS
ROCHESTER BREWING CO'S.
BEATS THE WORLD OVER FOR ITS PURITY.
FAMOUS BOTTLED BEER
HOME OFFICE & BREWERY ROCHESTER, N.Y.
NEW ENGLAND BRANCH
295-305 A STREET BOSTON
Free delivery in city and Suburbs
RIENZI, PREMIER, BOHEMIAN, BAVARIAN, STANDARD.

THE FALL RIVER LINE

OCCUPYING THE
LONG ISLAND SOUND ROUTE
BETWEEN

Boston and New York

Has the finest quintette of great steamboats that the world has ever seen. The

Priscilla, Puritan, Plymouth, Pilgrim, and Providence

Are the largest, best equipped, safest, and handsomest steamboats ever constructed. This route is one of the most attractive and naturally beautiful traversed by any transportation agency in the world. Trips of the Fall River Line are made throughout the year. Each steamboat has its own orchestra, and the service on each member of the fleet is maintained at the highest possible standard.

Tickets via this route are on sale at all of the principal Ticket Offices in the United States.

From **BOSTON**. Trains, connecting with steamers at Fall River in 80 minutes, leave Park Square Station, New York, New Haven & Hartford Railroad (Old Colony System), daily at 6 p.m.

From **NEW YORK**. Steamers leave Pier 19, North River, foot of Warren Street, daily at 5.30 p.m.

S. A. GARDNER, Superintendent, NEW YORK.
GEO. L. CONNOR, Passenger Traffic Manager, NEW HAVEN, CONN.
O. H. TAYLOR, General Passenger Agent, NEW YORK CITY.

HOTEL LANGWOOD,

Middlesex Fells Reservation.

P.O. Address, Melrose, Mass.   Wyoming Station, B. & M. R.R.

Twenty minutes by rail from Boston. Sixty trains daily. Hotel coaches meet trains each way. Four hundred feet above sea level. Beautiful rides, drives, and walks. Golf links, tennis courts, and ball grounds.

OPENS ABOUT MAY 20.

For plans and prices address:

F. W. GASKILL, Manager.

BOSTON OFFICE:
Hemenway Building, 10 Tremont Street, Room 29.

S.S. "Howard." Boston to Norfolk, 522 miles. Norfolk to Baltimore, 200 miles.

	1.	2.	3.
Boston	Leave July 2	July 16	August 19
	Arrive July 13	July 31	September 4

S.S. "Toronto." Toronto to Montreal, through the "Thousand Islands" and the "Rapids," 376 miles.

Third Season.

3 Ideal Outings

Personally conducted by
F. R. COMEE, Music Hall, Boston.

No. 1. Ten days. Saratoga-Lake George, 2,130 miles from Buffalo to Duluth, and return on the steamer "North-Land" through the Great Lakes, Erie, Huron, St. Clair, and Superior.

Nos. 2 and 3. Sixteen days. Exactly alike. 700 miles' ocean sail to Norfolk and Baltimore. Over Alleghany Mountains and a day in Chicago. Up Lake Michigan and three days at Mackinac Island. 1,546 miles on steamer "North-West" to Duluth and return to Buffalo through the Great Lakes. Niagara Falls to Toronto. Across Lake Ontario, through the Thousand Islands, and down the St. Lawrence River to Montreal and Boston.

SEND FOR CIRCULARS.

S.S. "Manitou." Chicago to Mackinac Island, across Lake Michigan, 350 miles.

"North-West." Mackinac Island to Duluth and return to Buffalo, 1,555 miles.

Allsopp's

ENGLISH ALE.
"The Red Hand Brand."

Bottled at the brewery, Burton-on-Trent, England, under the personal supervision of the Messrs. Allsopp.

Sold at these concerts.

SATURDAY, JUNE 10.

PROGRAMME.

1. MARCH, "Under the Double Eagle" — Wagner
2. OVERTURE, "Dame Blanche" — Boieldieu
3. KAISER WALTZ — Strauss
4. SELECTION from "The Serenade" — Herbert

5. OVERTURE, "Freischütz" — Weber
6. NORWEGIAN DANCE (First Time) — Grieg
7. SERENADE for String Orchestra (First Time) — Pierné

   The audience is respectfully requested to preserve silence during the performance of this number.

8. AMERICAN FANTASY — Herbert

9. OVERTURE, "Banditenstreiche" — Suppé
10. GAVOTTE, "Stephanie" — Czibulka
11. AT A GEORGIA CAMP-MEETING — Mills
12. MARCH from "The Bride Elect" — Sousa

The *only* Lithia Water sold at these concerts.

Hygeia Lithia Water

Sparkling and Still.

By its use you will avoid the germs of disease which natural MINERAL WATERS are liable to contain.

For Sale at these concerts and by

S. S. PIERCE CO.

FOR SALE AT THESE CONCERTS.

FAMOUS TANNHAEUSER EXPORT BEER

The finest Light Beer Extant.   Brewery Bottling.   Favorite of Connoisseurs.

Pure,   Palatable,   Perfect.

B. & E. Philadelphia Ale on Draught.
FOR SALE AT THESE CONCERTS.

The purity and keeping quality of the Tannhaeuser Export under all changes of temperature, its uniform excellence being guaranteed, together with its nutritious properties, make it the most pleasant, delicious, and convenient beverage for home consumption.

Put up in corked bottles, and packed in casks of 10 dozen white flint pints, and 6 dozen amber quarts.

Highest Awards wherever exhibited.

The BERGNER & ENGEL BREWING CO.'S N.E. Depot,
508 and 510 Atlantic Avenue, Boston.

Telephone 3805.   SOL. BACHARACH, Manager.

M. Steinert & Sons Co.,

STEINERT HALL BUILDING,

No. 162 Boylston Street, corner Carver, Boston.

STEINWAY & SONS,

HARDMAN,   GABLER,
EMERSON,   SINGER.

PIANOS.

The Æolian, Aeriol, Orchestrelle, and Pianola.

THE ÆOLIAN
AND
THE PIANOLA
FOR SUMMER HOMES.

At this season of the year we receive many orders for these instruments for Summer Residences, and therefore beg to call attention to our extensive assortment now on display, especially suited for this purpose.

The ÆOLIAN meets the requirements of country homes, furnishing, as it does, music suitable for every occasion. It practically takes the place of an orchestra — music for dancing — orchestral concerts, — in short, music of every style and description is always available.

The PIANOLA will appeal to many on account of the very little space it occupies. It will play any kind of a piano, and can also be used upon a rented piano without the slightest injury. For the above reasons it is bound to be very popular for small cottages.

We are glad to be able to announce that we can furnish PIANOLAS with no more than a week's delay, and, at times, the day the order is given.

Persons not familiar with these instruments are cordially invited to call at our warerooms and hear them, or a descriptive catalogue will be mailed free upon application.

M. STEINERT & SONS CO.,
Steinert Hall,   162 Boylston Street,   Boston.

ANHEUSER-BUSCH BREWING ASS'N,

ST. LOUIS, MO., U.S.A.

BREWERS OF HIGH=GRADE BEERS EXCLUSIVELY.

Black and Tan.   Faust.

Michelob.   Pale Lager.

Muenchener.   Anheuser Standard.

Served at the Music Hall Concerts.

Also at all first-class hotels, clubs, and bars, and on all Pullman and Wagner cars and ocean and lake steamers.

JACOB WIRTH,   Wholesale Dealer,   **Boston, Mass.**

THE MUSIC HALL
PROMENADE CONCERTS

SMOKE "LA CELESTINA," THE BEST ALL-HAVANA CIGAR. DANIEL, FRANK & CO.

SMOKE THE POPULAR "BARRISTER" CIGARS AT THE POPULAR CONCERTS

PUBLISHED BY
C. A. ELLIS,
MUSIC HALL.

BOSTON, FRIDAY, JUNE 9, 1899.

SUMMER SEASON.
Vol. XIV. No. 28.

THE MUSIC HALL

Promenade Concerts
FOURTEENTH SEASON.

C. A. ELLIS, Manager.   F. R. COMEE, Assistant Manager.
Mr. GUSTAV STRUBE, Conductor.

FRIDAY, JUNE 9.
LIGHT OPERA NIGHT.

PROGRAMME.

1. MARCH, "Am I a Wiz?" . . . . Herbert
2. SELECTION, "The Runaway Girl" . . . Ch. von Baar
3. WALTZ from "Die Fledermaus" . . . . Strauss
4. OVERTURE, "Sphinx" . . . . Thompson
5. SELECTION, "La Fille de Madame Angot" . . Lecocq
6. WALTZ AND PIZZICATO from Ballet Music, "Sylvia" Delibes
7. CAVATINA . . . . Raff
8. OVERTURE, "Tabasco" . . . . . . Chadwick
9. SELECTION, "The Belle of New York" . . . Kerker
10. WALTZ, "Vienna Blood" . . . . . . Strauss
11. ENTRÉE TRIOMPHALE DES BOYARDS . . Halvorsen
12. BOCCACCIO MARCH . . . . Suppé

Monday, June 12, Wagner Night.

To secure satisfactory service, patrons are URGED by the Management to report PROMPTLY any inattention. Complaints made so late that patrons cannot recall either the number of the table or the waiter are obviously useless.

ALBUMS OF SONGS,
Containing many popular compositions not published in single form.

IRISH FOLK SONGS, by Charles Wood,	$2.00
RUSSIAN SONGS, by F. Wishaw (2 vols.),	1.00
NINE SONGS, by S. Liddle,	1.00
NINE SONGS, by Liza Lehmann,	1.00
FIVE SONGS, by Francis Korbay,	2.00

Beautifully Illustrated by J. S. SARGENT, R.A.

BOOSEY & CO.,
9 East 17th Street,   New York.

YOU CAN
Have your last season's outfit dyed or cleansed and refinished so it will look like new, by our French process. Why discard soiled clothing when it can be overhauled and worn as second best? You can

RELY ON
Our methods of cleansing, and need not hesitate to trust us with articles of the most delicate textures. We dye or cleanse and refinish PROPERLY, *all* materials of household use and clothing of all kinds.

LEWANDO'S
W. L. Crosby, General Manager.
French Cleansers, Fancy Dyers, Fine Launderers.

PRINCIPAL OFFICES:
17 Temple Place, Boston.
479 Fifth Avenue, New York.
Established 70 years.
Largest in America.
Bundles called for and delivered.
Telephones in all offices.

If you are open
to conviction,
to-night
try one 10-cent box of

BETWEEN THE ACTS
Little Cigars

to smoke now—or at any time when you want a short smoke and haven't time for a long one. They are real cigars, but small ones.

They cost so little that you can use them every day as well as not and actually save on your daily cigar expense by substituting them for larger cigars.

FOR SALE HERE.

LAGER BEER
A Particularly Fine Lager for Family Use and Clubs.
Bottled in the most careful manner at our own bottling department, and sold by the S. S. Pierce Co. and all other leading grocers in New England.

Other Brands in Bottles:
"Norfolk India Pale Stock Ale."
"Norfolk Extra Golden Ale" (blue label).
"Norfolk Standard Lager."
Our "Cabinet" and "Bismarck Brau" are the most popular refreshments at these concerts.

HABICH & CO.
H. W. HABICH,   Telephone, 56 Roxbury
EDWARD BUHL.   or 1152 Boston.

ESTABROOK & EATON'S MARGUERITE PERFECTOS, 10c. EACH. CONCHAS, 10c., 3 FOR 25c., SOLD AT THE "POPS."

THE ICE-CREAM SERVED AT THESE CONCERTS IS FURNISHED BY WEBER, 25 Temple Place and 33 West Street.

MUSIC HALL PROMENADE PROGRAMME.
PUBLISHED EVERY EVENING DURING THE SUMMER SEASON.

NOTICE TO ADVERTISERS.
The advertising columns in the Programme are controlled SOLELY by F. R. Comee, Boston Music Hall Box Office, to whom all communications should be addressed.

The United States Hotel,
SARATOGA SPRINGS, N.Y.

Under a continuous management for 25 years.

Without a peer in its appointments, service, and liberal management.

The largest structure of its kind in the world.

Built entirely of brick.

The Hotel and court cover over seven acres.

For further information, rates, etc., etc., address

GAGE & PERRY,
Proprietors,
UNITED STATES HOTEL,
Saratoga Springs, N.Y.

Colonial Beer...

The Beer that's Brewed in Glass.

PURE, CLEAN, PALATABLE.

Order a Bottle.

SOUTHER BREWING CO.,
919 Parker Street,
Roxbury, Mass.

VEUVE CHAFFARD

PURE OLIVE OIL.

IN HONEST BOTTLES.

The Peer of all Cigarettes.
Save the band-label on each box for valuable premiums.

::: ALSO :::

Monopol
High-grade Egyptian Cigarettes

No. 8A Khedive,
No. 6A Nadine,
No. 9A Egyptian Belles,
No. 70A Princess Lillian

On sale at these concerts and all first-class dealers.

OCKENHEIMER BERG,
Near Bingen, GERMANY. On the Rhine.

PHILIP KRIM'S
OWN IMPORTATION OF
Rhine Wines,
FOR 30 YEARS
AT
163 Shawmut Avenue.
OUR WINES SOLD AT THESE CONCERTS.

HERRICK, COPLEY SQUARE, Telephones 608 and 950 (Back Bay), CHOICE TABLES for Music Hall "Pops."

D. LEIDEN'S SPARKLING MOSELLE,

The only Sparkling Wine sold at these Concerts.

SHINNECOCK

The Perfection of Scotch Whisky

Sold by
S. S. PIERCE COMPANY.

SATURDAY, JUNE 10.

PROGRAMME.

1. MARCH, "Under the Double Eagle" . . . Wagner
2. OVERTURE, "Dame Blanche" . . . Boieldieu
3. KAISER WALTZ . . . Strauss
4. SELECTION from "The Serenade" . . . Herbert

5. OVERTURE, "Freischütz" . . . Weber
6. NORWEGIAN DANCE . . . Grieg
    (First Time.)
7. SERENADE for String Orchestra . . . Pierne
    (First Time.)
   The audience is respectfully requested to preserve silence during the performance of this number.
8. AMERICAN FANTASY . . . Herbert

9. OVERTURE, "Banditenstreiche" . . . Suppé
10. GAVOTTE, "Stephanie" . . . Czibulka
11. AT A GEORGIA CAMP-MEETING . . . Mills
12. MARCH from "The Bride Elect" . . . Sousa

THE HAYWARD,
16 and 22 Hayward Place.
LADIES' AND GENTS' CAFÉ.   Open until 1 a.m.

SCIARRETTA'S NEAPOLITAN TRIO give concerts daily from 6 P.M. until 1 A.M.
Signor SALVATORE SCIARRETTI, Lyric Tenor,
Is highly endorsed by Vice-President Garret A. Hobart, Chauncey M. Depew, Eugene Ysaye, Raoul Pugno, Jean Gerardy, and many other prominent people.
SMITH & KERRISSEY, Proprietors.

AN HISTORIC RESORT.

The loveliest place on the New England coast to spend a short vacation or the whole season is the

MYLES STANDISH HOTEL,
at SOUTH DUXBURY, MASS.

Everything that money and intelligence can do has been done to make this hotel better, if possible, than it was last season.
The greatest pains will be taken to have the table service absolutely excellent. Of the house itself and its surroundings too much cannot be said. It is a resort of nice people, who come year after year, gaining strength, vitality, and pleasure.
Send for our 1899 booklet.

L. BOYER'S SONS, Proprietors,
27 Devonshire Street, Boston, Mass.,

Or ALFRED S. AMER, Manager,
90 Wall Street, New York
(Until June 1).

Myles Standish Hotel,
South Duxbury, Mass.

"AMERICA'S FINEST PRODUCT."

Bartholomay's "APOLLO"

LAGER BEER IN BOTTLES.

Sold at these Concerts.

ALBRECHT & KOELLNER,
SOLE AGENTS,
Telephone, Boston 1751.   295-305 A Street.

Also Agents for the "Crystal Rock" Mineral Water.

PURE BEER

PURE BEER

Sold at these Concerts,
IN BOTTLES ONLY
20¢ PER BOTTLE.

Inglenook Vineyard.

The only California Wines sold at these Concerts.

THE CODMAN & HALL CO.,
Opposite the South Union Station.

Sole Agents for New England.

IND. COOPE & CO.'S English Ale.

THE SECOND LARGEST BREWERY IN ENGLAND.

Brewers of the finest *light quality* ale. Very highly endorsed by the medical profession. : : : :

THE CODMAN & HALL CO.,
Opposite South Union Station.

Sole Agents for the United States.

DRINK only the PUREST WHISKEY

If you want purity and richness of flavor, try only genuine and original

OLD KENTUCKY TAYLOR,

Eight years old, own distillation, guaranteed pure Bottled and shipped direct from warehouses by None genuine without our signature on both labels. A sure ware of imitations. For consumption, indigestion, and ailments requiring stimulants, OLD KENTUCKY TAYLOR has no superior.

Sold by all first class druggists, grocers, and liquor dealers.

Wright & Taylor
Distillers,
Fine Kentucky Whiskies,
Louisville, Ky.

Hirshfield & Co.
New England Agents,
31 Doane Street,
Boston.

Instruct your waiter to bring a bottle of

Pfaff's "Monogram" Lager.

If you will do this, it will not be necessary for us to expatiate upon the good qualities of our production.
YOU CAN JUDGE FOR YOURSELF.

H. & J. PFAFF BREWING COMPANY,
Telephone 2608.   16 ARCH STREET, BOSTON.

TRY THE "COLUMBIA BRAND" VIENNA SAUSAGES. SERVED HOT OR COLD AT THESE CONCERTS.

They cannot sell you here
Canadian Club Whisky,
Ruinart Champagne,
Royal Liqueur Scotch,
Carstair's Philadelphia Rye,
Fort Hill Bourbon,
Alhambra Sherry,
All of which you will find
of excellent quality;

But you can get

Kaiser Water,

the most refreshing of all table waters,

*Chateau d'Arsac Claret,
N. Johnston & Sons' Medoc,*
and
California Inglenook Clarets.

SUPPLIED BY

CODMAN & HALL COMPANY,

WINE MERCHANTS,

Opposite New South Station.

MONDAY, JUNE 12.
WAGNER NIGHT.

PROGRAMME.

1. MARCH, "Nibelungen" . . . Sonntag
2. WALTZ, "Thousand and One Nights" . Strauss
3. TRÄUME . . . . Wagner
   (First Time.)
   Trumpet Solo, Mr. KLOEPFEL.
4. OVERTURE, "Rienzi" . . . . Wagner
5. INTRODUCTION, Act III., "Tannhäuser" . Wagner
   (First Time.)
6. EVENING STAR . . . . . Wagner
   Solo Trombone, Mr. HAMPE.
7. SAILORS' CHORUS from "The Flying Dutchman" Wagner
8. PRELUDE to "Meistersinger" . . . Wagner
9. PROCESSION OF WOMEN, from "Lohengrin" . Wagner
10. LOIN DU BAL . . . . . Gillet
11. POLKA, "Puppenfee" . . . . Bayer
12. MARCH, "Stars and Stripes Forever" . Sousa

COAL

Best Quality AT Lowest Prices

METROPOLITAN COAL COMPANY,
No. 30 Congress Street.

WILSON BELFAST GINGER ALE
and
Champagne Kola
are sold at these concerts.

DRINK
WILSON CHAMPAGNE KOLA.

It produces energy, activity, and force. Its medical virtues are endorsed by physicians.

The **Wilson** is acknowledged to be America's purest spring water. Bottled only in glass at the spring, North Raymond, Me.

In making our BELFAST GINGER ALE we use only the purest ginger.

Beware of Imitations.

Drink the **Wilson** and you are sure of the best.

Wilson Spring and Hotel Co.,
45 Arch Street,
Telephone 3129, Boston. Boston, Mass.

THE FALL RIVER LINE

OCCUPYING THE
LONG ISLAND SOUND ROUTE
BETWEEN

Boston and New York

Has the finest quintette of great steamboats that the world has ever seen. The

Priscilla, Puritan, Plymouth, Pilgrim, and Providence

Are the largest, best equipped, safest, and handsomest steamboats ever constructed. This route is one of the most attractive and naturally beautiful traversed by any transportation agency in the world. Trips of the Fall River Line are made throughout the year.

Each steamboat has its own orchestra, and the service on each member of the fleet is maintained at the highest possible standard.

Tickets via this route are on sale at all of the principal Ticket Offices in the United States.

From BOSTON. Trains, connecting with steamers at Fall River in 80 minutes leave Park Square Station, New York, New Haven & Hartford Railroad (Old Colony System), daily at 6 p.m.

From NEW YORK. Steamers leave Pier 19, North River, foot of Warren Street, daily at 5.30 p.m.

S. A. GARDNER, Superintendent, NEW YORK.
GEO. L. CONNOR, Passenger Traffic Manager, NEW HAVEN, CONN.
O. H. TAYLOR, General Passenger Agent, NEW YORK CITY.

HOTEL LANGWOOD,

Middlesex Fells Reservation.

P.O. Address, Melrose, Mass.   Wyoming Station, B. & M. R.R.

Twenty minutes by rail from Boston. Sixty trains daily. Hotel coaches meet trains each way. Four hundred feet above sea level. Beautiful rides, drives, and walks. Golf links, tennis courts, and ball grounds.

OPENS ABOUT MAY 20.

For plans and prices address:

F. W. GASKILL, Manager.

BOSTON OFFICE:
Hemenway Building, 10 Tremont Street, Room 29.

S.S. "Howard." Boston to Norfolk, 522 miles. Norfolk to Baltimore, 200 miles.

	1.	2.	3.
Boston	Leave July 2 Arrive July 12	July 15 July 31	August 19 September 4

S.S. "Toronto." Toronto to Montreal, through the "Thousand Islands" and the "Rapids," 376 miles.

Third Season.

3 Ideal Outings

Personally conducted by
F. R. COMEE, Music Hall, Boston.

No. 1. Ten days. **Saratoga, Lake George,** 2,130 miles from **Buffalo to Duluth,** and return on the steamer "North-Land" through the Great Lakes, Erie, Huron, St. Clair, and Superior.

Nos. 2 and 3. Sixteen days. Exactly alike. 700 miles' ocean sail to **Norfolk and Baltimore.** Over Alleghany Mountains and a day in **Chicago.** Up Lake Michigan and three days at **Mackinac Island.** 1,846 miles on steamer "North-West" to **Duluth** and return to Buffalo through the Great Lakes. **Niagara Falls to Toronto.** Across Lake Ontario, through the Thousand Islands, and down the St. Lawrence River to **Montreal** and **Boston.**

SEND FOR CIRCULARS.

S.S. "Manitou." Chicago to Mackinac Island, across Lake Michigan, 350 miles.

"North-West." Mackinac Island to Duluth and return to Buffalo, 1,555 miles.

Allsopp's

ENGLISH ALE.
"The Red Hand Brand."

Bottled at the brewery, Burton-on-Trent, England, under the personal supervision of the Messrs. Allsopp.

Sold at these concerts.

TUESDAY, JUNE 13.

PROGRAMME.

1. MARCH from "Le Prophète" — Meyerbeer
2. OVERTURE, "Fidelio" — Beethoven
3. GAVOTTE for String Orchestra — Bach
4. WALTZ, "Les Patineurs" — Waldteufel
5. OVERTURE, "William Tell" — Rossini
6. BALLET MUSIC from "Feramors" — Rubinstein
7. SPRING SONG — Mendelssohn
   The audience is respectfully requested to preserve silence during the performance of this number.
8. AN EVENING WITH BILSE — Schertz
9. SELECTION, "Fencing Master" — De Koven
10. WALTZ, "Wine, Woman, and Song" — Strauss
11. HUSARENRITT — Spindler
12. MARCH, "King Cotton" — Sousa

The *only* Lithia Water sold at these concerts.

Hygeia Lithia Water

Sparkling and Still.

By its use you will avoid the germs of disease which natural MINERAL WATERS are liable to contain.

For Sale at these concerts and by

S. S. PIERCE CO.

FOR SALE AT THESE CONCERTS.

FAMOUS TANNHAEUSER EXPORT BEER

The finest Light Beer Extant.   Brewery Bottling.   Favorite of Connoisseurs.

Pure,   Palatable,   Perfect.

B. & E. Philadelphia Ale on Draught.
FOR SALE AT THESE CONCERTS.

The purity and keeping quality of the Tannhaeuser Export under all changes of temperature, its uniform excellence being guaranteed, together with its nutritious properties, make it the most pleasant, delicious, and convenient beverage for home consumption.
Put up in corked bottles, and packed in casks of 10 dozen white flint pints, and 6 dozen amber quarts.

Highest Awards wherever exhibited.

The BERGNER & ENGEL BREWING CO.'S N.E. Depot,
508 and 510 Atlantic Avenue, Boston.

Telephone 3805.   SOL. BACHARACH, Manager.

M. Steinert & Sons Co.,

STEINERT HALL BUILDING,

No. 162 Boylston Street, corner Carver, Boston.

STEINWAY & SONS,

| HARDMAN, | GABLER, |
| EMERSON, | SINGER. |

PIANOS.

The Æolian, Aeriol, Orchestrelle, and Pianola.

THE ÆOLIAN
AND
THE PIANOLA
FOR SUMMER HOMES.

At this season of the year we receive many orders for these instruments for Summer Residences, and therefore beg to call attention to our extensive assortment now on display, especially suited for this purpose.

The ÆOLIAN meets the requirements of country homes, furnishing, as it does, music suitable for every occasion. It practically takes the place of an orchestra — music for dancing — orchestral concerts,— in short, music of every style and description is always available.

The PIANOLA will appeal to many on account of the very little space it occupies. It will play any kind of a piano, and can also be used upon a rented piano without the slightest injury. For the above reasons it is bound to be very popular for small cottages.

We are glad to be able to announce that we can furnish PIANOLAS with no more than a week's delay, and, at times, the day the order is given.

Persons not familiar with these instruments are cordially invited to call at our warerooms and hear them, or a descriptive catalogue will be mailed free upon application.

M. STEINERT & SONS CO.,
Steinert Hall,   162 Boylston Street,   Boston.

ANHEUSER-BUSCH BREWING ASS'N,

ST. LOUIS, MO., U.S.A.

BREWERS OF HIGH=GRADE BEERS EXCLUSIVELY.

Black and Tan.	Faust.
Michelob.	Pale Lager.
Muenchener.	Anheuser Standard.

Served at the Music Hall Concerts.

Also at all first-class hotels, clubs, and bars, and on all Pullman and Wagner cars and ocean and lake steamers.

JACOB WIRTH,   Wholesale Dealer,   **Boston, Mass.**

THE MUSIC HALL PROMENADE CONCERTS

BOSTON, SATURDAY, JUNE 10, 1899.

SUMMER SEASON. Vol. XIV. No. 29.

Published by C. A. ELLIS, Music Hall.

YOU CAN
Have your last season's outfit dyed or cleansed and refinished so it will look like new, by our French process. Why discard soiled clothing when it can be overhauled and worn as second best? You can

RELY ON

Our methods of cleansing, and need not hesitate to trust us with articles of the most delicate textures.

We dye or cleanse and refinish PROPERLY, *all* materials of household use and clothing of all kinds.

LEWANDO'S
W. L. Crosby, General Manager.
French Cleansers, Fancy Dyers, Fine Launderers.

PRINCIPAL OFFICES:
17 Temple Place, Boston.
479 Fifth Avenue, New York.
Established 70 years.
Largest in America.
Bundles called for and delivered.
Telephones in all offices.

Save half your money

do not throw it away in half-smoked cigars! You will find that 50% of your cigar money is thrown away every day if you recall how few cigars you really have time to smoke "up."

BETWEEN THE ACTS
Little Cigars

are pure — clean — all good tobacco, and are in every way a very satisfactory short smoke. While you are listening to the music to-night, try a 10-cent box. The waiter will get them for you as they are for sale here. You will enjoy them!

THE MUSIC HALL ... Promenade Concerts
FOURTEENTH SEASON.

C. A. ELLIS, Manager.   F. R. COMEE, Assistant Manager.

Mr. GUSTAV STRUBE, Conductor.

SATURDAY, JUNE 10.

PROGRAMME.

1. MARCH, "Under the Double Eagle" . . . . . Wagner
2. OVERTURE, "Dame Blanche" . . . . Boieldieu
3. KAISER WALTZ . . . . Strauss
4. SELECTION from "The Serenade" . . . . . Herbert
5. OVERTURE, "Freischütz" . . . . Weber
6. NORWEGIAN DANCE . . . . Grieg
   (First Time.)
7. SERENADE for String Orchestra . . . . . Pierné
   (First Time.)
   The audience is respectfully requested to preserve silence during the performance of this number.
8. AMERICAN FANTASY . . . . Herbert
9. OVERTURE, "Banditenstreiche" . . . . . Suppé
10. GAVOTTE, "Stephanie" . . . . Czibulka
11. AT A GEORGIA CAMP-MEETING . . . . . Mills
12. MARCH from "The Bride Elect" . . . . . . Sousa

Monday, June 12, Wagner Night.
Monday, June 19, Harvard Night.

To secure satisfactory service, patrons are URGED by the Management to report PROMPTLY any inattention. Complaints made so late that patrons cannot recall either the number of the table or the waiter are obviously useless.

THE TWO MOST POPULAR TWO-STEPS
OF THE SEASON.

THE RUNAWAY GIRL, by Van Baar, ... 60c.
THE CECIL, by Megone, ... 50c.
FOR ORCHESTRA OR PIANO SOLO.

BOOSEY & CO.,
9 EAST 17th STREET,   NEW YORK.

LAGER BEER
A Particularly Fine Lager for Family Use and Clubs.

Bottled in the most careful manner at our own bottling department, and sold by the S. S. Pierce Co. and all other leading grocers in New England.

Other Brands in Bottles:
"Norfolk India Pale Stock Ale,"
"Norfolk Extra Golden Ale" (blue label),
"Norfolk Standard Lager,"
Our "Cabinet" and "Bismarck Brown" are the most popular refreshments at these concerts.

HABICH & CO.
H. W. HABICH, } Telephone, 50 Roxbury
EDWARD RUHL. }   or 1152 Boston.

ESTABROOK & EATON'S MARGUERITE PERFECTOS, 10c. EACH. CONCHAS, 10c., 3 FOR 25c., **SOLD AT THE "POPS."**

SMOKE THE POPULAR "BARRISTER" CIGARS AT THE POPULAR CONCERTS.

SMOKE "LA CELESTINA," THE BEST ALL-HAVANA CIGAR. DANIEL FRANK & CO.

THE ICE-CREAM SERVED AT THESE CONCERTS IS FURNISHED BY WEBER, 25 Temple Place and 33 West Street.

MUSIC HALL PROMENADE PROGRAMME.

PUBLISHED EVERY EVENING DURING THE SUMMER SEASON.

NOTICE TO ADVERTISERS.

The advertising columns in the Programme are controlled SOLELY by F. R. Comee, Boston Music Hall Box Office, to whom all communications should be addressed.

The United States Hotel,

SARATOGA SPRINGS, N.Y.

Under a continuous management for 25 years.

Without a peer in its appointments, service, and liberal management.

The largest structure of its kind in the world.

Built entirely of brick.

The Hotel and court cover over seven acres.

For further information, rates, etc., etc., address

GAGE & PERRY,
Proprietors,
UNITED STATES HOTEL,
Saratoga Springs, N.Y.

The Beer that's Brewed in Glass.

Colonial Beer...

PURE, CLEAN, PALATABLE.

Order a Bottle.

SOUTHER BREWING CO.,
919 Parker Street,
Roxbury, Mass.

All The

IMPORTED CIGARS

Sold At These Concerts Are Supplied By The

S. S. PIERCE COMPANY.

The Peer of all Cigarettes.

Save the band-label on each box for valuable premiums.

::: ALSO :::

Monopol

High-grade Egyptian Cigarettes.

No. 8A Khedive,
No. 6½A Nadine,
No. 9A Egyptian Belles,
No. 70A Princess Lillian

On sale at these concerts and all first-class dealers.

OCKENHEIMER BERG, Near Bingen, GERMANY. On the Rhine.

PHILIP KRIM'S

OWN IMPORTATION OF

Rhine Wines,

FOR 30 YEARS AT

163 Shawmut Avenue.

OUR WINES SOLD AT THESE CONCERTS.

HERRICK, COPLEY SQUARE, Telephones 608 and 950 (Back Bay), CHOICE TABLES for Music Hall "Pops."

GREAT WESTERN
CHAMPAGNE

——A natural, genuine champagne, of the finest quality produced in America.

Sold by Wine Merchants, Grocers, and Druggists.

MONDAY, JUNE 12.
WAGNER NIGHT.

PROGRAMME.

1. MARCH, "Nibelungen" . . . . Sonntag
2. WALTZ, "Thousand and One Nights" . Strauss
3. TRÄUME . . . . . Wagner
   (First Time.)
   Trumpet Solo, Mr. KLOEPFEL.
4. OVERTURE, "Rienzi" . . . Wagner
5. INTRODUCTION, Act III., "Tannhäuser" . Wagner
   (First Time.)
6. EVENING STAR . . . . Wagner
   Solo Trombone, Mr. HAMPE.
7. SAILORS' CHORUS from "The Flying Dutchman" . Wagner
8. PRELUDE to "Meistersinger" . . Wagner
9. PROCESSION OF WOMEN, from "Lohengrin" . Wagner
10. LOIN DU BAL . . . . Gillet
11. POLKA, "Puppenfee" . . . Bayer
12. MARCH, "Stars and Stripes Forever" . Sousa

THE HAYWARD,
16 and 22 Hayward Place.
LADIES' AND GENTS' CAFE.   Open until 1 a.m.

SCIARRETTA'S NEAPOLITAN TRIO give concerts daily from 5 P.M. until 1 A.M.
Signor SALVATORE SCIARRETTI, Lyric Tenor, is highly endorsed by Vice-President Garrett A. Hobart, Chauncey M. Depew, Eugene Ysaye, Raoul Pugno, Jean Gerardy, and many other prominent people.

SMITH & KERRISSEY, Proprietors.

AN HISTORIC RESORT.

The loveliest place on the New England coast to spend a short vacation or the whole season is the

MYLES STANDISH HOTEL,
at SOUTH DUXBURY, MASS.

Everything that money and intelligence can do has been done to make this hotel better, if possible, than it was last season.

The greatest pains will be taken to have the table service absolutely excellent. Of the house itself and its surroundings too much cannot be said. It is a resort of nice people, who come year after year, gaining strength, vitality, and pleasure.

Send for our 1899 booklet.

L. BOYER'S SONS, Proprietors,
27 Devonshire Street, Boston, Mass.,

Or ALFRED S. AMER, Manager,
90 Wall Street, New York
(Until June 1).

Myles Standish Hotel,
South Duxbury, Mass.

"AMERICA'S FINEST PRODUCT."

Bartholomay's "APOLLO"
LAGER BEER IN BOTTLES.

Sold at these Concerts.

ALBRECHT & KOELLNER,
SOLE AGENTS,
Telephone, Boston 1751.   295-305 A Street.

Also Agents for the "Crystal Rock" Mineral Water.

PURE BEER
Harvard
BREW. CO'S $1000.00
PURE BEER
Sold at these Concerts,
IN BOTTLES ONLY
20¢ PER BOTTLE.

Inglenook Vineyard.

The only California Wines sold at these Concerts.

❧❧

THE CODMAN & HALL CO.,
Opposite the South Union Station.

Sole Agents for New England.

IND. COOPE & CO.'S English Ale.

THE SECOND LARGEST BREWERY IN ENGLAND.

Brewers of the finest *light quality* ale. Very highly endorsed by the medical profession. : : : : :

❧❧

THE CODMAN & HALL CO.,
Opposite South Union Station.

Sole Agents for the United States.

DRIN only th

PURE

WHIS

If you want p and richne flavor, try only gen and origin

OLD KENTU TAYLOR.

Eight years old own distillatio guaranteed p Bottled and shi direct from warehouses by None genuine out our signa on both labels ware of imitat For consump indigestion, an ailments requi stimulants, O KENTUCKY T LOR has superior.
Sold by all class drugs grocers, and li dealers.

Wright & Tay Distillers, Fine Kentuc Whiskies, Louisville, K

Hirshfield & New Englan Agents, 31 Doane Stre Boston.

Instruct your waiter to bring a bottle of **Pfaff's "Monogram" Lager.**

If you will do this, it will not be necessary for us to expatiate upon the good qualities of our production.
YOU CAN JUDGE FOR YOURSELF.

H. & J. PFAFF BREWING COMPANY,
Telephone 2608.   16 ARCH STREET, BOSTON.

TRY THE "COLUMBIA BRAND" VIENNA SAUSAGES. SERVED HOT OR COLD AT THESE CONCERTS.

They cannot sell you here
Canadian Club Whisky,
Ruinart Champagne,
Royal Liqueur Scotch,
Carstair's Philadelphia Rye,
Fort Hill Bourbon,
Alhambra Sherry,
All of which you will find
of excellent quality;

But you can get

Kaiser Water,

the most refreshing of all
table waters,

Chateau d'Arsac Claret,
N. Johnston & Sons' Medoc,
and
California Inglenook Clarets.

SUPPLIED BY

CODMAN & HALL COMPANY,

WINE MERCHANTS,

Opposite New South Station.

TUESDAY, JUNE 13.

PROGRAMME.

1. MARCH from "Le Prophète" . . . Meyerbeer
2. OVERTURE, "Fidelio" . . . Beethoven
3. GAVOTTE for String Orchestra . . . Bach
4. WALTZ, "Les Patineurs" . . . Waldteufel
5. OVERTURE, "William Tell" . . . Rossini
6. BALLET MUSIC from "Feramors" . . . Rubinstein
7. SPRING SONG . . . Mendelssohn
   The audience is respectfully requested to preserve silence during the performance of this number
8. AN EVENING WITH BILSE . . . Schertz
9. SELECTION, "Fencing Master" . . . De Koven
10. WALTZ, "Wine, Woman, and Song" . . . Strauss
11. HUSARENRITT . . . Spindler
12. MARCH, "King Cotton" . . . Sousa

COAL   Best Quality
         AT
         Lowest Prices

METROPOLITAN COAL COMPANY,
No. 30 Congress Street.

WILSON BELFAST GINGER ALE and **Champagne Kola** are sold at these concerts.

DRINK
WILSON CHAMPAGNE KOLA.

It produces energy, activity, and force. Its medical virtues are endorsed by physicians.

The **Wilson** is acknowledged to be America's purest spring water. Bottled only in glass at the spring, North Raymond, Me.

In making our BELFAST GINGER ALE we use only the purest ginger.

Beware of imitations.

Drink the Wilson and you are sure of the best.

Wilson Spring and Hotel Co.,
45 Arch Street.
Telephone 3129, Boston.   Boston, Mass.

"THE RECOGNIZED FAVORITE OF ALL BEERS."

THE ONLY BEER ON DRAUGHT AT THESE CONCERTS.

"the beer that's brewed"

Schlitz — THE BEER THAT MADE MILWAUKEE FAMOUS.

HIGHEST AWARD FOR PURITY.

Sold at these Concerts.   JOS. GAHM & CO., N.E. AGENTS, 125-127 PURCHASE ST.

THE FALL RIVER LINE

OCCUPYING THE
LONG ISLAND SOUND ROUTE
BETWEEN

Boston and New York

Has the finest quintette of great steamboats that the world has ever seen. The

Priscilla, Puritan, Plymouth, Pilgrim, and Providence

Are the largest, best equipped, safest, and handsomest steamboats ever constructed. This route is one of the most attractive and naturally beautiful traversed by any transportation agency in the world. Trips of the Fall River Line are made throughout the year. Each steamboat has its own orchestra, and the service on each member of the fleet is maintained at the highest possible standard.

Tickets via this route are on sale at all of the principal Ticket Offices in the United States.

From BOSTON. Trains, connecting with steamers at Fall River in 80 minutes, leave Park Square Station, New York, New Haven & Hartford Railroad (Old Colony System), daily at 6 p.m.

From NEW YORK. Steamers leave Pier 19, North River, foot of Warren Street, daily at 5.30 p.m.

S. A. GARDNER, Superintendent, NEW YORK.
GEO. L. CONNOR, Passenger Traffic Manager, NEW HAVEN, CONN.
O. H. TAYLOR, General Passenger Agent, NEW YORK CITY.

HOTEL LANGWOOD,

[Middlesex] Fells' Reservation.

P.O. Address, Melrose, Mass.   Wyoming Station, B. & M. R.R.

Twenty minutes by rail from Boston. Sixty trains daily. Hotel coaches meet trains each way. Four hundred feet above sea level. Beautiful rides, drives, and walks. Golf links, tennis courts, and ball grounds.

OPENS ABOUT MAY 20.

For plans and prices address:

F. W. GASKILL, Manager.

BOSTON OFFICE:
Hemenway Building, 10 Tremont Street, Room 29.

Third Season.

3 Ideal Outings

Personally conducted by
F. R. COMEE, Music Hall, Boston.

S.S. "Howard." Boston to Norfolk, 522 miles. Norfolk to Baltimore, 200 miles.

Boston	1. Leave July 2	2. July 15	3. August 19
	Arrive July 19	July 31	September 4

S.S. "Toronto." Toronto to Montreal, through the "Thousand Islands" and the "Rapids," 376 miles.

No. 1. Ten days. Saratoga, Lake George, 2,130 miles from Buffalo to Duluth, and return on the steamer "North-Land" through the Great Lakes, Erie, Huron, St. Clair, and Superior.

Nos. 2 and 3. Sixteen days. Exactly alike. 700 miles' ocean sail to Norfolk and Baltimore. Over Alleghany Mountains and a day in Chicago. Up Lake Michigan and three days at Mackinac Island. 1,546 miles on steamer "North-West" to Duluth and return to Buffalo through the Great Lakes. Niagara Falls to Toronto. Across Lake Ontario, through the Thousand Islands, and down the St. Lawrence River to Montreal and Boston.

SEND FOR CIRCULARS.

S.S. "Manitou." Chicago to Mackinac Island, across Lake Michigan, 350 miles.

"North-West." Mackinac Island to Duluth and return to Buffalo, 1,555 miles.

Allsopp's

ENGLISH ALE.
" The Red Hand Brand."

Protection for Ale Drinkers.

There is a strong and growing feeling abroad that all breweries should protect consumers by doing their own bottling. Allsopp's Ale is the only brand to-day that is bottled by its makers.

Sold at these concerts.

WEDNESDAY, JUNE 14.

PROGRAMME.

1. MARCH, " El Capitan " . . . . . Sousa
2. OVERTURE, " Masaniello " . . . . Auber
3. WALTZ, " Roses from the South " . . Strauss
4. WAR MARCH from " Rienzi " . . . Wagner

5. OVERTURE, " Mignon " . . . . . Thomas
6. HYMN TO ST. CECILIA . . . . . Gounod
   Violin Solo, Mr. ONDRICEK.
7. INTERMEZZO, " Naïla " . . . . . Delibes
8. HUNGARIAN RHAPSODY No. 12 . . Liszt
   (First Time)

9. SELECTION, " The Fortune-teller " . . Herbert
10. WALTZ, " Coquetry " . . . . . Waldteufel
11. MAZOURKA, " Libelle " . . . . . Strauss
12. MARCH, " Washington Post " . . . Sousa

The *only* Lithia Water sold at these concerts.

Hygeia Lithia Water

Sparkling and Still.

By its use you will avoid the germs of disease which natural MINERAL WATERS are liable to contain.

For Sale at these concerts and by

S. S. PIERCE CO.

FOR SALE AT THESE CONCERTS.
FAMOUS TANNHAEUSER EXPORT BEER

The finest Light Beer Extant.   Brewery Bottling.   Favorite of Connoisseurs.

Pure,   Palatable,   Perfect.
B. & E. Philadelphia Ale on Draught.
FOR SALE AT THESE CONCERTS.

The purity and keeping quality of the Tannhaeuser Export under all changes of temperature, its uniform excellence being guaranteed, together with its nutritious properties, make it the most pleasant, delicious, and convenient beverage for home consumption.
Put up in corked bottles, and packed in casks of 10 dozen white flint pints, and 6 dozen amber quarts.

Highest Awards wherever exhibited.

The BERGNER & ENGEL BREWING CO.'S N.E. Depot,
508 and 510 Atlantic Avenue, Boston.
Telephone 3805.   SOL. BACHARACH, Manager.

M. Steinert & Sons Co.,

STEINERT HALL BUILDING,

No. 162 Boylston Street, corner Carver, Boston.

STEINWAY & SONS,

HARDMAN,   GABLER,
EMERSON,   SINGER,

PIANOS.

The Æolian, Aeriol, Orchestrelle, and Pianola.

THE ÆOLIAN
AND
THE PIANOLA
FOR SUMMER HOMES.

At this season of the year we receive many orders for these instruments for Summer Residences, and therefore beg to call attention to our extensive assortment now on display, especially suited for this purpose.

The ÆOLIAN meets the requirements of country homes, furnishing, as it does, music suitable for every occasion. It practically takes the place of an orchestra — music for dancing — orchestral concerts, — in short, music of every style and description is always available.

The PIANOLA will appeal to many on account of the very little space it occupies. It will play any kind of a piano, and can also be used upon a rented piano without the slightest injury. For the above reasons it is bound to be very popular for small cottages.

We are glad to be able to announce that we can furnish PIANOLAS with no more than a week's delay, and, at times, the day the order is given.

Persons not familiar with these instruments are cordially invited to call at our warerooms and hear them, or a descriptive catalogue will be mailed free upon application.

M. STEINERT & SONS CO.,
Steinert Hall,   162 Boylston Street,   Boston.

ANHEUSER-BUSCH BREWING ASS'N,
ST. LOUIS, MO., U.S.A.
BREWERS OF HIGH=GRADE BEERS EXCLUSIVELY.

Black and Tan.   Faust.

Michelob.   Pale Lager.

Muenchener.   Anheuser Standard.

Served at the Music Hall Concerts.

Also at all first-class hotels, clubs, and bars, and on all Pullman and Wagner cars and ocean and lake steamers.

JACOB WIRTH,   Wholesale Dealer,   **Boston, Mass.**

THE MUSIC HALL PROMENADE CONCERTS

PUBLISHED BY
C. A. ELLIS,
MUSIC HALL.

BOSTON, MONDAY, JUNE 12, 1899.

SUMMER SEASON.
Vol. XIV. No. 30.

SMOKE "LA CELESTINA," THE BEST ALL-HAVANA CIGAR. DANIEL FRANK & CO.

SMOKE THE POPULAR "BARRISTER" CIGARS AT THE POPULAR CONCERTS.

YOU CAN

Have your last season's outfit dyed or cleansed and refinished so it will look like new, by our French process. Why discard soiled clothing when it can be overhauled and worn as second best? You can

RELY ON

Our methods of cleansing, and need not hesitate to trust us with article's of the most delicate textures.
We dye or cleanse and refinish PROPERLY, all materials of household use and clothing of all kinds.

LEWANDO'S

W. L. Crosby, General Manager.
French Cleansers, Fancy Dyers,
Fine Launderers.

PRINCIPAL OFFICES:
17 Temple Place, Boston.
479 Fifth Avenue, New York.
Established 70 years.
Largest in America.
Bundles called for and delivered.
Telephones in all offices.

In no other way

are men as wasteful and extravagant as in cigar smoking—because cigars are thrown away half smoked half the time.

BETWEEN THE ACTS Little Cigars

are just right for all short smokes. They light right, they burn right and taste right. Have you ever seen them? At all stores: 10 for 10 cts., or, as they are for sale here, you can try them to-night. Tell the waiter to bring you a 10-cent box of "Between the Acts." They will add to your enjoyment of this concert.

THE MUSIC HALL... Promenade Concerts
FOURTEENTH SEASON.

C. A. ELLIS, Manager.   F. R. COMEE, Assistant Manager.
Mr. GUSTAV STRUBE, Conductor.

MONDAY, JUNE 12.
WAGNER NIGHT.

PROGRAMME.

1. MARCH, "Nibelungen" . . . . . . Sonntag
2. WALTZ, "Thousand and One Nights" . . Strauss
3. TRÄUME . . . . Wagner
   (First Time.)
   Trumpet Solo, Mr. KLOEPFEL.
4. OVERTURE, "Rienzi" . . . . . Wagner
5. INTRODUCTION, Act III., "Tannhäuser" . Wagner
   (First Time.)
6. EVENING STAR . . . . Wagner
   Solo Trombone, Mr. HAMPE.
7. SAILORS' CHORUS from "The Flying Dutchman" . Wagner
8. PRELUDE to "Meistersinger" . . . . Wagner
9. PROCESSION OF WOMEN, from "Lohengrin" . Wagner
10. LOIN DU BAL . . . . Gillet
11. POLKA, " Puppenfee" . . . . . . Bayer
12. MARCH, "Stars and Stripes Forever" . . Sousa

Monday, June 19, Harvard Night.

To secure satisfactory service, patrons are URGED by the Management to report PROMPTLY any inattention. Complaints made so late that patrons cannot recall either the number of the table or the waiter are obviously useless.

Now the rage of the LONDON Concerts and Drawing-rooms:

YOU AND I, by Liza Lehmann, . . . 60c.
KING CHARLES, by M. V. White, . . 60c.
LIKE VIOLETS PALE, by F. Allitsen, . 60c.
WHEN THE WORLD IS FAIR, by F. H. Cowen, 60c.
QUEEN OF MY LIFE, by E. T. Lloyd, . 60c.

BOOSEY & CO.,
9 East 17th Street,   New York.

DRINK VAN NOSTRAND'S BOSTON CLUB LAGER
SOLD AT THESE CONCERTS

NORFOLK CABINET

LAGER BEER

A Particularly Fine Lager for Family Use and Clubs.
Bottled in the most careful manner at our own bottling department, and sold by the S. S. Pierce Co. and all other leading grocers in New England.

Other Brands in Bottles:
"Norfolk India Pale Stock Ale."
"Norfolk Extra Golden Ale" (blue label).
"Norfolk Standard Lager."
Our "Cabinets" and "Bismarck Brau" are the most popular refreshments at these concerts.

HABICH & CO.

H. W. HABICH, | Telephone, 56 Roxbury
EDWARD BUHL. | or 1152 Boston.

ESTABROOK & EATON'S MARGUERITE PERFECTOS, 10c. EACH.
CONCHAS, 10c., 3 FOR 25c.   SOLD AT THE "POPS."

THE ICE-CREAM SERVED AT THESE CONCERTS IS FURNISHED BY WEBER, 25 Temple Place and 33 West Street.

MUSIC HALL PROMENADE PROGRAMME.
PUBLISHED EVERY EVENING DURING THE SUMMER SEASON.

NOTICE TO ADVERTISERS.
The advertising columns in the Programme are controlled SOLELY by F. R. Comee, Boston Music Hall Box Office, to whom all communications should be addressed.

The United States Hotel,
SARATOGA SPRINGS, N.Y.

Under a continuous management for 25 years.

Without a peer in its appointments, service, and liberal management.

The largest structure of its kind in the world.

Built entirely of brick.

The Hotel and court cover over seven acres.

For further information, rates, etc., etc., address

GAGE & PERRY,
Proprietors,
UNITED STATES HOTEL,
Saratoga Springs, N.Y.

Colonial Beer...
The Beer that's Brewed in Glass.
PURE, CLEAN, PALATABLE.
Order a Bottle.
SOUTHER BREWING CO.,
919 Parker Street,
Roxbury, Mass.

VEUVE CHAFFARD

Pure Olive Oil.
IN HONEST BOTTLES.

The Peer of all Cigarettes.
Save the band-label on each box for valuable premiums.
::: ALSO :::

Monopol
High-grade Egyptian Cigarettes.

No. 8A Khedive,
No. 6A Nadine,
No. 9A Egyptian Belles,
No. 70A Princess Lillian

On sale at these concerts and all first-class dealers.

OCKENHEIMER BERG,
Near Bingen, GERMANY, On the Rhine.

PHILIP KRIM'S
OWN IMPORTATION OF
Rhine Wines.
FOR 30 YEARS AT
163 Shawmut Avenue.
OUR WINES SOLD AT THESE CONCERTS.

HERRICK, COPLEY SQUARE, Telephones 608 and 950 (Back Bay), CHOICE TABLES for Music Hall "Pops."

D. LEIDEN'S SPARKLING MOSELLE,

The only Sparkling Wine sold at these Concerts.

SHINNECOCK

The Perfection of

Scotch Whisky

Sold by
S. S. PIERCE COMPANY.

TUESDAY, JUNE 13.

PROGRAMME.

1. MARCH from "Le Prophète" . . . . Meyerbeer
2. OVERTURE, "Fidelio" . . . . Beethoven
3. GAVOTTE for String Orchestra . . . . Bach
4. WALTZ, "Les Patineurs" . . . . Waldteufel

5. OVERTURE, "William Tell" . . . . Rossini
6. BALLET MUSIC from "Feramors" . . . . Rubinstein
7. SPRING SONG . . . . Mendelssohn
   The audience is respectfully requested to preserve silence during the performance of this number
8. AN EVENING WITH BILSE . . . . Schertz

9. SELECTION, "Fencing Master" . . . . De Koven
10. WALTZ, "Wine, Woman, and Song" . . . . Strauss
11. HUSARENRITT . . . . Spindler
12. MARCH, "King Cotton" . . . . Sousa

THE HAYWARD,
16 and 22 Hayward Place.

LADIES' AND GENTS' CAFE.   Open until 1 a.m.

SCIARRETTA'S NEAPOLITAN TRIO give concerts daily from 6 p.m. until 1 a.m.

Signor SALVATORE SCIARRETTI, Lyric Tenor,
is highly endorsed by Vice-President Garret A. Hobart, Chauncey M. Depew, Eugene Ysaye, Raoul Pugno, Jean Gerardy, and many other prominent people

SMITH & KERRISSEY, Proprietors.

AN HISTORIC RESORT.

The loveliest place on the New England coast to spend a short vacation or the whole season is the

MYLES STANDISH HOTEL,
at SOUTH DUXBURY, MASS.

Everything that money and intelligence can do has been done to make this hotel better, if possible, than it was last season.

The greatest pains will be taken to have the table service absolutely excellent. Of the house itself and its surroundings too much cannot be said. It is a resort of nice people, who come year after year, gaining strength, vitality, and pleasure. Send for our 1899 booklet.

L. BOYER'S SONS, Proprietors,
27 Devonshire Street, Boston, Mass.,

Or ALFRED S. AMER, Manager,
90 Wall Street, New York
(Until June 1).

Myles Standish Hotel,
South Duxbury, Mass.

"AMERICA'S FINEST PRODUCT."

Bartholomay's "APOLLO"

LAGER BEER IN BOTTLES.

Sold at these Concerts.

ALBRECHT & KOELLNER,
SOLE AGENTS,

Telephone, Boston 1751.   295-305 A Street.

Also Agents for the "Crystal Rock" Mineral Water.

PURE BEER

BREW. CO'S $1000.00

PURE BEER

Sold at these Concerts,
IN BOTTLES ONLY
20¢ PER BOTTLE.

TABLE LINEN USED AT THESE CONCERTS LAUNDERED BY THE L. K. HUSTED LAUNDERING COMPANY, 27 and 29 BROADWAY, CHELSEA, MASS.

Inglenook Vineyard.

The only California Wines sold at these Concerts.

THE CODMAN & HALL CO.,
Opposite the South Union Station.

Sole Agents for New England.

IND. COOPE & CO.'S English Ale.

THE SECOND LARGEST BREWERY IN ENGLAND.

Brewers of the finest *light quality* ale. Very highly endorsed by the medical profession. : : : : :

THE CODMAN & HALL CO.,
Opposite South Union Station.

Sole Agents for the United States.

DRIN only the
PURE
WH[S]

If you want p
and richne
flavor, try
only gen u
and origin

OLD KENTU
TAYLOR,

Eight years old
own distillation
guaranteed p
Bottled and shi
direct from
warehouses by
None genuine v
out our signs
on both labels.
ware of imitati
For consump
indigestion, an
ailments requi
stimulants. O
KENTUCKY T
LOR has
superior.
Sold by all
class drugs
grocers, and li
dealers.

Wright & Tay
Distillers,
Fine Kentuck
Whiskies,
Louisville, K

Hirshfield &
New Englan
Agents,
31 Doane Stre
Boston.

Instruct your waiter to bring a bottle of **Pfaff's "Monogram" Lager.**

If you will do this, it will not be necessary for us to expatiate upon the good qualities of our production.
YOU CAN JUDGE FOR YOURSELF.

H. & J. PFAFF BREWING COMPANY,
Telephone 2608.   16 ARCH STREET, BOSTON.

TRY THE "COLUMBIA BRAND" VIENNA SAUSAGES. SERVED HOT OR COLD AT THESE CONCERTS.

They cannot sell you here
Canadian Club Whisky,
Ruinart Champagne,
Royal Liqueur Scotch,
Carstair's Philadelphia Rye,
Fort Hill Bourbon,
Alhambra Sherry,
All of which you will find
of excellent quality;

But you can get

Kaiser Water,

the most refreshing of all table waters.

*Chateau d'Arsac Claret,
N. Johnston & Sons' Medoc,*
and
California Inglenook Clarets.

SUPPLIED BY

CODMAN & HALL COMPANY,

WINE MERCHANTS,
Opposite New South Station.

WEDNESDAY, JUNE 14.

PROGRAMME.

1. MARCH, "El Capitan" — Sousa
2. OVERTURE, "Masaniello" — Auber
3. WALTZ, "Roses from the South" — Strauss
4. WAR MARCH from "Rienzi" — Wagner
5. OVERTURE, "Mignon" — Thomas
6. HYMN TO ST. CECILIA — Gounod
   Violin Solo, Mr. ONDRICEK.
7. INTERMEZZO, "Naila" — Delibes
8. HUNGARIAN RHAPSODY No. 12 — Liszt
   (First Time)
9. SELECTION, "The Fortune teller" — Herbert
10. WALTZ, "Coquetry" — Waldteufel
11. MAZOURKA, "Libelle" — Strauss
12. MARCH, "Washington Post" — Sousa

COAL

Best Quality
AT
Lowest Prices

METROPOLITAN COAL COMPANY,
No. 30 Congress Street.

WILSON BELFAST GINGER ALE
and
Champagne Kola
are sold at these concerts.

DRINK WILSON CHAMPAGNE KOLA.

It produces energy, activity, and force. Its medical virtues are endorsed by physicians.

The **Wilson** is acknowledged to be America's purest spring water. Bottled only in glass at the spring, North Raymond, Me.

In making our BELFAST GINGER ALE we use only the purest ginger.

Beware of imitations.

Drink the **Wilson** and you are sure of the best.

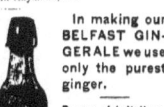

Wilson Spring and Hotel Co.,
45 Arch Street,
Telephone 3129, Boston. Boston, Mass.

"THE RECOGNIZED FAVORITE OF ALL BEERS."

Schlitz

THE BEER THAT MADE MILWAUKEE FAMOUS.

HIGHEST AWARD FOR PURITY.

Sold at these Concerts. JOS. GAHM & CO., N.E. AGENTS, 125-127 PURCHASE ST.

THE ONLY BEER ON DRAUGHT AT THESE CONCERTS.

"the beer that's brewed"

Rochester Brewing Co's

FAMOUS BOTTLED BEER

HOME OFFICE & BREWERY ROCHESTER, N.Y.
295-305 A STREET BOSTON
ENGLAND BRANCH

RIENZI, PREMIER, BOHEMIAN, BAVARIAN, STANDARD.

Free delivery in city and suburbs

THE FALL RIVER LINE

OCCUPYING THE
LONG ISLAND SOUND ROUTE
BETWEEN

Boston and New York

Has the finest quintette of great steamboats that the world has ever seen. The

Priscilla, Puritan, Plymouth, Pilgrim, and Providence

Are the largest, best equipped, safest, and handsomest steamboats ever constructed. This route is one of the most attractive and naturally beautiful traversed by any transportation agency in the world. Trips of the Fall River Line are made throughout the year. Each steamboat has its own orchestra, and the service on each member of the fleet is maintained at the highest possible standard.

Tickets via this route are on sale at all of the principal Ticket Offices in the United States.

From BOSTON. Trains connecting with steamers at Fall River in 80 minutes leave Park Square Station, New York, New Haven & Hartford Railroad (Old Colony System), daily at 6 p.m.

From NEW YORK. Steamers leave Pier 19, North River, foot of Warren Street, daily at 5.30 p.m.

S. A. GARDNER, Superintendent, NEW YORK.   GEO. L. CONNOR, Passenger Traffic Manager, NEW HAVEN, CONN.   O. H. TAYLOR, General Passenger Agent, NEW YORK CITY.

HOTEL LANGWOOD,

Middlesex Fells Reservation.

WYOMING STATION, B. & M. R.R.

NOW OPEN.

Twenty minutes by rail from Boston. Sixty trains daily. Hotel coaches meet trains each way. Four hundred feet above sea level. Beautiful rides, drives, and walks. Golf links, tennis courts, and ball grounds.

For plans and prices address:

F. W. GASKILL, Manager,

Telephone, 40 Melrose.   Melrose, Mass.

Third Season.

3 Ideal Outings

Personally conducted by
F. R. COMEE, Music Hall, Boston.

S.S. "Howard." Boston to Norfolk, 522 miles. Norfolk to Baltimore, 200 miles.

Boston	1.	2.	3.
Leave	July 2	July 15	August 19
Arrive	July 12	July 31	September 4

S.S. "Toronto." Toronto to Montreal, through the "Thousand Islands" and the "Rapids," 376 miles.

No. 1. Ten days. Saratoga, Lake George, 2,130 miles from Buffalo to Duluth, and return on the steamer "North-Land" through the Great Lakes, Erie, Huron, St. Clair, and Superior.

Nos. 2 and 3. Sixteen days. Exactly alike. 700 miles' ocean sail to Norfolk and Baltimore. Over Alleghany Mountains and a day in Chicago. Up Lake Michigan and three days at Mackinac Island. 1,546 miles on steamer "North-West" to Duluth and return to Buffalo through the Great Lakes. Niagara Falls to Toronto. Across Lake Ontario, through the Thousand Islands, and down the St. Lawrence River to Montreal and Boston.

SEND FOR CIRCULARS.

S.S. "Manitou." Chicago to Mackinac Island, across Lake Michigan, 350 miles.

"North-West." Mackinac Island to Duluth and return to Buffalo, 1,555 miles.

Allsopp's

ENGLISH ALE.
"The Red Hand Brand."

Protection for Ale Drinkers.

There is a strong and growing feeling abroad that all breweries should protect consumers by doing their own bottling. Allsopp's Ale is the only brand to-day that is bottled by its makers.

Sold at these concerts.

THURSDAY, JUNE 15.

PROGRAMME.

1. MARCH, "Merry War" — Strauss
2. OVERTURE, "Ruy Blas" — Mendelssohn
3. WALTZ, "Ocean Waves" — Metra
4. SELECTION, "Wizard of the Nile" — Herbert

---

5. OVERTURE, "Martha" — Flotow
6. LOVE SONG — Farwell
7. INTRODUCTION to Act III., "Lohengrin" — Wagner
8. CONGRESS OF MELODIES — Conradi

---

9. WALTZ, for String Orchestra — Keller
   (First Time.)
   The audience is respectfully requested to preserve silence during the performance of this number.
10. AMERICAN PATROL — Meacham
11. POLKA, "Hunter's Yarns" — Komzak
12. TABASCO MARCH — Chadwick

The *only* Lithia Water sold at these concerts.

Hygeia Lithia Water

Sparkling and Still.

By its use you will avoid the germs of disease which natural MINERAL WATERS are liable to contain.

For Sale at these concerts and by

S. S. PIERCE CO.

FOR SALE AT THESE CONCERTS.

FAMOUS TANNHAEUSER EXPORT BEER

The finest Light Beer Extant.   Brewery Bottling.   Favorite of Connoisseurs.

Pure,   Palatable,   Perfect.

B. & E. Philadelphia Ale on Draught.
FOR SALE AT THESE CONCERTS.

The BERGNER & ENGEL BREWING CO.'S N.E. Depot,
508 and 510 Atlantic Avenue, Boston.
Telephone 3805.   SOL. BACHARACH, Manager.

The purity and keeping quality of the Tannhaeuser Export under all changes of temperature, its uniform excellence being guaranteed, together with its nutritious properties, make it the most pleasant, delicious, and convenient beverage for home consumption.
Put up in corked bottles, and packed in casks of 10 dozen white flint pints, and 6 dozen amber quarts.

Highest Awards wherever exhibited.

M. Steinert & Sons Co.,
STEINERT HALL BUILDING,
No. 162 Boylston Street, corner Carver, Boston.

STEINWAY & SONS,

HARDMAN,   GABLER,
EMERSON,   SINGER,

PIANOS.

The Æolian, Aeriol, Orchestrelle, and Pianola.

THE ÆOLIAN
AND
THE PIANOLA
FOR SUMMER HOMES.

At this season of the year we receive many orders for these instruments for Summer Residences, and therefore beg to call attention to our extensive assortment now on display, especially suited for this purpose.

The ÆOLIAN meets the requirements of country homes, furnishing, as it does, music suitable for every occasion. It practically takes the place of an orchestra — music for dancing — orchestral concerts, — in short, music of every style and description is always available.

The PIANOLA will appeal to many on account of the very little space it occupies. It will play any kind of a piano, and can also be used upon a rented piano without the slightest injury. For the above reasons it is bound to be very popular for small cottages.

We are glad to be able to announce that we can furnish PIANOLAS with no more than a week's delay, and, at times, the day the order is given.

Persons not familiar with these instruments are cordially invited to call at our warerooms and hear them, or a descriptive catalogue will be mailed free upon application.

M. STEINERT & SONS CO.,
Steinert Hall,   162 Boylston Street,   Boston.

ANHEUSER-BUSCH BREWING ASS'N,
ST. LOUIS, MO., U.S.A.

BREWERS OF HIGH=GRADE BEERS EXCLUSIVELY.

Black and Tan.   Faust.

Michelob.   Pale Lager.

Muenchener.   Anheuser Standard.

Served at the Music Hall Concerts.
Also at all first-class hotels, clubs, and bars, and on all Pullman and Wagner cars and ocean and lake steamers.

JACOB WIRTH,   **Wholesale Dealer,**   **Boston, Mass.**

SMOKE "LA CELESTINA," THE BEST ALL-HAVANA CIGAR. DANIEL FRANK & CO.

SMOKE THE POPULAR "BARRISTER" CIGARS AT THE POPULAR CONCERTS.

THE MUSIC HALL
PROMENADE CONCERTS

PUBLISHED BY
C. A. ELLIS,
MUSIC HALL.

BOSTON, TUESDAY, JUNE 13, 1899.

SUMMER SEASON.
Vol. XIV. No. 31.

YOU CAN

Have your last season's outfit dyed or cleansed and refinished so it will look like new, by our French process. Why discard soiled clothing when it can be overhauled and worn as second best? You can

RELY ON

Our methods of cleansing, and need not hesitate to trust us with articles of the most delicate textures.
We dye or cleanse and refinish PROPERLY, *all* materials of household use and clothing of all kinds.

LEWANDO'S

W. L. Crosby, General Manager.
French Cleansers, Fancy Dyers, Fine Launderers.

PRINCIPAL OFFICES:
17 Temple Place, Boston.
479 Fifth Avenue, New York.
*Established 70 years.
Largest in America.*
Bundles called for and delivered.
Telephones in all offices.

If you are open
to conviction,
to-night

try one 10-cent box of

BETWEEN THE ACTS
Little Cigars

to smoke now—or at any time when you want a short smoke and haven't time for a long one. They are real cigars, but small ones.

They cost so little that you can use them every day as well as not and actually save on your daily cigar expense by substituting them for larger cigars.

FOR SALE HERE.

THE MUSIC HALL... Promenade Concerts
FOURTEENTH SEASON.

C. A. ELLIS, Manager.   F. R. COMEE, Assistant Manager.

Mr. GUSTAV STRUBE, Conductor.

TUESDAY, JUNE 13.

PROGRAMME.

1. MARCH from "Le Prophète" . . . . . Meyerbeer.
2. OVERTURE, "Fidelio" . . . . . Beethoven
3. GAVOTTE for String Orchestra . . . Bach
4. WALTZ, "Les Patineurs" . . . . . Waldteufel
5. OVERTURE, "William Tell" . . . . Rossini
6. BALLET MUSIC from "Feramors" . . . Rubinstein
7. SPRING SONG . . . . . . Mendelssohn
   The audience is respectfully requested to preserve silence during the performance of this number.
8. AN EVENING WITH BILSE . . . Schertz
9. SELECTION, "Fencing Master" . . . De Koven
10. WALTZ, "Wine, Woman, and Song" . . Strauss
11. HUSARENRITT . . . . . . Spindler
12. MARCH, "King Cotton" . . . . . Sousa

Monday, June 19, Harvard Night.

To secure satisfactory service, patrons are URGED by the Management to report PROMPTLY any inattention. Complaints made so late that patrons cannot recall either the number of the table or the waiter are obviously useless.

HERE ARE A FEW NAMES FROM OUR LIST OF COMPOSERS:

ENGLISH.— Stephen Adams, F. H. Cowen, S. Liddle, C. V. Stanford, A. C. Mackenzie, R. H. Walthew, H. R. Shelley, Goring Thomas, Frances Allitsen, Maude V. White, Edward German, Mary Carmichael, Liza Lehmann, etc.

FRENCH.— C. Chaminade, Jane Vieu, L. Denza, P. Delmet, Bemberg, Guy d'Hardelot, De Leva, F. P. Tosti, etc.

ITALIAN.— F. P. Tosti, P. Mascagni, G. Puccini, G. Verdi, Don Lorenzo Perosi, etc.

THE MOST REPRESENTATIVE PUBLISHING HOUSE IN AMERICA.

BOOSEY & CO., 9 East 17th Street, New York.

BEST BEER BREWED

"OH BE JOLLY"

DRINK VAN NOSTRAND'S P. B. ALE

SOLD AT THESE CONCERTS

NORFOLK CABINET
LAGER BEER

A Particularly Fine Lager for Family Use and Clubs.

Bottled in the most careful manner at our own bottling department, and sold by the S. S. Pierce Co. and all other leading grocers in New England.

Other Brands in Bottles:
"Norfolk India Pale Stock Ale"
"Norfolk Extra Golden Ale" (blue label).
"Norfolk Standard Lager."
Our "Cabinet" and "Bismarck Brau" are the most popular refreshments at these concerts.

HABICH & CO.

H. W. HABICH,   Telephone, 56 Roxbury
EDWARD RUHL.   or 1152 Boston.

ESTABROOK & EATON'S MARGUERITE PERFECTOS, 10c. EACH. CONCHAS, 10c., 3 FOR 25c., **SOLD AT THE "POPS."**

THE ICE-CREAM SERVED AT THESE CONCERTS IS FURNISHED BY **WEBER**, 25 Temple Place and 33 West Street.

MUSIC HALL PROMENADE PROGRAMME.

PUBLISHED EVERY EVENING DURING THE SUMMER SEASON.

NOTICE TO ADVERTISERS.

The advertising columns in the Programme are controlled SOLELY by F. R. Comee, Boston Music Hall Box Office, to whom all communications should be addressed.

The United States Hotel,

SARATOGA SPRINGS, N.Y.

Under a continuous management for 25 years.

Without a peer in its appointments, service, and liberal management.

The largest structure of its kind in the world.

Built entirely of brick.

The Hotel and court cover over seven acres.

For further information, rates, etc., address

GAGE & PERRY,
Proprietors,
UNITED STATES HOTEL,
Saratoga Springs, N.Y.

The Beer that's Brewed in Glass.

Colonial Beer...

PURE, CLEAN, PALATABLE.

Order a Bottle.

SOUTHER BREWING CO.,
919 Parker Street,
Roxbury, Mass.

All The **IMPORTED CIGARS**

Sold At These Concerts Are Supplied By The

S. S. PIERCE COMPANY.

The Peer of all Cigarettes.

Save the band-label on each box for valuable premiums.

::: ALSO :::

Monopol

High-grade Egyptian Cigarettes

No. 8½ Khedive,
No. 6½ Nadine,
No. 9A Egyptian Belles,
No. 7½ Princess Lillian

On sale at these concerts and all first-class dealers.

OCKENHEIMER BERG,
Near Bingen, GERMANY. On the Rhine.

PHILIP KRIM'S
OWN IMPORTATION OF
Rhine Wines.
FOR 30 YEARS
AT
163 Shawmut Avenue.
OUR WINES SOLD AT THESE CONCERTS.

HERRICK, COPLEY SQUARE, Telephones 608 and 950 (Back Bay), CHOICE TABLES for Music Hall "Pops."

GREAT WESTERN
CHAMPAGNE

—————— A natural,
genuine champagne, of
the finest quality pro-
duced in America.

Sold by Wine Merchants,
Grocers, and Druggists.

WEDNESDAY, JUNE 14.

PROGRAMME.

1. MARCH, "El Capitan" . . . . Sousa
2. OVERTURE, "Masaniello" . . . . . Auber
3. WALTZ, "Roses from the South" . . . Strauss
4. WAR MARCH from "Rienzi" . . . . Wagner
5. OVERTURE, "Mignon" . . . . . . Thomas
6. HYMN TO ST. CECILIA . . . . . Gounod
   Violin Solo, Mr. ONDRICEK.
7. INTERMEZZO, "Naila" . . . . . . Delibes
8. HUNGARIAN RHAPSODY No. 12 . . . Liszt
   (First Time)
9. SELECTION, "The Fortune-teller" . . Herbert
10. WALTZ, "Coquetry" . . . . . . Waldteufel
11. MAZOURKA, "Libelle" . . . . . Strauss
12. MARCH, "Washington Post" . . . . Sousa

THE HAYWARD,
16 and 22 Hayward Place.
LADIES' AND GENTS' CAFE.   Open until 1 a.m.
Table d'hôte dinner, including bottle of wine, 75c.,
served from 5 to 8.30 P.M.

SCIARRETTA'S NEAPOLITAN TRIO give concerts daily
from 6 P.M. until 1 A.M.
Signor SALVATORE SCIARRETTI, Lyric Tenor,
Is highly endorsed by Vice-President Garret A. Hobart, Chauncey M. Depew,
Eugene Ysaye, Raoul Pugno, Jean Gerardy, and many other prominent people.

SMITH & KERRISSEY, Proprietors.

AN
HISTORIC
RESORT.

The loveliest place on the New
England coast to spend a short
vacation or the whole season is the

MYLES STANDISH HOTEL,
at SOUTH DUXBURY, MASS.

Everything that money and intelligence can do has been done to make
this hotel better, if possible, than it
was last season.
The greatest pains will be taken
to have the table service absolutely
excellent. Of the house itself and
its surroundings too much cannot
be said. It is a resort of nice people,
who come year after year, gaining
strength, vitality, and pleasure.
Send for our 1899 booklet.

L. BOYER'S SONS, Proprietors,
27 Devonshire Street, Boston, Mass.,
Or ALFRED S. AMER, Manager,
90 Wall Street, New York
(Until June 1).

Myles Standish Hotel,
South Duxbury, Mass.

"AMERICA'S FINEST PRODUCT."
Bartholomay's "APOLLO"
LAGER BEER IN BOTTLES.

Sold at these Concerts.

ALBRECHT & KOELLNER,
SOLE AGENTS,
Telephone, Boston 1751.   295-305 A Street.

Also Agents for the "Crystal Rock" Mineral Water.

PURE BEER

BREW. CO'S $1000.⁰⁰
PURE BEER
Sold at these Concerts,
IN BOTTLES ONLY
20¢ PER BOTTLE.

Inglenook Vineyard.

The only California Wines sold at these Concerts.

❦❦

THE CODMAN & HALL CO.,
Opposite the South Union Station.

Sole Agents for New England.

IND. COOPE & CO.'S English Ale.

THE SECOND LARGEST BREWERY IN ENGLAND.

Brewers of the finest *light quality* ale. Very highly endorsed by the medical profession. : : : :

❦❦

THE CODMAN & HALL CO.,
Opposite South Union Station.

Sole Agents for the United States.

DRINK only the PUREST WHISK

If you want pu and richness flavor, try only genu and original

OLD KENTUC TAYLOR,

Eight years old, own distillation guaranteed pu Bottled and ship direct from warehouses by None genuine w out our signa on both labels. ware of imitati For consumpt indigestion and ailments requi stimulants, O KENTUCKY T. L O R ha superior.

Sold by all fi c l a s s drugg grocers, and li dealers.

Wright & Tay Distillers, Fine Kentuck Whiskies, Louisville, Ky

Hirshfield & New Englan Agents, 31 Doane Stre Boston.

Instruct your waiter to bring a bottle of **Pfaff's "Monogram" Lager.**

If you will do this, it will not be necessary for us to expatiate upon the good qualities of our production.
YOU CAN JUDGE FOR YOURSELF.

H. & J. PFAFF BREWING COMPANY,
Telephone 2608.   16 ARCH STREET, BOSTON.

TRY THE "COLUMBIA BRAND" VIENNA SAUSAGES. SERVED HOT OR COLD AT THESE CONCERTS.

They cannot sell you here
Canadian Club Whisky,
Ruinart Champagne,
Royal Liqueur Scotch,
Carstair's Philadelphia Rye,
Fort Hill Bourbon,
Alhambra Sherry,
All of which you will find
of excellent quality;

But you can get

Kaiser Water,

the most refreshing of all
table waters,

Chateau d'Arsac Claret,
N. Johnston & Sons' Medoc,
and
California Inglenook Clarets.

SUPPLIED BY

CODMAN & HALL COMPANY,

WINE MERCHANTS,

Opposite New South Station.

THURSDAY, JUNE 15.

PROGRAMME.

1. MARCH, "Merry War" . . . . Strauss
2. OVERTURE, "Ruy Blas" . . . . Mendelssohn
3. WALTZ, "Ocean Waves" . . . . Metra
4. SELECTION, "Wizard of the Nile" . . . Herbert

5. OVERTURE, "Martha" . . . . Flotow
6. LOVE SONG, (from an unfinished suite) . Farwell
7. INTRODUCTION to Act III. "Lohengrin" Wagner
8. CONGRESS OF MELODIES . . . . Conradi
9. (a) ELEGIE
   (b) SERENADE } for String Orchestra . . Strube
   (First Time.)
   The audience is respectfully requested to preserve silence during the performance of this number.
10. AMERICAN PATROL . . . . Meacham
11. POLKA, "Hunter's Yarns" . . . . Kumzak
12. TABASCO MARCH . . . . Chadwick

COAL — Best Quality AT Lowest Prices

METROPOLITAN COAL COMPANY,
No. 30 Congress Street.

WILSON BELFAST GINGER ALE

and **Champagne Kola** are sold at these concerts.

DRINK WILSON CHAMPAGNE KOLA.

It produces energy, activity, and force. Its medical virtues are endorsed by physicians.

The **Wilson** is acknowledged to be America's purest spring water. Bottled only in glass at the spring, North Raymond, Me.

In making our BELFAST GINGER ALE we use only the purest ginger.

Beware of Imitations.

Drink the **Wilson** and you are sure of the best.

Wilson Spring and Hotel Co.,

45 Arch Street.

Telephone 3129, Boston. Boston, Mass.

"THE RECOGNIZED FAVORITE OF ALL BEERS."

Sold at these Concerts. JOS. GAHM & CO., N.E. AGENTS, 125-127 PURCHASE ST.

THE ONLY BEER ON DRAUGHT AT THESE CONCERTS.

"the beer that's brewed"

THE FALL RIVER LINE

OCCUPYING THE
LONG ISLAND SOUND ROUTE
BETWEEN

Boston and New York

Has the finest quintette of great steamboats that the world has ever seen. The

Priscilla, Puritan, Plymouth, Pilgrim, and Providence

Are the largest, best equipped, safest, and handsomest steamboats ever constructed. This route is one of the most attractive and naturally beautiful traversed by any transportation agency in the world. Trips of the Fall River Line are made throughout the year.

Each steamboat has its own orchestra, and the service on each member of the fleet is maintained at the highest possible standard.

Tickets via this route are on sale at all of the principal Ticket Offices in the United States.

From BOSTON. Trains, connecting with steamers at Fall River in 80 minutes leave Park Square Station, New York, New Haven & Hartford Railroad (Old Colony System), daily at 6 p.m.

From NEW YORK. Steamers leave Pier 19, North River, foot of Warren Street, daily at 5.30 p.m.

S. A. GARDNER,   GEO. L. CONNOR,   O. H. TAYLOR,
Superintendent,   Passenger Traffic Manager,   General Passenger Agent,
NEW YORK.   NEW HAVEN, CONN.   NEW YORK CITY.

HOTEL LANGWOOD,

Middlesex Fells Reservation.

WYOMING STATION, B. & M. R.R.

NOW OPEN.

Twenty minutes by rail from Boston. Sixty trains daily. Hotel coaches meet trains each way. Four hundred feet above sea level. Beautiful rides, drives, and walks. Golf links, tennis courts, and ball grounds.

For plans and prices address:

F. W. GASKILL, Manager,

Telephone, 40 Melrose.   Melrose, Mass.

S.S. "Howard." Boston to Norfolk, 522 miles. Norfolk to Baltimore, 200 miles.

    1.   **2.**   **3.**

Boston | Leave | July 3 | July 15 | August 19
        | Arrive | July 12 | July 31 | September 4

S.S. "Toronto." Toronto to Montreal, through the "Thousand Islands" and the "Rapids," 376 miles.

Third Season.

3 Ideal Outings

Personally conducted by
F. R. COMEE, Music
Hall, Boston.

No. 1. Ten days. **Saratoga, Lake George.** 2,130 miles from Buffalo to Duluth, and return on the steamer "North-Land" through the **Great Lakes, Erie, Huron, St. Clair, and Superior.**

Nos. 2 and 3. Sixteen days. Exactly alike. 700 miles' ocean sail to **Norfolk** and **Baltimore.** Over Alleghany Mountains and a day in Chicago. Up Lake Michigan and three days at **Mackinac Island.** 1,546 miles on steamer "North-West" to **Duluth** and return to Buffalo through the **Great Lakes. Niagara Falls** to **Toronto.** Across Lake Ontario, through the Thousand Islands, and down the St. Lawrence River to **Montreal** and **Boston.**

SEND FOR CIRCULARS.

S.S. "Manitou." Chicago to Mackinac Island, across Lake Michigan, 350 miles.

"North-West." Mackinac Island to Duluth and return to Buffalo, 1,555 miles.

Allsopp's

ENGLISH ALE.
"The Red Hand Brand."

Protection for Ale Drinkers.

There is a strong and growing feeling abroad that all breweries should protect consumers by doing their own bottling. Allsopp's Ale is the only brand to-day that is bottled by its makers.

Sold at these concerts.

FRIDAY, JUNE 16.

PROGRAMME.

1. MARCH, " King Karl " . . . . Eilenberg
2. OVERTURE, " Stradella " . . . . . . Flotow
3. WALTZ, " Doctrinen " . . . . Strauss
4. SELECTION, " Faust " . . . . Gounod
5. INTRODUCTION to " Lohengrin " . . . Wagner
6. TWO MOVEMENTS from " Bal Costume " . Rubinstein
7. LE DÉLUGE . . . . Saint-Saens
   Solo Violin, Mr. ONDRICEK.
   The audience is respectfully requested to preserve silence during the performance of this number.
8. AUBADE PRINTANIÈRE . . . . Lacome
9. NOCTURNE AND WEDDING MARCH . . . Mendelssohn
10. ESTUDIANTINA . . . . Waldteufel
11. POLKA, " Rosebuds " . . . . Eilenberg
12. MARCH, " Wien, bleibt Wien " . . . . Schrammel

The *only* Lithia Water sold at these concerts.

Hygeia Lithia Water

Sparkling and Still.

By its use you will avoid the germs of disease which natural MINERAL WATERS are liable to contain.

For Sale at these concerts and by

S. S. PIERCE CO.

FOR SALE AT THESE CONCERTS.

FAMOUS TANNHAEUSER EXPORT BEER

The finest Light Beer Extant.   Brewery Bottling.   Favorite of Connoisseurs.

Pure,   Palatable,   Perfect.

B. & E. Philadelphia Ale on Draught.

FOR SALE AT THESE CONCERTS.

The purity and keeping quality of the Tannhaeuser Export under all changes of temperature, its uniform excellence being guaranteed, together with its nutritious properties, make it the most pleasant, delicious, and convenient beverage for home consumption.
Put up in corked bottles, and packed in casks of 10 dozen white flint pints, and 6 dozen amber quarts.

Highest Awards wherever exhibited.

The BERGNER & ENGEL BREWING CO.'S N.E. Depot,

508 and 510 Atlantic Avenue, Boston.

Telephone 3805.   SOL. BACHARACH, Manager.

M. Steinert & Sons Co.,

STEINERT HALL BUILDING,

No. 162 Boylston Street, corner Carver, Boston.

STEINWAY & SONS,

HARDMAN,   GABLER,
EMERSON,   SINGER,

PIANOS.

The Æolian, Aeriol, Orchestrelle, and Pianola.

THE ÆOLIAN
AND
THE PIANOLA
FOR SUMMER HOMES.

At this season of the year we receive many orders for these instruments for Summer Residences, and therefore beg to call attention to our extensive assortment now on display, especially suited for this purpose.

The ÆOLIAN meets the requirements of country homes, furnishing, as it does, music suitable for every occasion. It practically takes the place of an orchestra — music for dancing — orchestral concerts, — in short, music of every style and description is always available.

The PIANOLA will appeal to many on account of the very little space it occupies. It will play any kind of a piano, and can also be used upon a rented piano without the slightest injury. For the above reasons it is bound to be very popular for small cottages.

We are glad to be able to announce that we can furnish PIANOLAS with no more than a week's delay, and, at times, the day the order is given.

Persons not familiar with these instruments are cordially invited to call at our warerooms and hear them, or a descriptive catalogue will be mailed free upon application.

M. STEINERT & SONS CO.,
Steinert Hall,   162 Boylston Street,   Boston.

ANHEUSER-BUSCH BREWING ASS'N,

ST. LOUIS, MO., U.S.A.

BREWERS OF HIGH-GRADE BEERS EXCLUSIVELY.

Black and Tan.

Michelob.

Muenchener.

Faust.

Pale Lager.

Anheuser Standard.

Served at the Music Hall Concerts.

Also at all first-class hotels, clubs, and bars, and on all Pullman and Wagner cars and ocean and lake steamers.

JACOB WIRTH,   Wholesale Dealer,   Boston, Mass.

THE MUSIC HALL

Promenade Concerts

PUBLISHED BY
C. A. ELLIS,
MUSIC HALL.

BOSTON, WEDNESDAY, JUNE 14, 1899.

SUMMER SEASON.
Vol. XIV. No. 32.

SMOKE "LA CELESTINA," THE BEST ALL-HAVANA CIGAR. DANIEL FRANK & CO.

SMOKE THE POPULAR "BARRISTER" CIGARS AT THE POPULAR CONCERTS.

YOU CAN

Have your last season's outfit dyed or cleansed and refinished so it will look like new, by our French process. Why discard soiled clothing when it can be overhauled and worn as second best? You can

RELY ON

Our methods of cleansing, and need not hesitate to trust us with articles of the most delicate textures.

We dye or cleanse and refinish PROPERLY, *all* materials of household use and clothing of all kinds.

LEWANDO'S

W. L. Crosby, General Manager.
French Cleansers, Fancy Dyers,
Fine Launderers.

PRINCIPAL OFFICES:
17 Temple Place, Boston.
479 Fifth Avenue, New York.
*Established 70 years.
Largest in America.*
Bundles called for and delivered.
Telephones in all offices.

Knowledge
Experience. *differs from*

You may know "all about"

BETWEEN
THE ACTS
Little Cigars

but have you ever tried them yourself? Do you know how desirable they really are—how good they are—how economical they are—how convenient they are—how satisfactory they are? You can know—once for all—by having the waiter bring you a 10-cent box of ten—to smoke now—to-night—while you are enjoying this concert. They are for sale here.

THE MUSIC HALL.. Promenade Concerts

FOURTEENTH SEASON.

C. A. ELLIS, Manager.   F. R. COMEE, Assistant Manager.
Mr. GUSTAV STRUBE, Conductor.

WEDNESDAY, JUNE 14.

PROGRAMME.

1. MARCH, " El Capitan "	. . .	Sousa
2. OVERTURE, " Massaniello "	.	Auber
3. WALTZ, " Roses from the South "	.	Strauss
4. WAR MARCH from " Rienzi "	. .	Wagner
5. OVERTURE, " Mignon "	. .	Thomas
6. HYMN TO ST. CECILIA	. . .	Gounod
	Violin Solo, Mr. ONDRICEK.	
7. INTERMEZZO, " Naila "	. . .	Delibes
8. HUNGARIAN RHAPSODY No. 12	.	Liszt
	(First Time.)	
9. SELECTION, "The Fortune-teller "	.	Herbert
10. WALTZ, " Coquetry "	. . .	Waldteufel
11. MAZOURKA, " Libelle "	.	Strauss
12. MARCH, " Washington Post "	.	Sousa

Monday, June 19, Harvard Night.

To secure satisfactory service, patrons are URGED by the Management to report PROMPTLY any inattention. Complaints made so late that patrons cannot recall either the number of the table or the waiter are obviously useless.

ALBUMS OF SONGS,

Containing many popular compositions not published in single form.

IRISH FOLK SONGS, by Charles Wood,	$2.00
RUSSIAN SONGS, by F. Wishaw (2 vols.),	1.00
NINE SONGS, by S. Liddle,	1.00
NINE SONGS, by Liza Lehmann,	1.00
FIVE SONGS, by Francis Korbay,	2.00

Beautifully illustrated by J. S. SARGENT, R.A.

BOOSEY & CO.,
9 East 17th Street,   **New York.**

DRINK
VAN NOSTRAND'S
**BOSTON
CLUB
LAGER**
SOLD AT THESE CONCERTS

NORFOLK CABINET

LAGER BEER

A Particularly Fine Lager for Family Use and Clubs.

Bottled in the most careful manner at our own bottling department, and sold by the S. S. Pierce Co. and all other leading grocers in New England.

Other Brands in Bottles :
" Norfolk India Pale Stock Ale."
" Norfolk Extra Golden Ale " (blue label).
" Norfolk Standard Lager."
Our " Cabinet " and " Bismarck Bracu " are the most popular refreshments at these concerts.

HABICH & CO.

H. W. HABICH,   Telephone, 56 Roxbury
EDWARD HUHL.   or 1152 Boston.

ESTABROOK & EATON'S MARGUERITE PERFECTOS, 10c. EACH.
CONCHAS, 10c., 3 FOR 25c., SOLD AT THE " POPS."

THE ICE-CREAM SERVED AT THESE CONCERTS IS FURNISHED BY **WEBER,** 25 Temple Place and 33 West Street.

MUSIC HALL PROMENADE PROGRAMME.

PUBLISHED EVERY EVENING DURING THE SUMMER SEASON.

NOTICE TO ADVERTISERS.

The advertising columns in the Programme are controlled SOLELY by F. R. Comee, Boston Music Hall Box Office, to whom all communications should be addressed.

The United States Hotel,

SARATOGA SPRINGS, N.Y.

Under a continuous management for 25 years.

Without a peer in its appointments, service, and liberal management.

The largest structure of its kind in the world.

Built entirely of brick.

The Hotel and court cover over seven acres.

For further information, rates, etc., etc., address

GAGE & PERRY,
Proprietors,
UNITED STATES HOTEL,
Saratoga Springs, N.Y.

Colonial Beer...

The Beer that's Brewed in Glass.

PURE, CLEAN, PALATABLE.

Order a Bottle.

SOUTHER BREWING CO.,
919 Parker Street,
Roxbury, Mass.

VEUVE CHAFFARD

PURE OLIVE OIL.

IN HONEST BOTTLES.

The Peer of all Cigarettes.

Save the band-label on each box for valuable premiums.

::: ALSO :::

Monopol

High-grade Egyptian Cigarettes.

No. 8A Khedive,
No. 9A Nadine,
No. 9A Egyptian Belles,
No. 70A Princess Lillian

On sale at these concerts and all first-class dealers.

OCKENHEIMER BERG, Near Bingen, GERMANY, On the Rhine.

PHILIP KRIM'S OWN IMPORTATION OF **Rhine Wines,** FOR 30 YEARS AT **163 Shawmut Avenue.** OUR WINES SOLD AT THESE CONCERTS.

HERRICK, COPLEY SQUARE, Telephones 608 and 950 (Back Bay), CHOICE TABLES for Music Hall "Pops."

D. LEIDEN'S
SPARKLING
MOSELLE,

The only Sparkling Wine sold at these Concerts.

SHINNECOCK

The Perfection of

Scotch
Whisky

Sold by
S. S. PIERCE COMPANY.

THURSDAY, JUNE 15.

PROGRAMME.

1. MARCH, " Merry War " . . . . Strauss
2. OVERTURE, " Ruy Blas " . . . Mendelssohn
3. WALTZ, " Ocean Waves " . . . . Metra
4. SELECTION, " Wizard of the Nile " . . Herbert
5. OVERTURE, " Martha " . . . . Flotow
6. LOVE SONG (from an unfinished suite) . . Farwell
7. INTRODUCTION to Act III., " Lohengrin " . Wagner
8. CONGRESS OF MELODIES . . . Conradi
9. (a) ELEGIE . } for String Orchestra Strube
   (b) SERENADE }
   (First Time.)
   The audience is respectfully requested to preserve silence during the performance of this number.
10. AMERICAN PATROL . . . . Meecham
11. POLKA, " Hunter's Yarns " . . . Komzak
12. TABASCO MARCH . . . . . Chadwick

THE HAYWARD,
16 and 22 Hayward Place.
LADIES' AND GENTS' CAFE.   Open until 1 a.m.
Table d'hote dinner, including bottle of wine, 75c.,
served from 5 to 8.30 P.M.

SCIARRETTA'S NEAPOLITAN TRIO give concerts daily
from 6 P.M. until 1 A.M.
Signor SALVATORE SCIARRETTI, Lyric Tenor,
Is highly endorsed by Vice-President Garret A. Hobart, Chauncey M. Depew, Eugene Ysaye, Raoul Pugno, Jean Gerardy, and many other prominent people.
SMITH & KERRISSEY, Proprietors.

AN
HISTORIC
RESORT.

The loveliest place on the New England coast to spend a short vacation or the whole season is the

MYLES STANDISH HOTEL,
at SOUTH DUXBURY, MASS.

Everything that money and intelligence can do has been done to make this hotel better, if possible, than it was last season.
The greatest pains will be taken to have the table service absolutely excellent. Of the house itself and its surroundings too much cannot be said. It is a resort of nice people, who come year after year, gaining strength, vitality, and pleasure.
Send for our 1899 booklet.

L. BOYER'S SONS, Proprietors,
27 Devonshire Street, Boston, Mass.,
Or ALFRED S. AMER, Manager,
90 Wall Street, New York
(Until June 1).
Myles Standish Hotel,
South Duxbury, Mass.

"AMERICA'S FINEST PRODUCT."

Bartholomay's "APOLLO"

LAGER BEER IN BOTTLES.

Sold at these Concerts.

ALBRECHT & KOELLNER,
SOLE AGENTS,
Telephone, Boston 1751.   295-305 A Street.

Also Agents for the "Crystal Rock" Mineral Water.

PURE BEER
Harvard
BREW. CO'S $1000.00
PURE BEER
Sold at these Concerts,
IN BOTTLES ONLY
20¢ PER BOTTLE.

Inglenook Vineyard.

The only California Wines sold at these Concerts.

❦❦

THE CODMAN & HALL CO.,
Opposite the South Union Station.

Sole Agents for New England.

IND. COOPE & CO.'S English Ale.

THE SECOND LARGEST BREWERY IN ENGLAND.

Brewers of the finest *light quality* ale. Very highly endorsed by the medical profession. : : : : :

❦❦

THE CODMAN & HALL CO.,
Opposite South Union Station.

Sole Agents for the United States.

DRIN only th
PURE
WHIS

If you want p and richne flavor, try only genu and origin

OLD KENTU TAYLOR,

Eight years old own distillation guaranteed p Bottled and shi direct from warehouses by None genuine w out our sign on both labels. ware of imitati For consum indigestion, an ailments requi stimulants, O KENTUCKY T LOR has superior.
Sold by all class drug grocers, and li dealers.

Wright & Tay
Distillers,
Fine Kentuck
Whiskeys,
Louisville, K

Hirshfield &
New Englan
Agents,
31 Doane Stre
Boston.

Instruct your waiter to bring a bottle of **Pfaff's "Monogram" Lager.**

If you will do this, it will not be necessary for us to expatiate upon the good qualities of our production.
YOU CAN JUDGE FOR YOURSELF.

H. & J. PFAFF BREWING COMPANY,
Telephone 2608.   16 ARCH STREET, BOSTON.

TRY THE "COLUMBIA BRAND" VIENNA SAUSAGES. SERVED HOT OR COLD AT THESE CONCERTS.

They cannot sell you here
  Canadian Club Whisky,
  Ruinart Champagne,
  Royal Liqueur Scotch,
  Carstair's Philadelphia Rye,
  Fort Hill Bourbon,
  Alhambra Sherry,
All of which you will find of excellent quality;

But you can get

Kaiser Water,

the most refreshing of all table waters,

Chateau d'Arsac Claret,
N. Johnston & Sons' Medoc,
  and
California Inglenook Clarets.

SUPPLIED BY

CODMAN & HALL COMPANY,

WINE MERCHANTS,

Opposite New South Station.

FRIDAY, JUNE 16.

PROGRAMME.

1. MARCH, "King Karl" . . . . Eilenberg
2. OVERTURE, "Stradella" . . . . Flotow
3. WALTZ, "Doctrinen" . . . . Strauss
4. SELECTION, "Faust" . . . . Gounod
5. INTRODUCTION to "Lohengrin" . . . . Wagner
6. TWO MOVEMENTS from "Bal Costume" . Rubinstein
7. LE DÉLUGE . . . . Saint-Saens
   Solo Violin, Mr. ONDRICEK
   The audience is respectfully requested to preserve silence during the performance of this number.
8. AUBADE PRINTANIÈRE . . . . Lacome
9. NOCTURNE AND WEDDING MARCH . . . Mendelssohn
10. ESTUDIANTINA . . . . Waldteufel
11. POLKA, "Rosebuds" . . . . Eilenberg
12. MARCH, "Wien, bleibt Wien" . . . . . Schrammel

COAL
Best Quality AT Lowest Prices

METROPOLITAN COAL COMPANY,
No. 30 Congress Street.

WILSON BELFAST GINGER ALE
and
Champagne Kola
are sold at these concerts.

DRINK
WILSON CHAMPAGNE KOLA.

It produces energy, activity, and force. Its medical virtues are endorsed by physicians.

The **Wilson** is acknowledged to be America's purest spring water.
Bottled only in glass at the spring, North Raymond, Me.

In making our BELFAST GINGER ALE we use only the purest ginger.

Beware of imitations.

Drink the **Wilson** and you are sure of the best.

Wilson Spring and Hotel Co.,
45 Arch Street.
Telephone 3129, Boston. Boston, Mass.

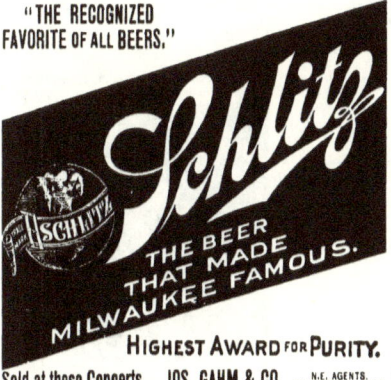

THE FALL RIVER LINE

OCCUPYING THE
LONG ISLAND SOUND ROUTE
BETWEEN

Boston and New York

Has the finest quintette of great steamboats
that the world has ever seen. The

Priscilla, Puritan, Plymouth, Pilgrim, and Providence

Are the largest, best equipped, safest, and handsomest steamboats ever constructed. This route is one of the most attractive and naturally beautiful traversed by any transportation agency in the world. Trips of the Fall River Line are made throughout the year.

Each steamboat has its own orchestra, and the service on each member of the fleet is maintained at the highest possible standard.

Tickets via this route are on sale at all of the principal Ticket Offices in the United States.

From BOSTON. Trains, connecting with steamers at Fall River in 80 minutes leave Park Square Station, New York, New Haven & Hartford Railroad (Old Colony System), daily at 6 p.m.

From NEW YORK. Steamers leave Pier 19, North River, foot of Warren Street, daily at 5.30 p.m.

S. A. GARDNER, Superintendent, NEW YORK.
GEO. L. CONNOR, Passenger Traffic Manager, NEW HAVEN, CONN.
O. H. TAYLOR, General Passenger Agent, NEW YORK CITY.

HOTEL LANGWOOD,

Middlesex Fells Reservation.

WYOMING STATION, B. & M. R.R.

NOW OPEN.

Twenty minutes by rail from Boston. Sixty trains daily. Hotel coaches meet trains each way. Four hundred feet above sea level. Beautiful rides, drives, and walks. Golf links, tennis courts, and ball grounds.

For plans and prices address:

F. W. GASKILL, Manager,

Telephone, 40 Melrose.   Melrose, Mass.

S.S. "Howard." Boston to Norfolk, 522 miles. Norfolk to Baltimore, 200 miles.

	1.	2.	3.
Boston	Leave July 2	July 15	August 19
	Arrive July 19	July 31	September 4

S.S. "Toronto." Toronto to Montreal, through the "Thousand Islands" and the "Rapids," 376 miles.

Third Season.

3 Ideal Outings

Personally conducted by
F. R. COMEE, Music Hall, Boston.

No. 1. Ten days. Saratoga, Lake George, 2,130 miles from Buffalo to Duluth, and return on the steamer "North-Land" through the Great Lakes, Erie, Huron, St. Clair, and Superior.

Nos. 2 and 3. Sixteen days. Exactly alike. 700 miles' ocean sail to Norfolk and Baltimore. Over Alleghany Mountains and a day in Chicago. Up Lake Michigan and three days at Mackinac Island. 1,540 miles on steamer "North-West" to Duluth and return to Buffalo through the Great Lakes. Niagara Falls to Toronto. Across Lake Ontario, through the Thousand Islands, and down the St. Lawrence River to Montreal and Boston.

SEND FOR CIRCULARS.

S.S. "Manitou." Chicago to Mackinac Island, across Lake Michigan, 350 miles.

"North-West." Mackinac Island to Duluth and return to Buffalo, 1,555 miles.

Allsopp's

ENGLISH ALE.
"The Red Hand Brand."

Protection for Ale Drinkers.

There is a strong and growing feeling abroad that all breweries should protect consumers by doing their own bottling. Allsopp's Ale is the only brand to-day that is bottled by its makers.

Sold at these concerts.

SATURDAY, JUNE 17.

PROGRAMME.

1. MARCH, "U. S. Volunteers" — Strube
2. OVERTURE, "Fra Diavolo" — Auber
3. WALTZ, "Amour et Printemps" — Waldteufel
4. SELECTION, "Fledermaus" — Strauss

5. OVERTURE, "Poet and Peasant" — Suppe
6. TWO MOVEMENTS from "Henry VIII." — Saint Saëns
7. LARGO. (Solo Violin, Mr. ONDRICEK.) — Handel
8. HUNGARIAN MARCH, from "Damnation of Faust" — Berlioz

9. PARAPHRASE on "Haste thee, Winter" (First Time.) — Loud
10. WALTZ, "Blue Danube" — Strauss
11. MAZOURKA, "Czarina" — Ganne
12. MARCH, "Hoch Habsburg" — Kral

The *only* Lithia Water sold at these concerts.

Hygeia Lithia Water

Sparkling and Still.

By its use you will avoid the germs of disease which natural MINERAL WATERS are liable to contain.

For Sale at these concerts and by

S. S. PIERCE CO.

FOR SALE AT THESE CONCERTS.

FAMOUS TANNHAEUSER EXPORT BEER

The finest Light Beer Extant. Brewery Bottling. Favorite of Connoisseurs.

Pure,   Palatable,   Perfect.

B. & E. Philadelphia Ale on Draught.

FOR SALE AT THESE CONCERTS.

The purity and keeping quality of the Tannhaeuser Export under all changes of temperature, its uniform excellence being guaranteed, together with its nutritious properties, make it the most pleasant, delicious, and convenient beverage for home consumption.

Put up in corked bottles, and packed in casks of 10 dozen white flint pints, and 6 dozen amber quarts.

Highest Awards wherever exhibited.

The BERGNER & ENGEL BREWING CO.'S N.E. Depot,

508 and 510 Atlantic Avenue, Boston.

Telephone 3805.   SOL. BACHARACH, Manager.

M. Steinert & Sons Co.,

STEINERT HALL BUILDING,

No. 162 Boylston Street, corner Carver, Boston.

STEINWAY & SONS,

HARDMAN,   GABLER,
EMERSON,   SINGER,

PIANOS.

The Æolian, Aeriol, Orchestrelle, and Pianola.

THE ÆOLIAN
AND
THE PIANOLA
FOR SUMMER HOMES.

At this season of the year we receive many orders for these instruments for Summer Residences, and therefore beg to call attention to our extensive assortment now on display, especially suited for this purpose.

The ÆOLIAN meets the requirements of country homes, furnishing, as it does, music suitable for every occasion. It practically takes the place of an orchestra — music for dancing — orchestral concerts, — in short, music of every style and description is always available.

The PIANOLA will appeal to many on account of the very little space it occupies. It will play any kind of a piano, and can also be used upon a rented piano without the slightest injury. For the above reasons it is bound to be very popular for small cottages.

We are glad to be able to announce that we can furnish PIANOLAS with no more than a week's delay, and, at times, the day the order is given.

Persons not familiar with these instruments are cordially invited to call at our warerooms and hear them, or a descriptive catalogue will be mailed free upon application.

M. STEINERT & SONS CO.,
Steinert Hall,   162 Boylston Street,   Boston.

ANHEUSER-BUSCH BREWING ASS'N,
ST. LOUIS, MO., U.S.A.

BREWERS OF HIGH=GRADE BEERS EXCLUSIVELY.

Black and Tan.   Faust.

Michelob.   Pale Lager.

Muenchener.   Anheuser Standard.

Served at the Music Hall Concerts.

Also at all first-class hotels, clubs, and bars, and on all Pullman and Wagner cars and ocean and lake steamers.

JACOB WIRTH,   Wholesale Dealer,   **Boston, Mass.**

THE MUSIC HALL
PROMENADE CONCERTS

C. A. ELLIS, PUBLISHED BY MUSIC HALL.

BOSTON, THURSDAY, JUNE 15, 1899.

SUMMER SEASON. Vol. XIV. No. 33.

YOU CAN
Have your last season's outfit dyed or cleansed and refinished so it will look like new, by our French process. Why discard soiled clothing when it can be overhauled and worn as second best? You can
RELY ON
Our methods of cleansing, and need not hesitate to trust us with articles of the most delicate textures.
We dye or cleanse and refinish PROPERLY, all materials of household use and clothing of all kinds.

LEWANDO'S
W. L. Crosby, General Manager, French Cleansers, Fancy Dyers, Fine Launderers.
PRINCIPAL OFFICES:
17 Temple Place, Boston.
479 Fifth Avenue, New York.
Established 70 years.
Largest in America.
Bundles called for and delivered.
Telephones in all offices.

THE MUSIC HALL Promenade Concerts
FOURTEENTH SEASON.

C. A. ELLIS, Manager.   F. R. COMEE, Assistant Manager.
Mr. GUSTAV STRUBE, Conductor.

THURSDAY, JUNE 15.
PROGRAMME.

1. MARCH, " Merry War " . . . . . Strauss
2. OVERTURE, " Ruy Blas " . . . . Mendelssohn
3. WALTZ, " Ocean Waves " . . . . . Metra
4. SELECTION, " Wizard of the Nile " . . . Herbert
5. OVERTURE, " Martha " . . . . . Flotow
6. LOVE SONG (from an unfinished suite) . . Farwell
7. INTRODUCTION to Act III., " Lohengrin " . Wagner
8. CONGRESS OF MELODIES . . . . Conradi
9. (a) ELEGIE }
   (b) SERENADE } for String Orchestra . Strube
   (First Time)
The audience is respectfully requested to preserve silence during the performance of this number.
10. AMERICAN PATROL . . . . . Meacham
11. POLKA, " Hunter's Yarns " . . . . Komzak
12. TABASCO MARCH . . . . . . Chadwick

Monday, June 19, Harvard Night.

To secure satisfactory service, patrons are URGED by the Management to report PROMPTLY any inattention. Complaints made so late that patrons cannot recall either the number of the table or the waiter are obviously useless.

THE TWO
MOST POPULAR TWO-STEPS
OF THE SEASON.

THE RUNAWAY GIRL, by Van Baar, ... 60c.
THE CECIL, by Megone, ... 30c.
FOR ORCHESTRA OR PIANO SOLO.

BOOSEY & CO.,
9 EAST 17th STREET,   NEW YORK.

Save half your money
do not throw it away in half-smoked cigars! You will find that 50% of your cigar money is thrown away every day if you recall how few cigars you really have time to smoke "up."

BETWEEN THE ACTS
Little Cigars

are pure—clean—all good tobacco, and are in every way a very satisfactory short smoke. While you are listening to the music to-night, try a 10-cent box. The waiter will get them for you as they are for sale here. You will enjoy them!

LAGER BEER
A Particularly Fine Lager for Family Use and Clubs.
Bottled in the most careful manner at our own bottling department, and sold by the N. N. Pierce Co. and all other leading grocers in New England.
Other Brands in Bottles:
" Norfolk India Pale Stock Ale."
" Norfolk Extra Golden Ale " (blue label).
" Norfolk Standard Lager."
Our " Cabinet " and " Bismarck Braun " are the most popular refreshments at these concerts.

HABICH & CO.
H. W. HABICH,   } Telephone, 56 Roxbury
EDWARD KUHL.   }   or 1152 Boston.

—— ESTABROOK & EATON'S MARGUERITE PERFECTOS, 10c. EACH. CONCHAS, 10c., 3 FOR 25c. **SOLD AT THE " POPS."**

THE ICE-CREAM SERVED AT THESE CONCERTS IS FURNISHED BY WEBER, 25 Temple Place and 33 West Street.

MUSIC HALL PROMENADE PROGRAMME.

PUBLISHED EVERY EVENING DURING THE SUMMER SEASON.

NOTICE TO ADVERTISERS.

The advertising columns in the Programme are controlled SOLELY by F. R. Comee, Boston Music Hall Box Office, to whom all communications should be addressed.

The United States Hotel,

SARATOGA SPRINGS, N.Y.

Under a continuous management for 25 years.

Without a peer in its appointments, service, and liberal management.

The largest structure of its kind in the world.

Built entirely of brick.

The Hotel and court cover over seven acres.

For further information, rates, etc., etc., address

GAGE & PERRY,
Proprietors,
UNITED STATES HOTEL,
Saratoga Springs, N.Y.

Colonial Beer...

The Beer that's Brewed in Glass.

PURE, CLEAN, PALATABLE.

Order a Bottle.

SOUTHER BREWING CO.,
919 Parker Street,
Roxbury, Mass.

All The IMPORTED CIGARS

Sold At These Concerts Are Supplied By The

S. S. PIERCE COMPANY.

The Peer of all Cigarettes.

Save the band-label on each box for valuable premiums.

::: ALSO :::

Monopol

High-grade Egyptian Cigarettes

No. 83 Khedive,
No. 65A Sultan,
No. 94 Egyptian Belles,
No. 30A Princess Lillian

On sale at these concerts and all first-class dealers.

PHILIP KRIM'S OWN IMPORTATION OF **Rhine Wines.**

FOR 30 YEARS AT **163 Shawmut Avenue.**

OUR WINES SOLD AT THESE CONCERTS.

HERRICK, COPLEY SQUARE, Telephones 608 and 950 (Back Bay), CHOICE TABLES for Music Hall "Pops."

GREAT WESTERN CHAMPAGNE

——— A natural, genuine champagne, of the finest quality produced in America.

Sold by Wine Merchants, Grocers, and Druggists.

FRIDAY, JUNE 16.

PROGRAMME.

1. MARCH, "King Karl" — Eilenberg
2. OVERTURE, "Stradella" — Flotow
3. WALTZ, "Doctrinen" — Strauss
4. SELECTION, "Faust" — Gounod
5. INTRODUCTION to "Lohengrin" — Wagner
6. TWO MOVEMENTS from "Bal Costumé" — Rubinstein
7. LE DÉLUGE — Saint-Saëns
   Solo Violin, Mr. ONDRICEK.
   The audience is respectfully requested to preserve silence during the performance of this number.
8. AUBADE PRINTANIÈRE — Lacome
9. NOCTURNE AND WEDDING MARCH — Mendelssohn
10. ESTUDIANTINA — Waldteufel
11. POLKA, "Rosebuds" — Eilenberg
12. MARCH, "Wien, bleibt Wien" — Schrammel

THE HAYWARD,
16 and 22 Hayward Place.
LADIES' AND GENTS' CAFÉ. Open until 1 a.m.
Table d'hote dinner, including bottle of wine, 75c.,
served from 5 to 8.30 P.M.

SCIARRETTA'S NEAPOLITAN TRIO give concerts daily from 6 P.M. until 1 A.M.
Signor SALVATORE SCIARRETTI, Lyric Tenor,
Is highly endorsed by Vice-President Garrett A. Hobart, Chauncey M. Depew, Eugene Ysaye, Raoul Pugno, Jean Gerardy, and many other prominent people.

SMITH & KERRISSEY, Proprietors.

AN HISTORIC RESORT.

The loveliest place on the New England coast to spend a short vacation or the whole season is the

MYLES STANDISH HOTEL,
at SOUTH DUXBURY, MASS.

Everything that money and intelligence can do has been done to make this hotel better, if possible, than it was last season.
The greatest pains will be taken to have the table service absolutely excellent. Of the house itself and its surroundings too much cannot be said. It is a resort of nice people, who come year after year, gaining strength, vitality, and pleasure.
Send for our 1899 booklet.

L. BOYER'S SONS, Proprietors,
27 Devonshire Street, Boston, Mass.,
Or ALFRED S. AMER, Manager,
90 Wall Street, New York
(Until June 1).
Myles Standish Hotel,
South Duxbury, Mass.

"AMERICA'S FINEST PRODUCT."
Bartholomay's "APOLLO"
LAGER BEER IN BOTTLES.

Sold at these Concerts.

ALBRECHT & KOELLNER,
SOLE AGENTS,
Telephone, Boston 1751.   295-305 A Street.

Also Agents for the "Crystal Rock" Mineral Water.

PURE BEER
Harvard BREW. CO'S $1000.00
PURE BEER
Sold at these Concerts
IN BOTTLES ONLY
20¢ PER BOTTLE.

Inglenook Vineyard.

The only California Wines sold at these Concerts.

❦❦

THE CODMAN & HALL CO.,
Opposite the South Union Station.

Sole Agents for New England.

IND. COOPE & CO.'S English Ale.

THE SECOND LARGEST BREWERY IN ENGLAND.

Brewers of the finest *light quality* ale. Very highly endorsed by the medical profession. : : : :

❦❦

THE CODMAN & HALL CO.,
Opposite South Union Station.

Sole Agents for the United States.

DRIN only th

PURE

WHIS

If you wa and rich flavor, tr only gen and origi

OLD KENT TAYLOR

Eight years ol own distillatic guaranteed p Bottled and sh direct from warehouses b None genuine out our sign on both labels ware of imita For consum indigestion, a ailments req stimulants, C KENTUCKY LOR has superior.
Sold by all class dru grocers, and dealers.

Wright & Te
Distillers
Fine Kentu
Whiskies
Louisville.

Hirshfield &
New Engl
Agents
31 Doane St
Boston.

Instruct your waiter to bring a bottle of

Pfaff's "Monogram" Lager.

If you will do this, it will not be necessary for us to expatiate upon the good qualities of our production.
YOU CAN JUDGE FOR YOURSELF.

H. & J. PFAFF BREWING COMPANY,
Telephone 2608. 16 ARCH STREET, BOSTON.

TABLE LINEN USED AT THESE CONCERTS LAUNDERED BY THE L. K. HUSTED LAUNDERING COMPANY, 27 and 29 BROADWAY, CHELSEA, MASS.

IBIA BRAND" VIENNA SAUSAGES. SERVED HOT OR COLD AT THESE CONCERTS.

SATURDAY, JUNE 17.

PROGRAMME.

1. MARCH, "U. S. Volunteers" ... Strube
2. OVERTURE, "Fra Diavolo" ... Auber
3. WALTZ, "Amour et Printemps" ... Waldteufel
4. SELECTION, "Fledermaus" ... Strauss
5. OVERTURE, "Poet and Peasant" ... Suppé
6. TWO MOVEMENTS from "Henry VIII." ... Saint Saens
7. LARGO ... Handel
   (Solo Violin, Mr. ONDRICEK)
8. HUNGARIAN MARCH, from "Damnation of Faust" ... Berlioz
9. PARAPHRASE on "Haste thee, Winter" ... Loud
   (First Time.)
10. WALTZ, "Blue Danube" ... Strauss
11. MAZOURKA, "Czarina" ... Ganne
12. MARCH, "Hoch Habsburg" ... Kral

WILSON BELFAST GINGER ALE
and
Champagne Kola
are sold at these concerts.

DRINK WILSON CHAMPAGNE KOLA.

It produces energy, activity, and force. Its medical virtues are endorsed by physicians.

The **Wilson** is acknowledged to be America's purest spring water. Bottled only in glass at the spring, North Raymond, Me.

In making our BELFAST GINGERALE we use only the purest ginger.

Beware of imitations.

Drink the Wilson and you are sure of the best.

Wilson Spring and Hotel Co.,
45 Arch Street,
Telephone 3129, Boston. **Boston, Mass.**

COAL
Best Quality AT Lowest Prices

METROPOLITAN COAL COMPANY,
No. 30 Congress Street.

THE ONLY BEER ON DRAUGHT AT THESE CONCERTS.

"the beer that's brewed"

SOLD AT THESE CONCERTS.

Rochester Brewing Co's.
NOTED THE WORLD OVER FOR ITS PURITY.

FAMOUS **BOTTLED BEER**

HOME OFFICE & BREWERY ROCHESTER, N.Y.
295-305 ENGLAND BRANCH
A STREET BOSTON ROCHESTER BREWING Co.
Free delivery in city and Suburbs

RIENZI, PREMIER, BOHEMIAN, BAVARIAN, STANDARD.

BEER MADE FAMOUS.

T AWARD FOR PURITY.
GAHM & CO., N.E. AGENTS,
125-127 PURCHASE ST.

THE FALL RIVER LINE

OCCUPYING THE
LONG ISLAND SOUND ROUTE
BETWEEN

Boston and New York

Has the finest quintette of great steamboats that the world has ever seen. The

Priscilla, Puritan, Plymouth, Pilgrim, and Providence

Are the largest, best equipped, safest, and handsomest steamboats ever constructed. This route is one of the most attractive and naturally beautiful traversed by any transportation agency in the world. Trips of the Fall River Line are made throughout the year. Each steamboat has its own orchestra, and the service on each member of the fleet is maintained at the highest possible standard.

Tickets via this route are on sale at all of the principal Ticket Offices in the United States.

From BOSTON, Trains, connecting with steamers at Fall River in 80 minutes leave Park Square Station, New York, New Haven & Hartford Railroad (Old Colony System), daily at 6 p.m.

From NEW YORK, Steamers leave Pier 19, North River, foot of Warren Street, daily at 5.30 p.m.

S. A. GARDNER,
Superintendent,
NEW YORK.

GEO. L. CONNOR,
Passenger Traffic Manager,
NEW HAVEN, CONN.

O. H. TAYLOR,
General Passenger Agent,
NEW YORK CITY.

HOTEL LANGWOOD,

Middlesex Fells Reservation.

WYOMING STATION, B. & M. R.R.

NOW OPEN.

Twenty minutes by rail from Boston. Sixty trains daily. Hotel coaches meet trains each way. Four hundred feet above sea level. Beautiful rides, drives, and walks. Golf links, tennis courts, and ball grounds.

For plans and prices address:

F. W. GASKILL, Manager,

Telephone, 40 Melrose.   Melrose, Mass.

THIRD SEASON.

3 Ideal Outings

Personally conducted by
F. R. COMEE,
Music Hall,
Boston.

	1.	2.	3.
Boston	Leave July 2	July 15	August 19
	Arrive July 12	July 31	September 4

No. 1. Ten days. **Saratoga, Lake George**, 2,130 miles from **Buffalo** to **Duluth**, and return on the steamer "North-Land" through the **Great Lakes, Erie, Huron, St. Clair**, and **Superior**.

Nos. 2 and 3. Sixteen days. Exactly alike. 700 miles' ocean sail to **Norfolk** and **Baltimore**. Over **Alleghany Mountains** and a day in **Chicago**. Up Lake Michigan and three days at **Mackinac Island**. 1,546 miles on steamer "North-West" to **Duluth** and return to **Buffalo** through the **Great Lakes, Niagara Falls** to **Toronto**. Across Lake **Ontario**, through the **Thousand Islands**, and down the **St. Lawrence River** to **Montreal** and **Boston**.

No country in the world can duplicate the journey of **1,065 miles in one steamer on fresh water** from **Buffalo** to **Duluth** through the Great Northern Lakes. These "Ideal Outings" are not cheap trips, as they are too extensive, trip No. 1 covering 3,000 miles, Nos. 2 and 3, which are exactly alike, covering 4,000 miles, and with only one night in a sleeping-car. There need be no fear of seasickness, as frequent experience has proved the Great Lakes to be unusually smooth in July and August. We travel first-class in every way. The parties are strictly limited, as it is impossible to secure equally good accommodations for a large number. The fatigue of too steady travel is avoided by from one to three days' rest at Old Point Comfort, Chicago, Mackinac Island, Duluth, Niagara Falls, Saratoga, etc. The average temperature through the Great Lakes in midsummer is 60°. No tourist who has made the journey has yet expressed disappointment: on the contrary, all are amazed at its extent and beauty.

SEND FOR CIRCULARS.

Allsopp's

ENGLISH ALE.
"The Red Hand Brand."

Protection for Ale Drinkers.

There is a strong and growing feeling abroad that all breweries should protect consumers by doing their own bottling. Allsopp's Ale is the only brand to-day that is bottled by its makers.

Sold at these concerts.

MONDAY, JUNE 19.
HARVARD NIGHT.

PROGRAMME.

1. MARCH, "University" . . . . Bruguière
2. OVERTURE, "Si J'étais Roi" . . . . Adam
3. WALTZ, "Jolly Fellows" . . . . Vollstedt
4. SELECTION, "Runaway Girl" . . . . . Ch. von Baar
5. AMERICAN FANTASY . . . . Herbert
6. OVERTURE to "Belles of Bellesley," Pi Eta Production, 1899.
7. SELECTION from "Hasty Pudding" Productions.
8. SERENADE . . . . Henry, '87
   (First Time.)
9. MARCH, "The Cruiser Harvard" . . . . . Strube
10. SELECTION, "Belle of New York" . . . . Kerker
11. FAIR HARVARD.
12. MARCH, "Up the Street" . . . . Morse, '96

The *only* Lithia Water sold at these concerts.

Hygeia Lithia Water

Sparkling and Still.

By its use you will avoid the germs of disease which natural MINERAL WATERS are liable to contain.

For Sale at these concerts and by

S. S. PIERCE CO.

FOR SALE AT THESE CONCERTS.

FAMOUS TANNHAEUSER EXPORT BEER

The finest Light Beer Extant.   Brewery Bottling.   Favorite of Connoisseurs.

Pure,   Palatable,   Perfect.

B. & E. Philadelphia Ale on Draught.
FOR SALE AT THESE CONCERTS.

The BERGNER & ENGEL BREWING CO.'S N.E. Depot,
508 and 510 Atlantic Avenue, Boston.

Telephone 3805.   SOL. BACHARACH, Manager.

The purity and keeping quality of the Tannhaeuser Export under all changes of temperature, its uniform excellence being guaranteed, together with its nutritious properties, make it the most pleasant, delicious, and convenient beverage for home consumption.
Put up in corked bottles, and packed in casks of 10 dozen white flint pints, and 6 dozen amber quarts.

Highest Awards wherever exhibited.

M. Steinert & Sons Co.,

STEINERT HALL BUILDING,

No. 162 Boylston Street, corner Carver, Boston.

STEINWAY & SONS,

HARDMAN,   GABLER,
EMERSON,   SINGER,

PIANOS.

The Æolian, Aeriol, Orchestrelle,

and Pianola.

THE ÆOLIAN
AND
THE PIANOLA
FOR SUMMER HOMES.

At this season of the year we receive many orders for these instruments for Summer Residences, and therefore beg to call attention to our extensive assortment now on display, especially suited for this purpose.

The ÆOLIAN meets the requirements of country homes, furnishing, as it does, music suitable for every occasion. It practically takes the place of an orchestra — music for dancing — orchestral concerts, — in short, music of every style and description is always available.

The PIANOLA will appeal to many on account of the very little space it occupies. It will play any kind of a piano, and can also be used upon a rented piano without the slightest injury. For the above reasons it is bound to be very popular for small cottages.

We are glad to be able to announce that we can furnish PIANOLAS with no more than a week's delay, and, at times, the day the order is given.

Persons not familiar with these instruments are cordially invited to call at our warerooms and hear them, or a descriptive catalogue will be mailed free upon application.

M. STEINERT & SONS CO.,
Steinert Hall,   162 Boylston Street,   Boston.

ANHEUSER-BUSCH BREWING ASS'N,

ST. LOUIS, MO., U.S.A.

BREWERS OF HIGH=GRADE BEERS EXCLUSIVELY.

Black and Tan.   Faust.

Michelob.   Pale Lager.

Muenchener.   Anheuser Standard.

Served at the Music Hall Concerts.

Also at all first-class hotels, clubs, and bars, and on all Pullman and Wagner cars and ocean and lake steamers.

JACOB WIRTH,   Wholesale Dealer,   **Boston, Mass.**

THE MUSIC HALL

PROMENADE CONCERTS

BOSTON, FRIDAY, JUNE 16, 1899.

SMOKE "LA CELESTINA," THE BEST ALL-HAVANA CIGAR. DANIEL FRANK & CO.

SMOKE THE POPULAR "BARRISTER" CIGARS AT THE POPULAR CONCERTS

PUBLISHED BY
C. A. ELLIS,
MUSIC HALL.

SUMMER SEASON.
Vol. XIV. No. 34.

YOU CAN
Have your last season's outfit dyed or cleansed and refinished so it will look like new, by our French process. Why discard soiled clothing when it can be overhauled and worn as second best? You can

RELY ON
Our methods of cleansing, and need not hesitate to trust us with articles of the most delicate textures.
We dye or cleanse and refinish PROPERLY, *all* materials of household use and clothing of all kinds.

LEWANDO'S
W. L. Crosby, General Manager.
French Cleansers, Fancy Dyers, Fine Launderers.

PRINCIPAL OFFICES:
17 Temple Place, Boston.
479 Fifth Avenue, New York.
Established 70 years.
Largest in America.
Bundles called for and delivered.
Telephones in all offices.

In no other way
are men as wasteful and extravagant as in cigar smoking — because cigars are thrown away half smoked half the time.

BETWEEN THE ACTS
Little Cigars
are just right for all short smokes. They light right, they burn right and taste right. Have you ever seen them? At all stores: 10 for 10 cts., or, as they are for sale here, you can try them to-night. Tell the waiter to bring you a 10-cent box of "Between the Acts." They will add to your enjoyment of this concert.

THE MUSIC HALL ... Promenade Concerts

FOURTEENTH SEASON.

C. A. ELLIS, Manager.   F. R. COMEE, Assistant Manager.

Mr. GUSTAV STRUBE, Conductor.

FRIDAY, JUNE 16.

PROGRAMME.

1. MARCH, "King Karl" . . . . Eilenberg
2. OVERTURE, "Stradella" . . . . Flotow
3. WALTZ, "Doctrinen" . . . . Strauss
4. SELECTION, "Faust" . . . . Gounod

5. INTRODUCTION to "Lohengrin" . . . . Wagner
6. TWO MOVEMENTS from "Bal Costumé" . Rubinstein
7. LE DÉLUGE . . . . Saint-Saëns
   Solo Violin, Mr. ONDRICEK.
   The audience is respectfully requested to preserve silence during the performance of this number.

8. AUBADE PRINTANIÈRE . . . . Lacome

9. NOCTURNE AND WEDDING MARCH . . Mendelssohn
10. ESTUDIANTINA . . . . Waldteufel
11. POLKA, "Rosebuds" . . . . Eilenberg
12. MARCH, "Wien, bleibt Wien" . . . . . Schrammel

Monday, June 19, Harvard Night.

To secure satisfactory service, patrons are URGED by the Management to report PROMPTLY any inattention. Complaints made so late that patrons cannot recall either the number of the table or the waiter are obviously useless.

Now the rage of the LONDON Concerts and Drawing-rooms:

YOU AND I, by Liza Lehmann, ... 60c.
KING CHARLES, by M. V. White, . . . 60c.
LIKE VIOLETS PALE, by F. Allitsen, . . 60c.
WHEN THE WORLD IS FAIR, by F. H. Cowen, 60c.
QUEEN OF MY LIFE, by E. T. Lloyd, . . 60c.

BOOSEY & CO.,
9 East 17th Street,   New York.

LAGER BEER
A Particularly Fine Lager for Family Use and Clubs.
Bottled in the most careful manner at our own bottling department, and sold by the S. S. Pierce Co. and all other leading grocers in New England.

Other Brands in Bottles:
"Norfolk India Pale Stock Ale."
"Norfolk Extra Golden Ale" (blue label).
"Norfolk Standard Lager."
Our "Cabinet" and "Bismarck Braeu" are the most popular refreshments at these concerts.

HABICH & CO.

H. W. HABICH, | Telephone, 36 Roxbury
EDWARD BUHL. | or 1182 Boston.

ESTABROOK & EATON'S MARGUERITE PERFECTOS, 10c. EACH. CONCHAS, 10c., 3 FOR 25c. SOLD AT THE "POPS."

THE ICE-CREAM SERVED AT THESE CONCERTS IS FURNISHED BY WEBER, 25 Temple Place and 33 West Street.

MUSIC HALL PROMENADE PROGRAMME.

PUBLISHED EVERY EVENING DURING THE SUMMER SEASON.

NOTICE TO ADVERTISERS.

The advertising columns in the Programme are controlled SOLELY by F. R. Comee, Boston Music Hall Box Office, to whom all communications should be addressed.

The United States Hotel,

SARATOGA SPRINGS, N.Y.

Under a continuous management for 25 years.

Without a peer in its appointments, service, and liberal management.

The largest structure of its kind in the world.

Built entirely of brick.

The Hotel and court cover over seven acres.

For further information, rates, etc., etc., address

GAGE & PERRY,
Proprietors,
UNITED STATES HOTEL,
Saratoga Springs, N.Y.

Colonial Beer

The Beer that's Brewed in Glass.

Colonial Beer...

PURE, CLEAN, PALATABLE.

Order a Bottle.

SOUTHER BREWING CO.,
919 Parker Street,
Roxbury, Mass.

VEUVE CHAFFARD

PURE OLIVE OIL.

IN HONEST BOTTLES.

The Peer of all Cigarettes.

Save the band-label on each box for valuable premiums.

::: ALSO :::

Monopol

High-grade Egyptian Cigarettes

No. 8A Khedive,
No. 6½ Nadine,
No. 9A Egyptian Belles,
No. 70A Princess Lillian

On sale at these concerts and all first-class dealers.

OCKENHEIMER BERG,
Near Bingen, GERMANY. On the Rhine.

PHILIP KRIM'S
OWN IMPORTATION OF
Rhine Wines.
FOR 30 YEARS AT
163 Shawmut Avenue.
OUR WINES SOLD AT THESE CONCERTS.

HERRICK, COPLEY SQUARE, Telephones 608 and 950 (Back Bay), CHOICE TABLES for Music Hall "Pops."

D. LEIDEN'S SPARKLING MOSELLE,

The only Sparkling Wine sold at these Concerts.

SHINNECOCK

The Perfection of Scotch Whisky

Sold by
S. S. PIERCE COMPANY.

SATURDAY, JUNE 17.

PROGRAMME.

1.	MARCH, "U. S. Volunteers"	Strube
2.	OVERTURE, "Fra Diavolo"	Auber
3.	WALTZ, "Amour et Printemps"	Waldteufel
4.	SELECTION, "Fledermaus"	Strauss
5.	OVERTURE, "Poet and Peasant"	Suppé
6.	TWO MOVEMENTS from "Henry VIII."	Saint Saëns
7.	LARGO, (Side Violin, Mr. ONDRICEK.)	Händel
8.	HUNGARIAN MARCH, from "Damnation of Faust"	Berlioz
9.	PARAPHRASE on "Haste thee, Winter" (First Time.)	Loud
10.	WALTZ, "Blue Danube"	Strauss
11.	MAZOURKA, "Czarina"	Ganne
12.	MARCH, "Hoch Habsburg"	Kral

THE HAYWARD,
16 and 22 Hayward Place.
LADIES' AND GENTS' CAFE.   Open until 1 a.m.
Table d'hôte dinner, including bottle of wine, 75c.,
served from 5 to 8.30 P.M.

SCIARRETTA'S NEAPOLITAN TRIO give concerts daily
from 6 P.M. until 1 A.M.
Signor SALVATORE SCIARRETTI, Lyric Tenor,
is highly endorsed by Vice-President Garrett A. Hobart, Chauncey M. Depew,
Eugene Ysaye, Raoul Pugno, Jean Gérardy, and many other prominent people.

SMITH & KERRISSEY, Proprietors.

AN HISTORIC RESORT.

The loveliest place on the New England coast to spend a short vacation or the whole season is the

MYLES STANDISH HOTEL,
at SOUTH DUXBURY, MASS.

Everything that money and intelligence can do has been done to make this hotel better, if possible, than it was last season.
The greatest pains will be taken to have the table service absolutely excellent. Of the house itself and its surroundings too much cannot be said. It is a resort of nice people, who come year after year, gaining strength, vitality, and pleasure.
Send for our 1899 booklet.

L. BOYER'S SONS, Proprietors,
27 Devonshire Street, Boston, Mass.,
Or ALFRED S. AMER, Manager,
90 Wall Street, New York
(Until June 1).

Myles Standish Hotel,
South Duxbury, Mass.

"AMERICA'S FINEST PRODUCT."

Bartholomay's "APOLLO"

LAGER BEER IN BOTTLES.

Sold at these Concerts.

ALBRECHT & KOELLNER,
SOLE AGENTS,
Telephone, Boston 1751.   295-305 A Street.

Also Agents for the "Crystal Rock" Mineral Water.

PURE BEER

Harvard BREW. CO'S $1000.⁰⁰

PURE BEER

Sold at these Concerts,
IN BOTTLES ONLY
20¢ PER BOTTLE.

Inglenook Vineyard.

The only California Wines sold at these Concerts.

THE CODMAN & HALL CO.,
Opposite the South Union Station.

Sole Agents for New England.

IND. COOPE & CO.'S English Ale.

THE SECOND LARGEST BREWERY IN ENGLAND.

Brewers of the finest *light quality* ale. Very highly endorsed by the medical profession. : : : : :

THE CODMAN & HALL CO.,
Opposite South Union Station.

Sole Agents for the United States.

DRINK only the

PURES

WHISK

If you want pu and richness flavor, try only genu and origina

OLD KENTUC TAYLOR,

Eight years old, own distillation guaranteed p u Bottled and ship direct from warehouses by None genuine w out our signat on both labels. ware of imitatio For consumpti indigestion, and ailments requir stimulants, O KENTUCKY T LOR has superior.
Sold by all fi class druggi grocers, and liq dealers.

Wright & Tayl
Distillers,
Fine Kentuck
Whiskies,
Louisville, Ky

Hirshfield &
New England
Agents,
31 Doane Stree
Boston.

Instruct your waiter to bring a bottle of

Pfaff's "Monogram" Lager.

If you will do this, it will not be necessary for us to expatiate upon the good qualities of our production.
YOU CAN JUDGE FOR YOURSELF.

H. & J. PFAFF BREWING COMPANY,
Telephone 2608.   16 ARCH STREET, BOSTON.

TRY THE "COLUMBIA BRAND" VIENNA SAUSAGES. SERVED HOT OR COLD AT THESE CONCERTS.

They cannot sell you here
Canadian Club Whisky,
Ruinart Champagne,
Royal Liqueur Scotch,
Carstair's Philadelphia Rye,
Fort Hill Bourbon,
Alhambra Sherry,
All of which you will find
of excellent quality;

But you can get

Kaiser Water,

the most refreshing of all
table waters.

*Chateau d'Arsac Claret,
N. Johnston & Sons' Medoc,*
and
California Inglenook Clarets.

SUPPLIED BY

CODMAN & HALL COMPANY,

WINE MERCHANTS,

Opposite New South Station.

MONDAY, JUNE 19.

HARVARD NIGHT.

PROGRAMME.

1. MARCH, "University" . . . . . Bruguière
2. OVERTURE, " Si j'étais Roi " . . . Adam
3. WALTZ, "Jolly Fellows" . . . . Vollstedt
4. SELECTION, "Runaway Girl" . . Ch. von Baar
5. AMERICAN FANTASY . . . . . Herbert
6. OVERTURE to "Belles of Bellesley," Pi Eta Production, 1899.
7. SELECTION from " Hasty Pudding " Productions.
8. SERENADE . . . . Henry, '87
    (First Time.)
9. MARCH, "The Cruiser Harvard" . . Strube
10. SELECTION, "Belle of New York" . Kerker
11. FAIR HARVARD.
12. MARCH, "Up the Street" . . . . Murse, '96

COAL Best Quality AT Lowest Prices

METROPOLITAN COAL COMPANY,
No. 30 Congress Street.

WILSON BELFAST GINGER ALE
and
Champagne Kola
are sold at these concerts.

DRINK
WILSON CHAMPAGNE KOLA.

It produces energy, activity, and force. Its medical virtues are endorsed by physicians.

The **Wilson** is acknowledged to be America's purest spring water. Bottled only in glass at the spring, North Raymond, Me.

In making our BELFAST GINGERALE we use only the purest ginger.

Beware of Imitations.

Drink the **Wilson** and you are sure of the best.

Wilson Spring and Hotel Co.,
45 Arch Street.
Telephone 3129, Boston. Boston, Mass.

THE FALL RIVER LINE

OCCUPYING THE
LONG ISLAND SOUND ROUTE
BETWEEN

Boston and New York

Has the finest quintette of great steamboats that the world has ever seen. The

Priscilla, Puritan, Plymouth, Pilgrim, and Providence

Are the largest, best equipped, safest, and handsomest steamboats ever constructed. This route is one of the most attractive and naturally beautiful traversed by any transportation agency in the world.

Trips of the Fall River Line are made throughout the year. Each steamboat has its own orchestra, and the service on each member of the fleet is maintained at the highest possible standard.

Tickets via this route are on sale at all of the principal Ticket Offices in the United States.

From BOSTON. Trains connecting with steamers at Fall River in 80 minutes leave Park Square Station, New York, New Haven & Hartford Railroad (Old Colony System), daily at 6 p.m.

From NEW YORK. Steamers leave Pier 19, North River, foot of Warren Street, daily at 5.30 p.m.

S. A. GARDNER,   GEO. L. CONNOR,   O. H. TAYLOR,
Superintendent,   Passenger Traffic Manager,   General Passenger Agent,
NEW YORK.   NEW HAVEN, CONN.   NEW YORK CITY.

HOTEL LANGWOOD,

Middlesex Fells Reservation.

WYOMING STATION, B. & M. R.R.

NOW OPEN.

Twenty minutes by rail from Boston. Sixty trains daily. Hotel coaches meet trains each way. Four hundred feet above sea level. Beautiful rides, drives, and walks. Golf links, tennis courts, and ball grounds.

For plans and prices address:

F. W. GASKILL, Manager,
Telephone, 40 Melrose.   Melrose, Mass.

THIRD SEASON.

3 Ideal Outings

Personally conducted by
F. R. COMEE,
Music Hall,
Boston.

	1.	2.	3.
Boston Leave	July 2	July 15	August 19
Boston Arrive	July 12	July 31	September 4

No. 1. Ten days. **Saratoga, Lake George**, 2,130 miles from **Buffalo to Duluth**, and return on the steamer "North-Land" through the **Great Lakes, Erie, Huron, St. Clair,** and **Superior**.

Nos. 2 and 3. Sixteen days. Exactly alike. 700 miles' ocean sail to **Norfolk** and **Baltimore**. Over **Alleghany Mountains** and a day in **Chicago**. Up **Lake Michigan** and three days at **Mackinac Island**. 1,546 miles on steamer "North-West" to **Duluth** and return to **Buffalo** through the **Great Lakes, Niagara Falls** to **Toronto**. Across **Lake Ontario**, through the **Thousand Islands**, and down the **St. Lawrence River** to **Montreal** and **Boston**.

No country in the world can duplicate the journey of 1,065 miles **in one steamer on fresh water** from **Buffalo to Duluth** through the Great Northern Lakes. These "Ideal Outings" are not cheap trips, as they are too extensive, trip No. 1 covering 3,000 miles, Nos. 2 and 3, which are exactly alike, covering 4,000 miles, and with only one night in a sleeping-car. There need be no fear of seasickness, as frequent experience has proved the Great Lakes to be unusually smooth in July and August. We travel first-class in every way. The parties are strictly limited, as it is impossible to secure equally good accommodations for a large number. The fatigue of too steady travel is avoided by from one to three days' rest at Old Point Comfort, Chicago, Mackinac Island, Duluth, Niagara Falls, Saratoga, etc. The average temperature through the Great Lakes in midsummer is 60°. No tourist who has made the journey has yet expressed disappointment: on the contrary, all are amazed at its extent and beauty.

SEND FOR CIRCULARS.

Allsopp's

ENGLISH ALE.
"The Red Hand Brand."

Protection for Ale Drinkers.

There is a strong and growing feeling abroad that all breweries should protect consumers by doing their own bottling. Allsopp's Ale is the only brand to-day that is bottled by its makers.

Sold at these concerts.

TUESDAY, JUNE 20.

PROGRAMME.

1. MARCH, "The Harvard Volunteers" . . . Grace Weston Lunt
   (First Time)
2. OVERTURE, "La Gazza Ladra" . . . Rossini
3. WALTZ, "Harlequin on a Voyage" . . . Zach
4. SELECTION, "The Brigands" . . . Offenbach

5. JUBEL OVERTURE . . . Weber
6. ANDANTE FOR STRING ORCHESTRA . . . Tchaikowsky
   The audience is respectfully requested to preserve silence during the performance of this number.
7. CZARDAS from "Der Geist des Wojewoden" . . . Grossmann
   (First Time.)
8. FINALE, Act I, "Lohengrin" . . . Wagner

9. SUITE DE BALLET . . . Levy
   (First Time.)
10. LOVE'S DREAM AFTER THE BALL . . . Czibulka
11. POLKA, "Love Letter" . . . Ziehrer
12. GEORGIA CAMP-MEETING . . . Mills

The *only* Lithia Water sold at these concerts.

Hygeia Lithia Water

Sparkling and Still.

By its use you will avoid the germs of disease which natural MINERAL WATERS are liable to contain.

For Sale at these concerts and by

S. S. PIERCE CO.

FOR SALE AT THESE CONCERTS.

FAMOUS TANNHAEUSER EXPORT BEER

The finest Light Beer Extant.   Brewery Bottling.   Favorite of Connoisseurs.

Pure,   Palatable,   Perfect.

B. & E. Philadelphia Ale on Draught.

FOR SALE AT THESE CONCERTS.

The purity and keeping quality of the Tannhaeuser Export under all changes of temperature, its uniform excellence being guaranteed, together with its nutritious properties, make it the most pleasant, delicious, and convenient beverage for home consumption.

Put up in corked bottles, and packed in casks of 10 dozen white flint pints, and 6 dozen amber quarts.

Highest Awards wherever exhibited.

The BERGNER & ENGEL BREWING CO.'S N.E. Depot,

508 and 510 Atlantic Avenue, Boston.

Telephone 3805.   SOL. BACHARACH, Manager.

M. Steinert & Sons Co.,

STEINERT HALL BUILDING,

No. 162 Boylston Street, corner Carver, Boston.

STEINWAY & SONS,

HARDMAN,   GABLER,
EMERSON,   SINGER,

PIANOS.

The Æolian, Aeriol, Orchestrelle, and Pianola.

THE ÆOLIAN
AND
THE PIANOLA
FOR SUMMER HOMES.

At this season of the year we receive many orders for these instruments for Summer Residences, and therefore beg to call attention to our extensive assortment now on display, especially suited for this purpose.

The ÆOLIAN meets the requirements of country homes, furnishing, as it does, music suitable for every occasion. It practically takes the place of an orchestra — music for dancing — orchestral concerts, — in short, music of every style and description is always available.

The PIANOLA will appeal to many on account of the very little space it occupies. It will play any kind of a piano, and can also be used upon a rented piano without the slightest injury. For the above reasons it is bound to be very popular for small cottages.

We are glad to be able to announce that we can furnish PIANOLAS with no more than a week's delay, and, at times, the day the order is given.

Persons not familiar with these instruments are cordially invited to call at our warerooms and hear them, or a descriptive catalogue will be mailed free upon application.

M. STEINERT & SONS CO.,
Steinert Hall,   162 Boylston Street,   Boston.

ANHEUSER-BUSCH BREWING ASS'N,
ST. LOUIS, MO., U.S.A.

BREWERS OF HIGH=GRADE BEERS EXCLUSIVELY.

Black and Tan.	Faust.
Michelob.	Pale Lager.
Muenchener.	Anheuser Standard.

Served at the Music Hall Concerts.

Also at all first-class hotels, clubs, and bars, and on all Pullman and Wagner cars and ocean and lake steamers.

JACOB WIRTH,   **Wholesale Dealer,**   **Boston, Mass.**

THE MUSIC HALL
PROMENADE CONCERTS

SMOKE "LA CELESTINA," THE BEST ALL-HAVANA CIGAR. DANIEL FRANK & CO.

SMOKE THE POPULAR "BARRISTER" CIGARS AT THE POPULAR CONCERTS

PUBLISHED BY
C. A. ELLIS,
MUSIC HALL.

BOSTON, SATURDAY, JUNE 17, 1899.

SUMMER SEASON.
Vol. XIV. No. 35.

YOU CAN

Have your last season's outfit dyed or cleansed and refinished so it will look like new, by our French process. Why discard soiled clothing when it can be overhauled and worn as second best? You can

RELY ON

Our methods of cleansing, and need not hesitate to trust us with articles of the most delicate textures.
We dye or cleanse and refinish PROPERLY, *all* materials of household use and clothing of all kinds.

LEWANDO'S
W. L. Crosby, General Manager.
French Cleansers, Fancy Dyers, Fine Launderers.
PRINCIPAL OFFICES:
17 Temple Place, Boston.
479 Fifth Avenue, New York.
Established 70 years.
Largest in America.
Bundles called for and delivered.
Telephones in all offices.

Knowledge
Experience.
differs from
You may know "all about"

BETWEEN THE ACTS
Little Cigars

but have you ever tried them yourself? Do you know how desirable they really are—how good they are—how economical they are—how convenient they are—how satisfactory they are? You can know—once for all—by having the waiter bring you a 10-cent box of ten—to smoke now—to-night—while you are enjoying this concert. They are for sale here.

THE MUSIC HALL Promenade Concerts
FOURTEENTH SEASON.

C. A. ELLIS, Manager.   F. R. COMEE, Assistant Manager.
Mr. GUSTAV STRUBE, Conductor.

SATURDAY, JUNE 17.

PROGRAMME.

1. MARCH, "U. S. Volunteers" . . . . . Strube
2. OVERTURE, "Fra Diavolo" . . . . . Auber
3. WALTZ, "Amour et Printemps" . . . . Waldteufel
4. SELECTION, "Fledermaus" . . . . . Strauss
5. OVERTURE, "Poet and Peasant" . . . . Suppé
6. TWO MOVEMENTS from "Henry VIII." . Saint Saëns
7. LARGO . . . . Händel
    (Solo Violin, Mr. ONDRICEK.)
8. HUNGARIAN MARCH, from "Damnation of Faust" . Berlioz
9. PARAPHRASE on "Haste thee, Winter" . . Loud
    (First Time.)
10. WALTZ, "Blue Danube" . . . . . . Strauss
11. MAZOURKA, "Czarina" . . . . . . Ganné
12. MARCH, "Hoch Habsburg" . . . . . Kral

Monday, June 19, Harvard Night.

To secure satisfactory service, patrons are URGED by the Management to report PROMPTLY any inattention. Complaints made so late that patrons cannot recall either the number of the table or the waiter are obviously useless.

HERE ARE A FEW NAMES FROM OUR LIST OF COMPOSERS:

ENGLISH.— Stephen Adams, F. H. Cowen, S. Liddle, C. V. Stanford, A. C. Mackenzie, R. H. Walthew, H. R. Shelley, Goring Thomas, Frances Allitsen, Maude V. White, Edward German, Mary Carmichael, Liza Lehmann, etc.

FRENCH.— C. Chaminade, Jane Vieu, L. Denza, P. Delmet, Bemberg, Guy d'Hardelot, De Leva, F. P. Tosti, etc.

ITALIAN.— F. P. Tosti, P. Mascagni, G. Puccini, G. Verdi, Don Lorenzo Perosi, etc.

THE MOST REPRESENTATIVE PUBLISHING HOUSE IN AMERICA.

BOOSEY & CO., 9 East 17th Street, New York.

BEST BEER BREWED

OH BE JOLLY!
DRINK VAN NOSTRAND'S
P. B. ALE
SOLD AT THESE CONCERTS

NORFOLK CABINET

LAGER BEER

A Particularly Fine Lager for Family Use and Clubs.
Bottled in the most careful manner at our own bottling department, and sold by the S. S. Pierce Co. and all other leading grocers in New England.

Other Brands in Bottles:
"Norfolk India Pale Stock Ale"
"Norfolk Extra Golden Ale" (blue label).
"Norfolk Standard Lager"
Our "Cabinet" and "Bismarck Brau" are the most popular refreshments at these concerts.

HABICH & CO.
H. W. HABICH,   Telephone, 56 Roxbury
EDWARD BUHL.   or 1151 Boston.

ESTABROOK & EATON'S MARGUERITE PERFECTOS, 10c. EACH; CONCHAS, 10c., 3 FOR 25c. **SOLD AT THE "POPS."**

THE ICE-CREAM SERVED AT THESE CONCERTS IS FURNISHED BY WEBER, 25 Temple Place and 33 West Street.

MUSIC HALL PROMENADE PROGRAMME.
PUBLISHED EVERY EVENING DURING THE SUMMER SEASON.

NOTICE TO ADVERTISERS.
The advertising columns in the Programme are controlled SOLELY by F. R. Comee, Boston Music Hall Box Office, to whom all communications should be addressed.

The United States Hotel,

SARATOGA SPRINGS, N.Y.

Under a continuous management for 25 years.

Without a peer in its appointments, service, and liberal management.

The largest structure of its kind in the world.

Built entirely of brick.

The Hotel and court cover over seven acres.

For further information, rates, etc., etc., address

GAGE & PERRY,
Proprietors,
UNITED STATES HOTEL,
Saratoga Springs, N.Y.

COLONIAL BEER

The Beer that's Brewed in Glass.

Colonial Beer...

PURE, CLEAN, PALATABLE.

Order a Bottle.

SOUTHER BREWING CO.,
919 Parker Street,
Roxbury, Mass.

All The
IMPORTED CIGARS

Sold At These Concerts Are Supplied By The

S. S. PIERCE COMPANY.

The Peer of all Cigarettes.
Save the band-label on each box for valuable premiums.

::: ALSO :::

Monopol

High-grade Egyptian Cigarettes.

No. 83 Khedive,
No. 93A Nadine,
No. 94 Egyptian Belles,
No. 104 Princess Lillian

On sale at these concerts and all first-class dealers.

OCKENHEIMER BERG,
Near Bingen, GERMANY, On the Rhine.

PHILIP KRIM'S
OWN IMPORTATION OF
Rhine Wines.
FOR 30 YEARS AT
163 Shawmut Avenue.
OUR WINES SOLD AT THESE CONCERTS.

HERRICK, COPLEY SQUARE, Telephones 608 and 950 (Back Bay), CHOICE TABLES for Music Hall "Pops."

GREAT WESTERN CHAMPAGNE

——— A natural, genuine champagne, of the finest quality produced in America.

Sold by Wine Merchants, Grocers, and Druggists.

MONDAY, JUNE 19.
HARVARD NIGHT.

PROGRAMME.

1. MARCH, "University" . . . . . Pruguère
2. OVERTURE, "Si j'etais Roi" . . . . Adam
3. WALTZ, "Jolly Fellows" . . . . Vollstedt
4. SELECTION, "Runaway Girl" . . . Ch. von Baur
5. AMERICAN FANTASY . . . . . Herbert
6. OVERTURE to "Belles of Belfesley," Pi Eta Production, 1899.
7. SELECTION from "Hasty Pudding" Productions.
8. SERENADE . . . . Henry, '87
 (First Time.)

9. MARCH, "The Cruiser Harvard" . . . Strube
10. SELECTION, "Belle of New York" . . Kerker
11. FAIR HARVARD.
12. MARCH, "Up the Street" . . . . Morse, '96

THE HAYWARD,
16 and 22 Hayward Place.
LADIES' AND GENTS' CAFE. Open until 1 a.m.
Table d'hôte dinner, including bottle of wine, 75c.,
served from 5 to 8.30 P.M.

SCIARRETTA'S NEAPOLITAN TRIO give concerts daily from 6 P.M. until 1 A.M.
Signor **SALVATORE SCIARRETTI, Lyric Tenor,**
is highly endorsed by Vice-President Garrett A. Hobart, Chauncey M. Depew, Eugene Ysaye, Raoul Pugno, Jean Gerardy, and many other prominent people.
SMITH & KERRISSEY, Proprietors.

AN HISTORIC RESORT.

The loveliest place on the New England coast to spend a short vacation or the whole season is the

MYLES STANDISH HOTEL,
at SOUTH DUXBURY, MASS.

Everything that money and intelligence can do has been done to make this hotel better, if possible, than it was last season.
The greatest pains will be taken to have the table service absolutely excellent. Of the house itself and its surroundings too much cannot be said. It is a resort of nice people, who come year after year, gaining strength, vitality, and pleasure.
Send for our 1899 booklet.

L. BOYER'S SONS, Proprietors,
27 Devonshire Street, Boston, Mass.,
Or ALFRED S. AMER, Manager,
90 Wall Street, New York
(Until June 1).
Myles Standish Hotel,
South Duxbury, Mass.

"AMERICA'S FINEST PRODUCT."

Bartholomay's "APOLLO"

LAGER BEER IN BOTTLES.

Sold at these Concerts.

ALBRECHT & KOELLNER,
SOLE AGENTS,
Telephone, Boston 1751.   295-305 A Street.

Also Agents for the "Crystal Rock" Mineral Water.

PURE BEER

BREW. CO'S $1000.00

PURE BEER
Sold at these Concerts,
IN BOTTLES ONLY
20¢ PER BOTTLE.

TABLE LINEN USED AT THESE CONCERTS. LAUNDERED BY THE L. K. HUSTED LAUNDERING COMPANY, 27 and 29 BROADWAY, CHELSEA, MASS.

Inglenook Vineyard.

The only California Wines sold at these Concerts.

THE CODMAN & HALL CO.,
Opposite the South Union Station.

Sole Agents for New England.

IND. COOPE & CO.'S English Ale.

THE SECOND LARGEST BREWERY IN ENGLAND.

Brewers of the finest *light quality* ale. Very highly endorsed by the medical profession. : : : : :

THE CODMAN & HALL CO.,
Opposite South Union Station.

Sole Agents for the United States.

DRIN
only th
PURE
WHIS

If you want p
and richne
flavor, try
only gen
and origin

OLD KENTU
TAYLOR,

Eight years old
own distillatio
guaranteed p
Bottled and shi
direct from
warehouses by
None genuine w
out our signa
on both labels.
ware of limitat
For consump
indigestion, an
ailments requi
stimulants, O
KENTUCKY T
LOR has
superior.
Sold by all t
class drugg
grocers, and li
dealers.

Wright & Tay
Distillers,
Fine Kentuc
Whiskies,
Louisville, K

Hirshfield &
New Englan
Agents,
31 Doane Stre
Boston.

Instruct your waiter to bring a bottle of

Pfaff's "Monogram" Lager.

If you will do this, it will not be necessary for us to expatiate upon the good qualities of our production.
YOU CAN JUDGE FOR YOURSELF.

H. & J. PFAFF BREWING COMPANY,
Telephone 2608.   16 ARCH STREET, BOSTON.

TRY THE "COLUMBIA BRAND" VIENNA SAUSAGES. SERVED HOT OR COLD AT THESE CONCERTS.

TUESDAY, JUNE 20.

PROGRAMME.

1. MARCH, "The Harvard Volunteers" . . . Grace Weston Lunt
   (First Time)
2. OVERTURE, "La Gazza Ladra" . . . Rossini
3. WALTZ, "Harlequin on a Voyage" . . . Zach
4. SELECTION, "The Brigands" . . . Offenbach
5. JUBEL OVERTURE . . . . . We'er
6. ANDANTE FOR STRING ORCHESTRA . . . Tchaikowsky
   The audience is respectfully requested to preserve silence during the performance of this number.
7. CZARDAS from "Der Geist des Wojewoden" . . . Grossmann
   (First Time)
8. FINALE, Act I., "Lohengrin" . . . Wagner
9. SUITE DE BALLET . . . . . Levy
   (First Time)
10. LOVE'S DREAM AFTER THE BALL . . . Czibulka
11. POLKA, "Love Letter" . . . Ziehrer
12. GEORGIA CAMP-MEETING . . . Mills

They cannot sell you here
Canadian Club Whisky,
Ruinart Champagne,
Royal Liqueur Scotch,
Carstair's Philadelphia Rye,
Fort Hill Bourbon,
Alhambra Sherry,
All of which you will find
of excellent quality ;

But you can get

Kaiser Water,

the most refreshing of all
table waters,

*Chateau d'Arsac Claret,
N. Johnston & Sons' Medoc,*
and
California Inglenook Clarets.

SUPPLIED BY

**CODMAN & HALL
COMPANY,**

WINE MERCHANTS,
Opposite New South
Station.

COAL Best Quality AT Lowest Prices

METROPOLITAN COAL COMPANY,
No. 30 Congress Street.

**WILSON
BELFAST
GINGER
ALE**
and
Champagne Kola
are sold at
these concerts.

**DRINK
WILSON
CHAMPAGNE
KOLA.**

It produces energy, activity, and force. Its medical virtues are endorsed by physicians.

The **Wilson** is acknowledged to be America's purest spring water.
Bottled only in glass at the spring.
North Raymond, Me.

In making our
BELFAST GINGER ALE we use
only the purest
ginger.

Beware of Imitations.

Drink the **Wilson**
and you are sure of the
best.

**Wilson Spring
and Hotel Co.,**
45 Arch Street.
Telephone
3129, Boston. Boston, Mass.

THE FALL RIVER LINE
OCCUPYING THE LONG ISLAND SOUND ROUTE BETWEEN
Boston and New York

Has the finest quintette of great steamboats that the world has ever seen. The **Priscilla, Puritan, Plymouth, Pilgrim, and Providence**

Are the largest, best equipped, safest, and handsomest steamboats ever constructed. This route is one of the most attractive and naturally beautiful traversed by any transportation agency in the world. Trips of the Fall River Line are made throughout the year. Each steamboat has its own orchestra, and the service on each member of the fleet is maintained at the highest possible standard.

Tickets via this route are on sale at all of the principal Ticket Offices in the United States.

From BOSTON. Trains, connecting with steamers at Fall River in 80 minutes leave Park Square Station, New York, New Haven & Hartford Railroad (Old Colony System), daily at 6 p.m.

From NEW YORK. Steamers leave Pier 19, North River, foot of Warren Street, daily at 5.30 p.m.

S. A. GARDNER, Superintendent, NEW YORK.
GEO. L. CONNOR, Passenger Traffic Manager, NEW HAVEN, CONN.
O. H. TAYLOR, General Passenger Agent, NEW YORK CITY.

HOTEL LANGWOOD,
Middlesex Fells Reservation.

WYOMING STATION, B. & M. R.R.

NOW OPEN.

Twenty minutes by rail from Boston. Sixty trains daily. Hotel coaches meet trains each way. Four hundred feet above sea level. Beautiful rides, drives, and walks. Golf links, tennis courts, and ball grounds.

For plans and prices address:

F. W. GASKILL, Manager,

Telephone, 40 Melrose.   Melrose, Mass.

THIRD SEASON.
3 Ideal Outings

Personally conducted by **F. R. COMEE,** Music Hall, Boston.

Boston	1.	2.	3.
Leave	July 2	July 15	August 19
Arrive	July 12	July 31	September 4

No. 1. Ten days. **Saratoga, Lake George,** 2,130 miles from **Buffalo** to **Duluth,** and return on the steamer "North-Land" through the **Great Lakes, Erie, Huron, St. Clair, and Superior.**

Nos. 2 and 3. Sixteen days. Exactly alike. 700 miles' ocean sail to **Norfolk** and **Baltimore.** Over **Alleghany Mountains** and a day in **Chicago.** Up **Lake Michigan** and three days at **Mackinac Island.** 1,546 miles on steamer "North-West" to **Duluth** and return to **Buffalo** through the **Great Lakes, Niagara Falls** to **Toronto.** Across **Lake Ontario,** through the **Thousand Islands,** and down the **St. Lawrence River** to **Montreal** and **Boston.**

No country in the world can duplicate the journey of 1,065 miles in one steamer on fresh water from Buffalo to Duluth through the Great Northern Lakes. These "Ideal Outings" are not cheap trips, as they are too extensive, trip No. 1 covering 3,000 miles, Nos. 2 and 3, which are exactly alike, covering 4,000 miles, and with only one night in a sleeping-car. There need be no fear of seasickness, as frequent experience has proved the Great Lakes to be unusually smooth in July and August. We travel first-class in every way. The parties are strictly limited, as it is impossible to secure equally good accommodations for a large number. The fatigue of too steady travel is avoided by from one to three days' rest at Old Point Comfort, Chicago, Mackinac Island, Duluth, Niagara Falls, Saratoga, etc. The average temperature through the Great Lakes in midsummer is 60°. No tourist who has made the journey has yet expressed disappointment; on the contrary, all are amazed at its extent and beauty.

SEND FOR CIRCULARS.

Allsopp's

ENGLISH ALE.
"The Red Hand Brand."

Protection for Ale Drinkers.

There is a strong and growing feeling abroad that all breweries should protect consumers by doing their own bottling. Allsopp's Ale is the only brand to-day that is bottled by its makers.

Sold at these concerts.

WEDNESDAY, JUNE 21.

PROGRAMME.

1. MARCH, "Hobson's Choice" — Strube
2. OVERTURE, "Felsenmühle" — Reissiger
3. WALTZ, "Violets" — Waldteufel
4. SELECTION, "Mikado" — Sullivan

5. OVERTURE, "Sakuntala" — Goldmark
6. a. "Reverie"
   b. "The Indian" } for String Orchestra. — Maquarre
   The audience is respectfully requested to preserve silence during the performance of this number.
7. INTRODUCTION, Act III., "Lohengrin" — Wagner
8. BACCHANALE, from "Samson and Delila" — Saint-Saëns

9. VISIONS IN A DREAM — Sumbye
   Zither Solo, Mr. KELLER.
10. OVERTURE, "Pique Dame" — Suppé
11. WALTZ, "Artist's Life" — Strauss
12. MARCH, "Austria" — Zach

The *only* Lithia Water sold at these concerts.

Hygeia Lithia Water

Sparkling and Still.

By its use you will avoid the germs of disease which natural MINERAL WATERS are liable to contain.

For Sale at these concerts and by

S. S. PIERCE CO.

The purity and keeping quality of the Tannhaeuser Export under all changes of temperature, its uniform excellence being guaranteed, together with its nutritious properties, make it the most pleasant, delicious, and convenient beverage for home consumption.
Put up in corked bottles, and packed in casks of 10 dozen white flint pints, and 6 dozen amber quarts.

Highest Awards wherever exhibited.

FOR SALE AT THESE CONCERTS.
FAMOUS TANNHAEUSER EXPORT BEER

The finest Light Beer Extant. Brewery Bottling. Favorite of Connoisseurs.

Pure, Palatable, Perfect.

B. & E. Philadelphia Ale on Draught.
FOR SALE AT THESE CONCERTS.

The BERGNER & ENGEL BREWING CO.'S N.E. Depot,
508 and 510 Atlantic Avenue, Boston.
Telephone 3805.   SOL. BACHARACH, Manager.

M. Steinert & Sons Co.,

STEINERT HALL BUILDING,

No. 162 Boylston Street, corner Carver, Boston.

STEINWAY & SONS,

HARDMAN,   GABLER,
EMERSON,   SINGER,

PIANOS.

The Æolian, Aeriol, Orchestrelle, and Pianola.

THE ÆOLIAN
AND
THE PIANOLA
FOR SUMMER HOMES.

At this season of the year we receive many orders for these instruments for Summer Residences, and therefore beg to call attention to our extensive assortment now on display, especially suited for this purpose.

The ÆOLIAN meets the requirements of country homes, furnishing, as it does, music suitable for every occasion. It practically takes the place of an orchestra — music for dancing — orchestral concerts, — in short, music of every style and description is always available.

The PIANOLA will appeal to many on account of the very little space it occupies. It will play any kind of a piano, and can also be used upon a rented piano without the slightest injury. For the above reasons it is bound to be very popular for small cottages.

We are glad to be able to announce that we can furnish PIANOLAS with no more than a week's delay, and, at times, the day the order is given.

Persons not familiar with these instruments are cordially invited to call at our warerooms and hear them, or a descriptive catalogue will be mailed free upon application.

M. STEINERT & SONS CO.,
Steinert Hall,   162 Boylston Street,   Boston.

ANHEUSER-BUSCH BREWING ASS'N,
ST. LOUIS, MO., U.S.A.
BREWERS OF HIGH=GRADE BEERS EXCLUSIVELY.

Black and Tan.   Faust.

Michelob.   Pale Lager.

Muenchener.   Anheuser Standard.

Served at the Music Hall Concerts.

Also at all first-class hotels, clubs, and bars, and on all Pullman and Wagner cars and ocean and lake steamers.

JACOB WIRTH,   **Wholesale Dealer,**   **Boston, Mass.**

THE MUSIC HALL
PROMENADE CONCERTS

SMOKE "LA CELESTINA," THE BEST ALL-HAVANA CIGAR. DANIEL FRANK & CO.

PUBLISHED BY A. ELLIS, MUSIC HALL.

BOSTON, MONDAY, JUNE 19, 1899.

SUMMER SEASON. Vol. XIV. No. 36.

YOU CAN

If your last season's outfit dyed, cleansed and refinished so it will look like new, by our French process. Why discard soiled cloth when it can be overhauled and made second best? You can

RELY ON

Our methods of cleansing, and need not hesitate to trust us with articles of the most delicate textures. We dye or cleanse and refinish PROPERLY, *all* materials of household use and clothing of all kinds.

LEWANDO'S

W. L. Crosby, General Manager.
French Cleansers, Fancy Dyers, Fine Launderers.

PRINCIPAL OFFICES:
17 Temple Place, Boston.
557 Fifth Avenue, New York
Established 70 years.
Largest in America.
Bundles called for and delivered
Telephone in all offices.

If you are open
to conviction,
to-night
try one 10-cent box of

BETWEEN
THE ACTS
Little Cigars

to smoke now — or at any time when you want a short smoke and haven't time for a long one. They are real cigars, but small ones.

They cost so little that you can use them every day as well as not and actually save on your daily cigar expense by substituting them for larger cigars.

FOR SALE HERE.

THE MUSIC HALL... Promenade Concerts
FOURTEENTH SEASON.

C. A. ELLIS, Manager.   F. R. COMEE, Assistant Manager.

Mr. GUSTAV STRUBE, Conductor.

MONDAY, JUNE 19.

PROGRAMME.

1. MARCH, "University" . . . . . Bruguière
2. OVERTURE, "Si j'etais Roi" . . . . . Adam
3. WALTZ, "Jolly Fellows" . . . . . Vollstedt
4. SELECTION, "Runaway Girl" . . . . . Ch. von Baar
5. AMERICAN FANTASY . . . . . Herbert
6. OVERTURE to "Belles of Bellesley," 18 Eta Production, 1899
7. SELECTION from "Hasty Pudding" Productions.
8. SERENADE . . . . . Henry, '87
   (First Time.)
9. MARCH, "The Cruiser Harvard" . . . . . Strube
10. SELECTION, "Belle of New York" . . . . . Kerker
11. FAIR HARVARD.
12. MARCH, "Up the Street" . . . . . Morse, '06

To secure satisfactory service, patrons are URGED by the Management to report PROMPTLY any inattention. Complaints made so late that patrons cannot recall either the number of the table or the waiter are obviously useless.

ALBUMS OF SONGS,

Containing many popular compositions not published in single form.

IRISH FOLK SONGS, by Charles Wood.	$2.00
RUSSIAN SONGS, by F. Wishaw (2 vols.),	1.00
NINE SONGS, by S. Liddle,	1.00
NINE SONGS, by Liza Lehmann,	1.00
FIVE SONGS, by Francis Korbay,	2.00

Beautifully illustrated by J. S. SARGENT, R.A.

BOOSEY & CO.,
9 East 17th Street,   **New York.**

A Particularly Fine Lager for Family Use and Clubs.

Bottled in the most careful manner at our own bottling department, and sold by the S. S. Pierce Co. and all other leading grocers in New England.

Other Brands in Bottles:
"Norfolk India Pale Stock Ale"
"Norfolk Extra Golden Ale" (blue label).
"Norfolk Standard Lager."
Bar "Cabinet" and "Bismarck Brau" are the most popular refreshments at these concerts.

HABICH & CO.

H. W. HABICH,
EDWARD RUHL. { Telephone, 56 Roxbury or 1182 Boston.

THE ICE-CREAM SERVED AT THESE CONCERTS IS FURNISHED BY, WEBER, 25 Temple Place and 33 West Street.

MUSIC HALL PROMENADE PROGRAMME.

PUBLISHED EVERY EVENING DURING THE SUMMER SEASON.

NOTICE TO ADVERTISERS.

The advertising columns in the Programme are controlled SOLELY by F. R. Comee, Boston Music Hall Box Office, to whom all communications should be addressed.

The United States Hotel,

SARATOGA SPRINGS, N.Y.

Under a continuous management for 25 years.

Without a peer in its appointments, service, and liberal management.

The largest structure of its kind in the world.

Built entirely of brick.

The Hotel and court cover over seven acres.

For further information, rates, etc., etc., address

GAGE & PERRY,
Proprietors,
UNITED STATES HOTEL,
Saratoga Springs, N.Y.

COLONIAL BEER

The Beer that's Brewed in Glass.

Colonial Beer...

PURE, CLEAN, PALATABLE.

Order a Bottle.

SOUTHER BREWING CO.,
919 Parker Street,
Roxbury, Mass.

VEUVE CHAFFARD

PURE OLIVE OIL.
IN HONEST BOTTLES.

The Peer of all Cigarettes.
Save the band label on each box for valuable premiums.

::: ALSO :::

Monopol

High-grade Egyptian Cigarettes.

No. 8½ Khedive,
No. 6½ Nadine,
No. 8½ Egyptian Belles.
No. 70½ Princess Lillian

On sale at these concerts and all first-class dealers.

OCKENHEIMER BERG,
Near Bingen, GERMANY. On the Rhine.

PHILIP KRIM'S

OWN IMPORTATION OF

Rhine Wines.

FOR 30 YEARS AT

163 Shawmut Avenue.

OUR WINES SOLD AT THESE CONCERTS.

HERRICK, COPLEY SQUARE, Telephones 608 and 950 (Back Bay), CHOICE TABLES for Music Hall "Pops."

D. LEIDEN'S
SPARKLING
MOSELLE,

The only Sparkling Wine sold at these Concerts.

SHINNECOCK

The Perfection of

Scotch Whisky

Sold by
S. S. PIERCE COMPANY.

TUESDAY, JUNE 20.

PROGRAMME.

1. MARCH, "The Harvard Volunteers" . . . Grace Weston Lunt
   (First Time.)
2. OVERTURE, "La Gazza Ladra" . . . . . . Rossini
3. WALTZ, "Harlequin on a Voyage" . . . . Zach
4. SELECTION, "The Brigands" . . . . . . Offenbach
5. JUBEL OVERTURE . . . . Weber
6. ANDANTE FOR STRING ORCHESTRA . . . Tchaikowsky
   The audience is respectfully requested to preserve silence during the performance of this number.
7. CZARDAS from "Der Geist des Wojewoden" . . Grossmann
   (First Time.)
8. FINALE, Act I., "Lohengrin" . . . . . . Wagner
9. SUITE DE BALLET . . . . Levy
   (First Time.)
10. LOVE'S DREAM AFTER THE BALL . . . . Czibulka
11. POLKA, "Love Letter" . . . . Ziehrer
12. GEORGIA CAMP-MEETING . . . . Mills

THE HAYWARD,
16 and 22 Hayward Place.
LADIES' AND GENTS' CAFÉ.   Open until 1 a.m.
Table d'hôte dinner, including bottle of wine, 75c.,
served from 5 to 8.30 P. M.

SCIARRETTA'S NEAPOLITAN TRIO give concerts daily from 6 P.M. until 1 A.M.
Signor SALVATORE SCIARRETTI, Lyric Tenor,
Is highly endorsed by Vice-President Garrett A. Hobart, Chauncey M. Depew, Eugene Ysaye, Raoul Pugno, Jean Gerardy, and many other prominent people.
SMITH & KERRISSEY, Proprietors.

AN
HISTORIC
RESORT.

The loveliest place on the New England coast to spend a short vacation or the whole season is the

MYLES STANDISH HOTEL,
at SOUTH DUXBURY, MASS.

Everything that money and intelligence can do has been done to make this hotel better, if possible, than it was last season.
The greatest pains will be taken to have the table service absolutely excellent. Of the house itself and its surroundings too much cannot be said. It is a resort of nice people, who come year after year, gaining strength, vitality, and pleasure.
Send for our 1899 booklet.

L. BOYER'S SONS, Proprietors,
27 Devonshire Street, Boston, Mass.,
Or ALFRED S. AMER, Manager,
90 Wall Street, New York
(Until June 1).
Myles Standish Hotel,
South Duxbury, Mass.

"AMERICA'S FINEST PRODUCT."

Bartholomay's "APOLLO"

LAGER BEER IN BOTTLES.

Sold at these Concerts.

ALBRECHT & KOELLNER,
SOLE AGENTS,
Telephone, Boston 1751. 295-305 A Street.

Also Agents for the "Crystal Rock" Mineral Water.

PURE BEER

Harvard
BREW. CO'S $1000.00

PURE BEER
Sold at these Concerts,
IN BOTTLES ONLY
20¢ PER BOTTLE.

Inglenook Vineyard.

The only California Wines sold at these Concerts.

❧❧

THE CODMAN & HALL CO.,

Opposite the South Union Station.

Sole Agents for New England.

IND. COOPE & CO.'S English Ale.

THE SECOND LARGEST BREWERY IN ENGLAND.

Brewers of the finest *light quality* ale. Very highly endorsed by the medical profession. : : : : :

❧❧

THE CODMAN & HALL CO.,

Opposite South Union Station.

Sole Agents for the United States.

Instruct your waiter to bring a bottle of

Pfaff's "Monogram" Lager.

If you will do this, it will not be necessary for us to expatiate upon the good qualities of our production.
YOU CAN JUDGE FOR YOURSELF.

H. & J. PFAFF BREWING COMPANY,

Telephone 2608.   16 ARCH STREET, BOSTON.

TRY THE "COLUMBIA BRAND" VIENNA SAUSAGES. SERVED HOT OR COLD AT THESE CONCERTS.

They cannot sell you here
Canadian Club Whisky,
Ruinart Champagne,
Royal Liqueur Scotch,
Carstair's Philadelphia Rye,
Fort Hill Bourbon,
Alhambra Sherry,
All of which you will find
of excellent quality;

But you can get

Kaiser Water,

the most refreshing of all table waters,

Chateau d'Arsac Claret,
N. Johnston & Sons' Medoc,
and
California Inglenook Clarets.

SUPPLIED BY

CODMAN & HALL COMPANY,

WINE MERCHANTS,
Opposite New South Station.

WEDNESDAY, JUNE 21.

PROGRAMME.

1. MARCH, "Hobson's Choice" . . . Strube
2. OVERTURE, "Felsenmuhle" . . . Keissiger
3. WALTZ, "Violets" . . . Waldteufel
4. SELECTION, "Mikado" . . . Sullivan
5. OVERTURE, "Sakuntala" . . . Goldmark
6. { a. "Reverie"
     b. "The Indian" } for String Orchestra . . Maquarre
   The audience is respectfully requested to preserve silence during the performance of this number.
7. INTRODUCTION, Act III, "Lohengrin" . . Wagner
8. BACCHANALE, from "Samson and Delila" . Saint-Saëns
9. VISIONS IN A DREAM . . . Sumbye
   Zuher Solo, Mr. KELLER.
10. OVERTURE, "Pique Dame" . . . Suppe
11. WALTZ, "Artist's Life" . . . Strauss
12. MARCH, "Austria" . . . Zach

COAL Best Quality AT Lowest Prices

METROPOLITAN COAL COMPANY,
No. 30 Congress Street.

WILSON BELFAST GINGER ALE and Champagne Kola are sold at these concerts.

DRINK

WILSON CHAMPAGNE KOLA.

It produces energy, activity, and force. Its medical virtues are endorsed by physicians.

The **Wilson** is acknowledged to be America's purest spring water. Bottled only in glass at the spring, North Raymond, Me.

In making our BELFAST GINGER ALE we use only the purest ginger.

Beware of Imitations.

Drink the **Wilson** and you are sure of the best.

Wilson Spring and Hotel Co.,
45 Arch Street.
Telephone 3129, Boston. Boston, Mass.

"THE RECOGNIZED FAVORITE OF ALL BEERS."

THE ONLY BEER ON DRAUGHT AT THESE CONCERTS.
"the beer that's brewed"

Sold at these Concerts. JOS. GAHM & CO., N.E. AGENTS, 125-127 PURCHASE ST.

THE FALL RIVER LINE

OCCUPYING THE LONG ISLAND SOUND ROUTE BETWEEN

Boston and New York

Has the finest quintette of great steamboats that the world has ever seen. The

Priscilla, Puritan, Plymouth, Pilgrim, and Providence

Are the largest, best equipped, safest, and handsomest steamboats ever constructed. This route is one of the most attractive and naturally beautiful traversed by any transportation agency in the world.

Trips of the Fall River Line are made throughout the year. Each steamboat has its own orchestra, and the service on each member of the fleet is maintained at the highest possible standard.

Tickets via this route are on sale at all of the principal Ticket Offices in the United States.

From BOSTON, Trains, connecting with steamers at Fall River in 80 minutes, leave Park Square Station, New York, New Haven & Hartford Railroad (Old Colony System), daily at 6 p.m.

From NEW YORK. Steamers leave Pier 19, North River, foot of Warren Street, daily at 5.30 p.m.

S. A. GARDNER, Superintendent, NEW YORK.
GEO. L. CONNOR, Passenger Traffic Manager, NEW HAVEN, CONN.
O. H. TAYLOR, General Passenger Agent, NEW YORK CITY.

HOTEL LANGWOOD,

Middlesex Fells Reservation.

WYOMING STATION, B. & M. R.R.

NOW OPEN.

Twenty minutes by rail from Boston. Sixty trains daily. Hotel coaches meet trains each way. Four hundred feet above sea level. Beautiful rides, drives, and walks. Golf links, tennis courts, and ball grounds.

For plans and prices address :

F. W. GASKILL, Manager,

Telephone, 40 Melrose.   Melrose, Mass.

THIRD SEASON.

3 Ideal Outings

Personally conducted by
F. R. COMEE,
Music Hall,
Boston.

	1.	2.	3.
Boston Leave	July 2	July 15	August 19
Arrive	July 12	July 31	September 4

No. 1. Ten days. **Saratoga, Lake George,** 2,130 miles from **Buffalo** to **Duluth,** and return on the steamer "North-Land" through the **Great Lakes, Erie, Huron, St. Clair,** and **Superior.**

Nos. 2 and 3. Sixteen days. Exactly alike. 700 miles' ocean sail to **Norfolk** and **Baltimore.** Over **Alleghany Mountains** and a day in **Chicago.** Up Lake **Michigan** and three days at **Mackinac Island.** 1,546 miles on steamer "North-West" to **Duluth** and return to **Buffalo** through the **Great Lakes, Niagara Falls** to **Toronto.** Across Lake **Ontario,** through the **Thousand Islands,** and down the **St. Lawrence River** to **Montreal** and **Boston.**

SEND FOR CIRCULARS.

No country in the world can duplicate the journey of 1,065 miles in one steamer on fresh water from **Buffalo** to **Duluth** through the Great Northern Lakes. These "Ideal Outings" are not cheap trips, as they are too extensive, trip No. 1 covering 3,000 miles, Nos. 2 and 3, which are exactly alike, covering 4,000 miles, and with only one night in a sleeping-car. There need be no fear of seasickness, as frequent experience has proved the Great Lakes to be unusually smooth in July and August. We travel first-class in every way. The parties are strictly limited, as it is impossible to secure equally good accommodations for a large number. The fatigue of too steady travel is avoided by from one to three days' rest at Old Point Comfort, Chicago, Mackinac Island, Duluth, Niagara Falls, Saratoga, etc. The average temperature through the Great Lakes in midsummer is 60°. No tourist who has made the journey has yet expressed disappointment; on the contrary, all are amazed at its extent and beauty.

Allsopp's

ENGLISH ALE.
"The Red Hand Brand."

Protection for Ale Drinkers.

There is a strong and growing feeling abroad that all breweries should protect consumers by doing their own bottling. Allsopp's Ale is the only brand to-day that is bottled by its makers.

Sold at these concerts.

THURSDAY, JUNE 22.

PROGRAMME.

1. LOUISBURG MARCH .... W. A. Rice
   (First Time)
2. OVERTURE, "Banditenstreiche" .... Suppé
3. WALTZ, "Vienna Blood" .... Strauss
4. SELECTION, "Trovatore" .... Verdi
5. OVERTURE, "Merry Wives of Windsor" .. Nicolai
6. SERENADE for String Orchestra ...... Moszkowski
   The audience is respectfully requested to preserve silence during the performance of this number.
7. TWO SLAVONIC DANCES .... Dvorak
8. POLONAISE .... Liszt
9. SELECTION, "Tabasco" .... Chadwick
10. WALTZ, "Donau Wellen" .... Ivanovici
11. THE DARKIES' DREAM .... Lansing
12. MARCH, "The Bride Elect" .... Sousa

The *only* Lithia Water sold at these concerts.

Hygeia Lithia Water

Sparkling and Still.

By its use you will avoid the germs of disease which natural MINERAL WATERS are liable to contain.

For Sale at these concerts and by

S. S. PIERCE CO.

The purity and keeping quality of the Tannhaeuser Export under all changes of temperature, its uniform excellence being guaranteed, together with its nutritious properties, make it the most pleasant, delicious, and convenient beverage for home consumption.

Put up in corked bottles, and packed in casks of 10 dozen white flint pints, and 6 dozen amber quarts.

Highest Awards wherever exhibited.

FOR SALE AT THESE CONCERTS.

FAMOUS TANNHAEUSER EXPORT BEER

The finest Light Beer Extant.   Brewery Bottling.   Favorite of Connoisseurs.

Pure,   Palatable,   Perfect.

B. & E. Philadelphia Ale on Draught.
FOR SALE AT THESE CONCERTS.

The BERGNER & ENGEL BREWING CO.'S N.E. Depot,
508 and 510 Atlantic Avenue, Boston.
Telephone 3805.   SOL. BACHARACH, Manager.

THE MUSIC HALL
PROMENADE CONCERTS

SMOKE THE POPULAR "BARRISTER" CIGARS AT THE POPULAR CONCERTS.

SMOKE: "LA CELESTINA," THE BEST ALL-HAVANA CIGAR. DANIEL FRANK & CO.

PUBLISHED BY
C. A. ELLIS,
MUSIC HALL.

BOSTON, TUESDAY, JUNE 20, 1899.

SUMMER SEASON.
Vol. XIV. No. 37.

YOU CAN
Have your last season's outfit dyed or cleansed and refinished so it will look like new, by our French process. Why discard soiled clothing when it can be overhauled and worn as second best? You can

RELY ON
Our methods of cleansing, and need not hesitate to trust us with articles of the most delicate textures.
We dye or cleanse and refinish PROPERLY, *all* materials of household use and clothing of all kinds.

LEWANDO'S
W. L. Crosby, General Manager.
French Cleansers, Fancy Dyers, Fine Launderers.

PRINCIPAL OFFICES:
17 Temple Place, Boston.
479 Fifth Avenue, New York.
Established 70 years.
Largest in America.
Bundles called for and delivered.
Telephones in all offices.

Save half your money

do not throw it away in half-smoked cigars! You will find that 50% of your cigar money is thrown away every day if you recall how few cigars you really have time to smoke "up."

BETWEEN THE ACTS
Little Cigars

are pure—clean—all good tobacco, and are in every way a very satisfactory short smoke. While you are listening to the music to-night, try a 10-cent box. The waiter will get them for you as they are for sale here. You will enjoy them!

THE MUSIC HALL ... Promenade Concerts
FOURTEENTH SEASON.

C. A. ELLIS, Manager.   F. R. COMEE, Assistant Manager.
Mr. GUSTAV STRUBE, Conductor.

TUESDAY, JUNE 20.
PROGRAMME.

1. MARCH, "The Harvard Volunteers" . . . Grace Weston Lunt
   (First Time)
2. OVERTURE, "La Gazza Ladra" . . . . Rossini
3. WALTZ, "Harlequin on a Voyage" . . . Zach
4. SELECTION, "The Brigands" . . . . Offenbach
5. JUBEL OVERTURE . . . . . . Weber
6. ANDANTE FOR STRING ORCHESTRA . . Tchaikowsky
   The audience is respectfully requested to preserve silence during the performance of this number
7. CZARDAS from "Der Geist des Wojewoden" . Grossmann
   (First Time.)
8. FINALE, Act I., "Lohengrin" . . . . Wagner
9. SUITE DE BALLET . . . . . . Levy
   (First Time.)
10. LOVE'S DREAM AFTER THE BALL . . Czibulka
11. POLKA, "Love Letter" . . . . . Ziehrer
12. GEORGIA CAMP-MEETING . . . . . Mills

Wednesday, June 21, Naval Night. Complimentary to the Officers of the North Atlantic Squadron.
Tuesday, June 27, Soloists' Night.
Friday, June 30, Request Night.

To secure satisfactory service, patrons are URGED by the Management to report PROMPTLY any inattention. Complaints made so late that patrons cannot recall either the number of the table or the waiter are obviously useless.

THE TWO
MOST POPULAR TWO-STEPS
OF THE SEASON.

THE RUNAWAY GIRL, by Van Baar, ... 60c.
THE CECIL, by Megone, ... 50c.
For Orchestra or Piano Solo.

BOOSEY & CO.,
9 EAST 17th STREET,   NEW YORK.

BEST BEER BREWED

OH BE JOLLY!
DRINK VAN NOSTRAND'S
P. B. ALE
SOLD AT THESE CONCERTS

NORFOLK CABINET

LAGER BEER
A Particularly Fine Lager for Family Use and Clubs.
Bottled in the most careful manner at our own bottling departments, and sold by the R. S. Pierce Co. and all other leading grocers in New England.
Other Brands in Bottles:
"Norfolk India Pale Stock Ale."
"Norfolk Extra Golden Ale" (blue label).
"Norfolk Standard Lager."
Our "Cabinet" and "Bismarck Brau" are the most popular refreshments at these concerts.

HABICH & CO.
H. W. HABICH,   Telephone, 51 Roxbury
EDWARD BUHL.   or 1182 Boston.

ESTABROOK & EATON'S MARGUERITE PERFECTOS, 10c. EACH CONCHAS, 10c., 3 FOR 25c., SOLD AT THE "POPS."

THE ICE-CREAM SERVED AT THESE CONCERTS IS FURNISHED BY WEBER, 25 Temple Place and 33 West Street.

MUSIC HALL PROMENADE PROGRAMME.

PUBLISHED EVERY EVENING DURING THE SUMMER SEASON.

NOTICE TO ADVERTISERS.

The advertising columns in the Programme are controlled SOLELY by F. R. Comee, Boston Music Hall Box Office, to whom all communications should be addressed.

The United States Hotel,

SARATOGA SPRINGS, N.Y.

Under a continuous management for 25 years.

Without a peer in its appointments, service, and liberal management.

The largest structure of its kind in the world.

Built entirely of brick.

The Hotel and court cover over seven acres.

For further information, rates, etc., etc., address

GAGE & PERRY,
Proprietors,
UNITED STATES HOTEL,
Saratoga Springs, N.Y.

Colonial Beer...

The Beer that's Brewed in Glass.

PURE, CLEAN, PALATABLE.

Order a Bottle.

SOUTHER BREWING CO.,
919 Parker Street,
Roxbury, Mass.

All The IMPORTED CIGARS

Sold At These Concerts Are Supplied By The

S. S. PIERCE COMPANY.

The Peer of all Cigarettes.

Save the band-label on each box for valuable premiums.

::: ALSO :::

Monopol

High-grade Egyptian Cigarettes.

No. 83 Kheilive,
No. 66A Nadine,
No. 84 Egyptian Belles,
No. 70A Princess Lillian

On sale at these concerts and all first-class dealers.

OCKENHEIMER BERG,
Near Bingen, GERMANY. On the Rhine.

PHILIP KRIM'S
OWN
IMPORTATION
OF

Rhine Wines.

FOR 30 YEARS
AT
163 Shawmut Avenue.

OUR WINES SOLD AT THESE CONCERTS.

HERRICK, COPLEY SQUARE, Telephones 608 and 950 (Back Bay), CHOICE TABLES for Music Hall "Pops."

GREAT WESTERN CHAMPAGNE

—————— A natural, genuine champagne, of the finest quality produced in America.

Sold by Wine Merchants, Grocers, and Druggists.

WEDNESDAY, JUNE 21.

Naval Night. Complimentary to the Officers of the North Atlantic Squadron.

PROGRAMME.

1. MARCH, "Under the Double Eagle" . . . . . Wagner
2. OVERTURE, "Felsenmühle" . . . . . Reissiger
3. WALTZ, "Violets" . . . . . Waldteufel
4. SELECTION, "Mikado" . . . . . Sullivan

5. OVERTURE, "Sakuntala" . . . . . Goldmark
6. { a. "Reverie" } for String Orchestra . . . Marquarre
   { b. "The Indian" }
   The audience is respectfully requested to preserve silence during the performance of this number.
7. INTRODUCTION, Act III., "Lohengrin" . . . Wagner
8. AMERICAN FANTASY . . . . . Herbert

9. MARCH, "Hobson's Choice" . . . . . Strube
10. OVERTURE, "Pique Dame" . . . . . Suppé
11. WALTZ, "Artist's Life" . . . . . Strauss
12. MARCH, "Austria" . . . . . Zach

THE HAYWARD,
16 and 22 Hayward Place.
LADIES' AND GENTS' CAFÉ.   Open until 1 a.m.
Table d'hôte dinner, including bottle of wine, 75c., served from 5 to 8.30 P.M.

SCIARRETTA'S NEAPOLITAN TRIO give concerts daily from 6 P.M. until 1 A.M.
Signor SALVATORE SCIARRETTI, Lyric Tenor,
Is highly endorsed by Vice-President Garrett A. Hobart, Chauncey M. Depew, Eugene Ysaye, Raoul Pugno, Jean Gerardy, and many other prominent people.

SMITH & KERRISSEY, Proprietors.

AN HISTORIC RESORT.

The loveliest place on the New England coast to spend a short vacation or the whole season is the

MYLES STANDISH HOTEL,
at SOUTH DUXBURY, MASS.

Everything that money and intelligence can do has been done to make this hotel better, if possible, than it was last season.
The greatest pains will be taken to have the table service absolutely excellent. Of the house itself and its surroundings too much cannot be said. It is a resort of nice people, who come year after year, gaining strength, vitality, and pleasure.
Send for our 1899 booklet.

L. BOYER'S SONS, Proprietors,
27 Devonshire Street, Boston, Mass.,
Or ALFRED S. AMER, Manager,
90 Wall Street, New York
(Until June 1).

Myles Standish Hotel,
South Duxbury, Mass.

"AMERICA'S FINEST PRODUCT."
Bartholomay's "APOLLO"
LAGER BEER IN BOTTLES.

Sold at these Concerts.

ALBRECHT & KOELLNER,
SOLE AGENTS,
Telephone, Boston 1751.   295-305 A Street.

Also Agents for the "Crystal Rock" Mineral Water.

PURE BEER
Harvard BREW. CO'S $1000.00
PURE BEER
Sold at these Concerts,
IN BOTTLES ONLY
20¢ PER BOTTLE.

Inglenook Vineyard.

The only California Wines sold at these Concerts.

❧❧

THE CODMAN & HALL CO.,
Opposite the South Union Station.

Sole Agents for New England.

IND. COOPE & CO.'S English Ale.

THE SECOND LARGEST BREWERY IN ENGLAND.

Brewers of the finest *light quality* ale. Very highly endorsed by the medical profession. : : : :

❧❧

THE CODMAN & HALL CO.,
Opposite South Union Station.

Sole Agents for the United States.

DRINK only the

PURE

WHIS

If you want pu
and richnes
flavor, try
only menu
and origina

OLD KENTU
TAYLOR,

Eight years old,
own distillation
guaranted pu
Bottled and ship
direct from
warehouses by
None genuine w
out our signat
on both labels.
ware of imitati
For consumpti
indigestion, and
ailments requir
stimulants. O
KENTUCKY T
LOR has
superior.
Sold by ll fi
class druggi
grocers, and liq
dealers.

Wright & Tayl
Distillers,
Fine Kentuck
Whiskies,
Louisville, Ky

Hirshfield & C
New England
Agents,
31 Doane Stree
Boston.

Instruct your waiter to bring a bottle of **Pfaff's "Monogram" Lager.**

If you will do this, it will not be necessary for us to expatiate upon the good qualities of our production.
YOU CAN JUDGE FOR YOURSELF.

H. & J. PFAFF BREWING COMPANY,
Telephone 2608.   16 ARCH STREET, BOSTON.

TABLE LINEN USED AT THESE CONCERTS LAUNDERED BY THE L. K. HÜSTED LAUNDERING COMPANY. 27 and 29 BROADWAY, CHELSEA, MASS.

BIA BRAND" VIENNA SAUSAGES. SERVED HOT OR COLD AT THESE CONCERTS.

THURSDAY, JUNE 22.

PROGRAMME.

1. LOUISBURG MARCH . . . . W. A. Rice
   (First Time)
2. OVERTURE, "Banditenstreiche" Suppé
3. WALTZ, "Vienna Blood" Strauss
4. SELECTION, "Trovatore" Verdi

5. OVERTURE, "Merry Wives of Windsor" . Nicola
6. SERENADE for String Orchestra . . . . Moszkowski
   The audience is respectfully requested to preserve silence during the performance of this number.
7. TWO SLAVONIC DANCES . . Dvorak
8. POLONAISE Liszt

9. SELECTION, "Tabasco" . Chadwick
10. WALTZ, "Donau Wellen" . Ivanovici
11. THE DARKIES' DREAM Lansing
12. MARCH, "The Bride Elect" Sousa

WILSON BELFAST GINGER ALE
and
Champagne Kola
are sold at these concerts.

DRINK WILSON CHAMPAGNE KOLA.

It produces energy, activity, and force. Its medical virtues are endorsed by physicians.

The **Wilson** is acknowledged to be America's purest spring water.
Bottled only in glass at the spring, North Raymond, Me.

In making our **BELFAST GINGER ALE** we use only the purest ginger.

Beware of imitations.

Drink the **Wilson** and you are sure of the best.

Wilson Spring and Hotel Co.,
45 Arch Street,
Telephone 3129, Boston. Boston, Mass.

COAL
Best Quality AT Lowest Prices

METROPOLITAN COAL COMPANY,
No. 30 Congress Street.

THE ONLY BEER ON DRAUGHT AT THESE CONCERTS.

"the beer that's brewed"

AWARD FOR PURITY.
GAHM & CO., N.E. AGENTS 175-127 PURCHASE ST.

THE FALL RIVER LINE

OCCUPYING THE
LONG ISLAND SOUND ROUTE
BETWEEN

Boston and New York

Has the finest quintette of great steamboats that the world has ever seen. The

Priscilla, Puritan, Plymouth, Pilgrim, and Providence

Are the largest, best equipped, safest, and handsomest steamboats ever constructed. This route is one of the most attractive and naturally beautiful traversed by any transportation agency in the world. Trips of the Fall River Line are made throughout the year. Each steamboat has its own orchestra, and the service on each member of the fleet is maintained at the highest possible standard.

Tickets via this route are on sale at all of the principal Ticket Offices in the United States.

From BOSTON. Trains, connecting with steamers at Fall River in 80 minutes leave Park Square Station, New York, New Haven & Hartford Railroad (Old Colony System), daily at 6 p.m.

From NEW YORK. Steamers leave Pier 19, North River, foot of Warren Street, daily at 5.30 p.m.

B. A. GARDNER, Superintendent, NEW YORK.
GEO. L. CONNOR, Passenger Traffic Manager, NEW HAVEN, CONN.
O. H. TAYLOR, General Passenger Agent, NEW YORK CITY.

HOTEL LANGWOOD,

Middlesex Fells Reservation.

WYOMING STATION, B. & M. R.R.

NOW OPEN.

Twenty minutes by rail from Boston. Sixty trains daily. Hotel coaches meet trains each way. Four hundred feet above sea level. Beautiful rides, drives, and walks. Golf links, tennis courts, and ball grounds.

For plans and prices address:

F. W. GASKILL, Manager,

Telephone, 40 Melrose.   Melrose, Mass.

THIRD SEASON.

3 Ideal Outings

Personally conducted by
F. R. COMEE,
Music Hall,
Boston.

	1.	2.	3.
Boston Leave	July 2	July 15	August 19
Arrive	July 12	July 31	September 4

No. 1. Ten days. **Saratoga, Lake George,** 2,130 miles from **Buffalo** to **Duluth,** and return on the steamer "North-Land" through the **Great Lakes, Erie, Huron, St. Clair,** and **Superior.**

Nos. 2 and 3. Sixteen days. Exactly alike. 700 miles' ocean sail to **Norfolk** and **Baltimore.** Over **Alleghany Mountains** and a day in **Chicago.** Up **Lake Michigan** and three days at **Mackinac Island.** 1,546 miles on steamer "North-West" to **Duluth** and return to **Buffalo** through the Great Lakes, Niagara Falls to **Toronto.** Across Lake Ontario, through the **Thousand Islands,** and down the St. Lawrence River to **Montreal** and **Boston.**

SEND FOR CIRCULARS.

No country in the world can duplicate the journey of 1,065 **miles in one steamer on fresh water** from Buffalo to Duluth through the Great Northern Lakes. These "Ideal Outings" are not cheap trips, as they are too extensive, trip No. 1 covering 3,000 miles, Nos. 2 and 3, which are exactly alike, covering 4,000 miles, and with only one night in a sleeping-car. There need be no fear of seasickness, as frequent experience has proved the Great Lakes to be unusually smooth in July and August. We travel first-class in every way. The parties are strictly limited, as it is impossible to secure equally good accommodations for a large number. The fatigue of too steady travel is avoided by from one to three days' rest at Old Point Comfort, Chicago, Mackinac Island, Duluth, Niagara Falls, Saratoga, etc. The average temperature through the Great Lakes in midsummer is 60°. No tourist who has made the journey has yet expressed disappointment; on the contrary, all are amazed at its extent and beauty.

Allsopp's

ENGLISH ALE.
"The Red Hand Brand."

Protection for Ale Drinkers.

There is a strong and growing feeling abroad that all breweries should protect consumers by doing their own bottling. Allsopp's Ale is the only brand to-day that is bottled by its makers.

Sold at these concerts.

FRIDAY, JUNE 23.

PROGRAMME.

1. MARCH, "Washington Post" . . . Sousa
2. OVERTURE, "Light Cavalry" . . . Suppe
3. WALTZ, "Bei uns zu Haus'" . . . Strauss
4. SELECTION, "Aïda" . . . Verdi
5. BALLET MUSIC from "Queen of Sheba" . . . Goldmark
   Violoncello Solo, Mr. KELLER
6. TWO MOVEMENTS from "Peer Gynt" . . . Grieg
7. MELODIE . . . Rubinstein
8. RIDE OF THE VALKYRIES . . . Wagner

9. LE DERNIER SOMMEIL DE LA VIERGE . . . Massenet
   The audience is respectfully requested to preserve silence during the performance of this number.
10. OVERTURE, "Orpheus" . . . Offenbach
11. WALTZ, "Meerleuchten" . . . Ziehrer
12. MARCH, "Stars and Stripes" . . . Sousa

The *only* Lithia Water sold at these concerts.

Hygeia Lithia Water

Sparkling and Still.

By its use you will avoid the germs of disease which natural MINERAL WATERS are liable to contain.

For Sale at these concerts and by

S. S. PIERCE CO.

FOR SALE AT THESE CONCERTS.

FAMOUS TANNHAEUSER EXPORT BEER

The finest Light Beer Extant.   Brewery Bottling.   Favorite of Connoisseurs.

Pure,   Palatable,   Perfect.

B. & E. Philadelphia Ale on Draught.

FOR SALE AT THESE CONCERTS.

The BERGNER & ENGEL BREWING CO.'S N.E. Depot,
508 and 510 Atlantic Avenue, Boston.
Telephone 3805.   **SOL. BACHARACH, Manager.**

The purity and keeping quality of the Tannhaeuser Export under all changes of temperature, its uniform excellence being guaranteed, together with its nutritious properties, make it the most pleasant, delicious, and convenient beverage for home consumption.
Put up in corked bottles, and packed in casks of 10 dozen white flint pints, and 6 dozen amber quarts.

Highest Awards wherever exhibited.

M. Steinert & Sons Co.,

STEINERT HALL BUILDING,

No. 162 Boylston Street, corner Carver, Boston.

STEINWAY & SONS,

HARDMAN,   GABLER,
EMERSON,   SINGER,

PIANOS.

The Æolian, Aeriol, Orchestrelle, and Pianola.

THE ÆOLIAN
AND
THE PIANOLA
FOR SUMMER HOMES.

At this season of the year we receive many orders for these instruments for Summer Residences, and therefore beg to call attention to our extensive assortment now on display, especially suited for this purpose.

The ÆOLIAN meets the requirements of country homes, furnishing, as it does, music suitable for every occasion. It practically takes the place of an orchestra — music for dancing — orchestral concerts, — in short, music of every style and description is always available.

The PIANOLA will appeal to many on account of the very little space it occupies. It will play any kind of a piano, and can also be used upon a rented piano without the slightest injury. For the above reasons it is bound to be very popular for small cottages.

We are glad to be able to announce that we can furnish PIANOLAS with no more than a week's delay, and, at times, the day the order is given.

Persons not familiar with these instruments are cordially invited to call at our warerooms and hear them, or a descriptive catalogue will be mailed free upon application.

M. STEINERT & SONS CO.,
Steinert Hall,   162 Boylston Street,   Boston.

ANHEUSER-BUSCH BREWING ASS'N,

ST. LOUIS, MO., U.S.A.

BREWERS OF HIGH=GRADE BEERS EXCLUSIVELY.

Black and Tan.	Faust.
Michelob.	Pale Lager.
Muenchener.	Anheuser Standard.

Served at the Music Hall Concerts.

Also at all first-class hotels, clubs, and bars, and on all Pullman and Wagner cars and ocean and lake steamers.

JACOB WIRTH,   Wholesale Dealer,   Boston, Mass.

THE MUSIC HALL
PROMENADE CONCERTS

PUBLISHED BY
C. A. ELLIS,
MUSIC HALL.

BOSTON, WEDNESDAY, JUNE 21, 1899.

SUMMER SEASON.
Vol. XIV. No. 38.

SMOKE THE POPULAR "BARRISTER" CIGARS AT THE POPULAR CONCERTS.
SMOKE "LA CELESTINA," THE BEST ALL-HAVANA CIGAR. DANIEL FRANK & CO.

YOU CAN

Have your last season's outfit dyed or cleansed and refinished so it will look like new, by our French process. Why discard soiled clothing when it can be overhauled and worn as second best? You can

RELY ON

Our methods of cleansing, and need not hesitate to trust us with articles of the most delicate textures. We dye or cleanse and refinish PROPERLY, *all* materials of household use and clothing of all kinds.

LEWANDO'S

W. L. Crosby, General Manager.
French Cleansers, Fancy Dyers, Fine Launderers.

PRINCIPAL OFFICES:
17 Temple Place, Boston.
479 Fifth Avenue, New York.
Established 70 years.
Largest in America.
Bundles called for and delivered.
Telephones in all offices.

In no other way

are men as wasteful and extravagant as in cigar smoking—because cigars are thrown away half smoked half the time.

BETWEEN THE ACTS
Little Cigars

are just right for all short smokes. They light right, they burn right and taste right. Have you ever seen them? At all stores: 10 for 10 cts., or, as they are for sale here, you can try them to-night. Tell the waiter to bring you a 10-cent box of "Between the Acts." They will add to your enjoyment of this concert.

THE MUSIC HALL :: Promenade Concerts

FOURTEENTH SEASON.

C. A. ELLIS, Manager.   F. R. COMEE, Assistant Manager.

Mr. GUSTAV STRUBE, Conductor.

WEDNESDAY, JUNE 21.

Naval Night. Complimentary to the Officers of the North Atlantic Squadron.

PROGRAMME.

1. MARCH, "Under the Double Eagle" . . . Wagner
2. OVERTURE, "Felsenmühle" . . . Reissiger
3. WALTZ, "Violets" . . . Waldteufel
4. SELECTION, "Mikado" . . . Sullivan
5. OVERTURE, "Sakuntala" . . . Goldmark
6. { a. "Reverie"
     b. "The Indian" } for String Orchestra . . . Maquarre

The audience is respectfully requested to preserve silence during the performance of this number.

7. INTRODUCTION, Act III., "Lohengrin" . . . Wagner
8. AMERICAN FANTASY . . . Herbert
9. MARCH, "Hobson's Choice" . . . Strube
10. OVERTURE, "Pique Dame" . . . Suppé
11. WALTZ, "Artist's Life" . . . Strauss
12. MARCH, "Austria" . . . Zach

Tuesday, June 27, Soloists' Night.
Friday, June 30, Request Night.

To secure satisfactory service, patrons are URGED by the Management to report PROMPTLY any inattention. Complaints made so late that patrons cannot recall either the number of the table or the waiter are obviously useless.

Now the rage of the LONDON Concerts and Drawing-rooms:

YOU AND I, by Liza Lehmann, . . . 60c.
KING CHARLES, by M. V. White, . . . 60c.
LIKE VIOLETS PALE, by F. Allitsen, . . . 60c.
WHEN THE WORLD IS FAIR, by F. H. Cowen, 60c.
QUEEN OF MY LIFE, by E. T. Lloyd, . . 60c.

BOOSEY & CO.,
9 East 17th Street,   New York.

DRINK VAN NOSTRAND'S BOSTON CLUB LAGER
SOLD AT THESE CONCERTS

NORFOLK CABINET

LAGER BEER

A Particularly Fine Lager for Family Use and Clubs.

Bottled in the most careful manner at our own bottling department, and sold by the B. S. Pierce Co. and all other leading grocers in New England.

Other Brands in Bottles:
"Norfolk India Pale Stock Ale."
"Norfolk Extra Golden Ale" (blue label).
"Norfolk Standard Lager."
Our "Cabinet" and "Bismarck Brau" are the most popular refreshments at these concerts.

HABICH & CO.

H. W. HABICH,   { Telephone, 56 Roxbury
EDWARD BUHL.   {   or 1152 Boston.

ESTABROOK & EATON'S MARGUERITE PERFECTOS, 10c. EACH.
CONCHAS, 10c., 3 FOR 25c. **SOLD AT THE "POPS."**

THE ICE-CREAM SERVED AT THESE CONCERTS IS FURNISHED BY WEBER, 25 Temple Place and 33 West Street.

MUSIC HALL PROMENADE PROGRAMME.
PUBLISHED EVERY EVENING DURING THE SUMMER SEASON.

NOTICE TO ADVERTISERS.
The advertising columns in the Programme are controlled SOLELY by F. R. Comee, Boston Music Hall Box Office, to whom all communications should be addressed.

The United States Hotel,
SARATOGA SPRINGS, N.Y.

Under a continuous management for 25 years.

Without a peer in its appointments, service, and liberal management.

The largest structure of its kind in the world.

Built entirely of brick.

The Hotel and court cover over seven acres.

For further information, rates, etc., address

GAGE & PERRY,
Proprietors,
UNITED STATES HOTEL,
Saratoga Springs, N.Y.

Colonial Beer...
The Beer that's Brewed in Glass.

PURE, CLEAN, PALATABLE.

Order a Bottle.

SOUTHER BREWING CO.,
919 Parker Street,
Roxbury, Mass.

The Peer of all Cigarettes.
Save the band-label on each box for valuable premiums.

::: ALSO :::

Monopol

High-grade Egyptian Cigarettes.

No. 8A Khedive,
No. 66A Nadine,
No. 9A Egyptian Belles,
No. 70A Princess Lillian

On sale at these concerts and all first-class dealers.

VEUVE CHAFFARD

PURE OLIVE OIL.
IN HONEST BOTTLES.

OCKENHEIMER BERG,
Near Bingen, GERMANY. On the Rhine.

PHILIP KRIM'S
OWN
IMPORTATION
OF
Rhine Wines,
FOR 30 YEARS
AT
163 Shawmut Avenue.
OUR WINES SOLD AT THESE CONCERTS.

HERRICK, COPLEY SQUARE, Telephones 608 and 950 (Back Bay), CHOICE TABLES for Music Hall "Pops."

THURSDAY, JUNE 22.

PROGRAMME.

1. LOUISBURG MARCH . . . . W. A. Rice
   (First Time.)
2. OVERTURE, "Banditenstreiche" . . . . . . Suppé
3. WALTZ, "Vienna Blood" . . . . Strauss
4. SELECTION, "Trovatore" . . . . Verdi
5. OVERTURE, "Merry Wives of Windsor" . . . Nicolai
6. SERENADE for String Orchestra . . . . Moszkowski
   The audience is respectfully requested to preserve silence during the performance of this number.
7. TWO SLAVONIC DANCES . . . . Dvorak
8. POLONAISE . . . . Liszt
9. SELECTION, "Tabasco" . . . . Chadwick
10. WALTZ, "Donau Wellen" . . . . Ivanovici
11. THE DARKIES' DREAM . . . . Lansing
12. MARCH, "The Bride Elect" . . . . Sousa

D. LEIDEN'S
SPARKLING
MOSELLE,

The only Sparkling Wine sold at these Concerts.

SHINNECOCK

The Perfection of

Scotch
Whisky

Sold by
S. S. PIERCE COMPANY.

THE HAYWARD,
16 and 22 Hayward Place.
LADIES' AND GENTS' CAFÉ.   Open until 1 a.m.
Table d'hôte dinner, including bottle of wine, 75c., served from 5 to 8.30 P.M.

SCIARRETTA'S NEAPOLITAN TRIO give concerts daily from 6 P.M. until 1 A.M.
Signor **SALVATORE SCIARRETTI**, Lyric Tenor,
Is highly endorsed by Vice-President Garret A. Hobart, Chauncey M. Depew, Eugene Ysaye, Raoul Pugno, Jean Gerardy, and many other prominent people.
SMITH & KERRISSEY, Proprietors.

AN
HISTORIC
RESORT.

The loveliest place on the New England coast to spend a short vacation or the whole season is the

MYLES STANDISH HOTEL,
at SOUTH DUXBURY, MASS.

Everything that money and intelligence can do has been done to make this hotel better, if possible, than it was last season.
The greatest pains will be taken to have the table service absolutely excellent. Of the house itself and its surroundings too much cannot be said. It is a resort of nice people, who come year after year, gaining strength, vitality, and pleasure.
Send for our 1899 booklet.

L. BOYER'S SONS, Proprietors,
27 Devonshire Street, Boston, Mass.,
Or ALFRED S. AMER, Manager,
90 Wall Street, New York
(Until June 1).
Myles Standish Hotel,
South Duxbury, Mass.

"AMERICA'S FINEST PRODUCT."

Bartholomay's "APOLLO"

LAGER BEER IN BOTTLES.

Sold at these Concerts.

ALBRECHT & KOELLNER,
SOLE AGENTS,
Telephone, Boston 1751.   295-305 A Street.

Also Agents for the "Crystal Rock" Mineral Water.

PURE BEER

BREW. CO'S **$1000.00**

PURE BEER

Sold at these Concerts,
IN BOTTLES ONLY
20¢ PER BOTTLE.

TABLE LINEN USED AT THESE CONCERTS THE L. K. HUSTED LAUNDERING COMPANY. 27 and 29 BROADWAY, CHELSEA, MASS.

Inglenook Vineyard.

The only California Wines sold at these Concerts.

❧❧

THE CODMAN & HALL CO.,
Opposite the South Union Station.

Sole Agents for New England.

IND. COOPE & CO.'S English Ale.

THE SECOND LARGEST BREWERY IN ENGLAND.

Brewers of the finest *light* quality ale. Very highly endorsed by the medical profession. : : : :

❧❧

THE CODMAN & HALL CO.,
Opposite South Union Station.

Sole Agents for the United States.

Instruct your waiter to bring a bottle of

Pfaff's "Monogram" Lager.

If you will do this, it will not be necessary for us to expatiate upon the good qualities of our production.
YOU CAN JUDGE FOR YOURSELF.

H. & J. PFAFF BREWING COMPANY,
Telephone 2608.   16 ARCH STREET, BOSTON.

DRIN only the PURE WHIS

If you want p and richnes flavor, try only gen and origin

OLD KENTU TAYLOR,

Eight years old own distillatio guaranteed p Bottled and shi direct from warehouses by None genuine w out our signa on both labels. ware of imitat for consump indigestion, an ailments requ stimulants, O KENTUCKY LOR has superior.
Sold by all class drug grocers, and li dealers.

Wright & Tay
Distillers,
Fine Kentuc
Whiskies,
Louisville, K

Hirshfield &
New Englan
Agents,
31 Doane Stre
Boston.

TRY THE "COLUMBIA BRAND" VIENNA SAUSAGES. SERVED HOT OR COLD AT THESE CONCERTS.

FRIDAY, JUNE 23

PROGRAMME.

1. MARCH, " Washington Post " . . . . . . Sousa
2. OVERTURE, "Light Cavalry " . . . . . Suppé
3. WALTZ, " Bei uns zu Haus' " . . . . . Strauss
4. SELECTION, " Aida " . . . . Verdi
5. BALLET MUSIC from " Queen of Sheba " . . Goldmark
   Violoncello Solo, Mr. KELLER.
6. TWO MOVEMENTS from " Peer Gynt " . . . Grieg
7. MELODIE . . . . Rubinstein
8. RIDE OF THE VALKYRIES . . . . . . Wagner
9. LE DERNIER SOMMEIL DE LA VIERGE . . . Massenet
   The audience is respectfully requested to preserve silence during the performance of this number.
10. OVERTURE, " Orpheus " . . . . . . Offenbach
11. WALTZ, " Meerleuchten " . . . . . . Ziehrer
12. MARCH, " Stars and Stripes " . . . . . Sousa

They cannot sell you here
Canadian Club Whisky,
Ruinart Champagne,
Royal Liqueur Scotch,
Carstair's Philadelphia Rye,
Fort Hill Bourbon,
Alhambra Sherry,
All of which you will find
of excellent quality;

But you can get

Kaiser Water,

the most refreshing of all table waters,

Chateau d'Arsac Claret,
N. Johnston & Sons' Medoc,
and
California Inglenook Clarets.

SUPPLIED BY

CODMAN & HALL COMPANY,

WINE MERCHANTS,

Opposite New South Station.

WILSON BELFAST GINGER ALE
and
Champagne Kola
are sold at these concerts.

DRINK
WILSON CHAMPAGNE KOLA.

It produces energy, activity, and force. Its medical virtues are endorsed by physicians.

The **Wilson** is acknowledged to be America's purest spring water. Bottled only in glass at the spring, North Raymond, Me.

In making our BELFAST GINGER ALE we use only the purest ginger.

Beware of Imitations.

Drink the **Wilson** and you are sure of the best.

Wilson Spring and Hotel Co.,
45 Arch Street,
Telephone 3129, Boston. Boston, Mass.

COAL Best Quality AT Lowest Prices

METROPOLITAN COAL COMPANY,
No. 30 Congress Street.

THE FALL RIVER LINE

OCCUPYING THE
LONG ISLAND SOUND ROUTE
BETWEEN

Boston and New York

Has the finest quintette of great steamboats that the world has ever seen. The

Priscilla, Puritan, Plymouth, Pilgrim, and Providence

Are the largest, best equipped, safest, and handsomest steamboats ever constructed. This route is one of the most attractive and naturally beautiful traversed by any transportation agency in the world.

Trips of the Fall River Line are made throughout the year. Each steamboat has its own orchestra, and the service on each member of the fleet is maintained at the highest possible standard.

Tickets via this route are on sale at all of the principal Ticket Offices in the United States.

From BOSTON. Trains, connecting with steamers at Fall River in 80 minutes leave Park Square Station, New York, New Haven & Hartford Railroad (Old Colony System), daily at 6 p.m.

From NEW YORK. Steamers leave Pier 19, North River, foot of Warren Street, daily at 5 30 p. m.

S. A. GARDNER, GEO. L. CONNOR, O. H. TAYLOR,
Superintendent, Passenger Traffic Manager, General Passenger Agent,
NEW YORK. NEW HAVEN, CONN. NEW YORK CITY.

HOTEL LANGWOOD.

Middlesex Fells Reservation.

WYOMING STATION, B. & M. R.R.

NOW OPEN.

Twenty minutes by rail from Boston. Sixty trains daily. Hotel coaches meet trains each way. Four hundred feet above sea level. Beautiful rides, drives, and walks. Golf links, tennis courts, and ball grounds.

For plans and prices address:

F. W. GASKILL, Manager,

Telephone, 40 Melrose. Melrose, Mass.

THIRD SEASON.

3 Ideal Outings

Personally conducted by
F. R. COMEE,
Music Hall,
Boston.

Boston | Leave July 2 | July 15 | August 19
           | Arrive July 12 | July 31 | September 4

No. 1. Ten days. **Saratoga, Lake George,** 2,130 miles from **Buffalo** to **Duluth,** and return on the steamer "**North-Land**" through the **Great Lakes, Erie, Huron, St. Clair,** and **Superior.**

Nos. 2 and 3. Sixteen days. Exactly alike. 700 miles' ocean sail to **Norfolk** and **Baltimore.** Over **Alleghany Mountains** and a day in **Chicago.** Up **Lake Michigan** and three days at **Mackinac Island.** 1,546 miles on steamer "**North-West**" to **Duluth** and return to **Buffalo** through the **Great Lakes, Niagara Falls** to **Toronto.** Across **Lake Ontario,** through the **Thousand Islands,** and down the **St. Lawrence River** to **Montreal** and **Boston.**

No country in the world can duplicate the journey of 1,065 miles in one steamer on fresh water from Buffalo to Duluth through the Great Northern Lakes. These "Ideal Outings" are not cheap trips, as they are too extensive, trip No. 1 covering 3,000 miles, Nos. 2 and 3, which are exactly alike, covering 4,000 miles, and with only one night in a sleeping-car. There need be no fear of seasickness, as frequent experience has proved the Great Lakes to be unusually smooth in July and August. We travel first-class in every way. The parties are strictly limited, as it is impossible to secure equally good accommodations for a large number. The fatigue of too steady travel is avoided by from one to three days' rest at Old Point Comfort, Chicago, Mackinac Island, Duluth, Niagara Falls, Saratoga, etc. The average temperature through the Great Lakes in midsummer is 60°. No tourist who has made the journey has yet expressed disappointment: on the contrary, all are amazed at its extent and beauty.

SEND FOR CIRCULARS.

Allsopp's

ENGLISH ALE.
"The Red Hand Brand."

Protection for Ale Drinkers.

There is a strong and growing feeling abroad that all breweries should protect consumers by doing their own bottling. Allsopp's Ale is the only brand to-day that is bottled by its makers.

Sold at these concerts.

SATURDAY, JUNE 24.

PROGRAMME.

1. MARCH, "Under the Double Eagle" . . . Wagner
2. OVERTURE, "Elisabeth" . . . Rossini
3. WALTZ, "Vienna Girls" . . . Ziehrer
4. SELECTION, "Carmen" . . . Bizet

5. MARCH, "Queen of Sheba" . . . Gounod
6. SELECTION, "La Grande Duchesse" . . . Offenbach
7. TWO SELECTIONS for String Orchestra . . . Kelley
   (First Time.)
8. OVERTURE, "Tannhäuser" . . . Wagner

9. MENUET . . . Heilman
   (First Time.)
10. TWO HUNGARIAN DANCES . . . Brahms
11. WALTZ, "Grubenlichter" . . . Zeller
12. MARCH, "Liberty Bell" . . . Sousa

The *only* Lithia Water sold at these concerts.

Hygeia Lithia Water

Sparkling and Still.

By its use you will avoid the germs of disease which natural MINERAL WATERS are liable to contain.

For Sale at these concerts and by

S. S. PIERCE CO.

FOR SALE AT THESE CONCERTS.

FAMOUS TANNHAEUSER EXPORT BEER

The finest Light Beer Extant.   Brewery Bottling.   Favorite of Connoisseurs.

Pure,   Palatable,   Perfect.

B. & E. Philadelphia Ale on Draught.
FOR SALE AT THESE CONCERTS.

The purity and keeping quality of the Tannhaeuser Export under all changes of temperature, its uniform excellence being guaranteed, together with its nutritious properties, make it the most pleasant, delicious, and convenient beverage for home consumption.
Put up in corked bottles, and packed in casks of 10 dozen white flint pints, and 6 dozen amber quarts.

Highest Awards wherever exhibited.

The BERGNER & ENGEL BREWING CO.'S N.E. Depot,
508 and 510 Atlantic Avenue, Boston.
Telephone 3805.   SOL. BACHARACH, Manager.

M. Steinert & Sons Co.,

STEINERT HALL BUILDING,

No. 162 Boylston Street, corner Carver, Boston.

STEINWAY & SONS,

HARDMAN,   GABLER,
EMERSON,   SINGER,

PIANOS.

The Æolian, Aeriol, Orchestrelle, and Pianola.

THE ÆOLIAN
AND
THE PIANOLA
FOR SUMMER HOMES.

At this season of the year we receive many orders for these instruments for Summer Residences, and therefore beg to call attention to our extensive assortment now on display, especially suited for this purpose.

The ÆOLIAN meets the requirements of country homes, furnishing, as it does, music suitable for every occasion. It practically takes the place of an orchestra — music for dancing — orchestral concerts, — in short, music of every style and description is always available.

The PIANOLA will appeal to many on account of the very little space it occupies. It will play any kind of a piano, and can also be used upon a rented piano without the slightest injury. For the above reasons it is bound to be very popular for small cottages.

We are glad to be able to announce that we can furnish PIANOLAS with no more than a week's delay, and, at times, the day the order is given.

Persons not familiar with these instruments are cordially invited to call at our warerooms and hear them, or a descriptive catalogue will be mailed free upon application.

M. STEINERT & SONS CO.,
Steinert Hall,   162 Boylston Street,   Boston.

ANHEUSER-BUSCH BREWING ASS'N,

ST. LOUIS, MO., U.S.A.

BREWERS OF HIGH-GRADE BEERS EXCLUSIVELY.

Black and Tan.

Michelob.

Muenchener.

Faust.

Pale Lager.

Anheuser Standard.

Served at the Music Hall Concerts.

Also at all first-class hotels, clubs, and bars, and on all Pullman and Wagner cars and ocean and lake steamers.

JACOB WIRTH,   **Wholesale Dealer,**   **Boston, Mass.**

THE MUSIC HALL
PROMENADE CONCERTS

SMOKE THE POPULAR "BARRISTER" CIGARS AT THE POPULAR CONCERTS.

SMOKE "LA CELESTINA," THE BEST ALL-HAVANA CIGAR. DANIEL FRANK & CO.

PUBLISHED BY C. A. ELLIS, MUSIC HALL.

BOSTON, THURSDAY, JUNE 22, 1899.

SUMMER SEASON. Vol. XIV. No. 39.

YOU CAN
Have your last season's outfit dyed or cleansed and refinished so it will look like new, by our French process. Why discard soiled clothing when it can be overhauled and worn as second best? You can

RELY ON
Our methods of cleaning, and need not hesitate to trust us with articles of the most delicate textures. We dye or cleanse and refinish PROPERLY, *all* materials of household use and clothing of all kinds.

LEWANDO'S
W. L. Crosby, General Manager.
French Cleansers, Fancy Dyers, Fine Launderers.

PRINCIPAL OFFICES:
17 Temple Place, Boston.
479 Fifth Avenue, New York.
Established 70 years.
Largest in America.
Bundles called for and delivered.
Telephones in all offices.

THE MUSIC HALL... Promenade Concerts
FOURTEENTH SEASON.

C. A. ELLIS, Manager.   F. R. COMEE, Assistant Manager.

Mr. GUSTAV STRUBE, Conductor.

THURSDAY, JUNE 22.

PROGRAMME.

1. LOUISBURG MARCH . . . . W. A. Rice
   (First Time.)
2. OVERTURE, "Banditenstreiche" . . . Suppé
3. WALTZ, "Vienna Blood" . . . . Strauss
4. SELECTION, "Trovatore" . . . . Verdi
5. OVERTURE, "Merry Wives of Windsor" . . . Nicolai
6. SERENADE for String Orchestra . . . Moszkowski
   The audience is respectfully requested to preserve silence during the performance of this number.
7. TWO SLAVONIC DANCES . . . . Dvorak
8. POLONAISE . . . . Liszt
9. SELECTION, "Tabasco" . . . . Chadwick
10. WALTZ, "Donau Wellen" . . . Ivanovici
11. THE DARKIES' DREAM . . . . Lansing
12. MARCH, "The Bride Elect" . . . Sousa

Tuesday, June 27, Soloists' Night.
Friday, June 30, Request Night.

To secure satisfactory service, patrons are URGED by the Management to report PROMPTLY any inattention. Complaints made so late that patrons cannot recall either the number of the table or the waiter are obviously useless.

HERE ARE A FEW NAMES FROM OUR LIST OF COMPOSERS:

ENGLISH.— Stephen Adams, F. H. Cowen, S. Liddle, C. V. Stanford, A. C. Mackenzie, R. H. Walthew, H. R. Shelley, Goring Thomas, Frances Allitsen, Maude V. White, Edward German, Mary Carmichael, Liza Lehmann, etc.

FRENCH.— C. Chaminade, Jane Vieu, L. Denza, P. Delmet, Bemberg, Guy d'Hardelot, De Leva, F. P. Tosti, etc.

ITALIAN.— F. P. Tosti, P. Mascagni, G. Puccini, G. Verdi, Don Lorenzo Perosi, etc.

THE MOST REPRESENTATIVE PUBLISHING HOUSE IN AMERICA.

BOOSEY & CO., 9 East 17th Street, New York.

Knowledge differs from Experience.
You may know "all about"

BETWEEN THE ACTS
Little Cigars
but have you ever tried them yourself? Do you know how desirable they really are—how good they are—how economical they are—how convenient they are—how satisfactory they are? You can know—once for all—by having the waiter bring you a 10-cent box of ten—to smoke now—to-night—while you are enjoying this concert. They are for sale here.

BEST BEER BREWED

"OH BE JOLLY!" DRINK VAN NOSTRAND'S P.B. ALE
SOLD AT THESE CONCERTS

NORFOLK CABINET LAGER BEER

A Particularly Fine Lager for Family Use and Clubs.
Bottled in the most careful manner at our own bottling department, and sold by the S. S. Pierce Co. and all other leading grocers in New England.

Other Brands in Bottles:
"Norfolk India Pale Stock Ale."
"Norfolk Extra Golden Ale" (blue label).
"Norfolk Standard Lager."
Our "Cabinet" and "Bismarck Braeu" are the most popular refreshments at these concerts.

HABICH & CO.
H. W. HABICH,   Telephone, 66 Roxbury
EDWARD HUHL.   or 1132 Boston.

ESTABROOK & EATON'S MARGUERITE PERFECTOS, 10c. EACH. CONCHAS, 10c., 3 FOR 25c., **SOLD AT THE "POPS."**

THE ICE-CREAM SERVED AT THESE CONCERTS IS FURNISHED BY: WEBER, 25 Temple Place and 33 West Street.

MUSIC HALL PROMENADE PROGRAMME.
PUBLISHED EVERY EVENING DURING THE SUMMER SEASON.

NOTICE TO ADVERTISERS.

The advertising columns in the Programme are controlled SOLELY by F. R. Comee, Boston Music Hall Box Office, to whom all communications should be addressed.

The United States Hotel,
SARATOGA SPRINGS, N.Y.

Under a continuous management for 25 years.

Without a peer in its appointments, service, and liberal management.

The largest structure of its kind in the world.

Built entirely of brick.

The Hotel and court cover over seven acres.

For further information, rates, etc., etc., address

GAGE & PERRY,
Proprietors,
UNITED STATES HOTEL,
Saratoga Springs, N.Y.

The Beer that's Brewed in Glass.

Colonial Beer...
PURE, CLEAN, PALATABLE.

Order a Bottle.

SOUTHER BREWING CO.,
919 Parker Street,
Roxbury, Mass.

All The IMPORTED CIGARS
Sold At These Concerts Are Supplied By The

S. S. PIERCE COMPANY.

The Peer of all Cigarettes.

Save the band-label on each box for valuable premiums.

::: ALSO :::

Monopol
High-grade Egyptian Cigarettes.

No. 9A Khedive.
No. 9GA Nadine.
No. 9A Egyptian Belles.
No. 70A Princess Lillian

☞ On sale at these concerts and all first-class dealers.

PHILIP KRIM'S
OWN IMPORTATION OF
Rhine Wines.
FOR 30 YEARS AT
163 Shawmut Avenue.
OUR WINES SOLD AT THESE CONCERTS.

HERRICK, COPLEY SQUARE, Telephones 608 and 950 (Back Bay), CHOICE TABLES for Music Hall "Pops."

GREAT WESTERN CHAMPAGNE

——————— A natural, genuine champagne, of the finest quality produced in America.

Sold by Wine Merchants, Grocers, and Druggists.

FRIDAY, JUNE 23.

PROGRAMME.

1. MARCH, " Washington Post " . . . Sousa
2. OVERTURE, " Light Cavalry " . . Suppé
3. WALTZ, " Bei uns zu Haus' " . . Strauss
4. SELECTION, " Aïda " . . . Verdi
5. BALLET MUSIC from " Queen of Sheba " . Goldmark
    Violoncello Solo, Mr. KELLER.
6. TWO MOVEMENTS from " Peer Gynt " . Grieg
7. MELODIE . . . . Rubinstein
8. RIDE OF THE VALKYRIES . . Wagner
9. LE DERNIER SOMMEIL DE LA VIERGE . Massenet
    The audience is respectfully requested to preserve silence during the performance of this number.
10. OVERTURE, " Orpheus " . . Offenbach
11. WALTZ, " Meerleuchten " . . Ziehrer
12. MARCH, " Stars and Stripes " . . Sousa

THE HAYWARD,
16 and 22 Hayward Place.
LADIES' AND GENTS' CAFÉ.   Open until 1 a.m.
Table d'hôte dinner, including bottle of wine, 75c., served from 5 to 8.30 P.M.

SCIARRETTA'S NEAPOLITAN TRIO give concerts daily from 6 P.M. until 1 A.M.
Signor SALVATORE SCIARRETTI, Lyric Tenor, is highly endorsed by Vice-President Garrett A. Hobart, Chauncey M. Depew, Eugene Ysaye, Raoul Pugno, Jean Gerardy, and many other prominent people.

SMITH & KERRISSEY, Proprietors.

AN HISTORIC RESORT.

The loveliest place on the New England coast to spend a short vacation or the whole season is the

MYLES STANDISH HOTEL,
at SOUTH DUXBURY, MASS.

Everything that money and intelligence can do has been done to make this hotel better, if possible, than it was last season.

The greatest pains will be taken to have the table service absolutely excellent. Of the house itself and its surroundings too much cannot be said. It is a resort of nice people, who come year after year, gaining strength, vitality, and pleasure.

Send for our 1899 booklet.

L. BOYER'S SONS, Proprietors,
27 Devonshire Street, Boston, Mass.,

Or ALFRED S. AMER, Manager,
90 Wall Street, New York
(Until June 1).

Myles Standish Hotel,
South Duxbury, Mass.

"AMERICA'S FINEST PRODUCT."
Bartholomay's "APOLLO"
LAGER BEER IN BOTTLES.

Sold at these Concerts.

ALBRECHT & KOELLNER,
SOLE AGENTS,
Telephone, Boston 1751.   295-305 A Street.

Also Agents for the "Crystal Rock" Mineral Water.

PURE BEER
Harvard BREW. CO'S $1000.00
PURE BEER
**Sold at these Concerts,
IN BOTTLES ONLY**
20¢ PER BOTTLE.

Inglenook Vineyard.

The only California Wines sold at these Concerts.

❦❦

THE CODMAN & HALL CO.,
Opposite the South Union Station.

Sole Agents for New England.

IND. COOPE & CO.'S English Ale.

THE SECOND LARGEST BREWERY IN ENGLAND.

Brewers of the finest *light quality* ale. Very highly endorsed by the medical profession. : : : :

❦❦

THE CODMAN & HALL CO.,
Opposite South Union Station.

Sole Agents for the United States.

Instruct your waiter to bring a bottle of

Pfaff's "Monogram" Lager.

If you will do this, it will not be necessary for us to expatiate upon the good qualities of our production.
YOU CAN JUDGE FOR YOURSELF.

H. & J. PFAFF BREWING COMPANY,
Telephone 2608.   16 ARCH STREET, BOSTON.

DRINK only th

PURE

WHIS

If you want p and richne flavor, try only gen and origin

OLD KENTU TAYLOR,

Eight years old own distillation guaranteed p Bottled and shi direct from warehouses by None genuine out our signa on both labels, ware of imita For consump indigestion, an ailments requ stimulants, O KENTUCKY LOR h s superior. Sold by all class drug grocers, and li dealers.

Wright & Tay
Distillers,
Fine Kentuck
Whiskies,
Louisville, K

Hirshfield &
New Englan
Agents,
31 Doane Stre
Boston.

TABLE LINEN USED AT THESE CONCERTS IS LAUNDERED BY THE L. K. HUSTED LAUNDERING COMPANY, 27 and 29 BROADWAY, CHELSEA, MASS.

TRY THE "COLUMBIA BRAND" VIENNA SAUSAGES. SERVED HOT OR COLD AT THESE CONCERTS.

SATURDAY, JUNE 24.

PROGRAMME.

1. MARCH, "Under the Double Eagle" . . . Wagner
2. OVERTURE, "Elisabeth" . . . Rossini
3. WALTZ, "Vienna Girls" . . . Ziehrer
4. SELECTION, "Carmen" . . . Bizet
5. MARCH, "Queen of Sheba" . . . Gounod
6. SELECTION, "La Grande Duchesse" . . . Offenbach
7. TWO SELECTIONS for String Orchestra . . . Keller
   (First Time.)
8. OVERTURE, "Tannhauser" . . . Wagner
9. MENUET . . . Heilman
   (First Time.)
10. TWO HUNGARIAN DANCES . . . Brahms
11. WALTZ, "Grubenlichter" . . . Zeller
12. MARCH, "Liberty Bell" . . . Sousa

They cannot sell you here
Canadian Club Whisky,
Ruinart Champagne,
Royal Liqueur Scotch,
Carstair's Philadelphia Rye,
Fort Hill Bourbon,
Alhambra Sherry,
All of which you will find
of excellent quality ;

But you can get

Kaiser Water,

the most refreshing of all table waters,

Chateau d'Arsac Claret,
N. Johnston & Sons' Medoc,
and
California Inglenook Clarets.

SUPPLIED BY

CODMAN & HALL COMPANY,

WINE MERCHANTS,
Opposite New South Station.

COAL
Best Quality
AT
Lowest Prices

METROPOLITAN COAL COMPANY,
No. 30 Congress Street.

WILSON BELFAST GINGER ALE
and
Champagne Kola
are sold at these concerts.

DRINK
WILSON CHAMPAGNE KOLA.

It produces energy, activity, and force. Its medical virtues are endorsed by physicians.

The **Wilson** is acknowledged to be America's purest spring water. Bottled only in glass at the spring, North Raymond, Me.

In making our BELFAST GINGERALE we use only the purest ginger.

Beware of imitations.

Drink the Wilson and you are sure of the best.

Wilson Spring and Hotel Co.,
45 Arch Street.
Telephone 3129, Boston. Boston, Mass.

"THE RECOGNIZED FAVORITE OF ALL BEERS."

THE BEER THAT MADE MILWAUKEE FAMOUS.

HIGHEST AWARD FOR PURITY.

Sold at these Concerts. JOS. GAHM & CO., N.E. AGENTS, 125-127 PURCHASE ST.

THE ONLY BEER ON DRAUGHT AT THESE CONCERTS.

"the beer that's brewed"

ROCHESTER BREWING CO'S.
FAMOUS BOTTLED BEER
RIENZI, PREMIER, BOHEMIAN, BAVARIAN, STANDARD.

HOME OFFICE & BREWERY ROCHESTER, N.Y.
NEW ENGLAND BRANCH
295-305 A STREET BOSTON
Free delivery in city and Suburbs

THE FALL RIVER LINE

OCCUPYING THE
LONG ISLAND SOUND ROUTE
BETWEEN

Boston and New York

Has the finest quintette of great steamboats that the world has ever seen. The

Priscilla, Puritan, Plymouth, Pilgrim, and Providence

Are the largest, best equipped, safest, and handsomest steamboats ever constructed. This route is one of the most attractive and naturally beautiful traversed by any transportation agency in the world.

Trips of the Fall River Line are made throughout the year. Each steamboat has its own orchestra, and the service on each member of the fleet is maintained at the highest possible standard.

Tickets via this route are on sale at all of the principal Ticket Offices in the United States.

From BOSTON. Trains, connecting with steamers at Fall River in 80 minutes, leave Park Square Station, New York, New Haven & Hartford Railroad (Old Colony System), daily at 6 p.m.
From NEW YORK. Steamers leave Pier 19, North River, foot of Warren Street, daily at 5.30 p.m.

S. A. GARDNER, Superintendent, NEW YORK.
GEO. L. CONNOR, Passenger Traffic Manager, NEW HAVEN, CONN.
O. H. TAYLOR, General Passenger Agent, NEW YORK CITY.

HOTEL LANGWOOD,

Middlesex Fells Reservation.

WYOMING STATION, B. & M. R.R.

NOW OPEN.

Twenty minutes by rail from Boston. Sixty trains daily. Hotel coaches meet trains each way. Four hundred feet above sea level. Beautiful rides, drives, and walks. Golf links, tennis courts, and ball grounds.

For plans and prices address:

F. W. GASKILL, Manager,

Telephone, 40 Melrose.   Melrose, Mass.

THIRD SEASON.

3 Ideal Outings

(Personally conducted by F. R. COMEE, Music Hall, Boston.

Boston	1.	2.	3.
Leave	July 2	July 15	August 19
Arrive	July 12	July 31	September 4

No. 1. Ten days. **Saratoga, Lake George,** 2,130 miles from **Buffalo** to **Duluth,** and return on the steamer "North-Land" through the **Great Lakes, Erie, Huron, St. Clair,** and **Superior.**

Nos. 2 and 3. Sixteen days. Exactly alike. 700 miles' ocean sail to **Norfolk** and **Baltimore.** Over **Alleghany Mountains** and a day in **Chicago.** Up **Lake Michigan** and three days at **Mackinac Island,** 1,546 miles on steamer "North-West" to **Duluth** and return to **Buffalo** through the **Great Lakes, Niagara Falls** to **Toronto.** Across **Lake Ontario,** through the **Thousand Islands,** and down the **St. Lawrence River** to **Montreal** and **Boston.**

No country in the world can duplicate the journey of **1,065 miles in one steamer on fresh water** from **Buffalo** to **Duluth** through the Great Northern Lakes. These "Ideal Outings" are not cheap trips, as they are too extensive, trip No. 1 covering 3,000 miles, Nos. 2 and 3, which are exactly alike, covering 4,000 miles, and with only one night in a sleeping-car. There need be no fear of seasickness, as frequent experience has proved the Great Lakes to be unusually smooth in July and August. We travel first-class in every way. The parties are strictly limited, as it is impossible to secure equally good accommodations for a large number. The fatigue of too steady travel is avoided by from one to three days' rest at Old Point Comfort, Chicago, Mackinac Island, Duluth, Niagara Falls, Saratoga, etc. The average temperature through the Great Lakes in midsummer is 60°. No tourist who has made the journey has yet expressed disappointment; on the contrary, all are amazed at its extent and beauty.

SEND FOR CIRCULARS.

Allsopp's

ENGLISH ALE.
"The Red Hand Brand."

Protection for Ale Drinkers.

There is a strong and growing feeling abroad that all breweries should protect consumers by doing their own bottling. Allsopp's Ale is the only brand to-day that is bottled by its makers.

Sold at these concerts.

MONDAY, JUNE 26.
GRADUATES' NIGHT.

PROGRAMME.

1.	MARCH, "'96" (First Time.)	Morse
2.	OVERTURE, "Raymond"	Thomas
3.	WALTZ, "Morgenblätter"	Strauss
4.	SELECTION, "Prince pro Tem."	Thompson
5.	OVERTURE, "Poet and Peasant"	Suppé
6.	WALTZ AND PIZZICATO from "Sylvia"	Delibes
7.	SELECTION, "The Fortune-teller"	Herbert
8.	MARCH FANTASY, "Alma Mater"	D'Andria
9.	COLLEGE OVERTURE	Moses
10.	AMERICAN PATROL	Meacham
11.	WALTZ, "Jolly Fellows"	Vollstedt
12.	MARCH, "Up the Street"	Morse

The *only* Lithia Water sold at these concerts.

Hygeia Lithia Water

Sparkling and Still.

By its use you will avoid the germs of disease which natural MINERAL WATERS are liable to contain.

For Sale at these concerts and by

S. S. PIERCE CO.

FOR SALE AT THESE CONCERTS.
FAMOUS TANNHAEUSER EXPORT BEER

The finest Light Beer Extant.   Brewery Bottling.   Favorite of Connoisseurs.

Pure,   Palatable,   Perfect.
B. & E. Philadelphia Ale on Draught.
FOR SALE AT THESE CONCERTS.

The purity and keeping quality of the Tannhaeuser Export under all changes of temperature, its uniform excellence being guaranteed, together with its nutritious properties, make it the most pleasant, delicious, and convenient beverage for home consumption.
Put up in corked bottles, and packed in casks of 10 dozen white flint pints, and 6 dozen amber quarts.

Highest Awards wherever exhibited.

The BERGNER & ENGEL BREWING CO.'S N.E. Depot,
508 and 510 Atlantic Avenue, Boston.
Telephone 3805.   **SOL. BACHARACH, Manager.**

M. Steinert & Sons Co.,

STEINERT HALL BUILDING,

No. 162 Boylston Street, corner Carver, Boston.

STEINWAY & SONS,

HARDMAN,   GABLER,
EMERSON,   SINGER,

PIANOS.

The Æolian, Aeriol, Orchestrelle, and Pianola.

THE ÆOLIAN
AND
THE PIANOLA
FOR SUMMER HOMES.

At this season of the year we receive many orders for these instruments for Summer Residences, and therefore beg to call attention to our extensive assortment now on display, especially suited for this purpose.

The ÆOLIAN meets the requirements of country homes, furnishing, as it does, music suitable for every occasion. It practically takes the place of an orchestra — music for dancing — orchestral concerts, — in short, music of every style and description is always available.

The PIANOLA will appeal to many on account of the very little space it occupies. It will play any kind of a piano, and can also be used upon a rented piano without the slightest injury. For the above reasons it is bound to be very popular for small cottages.

We are glad to be able to announce that we can furnish PIANOLAS with no more than a week's delay, and, at times, the day the order is given.

Persons not familiar with these instruments are cordially invited to call at our warerooms and hear them, or a descriptive catalogue will be mailed free upon application.

M. STEINERT & SONS CO.,
Steinert Hall,   162 Boylston Street,   Boston.

ANHEUSER-BUSCH BREWING ASS'N,

ST. LOUIS, MO., U.S.A.

BREWERS OF HIGH=GRADE BEERS EXCLUSIVELY.

Black and Tan.	Faust.
Michelob.	Pale Lager.
Muenchener.	Anheuser Standard.

Served at the Music Hall Concerts.

Also at all first-class hotels, clubs, and bars, and on all Pullman and Wagner cars and ocean and lake steamers.

JACOB WIRTH,   Wholesale Dealer,   **Boston, Mass.**

THE MUSIC HALL
PROMENADE CONCERTS

SMOKE THE POPULAR "BARRISTER" CIGARS AT THE POPULAR CONCERTS.

SMOKE "LA CELESTINA," THE BEST ALL-HAVANA CIGAR. DANIEL FRANK & CO.

PUBLISHED BY
C. A. ELLIS,
MUSIC HALL.

BOSTON, FRIDAY, JUNE 23, 1899.

SUMMER SEASON.
Vol. XIV. No. 40.

YOU CAN
Have your last season's outfit dyed or cleansed and refinished so it will look like new, by our French process. Why discard soiled clothing when it can be overhauled and worn as second best? You can

RELY ON
Our methods of cleansing, and need not hesitate to trust us with articles of the most delicate textures.
We dye or cleanse and refinish PROPERLY, *all* materials of household use and clothing of all kinds.

LEWANDO'S
W. L. Crosby, General Manager.
French Cleansers, Fancy Dyers, Fine Launderers.

PRINCIPAL OFFICES:
17 Temple Place, Boston.
479 Fifth Avenue, New York.
Established 70 years.
Largest in America.
Bundles called for and delivered.
Telephones in all offices.

If you are open to conviction, to-night

try one 10-cent box of

BETWEEN THE ACTS
Little Cigars

to smoke now — or at any time when you want a short smoke and haven't time for a long one. They are real cigars, but small ones.

They cost so little that you can use them every day as well as not and actually save on your daily cigar expense by substituting them for larger cigars.

FOR SALE HERE.

THE MUSIC HALL
Promenade Concerts
FOURTEENTH SEASON.

C. A. ELLIS, Manager. F. R. COMEE, Assistant Manager.
Mr. GUSTAV STRUBE, Conductor.

FRIDAY, JUNE 23.
PROGRAMME.

1. MARCH, "Washington Post" . . . . Sousa
2. OVERTURE, "Light Cavalry" . . . . Suppé
3. WALTZ, "Bei uns au Haus" . . . . Strauss
4. SELECTION, "Aïda" . . . . Verdi
5. BALLET MUSIC from "Queen of Sheba" . . . Goldmark
   Violoncello Solo, Mr. KELLER.
6. TWO MOVEMENTS from "Peer Gynt" . . . . Grieg
7. MELODIE . . . . Rubinstein
8. RIDE OF THE VALKYRIES . . . . Wagner
9. LE DERNIER SOMMEIL DE LA VIERGE . . . Massenet
   The audience is respectfully requested to preserve silence during the performance of this number.
10. OVERTURE, "Orpheus" . . . . Offenbach
11. WALTZ, "Meerleuchten" . . . . Ziehrer
12. MARCH, "Stars and Stripes" . . . . Sousa

Tuesday, June 27, Soloists' Night.
Friday, June 30, Request Night.

To secure satisfactory service, patrons are URGED by the Management to report PROMPTLY any inattention. Complaints made so late that patrons cannot recall either the number of the table or the waiter are obviously useless.

ALBUMS OF SONGS,
Containing many popular compositions not published in single form.

IRISH FOLK SONGS, by Charles Wood, . . $2.00
RUSSIAN SONGS, by F. Wishaw (2 vols.), . 1.00
NINE SONGS, by S. Liddle, ... 1.00
NINE SONGS, by Liza Lehmann, ... 1.00
FIVE SONGS, by Francis Korbay, ... 2.00
Beautifully Illustrated by J. S. SARGENT, R.A.

BOOSEY & CO.,
9 East 17th Street,   New York.

LAGER BEER

A Particularly Fine Lager for Family Use and Clubs.

Bottled in the most careful manner at our own bottling department, and sold by the S. S. Pierce Co. and all other leading grocers in New England.

Other Brands in Bottles:
"Norfolk India Pale Stock Ale."
"Norfolk Extra Golden Ale" (blue label).
"Norfolk Standard Lager."
Our "Cabinet" and "Bismarck Brau" are the most popular refreshments at these concerts.

HABICH & CO.

H. W. HARER. | Telephone, 56 Roxbury
EDWARD BUHL. | or 1152 Boston.

ESTABROOK & EATON'S MARGUERITE PERFECTOS, 10c. EACH. CONCHAS, 10c., 3 FOR 25c. SOLD AT THE "POPS."

THE ICE-CREAM SERVED AT THESE CONCERTS IS FURNISHED BY **WEBER,** 25 Temple Place and 33 West Street.

MUSIC HALL PROMENADE PROGRAMME.

PUBLISHED EVERY EVENING DURING THE SUMMER SEASON.

NOTICE TO ADVERTISERS.

The advertising columns in the Programme are controlled SOLELY by F. R. Comee, Boston Music Hall Box Office, to whom all communications should be addressed.

The United States Hotel,

SARATOGA SPRINGS, N.Y.

Under a continuous management for 25 years.

Without a peer in its appointments, service, and liberal management.

The largest structure of its kind in the world.

Built entirely of brick.

The Hotel and court cover over seven acres.

For further information, rates, etc., address

GAGE & PERRY,
Proprietors,
UNITED STATES HOTEL,
Saratoga Springs, N.Y.

Colonial Beer...

The Beer that's Brewed in Glass.

PURE, CLEAN, PALATABLE.

Order a Bottle.

SOUTHER BREWING CO.,
919 Parker Street,
Roxbury, Mass.

The Peer of all Cigarettes.

Save the band-label on each box for valuable premiums.

::: ALSO :::

Monopol

High-grade Egyptian Cigarettes.

No. 83 Khedive.
No. 6A Nadine.
No. 8A Egyptian Belles.
No. 70A Princess Lillian

On sale at these concerts and all first-class dealers.

VEUVE CHAFFARD

PURE OLIVE OIL.

IN HONEST BOTTLES.

OCKENHEIMER BERG, Near Bingen, **GERMANY.** On the Rhine.

PHILIP KRIM'S

OWN IMPORTATION OF

Rhine Wines.

FOR 30 YEARS AT

163 Shawmut Avenue.

OUR WINES SOLD AT THESE CONCERTS.

HERRICK, COPLEY SQUARE, Telephones 608 and 950 (Back Bay), CHOICE TABLES for Music Hall "Pops."

D. LEIDEN'S SPARKLING MOSELLE,

The only Sparkling Wine sold at these Concerts.

SHINNECOCK

The Perfection of Scotch Whisky

Sold by
S. S. PIERCE COMPANY.

SATURDAY, JUNE 24.

PROGRAMME.

1. MARCH, "Under the Double Eagle" . . . Wagner
2. OVERTURE, "Elisabeth" . . . Rossini
3. WALTZ, "Vienna Girls" . . . Ziehrer
4. SELECTION, "Carmen" . . . Bizet
5. MARCH, "Queen of Sheba" . . . Gounod
6. SELECTION, "La Grande Duchesse" . . . Offenbach
7. TWO SELECTIONS for String Orchestra . . . Keller
   (First Time.)
8. OVERTURE, "Tannhäuser" . . . Wagner
9. MENUET . . . Heilman
   (First Time.)
10. TWO HUNGARIAN DANCES . . . Brahms
11. WALTZ, "Grubenlichter" . . . Zeller
12. MARCH, "Liberty Bell" . . . Sousa

THE HAYWARD,
16 and 22 Hayward Place.
LADIES' AND GENTS' CAFE.   Open until 1 a.m.
Table d'hôte dinner, including bottle of wine, 75c.,
served from 5 to 8.30 P. M.

SCIARRETTA'S NEAPOLITAN TRIO give concerts daily
from 6 P.M. until 1 A.M.

Signor SALVATORE SCIARRETTI, Lyric Tenor,
Is highly endorsed by Vice-President Garrett A. Hobart, Chauncey M. Depew,
Eugene Ysaye, Raoul Pugno, Jean Gerardy, and many other prominent people.

SMITH & KERRISSEY, Proprietors.

AN HISTORIC RESORT.

The loveliest place on the New England coast to spend a short vacation or the whole season is the

MYLES STANDISH HOTEL,
at SOUTH DUXBURY, MASS.

Everything that money and intelligence can do has been done to make this hotel better, if possible, than it was last season.
The greatest pains will be taken to have the table service absolutely excellent. Of the house itself and its surroundings too much cannot be said. It is a resort of nice people, who come year after year, gaining strength, vitality, and pleasure.
Send for our 1899 booklet.

L. BOYER'S SONS, Proprietors,
27 Devonshire Street, Boston, Mass.,
Or ALFRED S. AMER, Manager,
90 Wall Street, New York
(Until June 1).
Myles Standish Hotel,
South Duxbury, Mass.

"AMERICA'S FINEST PRODUCT."

Bartholomay's "APOLLO"
LAGER BEER IN BOTTLES.

Sold at these Concerts.

ALBRECHT & KOELLNER,
SOLE AGENTS,
Telephone, Boston 1751.   295-305 A Street.

Also Agents for the "Crystal Rock" Mineral Water.

PURE BEER

BREW. CO'S $1000.00

PURE BEER
Sold at these Concerts,
IN BOTTLES ONLY
20¢ PER BOTTLE.

USED AT THESE CONCERTS THE L. K. HUSTED LAUNDERING COMPANY, 27 and 29 BROADWAY, CHELSEA, MASS.
TABLE LINEN LAUNDERED BY

Inglenook Vineyard.

The only California Wines sold at these Concerts.

THE CODMAN & HALL CO.,
Opposite the South Union Station.

Sole Agents for New England.

IND. COOPE & CO.'S English Ale.

THE SECOND LARGEST BREWERY IN ENGLAND.

Brewers of the finest *light quality* ale. Very highly endorsed by the medical profession. : : : : :

THE CODMAN & HALL CO.,
Opposite South Union Station.

Sole Agents for the United States.

DRINK only the PUREST WHISK

If you want purity and richness of flavor, try only genuine and original

OLD KENTUCKY TAYLOR,

Eight years old, of own distillation; guaranteed pure. Bottled and shipped direct from our warehouses by us. None genuine without our signature on both labels. Beware of imitations. For consumption, indigestion, and ailments requiring stimulants, OLD KENTUCKY TAYLOR has no superior.
Sold by all first class druggists, grocers, and liquor dealers.

Wright & Taylor, Distillers, Fine Kentucky Whiskies. Louisville, Ky.

Hirshfield & Co. New England Agents, 31 Doane Street, Boston.

Instruct your waiter to bring a bottle of

Pfaff's "Monogram" Lager.

If you will do this, it will not be necessary for us to expatiate upon the good qualities of our production.
YOU CAN JUDGE FOR YOURSELF.

H. & J. PFAFF BREWING COMPANY,
Telephone 2608.   16 ARCH STREET, BOSTON.

TRY THE "COLUMBIA BRAND" VIENNA SAUSAGES. SERVED HOT OR COLD AT THESE CONCERTS.

They cannot sell you here
Canadian Club Whisky,
Ruinart Champagne,
Royal Liqueur Scotch,
Carstair's Philadelphia Rye,
Fort Hill Bourbon,
Alhambra Sherry,
All of which you will find
of excellent quality;

But you can get

Kaiser Water,

the most refreshing of all
table waters.

Chateau d'Arsac Claret,
N. Johnston & Sons' Medoc,
and
California Inglenook Clarets.

SUPPLIED BY

CODMAN & HALL COMPANY,

WINE MERCHANTS,
Opposite New South Station.

MONDAY, JUNE 26.
GRADUATES' NIGHT.

PROGRAMME.

1. MARCH, "'96" . . . . Morse
   (First Time.)
2. OVERTURE, "Raymond" . . Thomas
3. WALTZ, "Morgenblätter" . . Strauss
4. SELECTION, "Prince pro Tem." Thompson

5. OVERTURE, "Poet and Peasant" Suppé
6. WALTZ AND PIZZICATO from "Sylvia" Delibes
7. SELECTION, "The Fortune-teller" Herbert
8. MARCH FANTASY, "Alma Mater" D'Andria

9. COLLEGE OVERTURE Moses
10. AMERICAN PATROL Meacham
11. WALTZ, "Jolly Fellows" Vollstedt
12. MARCH, "Up the Street" Morse

COAL
Best Quality
AT
Lowest Prices

METROPOLITAN COAL COMPANY,
No. 30 Congress Street.

WILSON BELFAST GINGER ALE
and
Champagne Kola

are sold at these concerts.

DRINK WILSON CHAMPAGNE KOLA

It produces energy, activity, and force. Its medical virtues are endorsed by physicians.

The **Wilson** is acknowledged to be America's purest spring water. Bottled only in glass at the spring, North Raymond, Me.

In making our BELFAST GINGERALE we use only the purest ginger.

Beware of imitations.

Drink the Wilson and you are sure of the best.

Wilson Spring and Hotel Co.,
45 Arch Street.
Telephone 3129, Boston. Boston, Mass.

"THE RECOGNIZED FAVORITE OF ALL BEERS."

Schlitz
THE BEER THAT MADE MILWAUKEE FAMOUS.

HIGHEST AWARD for PURITY.

Sold at these Concerts. JOS. GAHM & CO., N.E. AGENTS, 125-127 PURCHASE ST.

THE ONLY BEER ON DRAUGHT AT THESE CONCERTS.

"the beer that's brewed"

THE FALL RIVER LINE
OCCUPYING THE
LONG ISLAND SOUND ROUTE
BETWEEN

Boston and New York

Has the finest quintette of great steamboats that the world has ever seen. The

Priscilla, Puritan, Plymouth, Pilgrim, and Providence

Are the largest, best equipped, safest, and handsomest steamboats ever constructed. This route is one of the most attractive and naturally beautiful traversed by any transportation agency in the world.

Trips of the Fall River Line are made throughout the year. Each steamboat has its own orchestra, and the service on each member of the fleet is maintained at the highest possible standard.

Tickets via this route are on sale at all of the principal Ticket Offices in the United States.

From BOSTON. Trains, connecting with steamers at Fall River in 80 minutes, leave Park Square Station, New York, New Haven & Hartford Railroad (Old Colony System), daily at 6 p.m.

From NEW YORK. Steamers leave Pier 19, North River, foot of Warren Street, daily at 5.30 p.m.

| S. A. GARDNER, Superintendent, NEW YORK. | GEO. L. CONNOR, Passenger Traffic Manager, NEW HAVEN, CONN. | O. H. TAYLOR, General Passenger Agent, NEW YORK CITY. |

HOTEL LANGWOOD,
Middlesex Fells Reservation.

WYOMING STATION, B. & M. R.R.

NOW OPEN.

Twenty minutes by rail from Boston. Sixty trains daily. Hotel coaches meet trains each way. Four hundred feet above sea level. Beautiful rides, drives, and walks. Golf links, tennis courts, and ball grounds.

For plans and prices address:

F. W. GASKILL, Manager,

Telephone, 40 Melrose.   Melrose, Mass.

---

3 Ideal Outings

THIRD SEASON.

Personally conducted by
F. R. COMEE,
Music Hall,
Boston.

Boston	1.	2.	3.
Leave	July 2	July 15	August 19
Arrive	July 12	July 31	September 4

No. 1. Ten days. **Saratoga, Lake George,** 2,130 miles from **Buffalo** to **Duluth,** and return on the steamer "North-Land" through the **Great Lakes, Erie, Huron, St. Clair,** and **Superior.**

Nos. 2 and 3. Sixteen days. Exactly alike. 700 miles' ocean sail to **Norfolk** and **Baltimore.** Over **Alleghany Mountains** and a day in **Chicago.** Up **Lake Michigan** and three days at **Mackinac Island.** 1,546 miles on steamer "North-West" to **Duluth** and return to **Buffalo** through the **Great Lakes, Niagara Falls** to **Toronto.** Across **Lake Ontario,** through the **Thousand Islands,** and down the St. Lawrence River to **Montreal** and **Boston.**

No country in the world can duplicate the journey of 1,065 miles in one steamer on fresh water from Buffalo to Duluth through the Great Northern Lakes. These "Ideal Outings" are not cheap trips, as they are too extensive, trip No. 1 covering 3,000 miles, Nos. 2 and 3, which are exactly alike, covering 4,000 miles, and with only one night in a sleeping-car. There need be no fear of seasickness, as frequent experience has proved the Great Lakes to be unusually smooth in July and August. We travel first-class in every way. The parties are strictly limited, as it is impossible to secure equally good accommodations for a large number. The fatigue of too steady travel is avoided by from one to three days' rest at Old Point Comfort, Chicago, Mackinac Island, Duluth, Niagara Falls, Saratoga, etc. The average temperature through the Great Lakes in midsummer is 60°. No tourist who has made the journey has yet expressed disappointment: on the contrary, all are amazed at its extent and beauty.

SEND FOR CIRCULARS.

Allsopp's

ENGLISH ALE.

"The Red Hand Brand."

Protection for Ale Drinkers.

There is a strong and growing feeling abroad that all breweries should protect consumers by doing their own bottling. Allsopp's Ale is the only brand to-day that is bottled by its makers.

Sold at these concerts.

TUESDAY, JUNE 27.
SOLOISTS' NIGHT.

PROGRAMME.

1. MARCH, "Obersteiger" . . . Zeller
2. WALTZ, "Lagunen" . . . Strauss
3. OVERTURE, "Robinson Crusoe" . Heberlein
    (First Time.)
4. LES RAMEAUX . . . Faure
    Baritone Solo, De G. de AMEZAGA.

5. OVERTURE, "Tell" . . . Rossini
6. INVITATION TO DANCE . . Weber
7. { a. LÉGENDE }
   { b. MAZOURKA } . . . Wieniawski
   Violin Solo, Mr. ONDRICEK.
   Piano Accompaniment by Mr. NAGEL.
8. BACCHANALE, from "Samson and Dalila" . Saint-Saëns

9. MARCH, from "Strawberry Leaves" . . Tippett
10. OVERTURE, "Frau Meisterin" . . Suppé
    (First Time.)
11. WALTZ, "Amour et Printemps" . Waldteufel
12. MARCH, "Wien bleibt Wien" . . Schrammel

The *only* Lithia Water sold at these concerts.

Hygeia Lithia Water

Sparkling and Still.

By its use you will avoid the germs of disease which natural MINERAL WATERS are liable to contain.

For Sale at these concerts and by

S. S. PIERCE CO.

FOR SALE AT THESE CONCERTS.
FAMOUS TANNHAEUSER EXPORT BEER

The finest Light Beer Extant.   Brewery Bottling.   Favorite of Connoisseurs.

Pure,   Palatable,   Perfect.

B. & E. Philadelphia Ale on Draught.
FOR SALE AT THESE CONCERTS.

The purity and keeping quality of the Tannhaeuser Export under all changes of temperature, its uniform excellence being guaranteed, together with its nutritious properties, make it the most pleasant, delicious, and convenient beverage for home consumption.
Put up in corked bottles, and packed in casks of 10 dozen white flint pints, and 6 dozen amber quarts.

Highest Awards wherever exhibited.

The BERGNER & ENGEL BREWING CO.'S N.E. Depot,
508 and 510 Atlantic Avenue, Boston.
Telephone 3805.   SOL. BACHARACH, Manager.

M. Steinert & Sons Co.,

STEINERT HALL BUILDING,

No. 162 Boylston Street, corner Carver, Boston.

STEINWAY & SONS,

HARDMAN,   GABLER,
EMERSON,   SINGER,

PIANOS.

The Æolian, Aeriol, Orchestrelle, and Pianola.

THE ÆOLIAN
AND
THE PIANOLA
FOR SUMMER HOMES.

At this season of the year we receive many orders for these instruments for Summer Residences, and therefore beg to call attention to our extensive assortment now on display, especially suited for this purpose.

The ÆOLIAN meets the requirements of country homes, furnishing, as it does, music suitable for every occasion. It practically takes the place of an orchestra — music for dancing — orchestral concerts,— in short, music of every style and description is always available.

The PIANOLA will appeal to many on account of the very little space it occupies. It will play any kind of a piano, and can also be used upon a rented piano without the slightest injury. For the above reasons it is bound to be very popular for small cottages.

We are glad to be able to announce that we can furnish PIANOLAS with no more than a week's delay, and, at times, the day the order is given.

Persons not familiar with these instruments are cordially invited to call at our warerooms and hear them, or a descriptive catalogue will be mailed free upon application.

M. STEINERT & SONS CO.,
Steinert Hall,   162 Boylston Street,   Boston.

ANHEUSER-BUSCH BREWING ASS'N,

ST. LOUIS, MO., U.S.A.

BREWERS OF HIGH=GRADE BEERS EXCLUSIVELY.

Black and Tan.		Faust.
Michelob.		Pale Lager.
Muenchener.		Anheuser Standard.

Served at the Music Hall Concerts.

Also at all first-class hotels, clubs, and bars, and on all Pullman and Wagner cars and ocean and lake steamers.

JACOB WIRTH,   Wholesale Dealer,   **Boston, Mass.**

THE MUSIC HALL
PROMENADE CONCERTS

C. A. ELLIS, { PUBLISHED BY MUSIC HALL. }

BOSTON, SATURDAY, JUNE 24, 1899.

SUMMER SEASON.
Vol. XIV. No. 41.

YOU CAN

Have your last season's outfit dyed or cleansed and refinished so it will look like new, by our French process. Why discard soiled clothing when it can be overhauled and worn as second best? You can

RELY ON

Our methods of cleansing, and need not hesitate to trust us with articles of the most delicate textures.

We dye or cleanse and refinish PROPERLY, *all* materials of household use and clothing of all kinds.

LEWANDO'S

W. L. Crosby, General Manager.
French Cleansers, Fancy Dyers, Fine Launderers.

PRINCIPAL OFFICES:
17 Temple Place, Boston.
479 Fifth Avenue, New York.
Established 70 years.
Largest in America.
Bundles called for and delivered.
Telephones in all offices.

Save half your money

do not throw it away in half-smoked cigars! You will find that 50% of your cigar money is thrown away every day if you recall how few cigars you really have time to smoke "up."

BETWEEN THE ACTS
Little Cigars

are pure—clean—all good tobacco, and are in every way a very satisfactory short smoke. While you are listening to the music to-night, try a 10-cent box. The waiter will get them for you as they are for sale here. You will enjoy them!

THE MUSIC HALL.. **Promenade Concerts**

FOURTEENTH SEASON.

C. A. ELLIS, Manager.   F. R. COMEE, Assistant Manager.

Mr. GUSTAV STRUBE, Conductor.

SATURDAY, JUNE 24.

PROGRAMME.

1. MARCH, "Under the Double Eagle" . . . . . . Wagner
2. OVERTURE, "Elisabeth" . . . . Rossini
3. WALTZ, "Vienna Girls" . . . . Ziehrer
4. SELECTION, "Carmen" . . . . Bizet
5. MARCH, "Queen of Sheba" . . . . Gounod
6. SELECTION, "La Grande Duchesse" . . . . Offenbach
7. (a) ERINNERUNG } for String Orchestra . . . Keller
   (b) VALSE CAPRICE }
   (First Time.)
8. OVERTURE, "Tannhäuser" . . . . Wagner
9. MENUET . . . . Heilman
   (First Time.)
10. TWO HUNGARIAN DANCES . . . . Brahms
11. WALTZ, "Grubenlichter" . . . . Zeller
12. MARCH, "Liberty Bell" . . . . Sousa

Tuesday, June 27, Soloists' Night.
Friday, June 30, Request Night.

To secure satisfactory service, patrons are URGED by the Management to report PROMPTLY any inattention. Complaints made so late that patrons cannot recall either the number of the table or the waiter are obviously useless.

THE TWO
MOST POPULAR TWO-STEPS
OF THE SEASON.

THE RUNAWAY GIRL, by Van Baar, ... 60c.
THE CECIL, by Megone, ... 50c.
For Orchestra or Piano Solo.

BOOSEY & CO.,
9 EAST 17th STREET,   NEW YORK.

H. W. HABICH, | Telephone, 50 Roxbury
EDWARD RUHL. | or 1152 Boston.

HABICH & CO.

ESTABROOK & EATON'S MARGUERITE   PERFECTOS, 10c. EACH.
CONCHAS, 10c., 3 FOR 25c.,   SOLD AT THE "POPS."

THE ICE-CREAM SERVED AT THESE CONCERTS IS FURNISHED BY. WEBER, 25 Temple Place and 33 West Street.

MUSIC HALL PROMENADE PROGRAMME.

PUBLISHED EVERY EVENING DURING THE SUMMER SEASON.

NOTICE TO ADVERTISERS.

The advertising columns in the Programme are controlled SOLELY by F. R. Comee, Boston Music Hall Box Office, to whom all communications should be addressed.

The United States Hotel,

SARATOGA SPRINGS, N.Y.

Under a continuous management for 25 years.

Without a peer in its appointments, service, and liberal management.

The largest structure of its kind in the world.

Built entirely of brick.

The Hotel and court cover over seven acres.

For further information, rates, etc., address

GAGE & PERRY,
Proprietors,
UNITED STATES HOTEL,
Saratoga Springs, N.Y.

COLONIAL BEER

The Beer that's Brewed in Glass.

Colonial Beer...

PURE, CLEAN, PALATABLE.

Order a Bottle.

SOUTHER BREWING CO.,
919 Parker Street,
Roxbury, Mass.

All The

IMPORTED CIGARS

Sold At These Concerts Are Supplied By The

S. S. PIERCE COMPANY.

The Peer of all Cigarettes.

Save the band label on each box for valuable premiums.

!!! ALSO !!!

Monopol

High-grade Egyptian Cigarettes.

No. 8A Khedive,
No. 6½ Nadine,
No. 9A Egyptian Belles,
No. 7½ Princess Lillian

On sale at these concerts and all first-class dealers.

OCKENHEIMER BERG, Near Bingen, GERMANY. On the Rhine.

PHILIP KRIM'S OWN IMPORTATION OF Rhine Wines.

FOR 30 YEARS AT

163 Shawmut Avenue.

OUR WINES SOLD AT THESE CONCERTS.

HERRICK, COPLEY SQUARE, Telephones 608 and 950 (Back Bay), CHOICE TABLES for Music Hall "Pops."

GREAT WESTERN CHAMPAGNE

——————— A natural, genuine champagne, of the finest quality produced in America.

Sold by Wine Merchants, Grocers, and Druggists.

MONDAY, JUNE 26.
GRADUATES' NIGHT.

PROGRAMME.

1.	MARCH, " '96 "	Morse
	(First Time)	
2.	OVERTURE, "Raymond"	Thomas
3.	WALTZ, "Morgenblätter"	Strauss
4.	SELECTION, " Prince pro Tem."	Thompson
5.	OVERTURE, "Poet and Peasant"	Suppé
6.	WALTZ AND PIZZICATO from "Sylvia"	Delibes
7.	SELECTION, "The Fortune-teller"	Herbert
8.	MARCH FANTASY, "Alma Mater"	D'Andria
9.	COLLEGE OVERTURE	Moses
10.	AMERICAN PATROL	Meecham
11.	WALTZ, "Jolly Fellows"	Vollstedt
12.	MARCH, "Up the Street"	Morse

THE HAYWARD,
16 and 22 Hayward Place.

LADIES' AND GENTS' CAFE. Open until 1 a.m.

Table d'hôte dinner, including bottle of wine, 75c., served from 5 to 8:30 P.M.

SCIARRETTA'S NEAPOLITAN TRIO give concerts daily from 6 P.M. until 1 A.M.

Signor SALVATORE SCIARRETTI, Lyric Tenor, Is highly endorsed by Vice-President Garrett A. Hobart, Chauncey M. Depew, Eugene Ysaye, Raoul Pugno, Jean Gerardy, and many other prominent people.

SMITH & KERRISSEY, Proprietors.

AN HISTORIC RESORT.

The loveliest place on the New England coast to spend a short vacation or the whole season is the

MYLES STANDISH HOTEL,
at SOUTH DUXBURY, MASS.

Everything that money and intelligence can do has been done to make this hotel better, if possible, than it was last season.

The greatest pains will be taken to have the table service absolutely excellent. Of the house itself and its surroundings too much cannot be said. It is a resort of nice people, who come year after year, gaining strength, vitality, and pleasure. Send for our 1899 booklet.

L. BOYER'S SONS, Proprietors,
27 Devonshire Street, Boston, Mass.,
Or ALFRED S. AMES, Manager,
90 Wall Street, New York
(Until June 1).

Myles Standish Hotel,
South Duxbury, Mass.

"AMERICA'S FINEST PRODUCT."

Bartholomay's "APOLLO"

LAGER BEER IN BOTTLES.

Sold at these Concerts.

ALBRECHT & KOELLNER,
SOLE AGENTS,
Telephone, Boston 1751.   295-305 A Street.

Also Agents for the "Crystal Rock" Mineral Water.

PURE BEER

Harvard BREW. CO'S $1000.00

PURE BEER

Sold at these Concerts.
IN BOTTLES ONLY
20¢ PER BOTTLE.

Inglenook Vineyard.

The only California Wines sold at these Concerts.

❧❧

THE CODMAN & HALL CO.,
Opposite the South Union Station.

Sole Agents for New England.

IND. COOPE & CO.'S English Ale.

THE SECOND LARGEST BREWERY IN ENGLAND.

Brewers of the finest *light quality* ale. Very highly endorsed by the medical profession. : : : : :

❧❧

THE CODMAN & HALL CO.,
Opposite South Union Station.

Sole Agents for the United States.

DRIN only the PURE WHIS

If you want pu and richnes flavor, try only genu and origin

OLD KENTU TAYLOR,

Eight years old own distillation guaranteed pu Bottled and ship direct from warehouses by None genuine w out our signa on both labels. ware of imitati For consumpt indigestion, and ailments requi stimulants, O KENTUCKY T LOR has superior.
Sold by all fi class drugg grocers, and li dealers.

Wright & Tay
Distillers,
Fine Kentuck Whiskies,
Louisville, Ky

Hirshfield & C
New Englan Agents,
31 Doane Stree Boston.

Instruct your waiter to bring a bottle of **Pfaff's "Monogram" Lager.**

If you will do this, it will not be necessary for us to expatiate upon the good qualities of our production.
YOU CAN JUDGE FOR YOURSELF.

H. & J. PFAFF BREWING COMPANY,
Telephone 2608.   16 ARCH STREET, BOSTON.

TRY THE "COLUMBIA BRAND" VIENNA SAUSAGES. SERVED HOT OR COLD AT THESE CONCERTS.

They cannot sell you here
Canadian Club Whisky,
Ruinart Champagne,
Royal Liqueur Scotch,
Carstair's Philadelphia Rye,
Fort Hill Bourbon,
Alhambra Sherry,
All of which you will find
of excellent quality;

But you can get

Kaiser Water,

the most refreshing of all
table waters,

Chateau d'Arsac Claret,
N. Johnston & Sons' Medoc,
and
California Inglenook Clarets.

SUPPLIED BY

CODMAN & HALL COMPANY,

WINE MERCHANTS,

Opposite New South Station.

TUESDAY, JUNE 27.
SOLOISTS' NIGHT.

PROGRAMME.

1. MARCH, "Obersteiger" . . . . Zeller
2. WALTZ, "Lagunen" . . . . Strauss
3. OVERTURE, "Robinson Crusoe" . . . . . Heberlein
   (First Time.)
4. LES RAMEAUX . . . . Faure
   Baritone Solo, Da. G. tot AMEZAGA.
5. OVERTURE, "Tell" . . . . Rossini
6. INVITATION TO DANCE . . . . Weber
7. { a. LÉGENDE }
   { b. MAZOURKA } . . . . Wieniawski
   Violin Solo, Mr. ONDRICEK.
   Piano Accompaniment by Mr. NAGEL.
8. BACCHANALE, from "Samson and Dalila" . . Saint-Saëns
9. MARCH, from "Strawberry Leaves" . . . . Tippett
10. OVERTURE, "Frau Meisterin" . . . . . Suppé
    (First Time.)
11. WALTZ, "Amour et Printemps" . . . . . Waldteufel
12. MARCH, "Wien bleibt Wien" . . . . . Schrammel

COAL Best Quality AT Lowest Prices

METROPOLITAN COAL COMPANY,
No. 30 Congress Street.

WILSON BELFAST GINGER ALE
and
Champagne Kola
are sold at these concerts.

DRINK WILSON CHAMPAGNE KOLA.

It produces energy, activity, and force. Its medical virtues are endorsed by physicians.

The **Wilson** is acknowledged to be America's purest spring water.
Bottled only in glass at the spring, North Raymond, Me.

In making our BELFAST GINGER ALE we use only the purest ginger.

Beware of imitations.

Drink the **Wilson** and you are sure of the best.

Wilson Spring and Hotel Co.,
45 Arch Street.
Telephone 3129, Boston. Boston, Mass.

"THE RECOGNIZED FAVORITE OF ALL BEERS."

Schlitz
THE BEER THAT MADE MILWAUKEE FAMOUS.

HIGHEST AWARD for PURITY.

Sold at these Concerts. JOS. GAHM & CO., N.E. AGENTS, 125-127 PURCHASE ST.

THE ONLY BEER ON DRAUGHT AT THESE CONCERTS.

"the beer that's brewed"

SOLD AT THESE CONCERTS
ROCHESTER BREWING CO'S
NOTED THE WORLD OVER FOR ITS PURITY.
FAMOUS BOTTLED BEER

HOME OFFICE & BREWERY ROCHESTER, N.Y.
NEW ENGLAND BRANCH, ROCHESTER BREWING CO.
295-305 A STREET BOSTON
Free delivery in city and Suburbs

RIENZI, PREMIER, BOHEMIAN, BAVARIAN, STANDARD.

THE FALL RIVER LINE

OCCUPYING THE LONG ISLAND SOUND ROUTE BETWEEN

Boston and New York

Has the finest quintette of great steamboats that the world has ever seen. The

Priscilla, Puritan, Plymouth, Pilgrim, and Providence

Are the largest, best equipped, safest, and handsomest steamboats ever constructed. This route is one of the most attractive and naturally beautiful traversed by any transportation agency in the world. Trips of the Fall River Line are made throughout the year. Each steamboat has its own orchestra, and the service on each member of the fleet is maintained at the highest possible standard.

Tickets via this route are on sale at all of the principal Ticket Offices in the United States.

From **BOSTON.** Trains, connecting with steamers at Fall River in 80 minutes, leave Park Square Station, New York, New Haven & Hartford Railroad (Old Colony System), daily at 6 p.m.

From **NEW YORK.** Steamers leave Pier 19, North River, foot of Warren Street, daily at 5.30 p.m.

S. A. GARDNER, Superintendent, NEW YORK.   GEO. L. CONNOR, Passenger Traffic Manager, NEW HAVEN, CONN.   O. H. TAYLOR, General Passenger Agent, NEW YORK CITY.

HOTEL LANGWOOD,

Middlesex Fells Reservation.

WYOMING STATION, B. & M. R.R.

NOW OPEN.

Twenty minutes by rail from Boston. Sixty trains daily. Hotel coaches meet trains each way. Four hundred feet above sea level. Beautiful rides, drives, and walks. Golf links, tennis courts, and ball grounds.

For plans and prices address:

F. W. GASKILL, Manager,

Telephone, 40 Melrose.   Melrose, Mass.

THIRD SEASON.

3 Ideal Outings

Personally conducted by
F. R. COMEE,
Music Hall,
Boston.

	1.	2.	3.
Boston Leave	July 2	July 15	August 19
Arrive	July 12	July 31	September 4

No. 1. Ten days. **Saratoga, Lake George,** 2,130 miles from **Buffalo** to **Duluth,** and return on the steamer "**North-Land**" through the **Great Lakes, Erie, Huron, St. Clair,** and **Superior.**

Nos. 2 and 3. Sixteen days. Exactly alike. 700 miles' ocean sail to **Norfolk** and **Baltimore.** Over **Alleghany Mountains** and a day in **Chicago.** Up **Lake Michigan** and three days at **Mackinac Island.** 1,546 miles on steamer "**North-West**" to **Duluth** and return to **Buffalo** through the **Great Lakes, Niagara Falls** to **Toronto.** Across **Lake Ontario,** through the **Thousand Islands,** and down the **St. Lawrence River** to **Montreal** and **Boston.**

No country in the world can duplicate the journey of 1,065 miles in one steamer on fresh water from **Buffalo** to **Duluth** through the Great Northern Lakes. These "Ideal Outings" are not cheap trips, as they are too extensive, trip No. 1 covering 3,000 miles, Nos. 2 and 3, which are exactly alike, covering 4,000 miles, and with only one night in a sleeping-car. There need be no fear of seasickness, as frequent experience has proved the Great Lakes to be unusually smooth in July and August. We travel first-class in every way. The parties are strictly limited, as it is impossible to secure equally good accommodations for a large number. The fatigue of too steady travel is avoided by from one to three days' rest at Old Point Comfort, Chicago, Mackinac Island, Duluth, Niagara Falls, Saratoga, etc. The average temperature through the Great Lakes in midsummer is 60°. No tourist who has made the journey has yet expressed disappointment; on the contrary, all are amazed at its extent and beauty.

SEND FOR CIRCULARS.

Allsopp's

ENGLISH ALE.

"The Red Hand Brand."

Protection for Ale Drinkers.

There is a strong and growing feeling abroad that all breweries should protect consumers by doing their own bottling. Allsopp's Ale is the only brand to-day that is bottled by its makers.

Sold at these concerts.

WEDNESDAY, JUNE 28.

PROGRAMME.

1. MARCH OF THE PRÆTORIAN GUARD . . . Noll
2. OVERTURE, "Pique Dame" . . . Suppé
3. WALTZ, "In's Centrum" . . . Strauss
4. SELECTION, "Wizard of the Nile" . . . Herbert
5. { a. "Der Lindenaum"
     b. "Annie Laurie" } . . . Schubert
   Boston Trombone Quartette: Messrs. HAMPE, MAUSEBACH, MEYER, THOMAS.
6. OVERTURE, "Zampa" . . . Hérold
7. { a. "Spring Song"
     b. "Aubade Printanière" } . . . Mendelssohn / Lacome
8. SELECTION, "Robin Hood" . . . De Koven
9. VISIONS IN A DREAM . . . Lumbye
   Zither Solo, Mr. KELLER.
   The audience is respectfully requested to preserve silence during the performance of this number.
10. OVERTURE, "Stradella" . . . Flotow
11. WALTZ, "España" . . . Waldteufel
12. MARCH, "With our Soldier Boys at Tampa Bay" . . . Slocum

The *only* Lithia Water sold at these concerts.

Hygeia Lithia Water

Sparkling and Still.

By its use you will avoid the germs of disease which natural MINERAL WATERS are liable to contain.

For Sale at these concerts and by

S. S. PIERCE CO.

FOR SALE AT THESE CONCERTS.

FAMOUS TANNHAEUSER EXPORT BEER

The finest Light Beer Extant.   Brewery Bottling.   Favorite of Connoisseurs.

Pure,   Palatable,   Perfect.

B. & E. Philadelphia Ale on Draught.

FOR SALE AT THESE CONCERTS.

The purity and keeping quality of the Tannhaeuser Export under all changes of temperature, its uniform excellence being guaranteed, together with its nutritious properties, make it the most pleasant, delicious, and convenient beverage for home consumption.

Put up in corked bottles, and packed in casks of 10 dozen white flint pints, and 6 dozen amber quarts.

Highest Awards wherever exhibited.

The BERGNER & ENGEL BREWING CO.'S N.E. Depot,
508 and 510 Atlantic Avenue, Boston.
Telephone 3805.   **SOL. BACHARACH, Manager.**

M. Steinert & Sons Co.,

STEINERT HALL BUILDING,

No. 162 Boylston Street, corner Carver, Boston.

STEINWAY & SONS,

HARDMAN,   GABLER,
EMERSON,   SINGER,

PIANOS.

The Æolian, Aeriol, Orchestrelle, and Pianola.

THE ÆOLIAN
AND
THE PIANOLA
FOR SUMMER HOMES.

At this season of the year we receive many orders for these instruments for Summer Residences, and therefore beg to call attention to our extensive assortment now on display, especially suited for this purpose.

The ÆOLIAN meets the requirements of country homes, furnishing, as it does, music suitable for every occasion. It practically takes the place of an orchestra — music for dancing — orchestral concerts, — in short, music of every style and description is always available.

The PIANOLA will appeal to many on account of the very little space it occupies. It will play any kind of a piano, and can also be used upon a rented piano without the slightest injury. For the above reasons it is bound to be very popular for small cottages.

We are glad to be able to announce that we can furnish PIANOLAS with no more than a week's delay, and, at times, the day the order is given.

Persons not familiar with these instruments are cordially invited to call at our warerooms and hear them, or a descriptive catalogue will be mailed free upon application.

M. STEINERT & SONS CO.,
Steinert Hall,   162 Boylston Street,   Boston.

ANHEUSER-BUSCH BREWING ASS'N,
ST. LOUIS, MO., U.S.A.
BREWERS OF HIGH=GRADE BEERS EXCLUSIVELY.

Black and Tan.	Faust.
Michelob.	Pale Lager.
Muenchener.	Anheuser Standard.

Served at the Music Hall Concerts.

Also at all first-class hotels, clubs, and bars, and on all Pullman and Wagner cars and ocean and lake steamers.

JACOB WIRTH,   Wholesale Dealer,   **Boston, Mass.**

THE MUSIC HALL
PROMENADE CONCERTS

PUBLISHED BY
C. A. ELLIS, MUSIC HALL.

SUMMER SEASON.
Vol. XIV. No. 42.

BOSTON, MONDAY, JUNE 26, 1899.

SMOKE "LA CELESTINA," THE BEST ALL-HAVANA CIGAR. DANIEL FRANK & CO.

SMOKE THE POPULAR "BARRISTER" CIGARS AT THE POPULAR CONCERTS.

YOU CAN
Have your last season's outfit dyed or cleansed and refinished so it will look like new, by our French process. Why discard soiled clothing when it can be overhauled and worn as second best? You are

RELY ON
Our methods of cleansing, and need not hesitate to trust us with articles of the most delicate textures.
We dye or cleanse and refinish PROPERLY, *all* materials of household use and clothing of all kinds.

LEWANDO'S
W. L. Crosby, General Manager.
French Cleansers, Fancy Dyers, Fine Launderers.

PRINCIPAL OFFICES:
17 Temple Place, Boston.
479 Fifth Avenue, New York.
Established 70 years.
Largest in America.
Bundles called for and delivered.
Telephones in all offices.

In no other way are men as wasteful and extravagant as in cigar smoking—because cigars are thrown away half smoked half the time.

BETWEEN THE ACTS
Little Cigars
are just right for all short smokes. They light right, they burn right and taste right. Have you ever seen them? At all stores; 10 for 10 cts., or, as they are for sale here, you can try them to-night. Tell the waiter to bring you a 10-cent box of "Between the Acts." They will add to your enjoyment of this concert.

THE MUSIC HALL ... Promenade Concerts
FOURTEENTH SEASON.

C. A. ELLIS, Manager.   F. R. COMEE, Assistant Manager.
Mr. GUSTAV STRUBE, Conductor.

MONDAY, JUNE 26.
GRADUATES' NIGHT.

PROGRAMME.

1.	MARCH, "'96"	Morse
	(First Time.)	
2.	OVERTURE, "Raymond"	Thomas
3.	WALTZ, "Morgenblätter"	Strauss
4.	SELECTION, "Prince pro Tem."	Thompson
5.	OVERTURE, "Poet and Peasant"	Suppé
	'Cello Obligato, Mr. KELLER.	
6.	WALTZ AND PIZZICATO from "Sylvia"	Delibes
7.	SELECTION, "The Fortune-teller"	Herbert
8.	MARCH FANTASY, "Alma Mater"	D'Andria
9.	COLLEGE OVERTURE	Moses
10.	AMERICAN PATROL	Meacham
11.	WALTZ, "Jolly Fellows"	Vollstedt
12.	MARCH, "Up the Street"	Morse

Tuesday, June 27, Soloists' Night.
Friday, June 30, Request Night.
Saturday, July 1, Closing Night.

To secure satisfactory service, patrons are URGED by the Management to report PROMPTLY any inattention. Complaints made so late that patrons cannot recall either the number of the table or the waiter are practically useless.

Now the rage of the LONDON Concerts and Drawing-rooms:

YOU AND I, by Liza Lehmann,	60c.
KING CHARLES, by M. V. White,	60c.
LIKE VIOLETS PALE, by F. Allitsen,	60c.
WHEN THE WORLD IS FAIR, by F. H. Cowen,	60c.
QUEEN OF MY LIFE, by E. T. Lloyd,	60c.

BOOSEY & CO.,
9 East 17th Street,   New York.

DRINK
VAN NOSTRAND'S
BOSTON CLUB LAGER
SOLD AT THESE CONCERTS

NORFOLK CABINET
LAGER BEER

A Particularly Fine Lager for Family Use and Clubs.

Bottled in the most careful manner at our own bottling department, and sold by the S. S. Pierce Co. and all other leading grocers in New England.

Other Brands in Bottles:
"Norfolk India Pale Stock Ale."
"Norfolk Extra Golden Ale" (blue label).
"Norfolk Standard Lager."
Our "Cabinet" and "Bismarck Brau" are the most popular refreshments at these concerts.

HABICH & CO.

H. W. HABICH, | Telephone, 36 Roxbury
EDWARD KUHL. | or 1152 Boston.

ESTABROOK & EATON'S MARGUERITE PERFECTOS, 10c. EACH. CONCHAS, 10c., 3 FOR 25c. **SOLD AT THE "POPS."**

THE ICE-CREAM SERVED AT THESE CONCERTS IS FURNISHED BY **WEBER,** 25 Temple Place and 33 West Street.

MUSIC HALL PROMENADE PROGRAMME.

PUBLISHED EVERY EVENING DURING THE SUMMER SEASON.

NOTICE TO ADVERTISERS.

The advertising columns in the Programme are controlled SOLELY by F. R. Comee, Boston Music Hall Box Office, to whom all communications should be addressed.

The United States Hotel,

SARATOGA SPRINGS, N.Y.

Under a continuous management for 25 years.

Without a peer in its appointments, service, and liberal management.

The largest structure of its kind in the world.

Built entirely of brick.

The Hotel and court cover over seven acres.

For further information, rates, etc., etc., address

GAGE & PERRY,
Proprietors,
UNITED STATES HOTEL,
Saratoga Springs, N.Y.

Colonial Beer...

The Beer that's Brewed in Glass.

PURE, CLEAN, PALATABLE.

Order a Bottle.

SOUTHER BREWING CO.,
919 Parker Street,
Roxbury, Mass.

VEUVE CHAFFARD

PURE OLIVE OIL.

IN HONEST BOTTLES.

The Peer of all Cigarettes.

Save the band-label on each box for valuable premiums.

::: ALSO :::

Monopol

High-grade Egyptian Cigarettes.

No. 8A Khedive.
No. 6A Nadine.
No. 9A Egyptian Belle.
No. 7SA Princess Lillian

On sale at these concerts and all first-class dealers.

OCKENHEIMER BERG,
Near Bingen, GERMANY. On the Rhine.

PHILIP KRIM'S OWN IMPORTATION OF Rhine Wines,

FOR 30 YEARS AT

163 Shawmut Avenue.

OUR WINES SOLD AT THESE CONCERTS.

HERRICK, COPLEY SQUARE, Telephones 608 and 950 (Back Bay), CHOICE TABLES for Music Hall "Pops."

D. LEIDEN'S SPARKLING MOSELLE,

The only Sparkling Wine sold at these Concerts.

SHINNECOCK

The Perfection of Scotch Whisky

Sold by
S. S. PIERCE COMPANY.

TUESDAY, JUNE 27.
SOLOISTS' NIGHT.

PROGRAMME.

1.	MARCH, "Obersteiger"	Zeller
2.	WALTZ, "Lagunen"	Strauss
3.	OVERTURE, "Robinson Crusoe" (First Time.)	Heberlein
4.	LES RAMEAUX Baritone Solo, Du. G. de AMEZAGA.	Faure
5.	OVERTURE, "Tell"	Rossini
6.	INVITATION TO DANCE	Weber
7.	{ a LEGENDE { A. MAZOURKA } Violin Solo, Mr. ONDRICEK. Piano Accompaniment by Mr. NAGEL.	Wieniawski
8.	BACCHANALE, from "Samson and Da'ila"	Saint-Saëns
9.	MARCH, from "Strawberry Leaves"	Tippett
10.	OVERTURE, "Frau Meisterin" (First Time.)	Suppé
11.	WALTZ, "Amour et Printemps"	Waldteufel
12.	MARCH, "Wien bleibt Wien"	Schrammel

THE HAYWARD,
16 and 22 Hayward Place.
LADIES' AND GENTS' CAFE.   Open until 1 a.m.
Table d'hôte dinner, including bottle of wine, 75c.,
served from 5 to 8.30 P.M.

SCIARRETTA'S NEAPOLITAN TRIO give concerts daily
from 6 P.M. until 1 A.M.
Signor **SALVATORE SCIARRETTI**, Lyric Tenor,
Is high y endorsed by Vice-President Garrett A. Hobart, Chauncey M. Depew,
Eugene Ysaye, Raoul Pugno, Jean Gerardy, and many other prominent people.

SMITH & KERRISSEY, Proprietors.

M. S. Ginger Ale.

We desire to advise the public that hereafter the

Codman & Hall Co.,

opposite new South Station, will be our sole New England Agents for our carbonated preparations,

GINGER ALE,
SARSAPARILLA, Etc.,

all of which are made with water from the famous

MYLES STANDISH SPRING,

at South Duxbury, Mass.

L. BOYER'S SONS,
90 Wall Street, NEW YORK.

"AMERICA'S FINEST PRODUCT."

Bartholomay's "APOLLO"
LAGER BEER IN BOTTLES.

Sold at these Concerts.

ALBRECHT & KOELLNER,
SOLE AGENTS,
Telephone, Boston 1751.   295-305 A Street.

Also Agents for the "Crystal Rock" Mineral Water.

PURE BEER
Harvard
BREW. CO'S $1000.⁰⁰
PURE BEER
**Sold at these Concerts,
IN BOTTLES ONLY**
20¢ PER BOTTLE.

Inglenook Vineyard.

The only California Wines sold at these Concerts.

❧❧

THE CODMAN & HALL CO.,
Opposite the South Union Station.

Sole Agents for New England.

IND. COOPE & CO.'S English Ale.

THE SECOND LARGEST BREWERY IN ENGLAND.

Brewers of the finest *light quality* ale. Very highly endorsed by the medical profession. : : : : :

❧❧

THE CODMAN & HALL CO.,
Opposite South Union Station.

Sole Agents for the United States.

Instruct your waiter to bring a bottle of

Pfaff's "Monogram" Lager.

If you will do this, it will not be necessary for us to expatiate upon the good qualities of our production.
YOU CAN JUDGE FOR YOURSELF.

H. & J. PFAFF BREWING COMPANY,
Telephone 2608.   16 ARCH STREET, BOSTON.

DRIN only th
PURE
WHIS

If you want p and richne flavor, try only gen and origi

OLD KENTU TAYLOR

Eight years old own distillatio guaranteed p Bottled and shi direct from warehouses by None genuine out our signs on both labels. ware of imitat For consump indigestion, an ailments requ stimulants O KENTUCKY T L O R h s superior.
Sold by all class drugs grocers, and li dealers.

Wright & Tay
Distillers,
Fine Kentuck Whiskies,
Louisville, K

Hirstfield &
New Englan Agents,
31 Duane Stre Boston.

TRY THE "COLUMBIA BRAND" VIENNA SAUSAGES. SERVED HOT OR COLD AT THESE CONCERTS.

They cannot sell you here
Canadian Club Whisky,
Ruinart Champagne,
Royal Liqueur Scotch,
Carstair's Philadelphia Rye,
Fort Hill Bourbon,
Alhambra Sherry,
All of which you will find
of excellent quality;

But you can get

Kaiser Water,

the most refreshing of all table waters,

Chateau d'Arsac Claret,
N. Johnston & Sons' Medoc,
and
California Inglenook Clarets.

SUPPLIED BY

CODMAN & HALL COMPANY,

WINE MERCHANTS,
Opposite New South Station.

WEDNESDAY, JUNE 28.

PROGRAMME.

1. MARCH OF THE PRÆTORIAN GUARD . . . Noll
2. OVERTURE, "Pique Dame" . . . Suppé
3. WALTZ, "In's Centrum" . . . Strauss
4. SELECTION, "Wizard of the Nile" . . . Herbert
5. { a. "Der Lindenbaum"
     b. "Annie Laurie" } . . . Schubert
   Boston Trombone Quartette: Messrs. HAMPE, MAUSEBACH, MEYER, THOMAE.
6. OVERTURE, "Zampa" . . . Hérold
7. { a. "Spring Song" . . . Mendelssohn
     b. "Aubade Printanière" . . . Lacome
8. SELECTION, "Robin Hood" . . . De Koven
9. VISIONS IN A DREAM . . . Lumbye
   Zither Solo, Mr. KELLER.
   The audience is respectfully requested to preserve silence during the performance of this number.
10. OVERTURE, "Stradella" . . . Flotow
11. WALTZ, "España" . . . Waldteufel
12. MARCH, "With our Soldier Boys at Tampa Bay" . . . Slocum

COAL

Best Quality AT Lowest Prices

**METROPOLITAN COAL COMPANY,
No. 30 Congress Street.**

WILSON BELFAST GINGER ALE

and

Champagne Kola

are sold at these concerts.

DRINK
WILSON CHAMPAGNE KOLA.

It produces energy, activity, and force. Its medical virtues are endorsed by physicians.

The **Wilson** is acknowledged to be America's purest spring water. Bottled only in glass at the spring, North Raymond, Me.

In making our BELFAST GIN-GERALE we use only the purest ginger.

Beware of Imitations.

Drink the **Wilson** and you are sure of the best.

Wilson Spring and Hotel Co.,
45 Arch Street.
Telephone 3129, Boston. Boston, Mass.

"THE RECOGNIZED FAVORITE OF ALL BEERS."

Schlitz
THE BEER THAT MADE MILWAUKEE FAMOUS.

HIGHEST AWARD FOR PURITY.

Sold at these Concerts. JOS. GAHM & CO., N.E. AGENTS. 125-127 PURCHASE ST.

THE ONLY BEER ON DRAUGHT AT THESE CONCERTS.
"the beer that's brewed"

Rochester Brewing Co's
FAMOUS BOTTLED BEER

THE FALL RIVER LINE

OCCUPYING THE
LONG ISLAND SOUND ROUTE
BETWEEN

Boston and New York

Has the finest quintette of great steamboats that the world has ever seen. The

Priscilla, Puritan, Plymouth, Pilgrim, and Providence

Are the largest, best equipped, safest, and handsomest steamboats ever constructed. This route is one of the most attractive and naturally beautiful traversed by any transportation agency in the world.

Trips of the Fall River Line are made throughout the year. Each steamboat has its own orchestra, and the service on each member of the fleet is maintained at the highest possible standard.

Tickets via this route are on sale at all of the principal Ticket Offices in the United States.

From BOSTON. Trains, connecting with steamers at Fall River in 80 minutes, leave Park Square Station, New York, New Haven & Hartford Railroad (Old Colony System), daily at 6 p.m.

From NEW YORK. Steamers leave Pier 19, North River, foot of Warren Street, daily at 5.30 p.m.

S. A. GARDNER, GEO. L. CONNOR, O. H. TAYLOR,
Superintendent, Passenger Traffic Manager, General Passenger Agent,
NEW YORK. NEW HAVEN, CONN. NEW YORK CITY.

HOTEL LANGWOOD,

Middlesex Fells Reservation.

WYOMING STATION, B. & M. R.R.

NOW OPEN.

Twenty minutes by rail from Boston. Sixty trains daily. Hotel coaches meet trains each way. Four hundred feet above sea level. Beautiful rides, drives, and walks. Golf links, tennis courts, and ball grounds.

For plans and prices address:

F. W. GASKILL, Manager,

Telephone, 40 Melrose.   Melrose, Mass.

THIRD SEASON.

3 Ideal Outings

Personally conducted by
F. R. COMEE,
Music Hall,
Boston.

	1.	2.	3.
Boston Leave	July 2	July 15	August 19
Arrive	July 12	July 31	September 4

No. 1. Ten days. **Saratoga, Lake George,** 2,130 miles from **Buffalo** to **Duluth,** and return on the steamer "North-Land" through the **Great Lakes, Erie, Huron, St. Clair,** and **Superior.**

Nos. 2 and 3. Sixteen days. Exactly alike. 700 miles' ocean sail to **Norfolk** and **Baltimore.** Over **Alleghany Mountains** and a day in **Chicago.** Up **Lake Michigan** and three days at **Mackinac Island.** 1,546 miles on steamer "North-West" to **Duluth** and return to **Buffalo** through the **Great Lakes, Niagara Falls** to **Toronto.** Across **Lake Ontario,** through the **Thousand Islands,** and down the **St. Lawrence River** to **Montreal** and **Boston.**

SEND FOR CIRCULARS.

No country in the world can duplicate the journey of 1,065 miles in one steamer on fresh water from **Buffalo** to **Duluth** through the Great Northern Lakes. These "Ideal Outings" are not cheap trips, as they are too extensive, trip No. 1 covering 3,000 miles, Nos. 2 and 3, which are exactly alike, covering 4,000 miles, and with only one night in a sleeping-car. There need be no fear of seasickness, as frequent experience has proved the Great Lakes to be unusually smooth in July and August. We travel first-class in every way. The parties are strictly limited, as it is impossible to secure equally good accommodations for a large number. The fatigue of too steady travel is avoided by from one to three days' rest at Old Point Comfort, Chicago, Mackinac Island, Duluth, Niagara Falls, Saratoga, etc. The average temperature through the Great Lakes in midsummer is 60°. No tourist who has made the journey has yet expressed disappointment: on the contrary, all are amazed at its extent and beauty.

Allsopp's

ENGLISH ALE.

"The Red Hand Brand."

Protection for Ale Drinkers.

There is a strong and growing feeling abroad that all breweries should protect consumers by doing their own bottling. Allsopp's Ale is the only brand to-day that is bottled by its makers.

Sold at these concerts.

THURSDAY, JUNE 29.

PROGRAMME.

1. MARCH, "Uncle Ruff's Jubilee" . . . . . . Rollinson
2. OVERTURE, "A Night in Granada" . . . . . Kreutzer
3. WALTZ, "O schöner Mai" . . . . Strauss
4. SELECTION, "Fatinitza" . . . . Suppé

5. OVERTURE, "Freischutz" . . . . Weber
6. TRÄUMEREI . . . . Schumann
   The audience is respectfully requested to preserve silence during the performance of this number.
7. INTERMEZZO, "Naila" . . . . Delibes
8. FINALE, "Lohengrin" . . . . Wagner

9. EINZUGS-MARSCH . . . . Stearns
10. OFFENBACHIANA . . . . Conradi
11. WALTZ, "Grubenlichter" . . . . Zeller
12. MARCH, "The Pearl of the Orient" . . . . Krogmann

The *only* Lithia Water sold at these concerts.

Hygeia Lithia Water

Sparkling and Still.

By its use you will avoid the germs of disease which natural MINERAL WATERS are liable to contain.

For Sale at these concerts and by

S. S. PIERCE CO.

FOR SALE AT THESE CONCERTS.

FAMOUS TANNHAEUSER EXPORT BEER

The finest Light Beer Extant.   Brewery Bottling.   Favorite of Connoisseurs.

Pure,   Palatable,   Perfect.

B. & E. Philadelphia Ale on Draught.

FOR SALE AT THESE CONCERTS.

The purity and keeping quality of the Tannhaeuser Export under all changes of temperature, its uniform excellence being guaranteed, together with its nutritious properties, make it the most pleasant, delicious, and convenient beverage for home consumption.
Put up in corked bottles, and packed in casks of 10 dozen white flint pints, and 6 dozen amber quarts.

Highest Awards wherever exhibited.

The BERGNER & ENGEL BREWING CO.'S N.E. Depot,

508 and 510 Atlantic Avenue, Boston.

Telephone 3805.   **SOL. BACHARACH, Manager.**

M. Steinert & Sons Co.,

STEINERT HALL BUILDING,

No. 162 Boylston Street, corner Carver, Boston.

STEINWAY & SONS,

HARDMAN,   GABLER,
EMERSON,   SINGER,

PIANOS.

The Æolian, Aeriol, Orchestrelle, and Pianola.

THE ÆOLIAN
AND
THE PIANOLA
FOR SUMMER HOMES.

At this season of the year we receive many orders for these instruments for Summer Residences, and therefore beg to call attention to our extensive assortment now on display, especially suited for this purpose.

The ÆOLIAN meets the requirements of country homes, furnishing, as it does, music suitable for every occasion. It practically takes the place of an orchestra — music for dancing — orchestral concerts, — in short, music of every style and description is always available.

The PIANOLA will appeal to many on account of the very little space it occupies. It will play any kind of a piano, and can also be used upon a rented piano without the slightest injury. For the above reasons it is bound to be very popular for small cottages.

We are glad to be able to announce that we can furnish PIANOLAS with no more than a week's delay, and, at times, the day the order is given.

Persons not familiar with these instruments are cordially invited to call at our warerooms and hear them, or a descriptive catalogue will be mailed free upon application.

M. STEINERT & SONS CO.,
Steinert Hall,   162 Boylston Street,   Boston.

ANHEUSER-BUSCH BREWING ASS'N,
ST. LOUIS, MO., U.S.A.

BREWERS OF HIGH=GRADE BEERS EXCLUSIVELY.

Black and Tan.   Faust.

Michelob.   Pale Lager.

Muenchener.   Anheuser Standard.

Served at the Music Hall Concerts.

Also at all first-class hotels, clubs, and bars, and on all Pullman and Wagner cars and ocean and lake steamers.

JACOB WIRTH,   Wholesale Dealer,   **Boston, Mass.**

THE MUSIC HALL
PROMENADE CONCERTS

PUBLISHED BY
C. A. ELLIS, MUSIC HALL.

BOSTON, TUESDAY, JUNE 27, 1899.

SUMMER SEASON.
Vol. XIV. No. 43.

SMOKE "LA CELESTINA," THE BEST ALL-HAVANA CIGAR. DANIEL FRANK & CO.

SMOKE THE POPULAR "BARRISTER" CIGARS AT THE POPULAR CONCERTS.

YOU CAN
Have your last season's outfit dyed or cleansed and refinished so it will look like new, by our French process. Why discard soiled clothing when it can be overhauled and worn as second best? You can

RELY ON

Our methods of cleansing, and need not hesitate to trust us with articles of the most delicate textures.

We dye or cleanse and refinish PROPERLY, *all* materials of household use and clothing of all kinds.

LEWANDO'S
W. L. Crosby, General Manager.
French Cleansers, Fancy Dyers, Fine Launderers.

PRINCIPAL OFFICES:
17 Temple Place, Boston.
179 Fifth Avenue, New York.
Established 70 years.
Largest in America.
Bundles called for and delivered.
Telephones in all offices.

Knowledge differs from **Experience.**

You may know "all about"

BETWEEN THE ACTS
Little Cigars

but have you ever tried them yourself? Do you know how desirable they really are—how good they are—how economical they are—how convenient they are—how satisfactory they are? You can know—once for all—by having the waiter bring you a 10-cent box of ten—to smoke now—to-night—while you are enjoying this concert. They are for sale here.

THE MUSIC HALL
Promenade Concerts
FOURTEENTH SEASON.

C. A. ELLIS, Manager.　　F. R. COMEE, Assistant Manager.

Mr. GUSTAV STRUBE, Conductor.

TUESDAY, JUNE 27.
SOLOISTS' NIGHT.
PROGRAMME.

1. MARCH, "Obersteiger" . . . . . Zeller
2. WALTZ, "Lagunen" . . . . . Strauss
3. OVERTURE, "Robinson Crusoe" . . Haeberlein
　　　　(First Time.)
4. LES RAMEAUX . . . . . . Faure
　　Baritone Solo, Dr. G. DE AMEZAGA.

5. OVERTURE, "Tell" . . . . . Rossini
6. INVITATION TO DANCE . . . . Weber
7. { a. LÉGENDE　　　　　 } Wieniawski
　　{ b. MAZOURKA }
　　Violin Solo, Mr. ONDRICEK.
　　Piano Accompaniment by Mr. NAGEL.
8. BACCHANALE, from "Samson and Dalila" . Saint-Saëns
9. MARCH, from "Strawberry Leaves" . . Tippett
10. OVERTURE, "Frau Meisterin" . . . Suppé
　　　　(First Time.)
11. WALTZ, "Amour et Printemps" . . Waldteufel
12. MARCH, "Wien bleibt Wien" . . . Schrammel

Friday, June 30, Request Night.
Saturday, July 1, Closing Night.

To secure satisfactory service, patrons are URGED by the Management to report PROMPTLY any inattention. Complaints made so late that patrons cannot recall either the number of the table or the waiter are obviously useless.

HERE ARE A FEW NAMES FROM OUR LIST OF COMPOSERS:

ENGLISH.— Stephen Adams, F. H. Cowen, S. Liddle, C. V. Stanford, A. C. Mackenzie, R. H. Walthew, H. R. Shelley, Goring Thomas, Frances Allitsen, Maude V. White, Edward German, Mary Carmichael, Liza Lehmann, etc.

FRENCH.— C. Chaminade, Jane Vieu, L. Denza, P. Delmet, Hemberg, Guy d'Hardelot, De Leva, F. P. Tosti, etc.

ITALIAN.— F. P. Tosti, P. Mascagni, G. Puccini, G. Verdi, Don Lorenzo Perosi, etc.

THE MOST REPRESENTATIVE PUBLISHING HOUSE IN AMERICA,
BOOSEY & CO., 9 East 17th Street, New York.

BEST BEER BREWED

"OH BE JOLLY!"

DRINK VAN NOSTRAND'S
P. B. ALE
SOLD AT THESE CONCERTS

NORFOLK CABINET

LAGER BEER

A Particularly Fine Lager for Family Use and Clubs.

Bottled in the most careful manner at our own bottling department, and sold by the S. S. Pierce Co. and all other leading grocers in New England.

Other Brands in Bottles:
" Norfolk India Pale Stock Ale."
" Norfolk Extra Golden Ale" (blue label).
" Norfolk Standard Lager."
Our "Cabinet" and " Bismarck Braeu" are the finest popular refreshments at these concerts.

HABICH & CO.
H. W. HABICH.　　| Telephone, 86 Roxbury
EDWARD BUHL.　　| or 1185 Boston.

ESTABROOK & EATON'S MARGUERITE PERFECTOS, 10c. EACH, DONOHAR, 10c., 3 FOR 25c., SOLD AT THE "POPS."

THE ICE-CREAM SERVED AT THESE CONCERTS IS FURNISHED BY WEBER, 25 Temple Place and 33 West Street.

MUSIC HALL PROMENADE PROGRAMME.

PUBLISHED EVERY EVENING DURING THE SUMMER SEASON.

NOTICE TO ADVERTISERS.
The advertising columns in the Programme are controlled SOLELY by F. R. Comee, Boston Music Hall Box Office, to whom all communications should be addressed.

The United States Hotel,

SARATOGA SPRINGS, N.Y.

Under a continuous management for 25 years.

Without a peer in its appointments, service, and liberal management.

The largest structure of its kind in the world.

Built entirely of brick.

The Hotel and court cover over seven acres.

For further information, rates, etc., etc., address

GAGE & PERRY,
Proprietors,
UNITED STATES HOTEL,
Saratoga Springs, N.Y.

The Beer that's Brewed in Glass.

Colonial Beer...

PURE, CLEAN, PALATABLE.

Order a Bottle.

SOUTHER BREWING CO.,
919 Parker Street,
Roxbury, Mass.

All The IMPORTED CIGARS

Sold At These Concerts Are Supplied By The

S. S. PIERCE COMPANY.

The Peer of all Cigarettes.
Save the band-label on each box for valuable premiums.

::: ALSO :::

Monopol

High-grade Egyptian Cigarettes.

No. 8A Khedive,
No. 9A Nadine,
No. 9A Egyptian Belles,
No. 70A Princess Lillian

On sale at these concerts and all first-class dealers.

OCKENHEIMER BERG, Near Bingen, GERMANY. On the Rhine.

PHILIP KRIM'S

OWN IMPORTATION OF

Rhine Wines,

FOR 30 YEARS AT

163 Shawmut Avenue,

OUR WINES SOLD AT THESE CONCERTS.

HERRICK, COPLEY SQUARE, Telephones 608 and 950 (Back Bay), CHOICE TABLES for Music Hall "Pops."

GREAT WESTERN CHAMPAGNE

—————— A natural, genuine champagne, of the finest quality produced in America.

Sold by Wine Merchants, Grocers, and Druggists.

WEDNESDAY, JUNE 28.

PROGRAMME.

1. MARCH OF THE PRETORIAN GUARD . . . Noll
2. OVERTURE, "Pique Dame" . . . Suppé
3. WALTZ, "In's Centrum" . . . Strauss
4. SELECTION, "Wizard of the Nile" . . . Herbert
5. { a. "Der Lindenbaum"
     b. "Annie Laurie" } . . . Schubert
   Boston Trombone Quartette: Messrs. HAMPE, MAUSEBACH, MEYER, THOMAE.
6. OVERTURE, "Zampa" . . . Hérold
7. { a. "Spring Song" . . . Mendelssohn
     b. "Aubade Printanière" . . . Lacome }
8. SELECTION, "Robin Hood" . . . De Koven
9. VISIONS IN A DREAM . . . Lumbye
   Zither Solo, Mr. KELLER.
   The audience is respectfully requested to preserve silence during the performance of this number.
10. OVERTURE, "Stradella" . . . Flotow
11. WALTZ, "España" . . . Waldteufel
12. MARCH, "With our Soldier Boys at Tampa Bay" . . . Slocum

THE HAYWARD,
16 and 22 Hayward Place.
LADIES' AND GENTS' CAFÉ. Open until 1 a.m.
Table d'hôte dinner, including bottle of wine, 75c., served from 5 to 8.30 P.M.
SCIARRETTA'S NEAPOLITAN TRIO give concerts daily from 6 P.M. until 1 A.M.
Signor SALVATORE SCIARRETTI, Lyric Tenor, is highly endorsed by Vice-President Garrett A. Hobart, Chauncey M. Depew, Eugene Ysaye, Raoul Pugno, Jean Gerardy, and many other prominent people.
SMITH & KERRISSEY, Proprietors.

M. S. Ginger Ale.

We desire to advise the public that hereafter the

Codman & Hall Co.,

opposite new South Station, will be our sole New England Agents for our carbonated preparations,

GINGER ALE, SARSAPARILLA, Etc.,

all of which are made with water from the famous

MYLES STANDISH SPRING,

at South Duxbury, Mass.

———

L. BOYER'S SONS,
90 Wall Street, NEW YORK.

"AMERICA'S FINEST PRODUCT."
Bartholomay's "APOLLO"
LAGER BEER IN BOTTLES.

Sold at these Concerts.

ALBRECHT & KOELLNER,
SOLE AGENTS,
Telephone, Boston 1751.   295-305 A Street.

Also Agents for the "Crystal Rock" Mineral Water.

PURE BEER

Harvard BREW. CO'S $1000.00

PURE BEER
Sold at these Concerts, IN BOTTLES ONLY
20¢ PER BOTTLE.

TABLE LINEN USED AT THESE CONCERTS THE L. K. HUSTED LAUNDERING COMPANY. 27 and 29 BROADWAY. CHELSEA, MASS.

Inglenook Vineyard.

The only California Wines sold at these Concerts.

≈≈

THE CODMAN & HALL CO.,
Opposite the South Union Station.

Sole Agents for New England.

IND. COOPE & CO.'S English Ale.

THE SECOND LARGEST BREWERY IN ENGLAND.

Brewers of the finest *light quality* ale. Very highly endorsed by the medical profession. : : : :

≈≈

THE CODMAN & HALL CO.,
Opposite South Union Station.

Sole Agents for the United States.

DRINK only the PUREST WHISKY

If you want purity and richness of flavor, try the only genuine and original

OLD KENTUCKY TAYLOR,

Eight years old, our own distillation and guaranteed pure. Bottled and shipped direct from our warehouses by us. None genuine without our signature on both labels. Beware of imitation. For consumption, indigestion, and all ailments requiring stimulants, OLD KENTUCKY TAYLOR has no superior.

Sold by all first class druggists, grocers, and liquor dealers.

Wright & Taylor
Distillers,
Fine Kentucky Whiskies,
Louisville, Ky.

Hirshfield & Co.
New England Agents,
31 Doane Street
Boston.

Instruct your waiter to bring a bottle of

Pfaff's "Monogram" Lager.

If you will do this, it will not be necessary for us to expatiate upon the good qualities of our production.
YOU CAN JUDGE FOR YOURSELF.

H. & J. PFAFF BREWING COMPANY,
Telephone 2608. 16 ARCH STREET, BOSTON.

TRY THE "COLUMBIA BRAND" VIENNA SAUSAGES. SERVED HOT OR COLD AT THESE CONCERTS.

They cannot sell you here
Canadian Club Whisky,
Ruinart Champagne,
Royal Liqueur Scotch,
Carstair's Philadelphia Rye,
Fort Hill Bourbon,
Alhambra Sherry,
All of which you will find
of excellent quality;

But you can get

Kaiser Water,

the most refreshing of all table waters,

Chateau d' Arsac Claret,
N. Johnston & Sons' Medoc,
and
California Inglenook Clarets.

SUPPLIED BY

CODMAN & HALL COMPANY,

WINE MERCHANTS,

Opposite New South Station.

THURSDAY, JUNE 29.

PROGRAMME.

1. MARCH, " Uncle Ruff's Jubilee " . . . . . Rollinson
2. OVERTURE, " A Night in Granada " . . . . Kreutzer
3. WALTZ, " O schöner Mai " . . . . . . Strauss
4. SELECTION, " Fatinitza " . . . . . . Suppé
5. OVERTURE, " Freischütz " . . . . . . Weber
6. TRÄUMEREI . . . . Schumann
   The audience is respectfully requested to preserve silence during the performance of this number.
7. SERENADE, " Espagnole," for Xylophone . . . Metra
   (Solo by MR. RETTBERG.)
8. FINALE, " Lohengrin " . . . . Wagner
9. EINZUGS-MARSCH . . . . Stearns
10. OFFENBACHIANA . . . . Conradi
11. WALTZ, " Grubenlichter " . . . . . . Zeller
12. MARCH, " The Pearl of the Orient " . . . . Krogmann

COAL Best Quality AT Lowest Prices

METROPOLITAN COAL COMPANY,

No. 30 Congress Street.

WILSON BELFAST GINGER ALE and Champagne Kola are sold at these concerts.

DRINK WILSON CHAMPAGNE KOLA.

It produces energy, activity, and force. Its medical virtues are endorsed by physicians.

The **Wilson** is acknowledged to be America's purest spring water. Bottled only in glass at the spring, North Raymond, Me.

In making our BELFAST GINGER ALE we use only the purest ginger.

Beware of imitations.

Drink the **Wilson** and you are sure of the best.

Wilson Spring and Hotel Co.,
45 Arch Street,
Telephone 3129, Boston. Boston, Mass.

THE FALL RIVER LINE

OCCUPYING THE
LONG ISLAND SOUND ROUTE
BETWEEN

Boston and New York

Has the finest quintette of great steamboats that the world has ever seen. The
Priscilla, Puritan, Plymouth, Pilgrim, and Providence

Are the largest, best equipped, safest, and handsomest steamboats ever constructed. This route is one of the most attractive and naturally beautiful traversed by any transportation agency in the world. Trips of the Fall River Line are made throughout the year. Each steamboat has its own orchestra, and the service on each member of the fleet is maintained at the highest possible standard.

Tickets via this route are on sale at all of the principal Ticket Offices in the United States.

From BOSTON. Trains, connecting with steamers at Fall River in 80 minutes, leave Park Square Station, New York, New Haven & Hartford Railroad (Old Colony System), daily at 6 p.m.

From NEW YORK. Steamers leave Pier 19, North River, foot of Warren Street, daily at 5.30 p.m.

R. A. GARDNER, Superintendent, NEW YORK.
GEO. L. CONNOR, Passenger Traffic Manager, NEW HAVEN, CONN.
O. H. TAYLOR, General Passenger Agent, NEW YORK CITY.

HOTEL LANGWOOD,

Middlesex Fells Reservation.

WYOMING STATION, B. & M. R.R.

NOW OPEN.

Twenty minutes by rail from Boston. Sixty trains daily. Hotel coaches meet trains each way. Four hundred feet above sea level. Beautiful rides, drives, and walks. Golf links, tennis courts, and ball grounds.

For plans and prices address:

F. W. GASKILL, Manager,

Telephone, 40 Melrose.   Melrose, Mass.

THIRD SEASON.

3 Ideal Outings

Personally conducted by
F. R. COMEE,
Music Hall,
Boston.

	1.	2.	3.
Boston Leave	July 2	July 15	August 19
Boston Arrive	July 12	July 31	September 4

No. 1. Ten days. **Saratoga, Lake George,** 2,130 miles from **Buffalo** to **Duluth,** and return on the steamer "**North-Land**" through the **Great Lakes, Erie, Huron, St. Clair,** and **Superior.**

Nos. 2 and 3. Sixteen days. Exactly alike. 700 miles' ocean sail to **Norfolk** and **Baltimore.** Over **Alleghany Mountains** and a day in **Chicago.** Up **Lake Michigan** and three days at **Mackinac Island.** 1,546 miles on steamer "**North-West**" to **Duluth** and return to **Buffalo** through the **Great Lakes, Niagara Falls** to **Toronto.** Across **Lake Ontario,** through the **Thousand Islands,** and down the **St. Lawrence River** to **Montreal** and **Boston.**

SEND FOR CIRCULARS.

No country in the world can duplicate the journey of 1,065 miles in one steamer on fresh water from **Buffalo** to **Duluth** through the Great Northern Lakes. These "Ideal Outings" are not cheap trips, as they are too extensive, trip No. 1 covering 3,000 miles, Nos. 2 and 3, which are exactly alike, covering 4,000 miles, and with only one night in a sleeping-car. There need be no fear of seasickness, as frequent experience has proved the Great Lakes to be unusually smooth in July and August. We travel first-class in every way. The parties are strictly limited, as it is impossible to secure equally good accommodations for a larger number. The fatigue of too steady travel is avoided by from one to three days' rest at Old Point Comfort, Chicago, Mackinac Island, Duluth, Niagara Falls, Saratoga, etc. The average temperature through the Great Lakes in midsummer is 60°. No tourist who has made the journey has yet expressed disappointment: on the contrary, all are amazed at its extent and beauty.

Allsopp's

ENGLISH ALE.
"The Red Hand Brand."

Protection for Ale Drinkers.

There is a strong and growing feeling abroad that all breweries should protect consumers by doing their own bottling. Allsopp's Ale is the only brand to-day that is bottled by its makers.

Sold at these concerts.

FRIDAY, JUNE 30.
REQUEST NIGHT.

PROGRAMME.

1. MARCH, "Tannhäuser" — Wagner
2. WALTZ, "Kaiser" — Strauss
3. OVERTURE, "Martha" — Flotow
4. SELECTION, "Cavalleria Rusticana" — Mascagni

5. MARCH, "U. S. Volunteers" — Strube
6. OVERTURE, "Mignon" — Thomas
7. TWO MOVEMENTS from "Peer Gynt" — Grieg
8. INTRODUCTION, "Lohengrin" — Wagner

9. GROSSMÜTTERCHEN — Langer
   Violin Solo, Messrs. ONDRICEK and HOFFMANN.
   The audience is respectfully requested to preserve silence during the performance of this number.
10. OVERTURE, "Fra Diavolo" — Auber
11. WALTZ, "Coquetry" — Waldteufel
12. MARCH, "Runaway Girl" — Van Baar

The *only* Lithia Water sold at these concerts.

Hygeia Lithia Water

Sparkling and Still.

By its use you will avoid the germs of disease which natural MINERAL WATERS are liable to contain.

For Sale at these concerts and by

S. S. PIERCE CO.

FOR SALE AT THESE CONCERTS.

FAMOUS TANNHAEUSER EXPORT BEER

The finest Light Beer Extant.   Brewery Bottling.   Favorite of Connoisseurs.

Pure,   Palatable,   Perfect.

B. & E. Philadelphia Ale on Draught.
FOR SALE AT THESE CONCERTS.

The BERGNER & ENGEL BREWING CO.'S N.E. Depot,
508 and 510 Atlantic Avenue, Boston.
Telephone 3805.   **SOL. BACHARACH, Manager.**

The purity and keeping quality of the Tannhaeuser Export under all changes of temperature, its uniform excellence being guaranteed, together with its nutritious properties, make it the most pleasant, delicious, and convenient beverage for home consumption.
Put up in corked bottles, and packed in casks of 10 dozen white flint pints, and 6 dozen amber quarts.

Highest Awards wherever exhibited.

M. Steinert & Sons Co.,

STEINERT HALL BUILDING,

No. 162 Boylston Street, corner Carver, Boston.

STEINWAY & SONS,

HARDMAN,   GABLER,
EMERSON,   SINGER,

PIANOS.

The Æolian, Aeriol, Orchestrelle, and Pianola.

THE ÆOLIAN
AND
THE PIANOLA
FOR SUMMER HOMES.

At this season of the year we receive many orders for these instruments for Summer Residences, and therefore beg to call attention to our extensive assortment now on display, especially suited for this purpose.

The ÆOLIAN meets the requirements of country homes, furnishing, as it does, music suitable for every occasion. It practically takes the place of an orchestra — music for dancing — orchestral concerts, — in short, music of every style and description is always available.

The PIANOLA will appeal to many on account of the very little space it occupies. It will play any kind of a piano, and can also be used upon a rented piano without the slightest injury. For the above reasons it is bound to be very popular for small cottages.

We are glad to be able to announce that we can furnish PIANOLAS with no more than a week's delay, and, at times, the day the order is given.

Persons not familiar with these instruments are cordially invited to call at our warerooms and hear them, or a descriptive catalogue will be mailed free upon application.

M. STEINERT & SONS CO.,
Steinert Hall,   162 Boylston Street,   Boston.

ANHEUSER-BUSCH BREWING ASS'N,
ST. LOUIS, MO., U.S.A.

BREWERS OF HIGH=GRADE BEERS EXCLUSIVELY.

Black and Tan.   Faust.

Michelob.   Pale Lager.

Muenchener.   Anheuser Standard.

Served at the Music Hall Concerts.

Also at all first-class hotels, clubs, and bars, and on all Pullman and Wagner cars and ocean and lake steamers.

JACOB WIRTH,   **Wholesale Dealer,**   **Boston, Mass.**

PUBLISHED BY
C. A. ELLIS, MUSIC HALL.

BOSTON, WEDNESDAY, JUNE 28, 1899.

SUMMER SEASON.
Vol. XIV. No. 44.

THE MUSIC HALL — Promenade Concerts

FOURTEENTH SEASON.

C. A. ELLIS, Manager.　　F. R. COMEE, Assistant Manager.

Mr. GUSTAV STRUBE, Conductor.

WEDNESDAY, JUNE 28.

PROGRAMME.

1. MARCH OF THE PRÆTORIAN GUARD . . . . . . Noll
2. OVERTURE, "Pique Dame" . . . . Suppé
3. WALTZ, "In's Centrum" . . . . Strauss
4. SELECTION, "Wizard of the Nile" . . . . . Herbert
5. { a. "Der Lindenbaum" . . . . Schubert
   { b. "Annie Laurie" . . . . Old Scotch Song
   Boston Trombone Quartette: Messrs. HAMPE, MAUSEBACH, MEYER, THOMAE.
6. OVERTURE, "Zampa" . . . . Hérold
7. { a. "Spring Song" . . . . Mendelssohn
   { b. "Aubade Printanière" . . . . Lacome
8. SELECTION, "Robin Hood" . . . . De Koven
9. VISIONS IN A DREAM . . . . Lumbye
   Zither Solo, Mr. KELLER.
   The audience is respectfully requested to preserve silence during the performance of this number.
10. OVERTURE, "Stradella" . . . . Flotow
11. WALTZ, "España" . . . . Waldteufel
12. MARCH, "With our Soldier Boys at Tampa Bay" . . Slocum

Friday, June 30, Request Night.
Saturday, July 1, Closing Night.

To secure satisfactory service, patrons are URGED by the Management to report PROMPTLY any inattention. Complaints made so late that patrons cannot recall either the number of the table or the waiter are obviously useless.

ALBUMS OF SONGS,

Containing many popular compositions not published in single form.

IRISH FOLK SONGS, by Charles Wood, .	$2.00
RUSSIAN SONGS, by F. Wishaw (2 vols.), .	1.00
NINE SONGS, by S. Liddle, ...	1.00
NINE SONGS, by Liza Lehmann, . . .	1.00
FIVE SONGS, by Francis Korbay, . . .	2.00

Beautifully Illustrated by J. S. SARGENT, R.A.

BOOSEY & CO.,
9 East 17th Street,　　　　　New York.

SMOKE THE POPULAR "BARRISTER" CIGARS AT THE POPULAR CONCERTS.

YOU CAN

Have your last season's outfit dyed or cleansed and refinished so it will look like new, by our French process. Why discard soiled clothing when it can be overhauled and worn as second best? You can

RELY ON

Our methods of cleansing, and need not hesitate to trust us with articles of the most delicate textures. We dye or cleanse and refinish PROPERLY, all materials of household use and clothing of all kinds.

LEWANDO'S

W. L. Crosby, General Manager.
French Cleansers, Fancy Dyers, Fine Launderers.

PRINCIPAL OFFICES:
17 Temple Place, Boston.
479 Fifth Avenue, New York.
Established 70 years.
Largest in America.
Bundles called for and delivered.
Telephones in all offices.

If you are open
to conviction,
to-night
try one 10-cent box of

BETWEEN THE ACTS
Little Cigars

to smoke now — or at any time when you want a short smoke and haven't time for a long one. They are real cigars, but small ones.

They cost so little that you can use them every day as well as not and actually save on your daily cigar expense by substituting them for larger cigars.

FOR SALE HERE.

LAGER BEER

A Particularly Fine Lager for Family Use and Clubs.

Bottled in the most careful manner at our own bottling department, and sold by the R. R. Pierce Co. and all other leading grocers in New England.

Other Brands in Bottles:
"Norfolk India Pale Stock Ale."
"Norfolk Extra Golden Ale" (blue label).
"Norfolk Standard Lager."
Our "Cabinet" and "Bismarck Brau" are the most popular refreshments at these concerts.

HABICH & CO.

| H. W. HABICH, | Telephone, St. Roxbury |
| EDWARD BUHL. | or 1152 Boston. |

ESTABROOK & EATON'S MARGUERITE PERFECTOS, 10c. EACH, CONCHAS, 10c., 3 FOR 25c., SOLD AT THE "POPS."

THE ICE-CREAM SERVED AT THESE CONCERTS IS FURNISHED BY WEBER, 25 Temple Place and 33 West Street.

MUSIC HALL PROMENADE PROGRAMME.

PUBLISHED EVERY EVENING DURING THE SUMMER SEASON.

NOTICE TO ADVERTISERS.

The advertising columns in the Programme are controlled SOLELY by F. R. Comee, Boston Music Hall Box Office, to whom all communications should be addressed.

The United States Hotel,

SARATOGA SPRINGS, N.Y.

Under a continuous management for 25 years.

Without a peer in its appointments, service, and liberal management.

The largest structure of its kind in the world.

Built entirely of brick.

The Hotel and court cover over seven acres.

For further information, rates, etc., etc., address

GAGE & PERRY,
Proprietors,
UNITED STATES HOTEL,
Saratoga Springs, N.Y.

Colonial Beer...

The Beer that's Brewed in Glass.

PURE, CLEAN, PALATABLE.

Order a Bottle.

SOUTHER BREWING CO.,
919 Parker Street,
Roxbury, Mass.

VEUVE CHAFFARD

PURE OLIVE OIL.
IN HONEST BOTTLES.

The Peer of all Cigarettes.

Save the band-label on each box for valuable premiums.

::: ALSO :::

Monopol

High-grade Egyptian Cigarettes

No. 8A Khedive,
No. 66A Nadine,
No. 9A Egyptian Belles,
No. 70A Princess Lillian

On sale at these concerts and all first-class dealers.

OCKENHEIMER BERG,
Near Bingen, GERMANY. On the Rhine.

PHILIP KRIM'S OWN IMPORTATION OF **Rhine Wines,**
FOR 30 YEARS AT
163 Shawmut Avenue.

OUR WINES SOLD AT THESE CONCERTS.

HERRICK, COPLEY SQUARE, Telephones 608 and 950 (Back Bay), CHOICE TABLES for Music Hall "Pops."

D. LEIDEN'S SPARKLING MOSELLE,

The only Sparkling Wine sold at these Concerts.

SHINNECOCK

The Perfection of Scotch Whisky

Sold by
S. S. PIERCE COMPANY.

THURSDAY, JUNE 29.

PROGRAMME.

1. MARCH, "Uncle Ruff's Jubilee" . . . . . Kollinson
2. OVERTURE, "A Night in Granada" . . . . . Kreutzer
3. WALTZ, "O schoner Mai" . . . . Strauss
4. SELECTION, "Fatinitza" . . . . Suppé
5. OVERTURE, "Frei-schütz" . . . . Weber
6. TRÄUMEREI . . . . Schumann
   The audience is respectfully requested to preserve silence during the performance of this number.
7. SERENADE, "Espagnole," for Xylophone . . . Metra
   (Solo by Mr. RETTBERG.)
8. FINALE, "Lohengrin" . . . . Wagner
9. EINZUGS-MARSCH . . . . Stearns
10. OFFENBACHIANA . . . . Conradi
11. WALTZ, "Grabenlichter" . . . . Zeller
12. MARCH, "The Pearl of the Orient" . . . . Krugmann

THE HAYWARD,
16 and 22 Hayward Place.
LADIES' AND GENTS' CAFÉ. Open until 1 a.m.
Table d'hôte dinner, including bottle of wine, 75c., served from 5 to 8.30 P.M.

SCIARRETTA'S NEAPOLITAN TRIO give concerts daily from 6 P.M. until 1 A.M.
Signor SALVATORE SCIARRETTI, Lyric Tenor,
Is highly endorsed by Vice-President Garrett A. Hobart, Chauncey M. Depew, Eugene Ysaye, Raoul Pugno, Jean Gerardy, and many other prominent people.

SMITH & KERRISSEY, Proprietors.

M. S. Ginger Ale.

We desire to advise the public that hereafter the

Codman & Hall Co.,

opposite new South Station, will be our sole New England Agents for our carbonated preparations,

GINGER ALE, SARSAPARILLA, Etc.,

all of which are made with water from the famous

MYLES STANDISH SPRING,

at South Duxbury, Mass.

L. BOYER'S SONS,
90 Wall Street, NEW YORK.

"AMERICA'S FINEST PRODUCT."
Bartholomay's "APOLLO"
LAGER BEER IN BOTTLES.

Sold at these Concerts.

ALBRECHT & KOELLNER,
SOLE AGENTS,
Telephone, Boston 1751.   295-305 A Street.

Also Agents for the "Crystal Rock" Mineral Water.

PURE BEER
Harvard BREW. CO'S $1000.00
PURE BEER
Sold at these Concerts
IN BOTTLES ONLY
20¢ PER BOTTLE.

Inglenook Vineyard.

The only California Wines sold at these Concerts.

❦❦

THE CODMAN & HALL CO.,
Opposite the South Union Station.

Sole Agents for New England.

IND. COOPE & CO.'S English Ale.

THE SECOND LARGEST BREWERY IN ENGLAND.

Brewers of the finest *light quality* ale. Very highly endorsed by the medical profession. : : : :

❦❦

THE CODMAN & HALL CO.,
Opposite South Union Station.

Sole Agents for the United States.

DRINK only the PURE WHISK

If you want pu and richness flavor, try only genu and original

OLD KENTU TAYLOR,

Eight years old, own distillation guaranteed p u Bottled and ship direct from warehouses w None genuine w out our signat on both labels. ware of imitati For consumpt indigestion, and ailments requir stimulants, O KENTUCKY T LOR has superior.
Sold by all fi class drugg grocers and liq dealers.

Wright & Tay Distillers, Fine Kentuck Whiskies, Louisville, Ky

Hirshfield & C New Englan Agents, 31 Doane Stree Boston.

Instruct your waiter to bring a bottle of **Pfaff's "Monogram" Lager.**

If you will do this, it will not be necessary for us to expatiate upon the good qualities of our production.
YOU CAN JUDGE FOR YOURSELF.

H. & J. PFAFF BREWING COMPANY,
Telephone 2608.   16 ARCH STREET, BOSTON.

TRY THE "COLUMBIA BRAND" VIENNA SAUSAGES. SERVED HOT OR COLD AT THESE CONCERTS.

They cannot sell you here
Canadian Club Whisky,
Ruinart Champagne,
Royal Liqueur Scotch,
Carstair's Philadelphia Rye,
Fort Hill Bourbon,
Alhambra Sherry,
All of which you will find
of excellent quality;

But you can get

Kaiser Water,

the most refreshing of all table waters,

Chateau d'Arsac Claret,
N. Johnston & Sons' Medoc,
and
California Inglenook Clarets.

SUPPLIED BY

CODMAN & HALL COMPANY,

WINE MERCHANTS,

Opposite New South Station.

FRIDAY, JUNE 30.
REQUEST NIGHT.

PROGRAMME.

1. MARCH, "Tannhäuser" . . . . Wagner
2. WALTZ, "Kaiser" . . . . Strauss
3. OVERTURE, "Martha" . . . . Flotow
4. SELECTION, "Cavalleria Rusticana" . . . . Mascagni
5. MARCH, "U. S. Volunteers" . . . . Strube
6. OVERTURE, "Mignon" . . . . Thomas
7. TWO MOVEMENTS from "Peer Gynt" . . . . Grieg
8. INTRODUCTION, "Lohengrin" . . . . Wagner
9. GROSSMÜTTERCHEN . . . . Langer
   Violin Solo, Messrs. ONDRICEK and HOFFMANN.
   The audience is respectfully requested to preserve silence during the performance of this number.
10. OVERTURE, "Fra Diavolo" . . . . Auber
11. WALTZ, "Coquetry" . . . . Waldteufel
12. MARCH, "Runaway Girl" . . . . Van Baar

COAL
Best Quality
AT
Lowest Prices

METROPOLITAN COAL COMPANY,
No. 30 Congress Street.

WILSON BELFAST GINGER ALE
and
Champagne Kola
are sold at these concerts.

DRINK
WILSON CHAMPAGNE KOLA.

It produces energy, activity, and force. Its medical virtues are endorsed by physicians.

The **Wilson** is acknowledged to be America's purest spring water. Bottled only in glass at the spring, North Raymond, Me.

In making our BELFAST GINGER ALE we use only the purest ginger.

Beware of imitations.

Drink the **Wilson** and you are sure of the best.

Wilson Spring and Hotel Co.,
45 Arch Street.
Telephone 3129, Boston. Boston, Mass.

"THE RECOGNIZED FAVORITE OF ALL BEERS."

Sold at these Concerts. JOS. GAHM & CO., N.E. AGENTS. 125-127 PURCHASE ST.

THE ONLY BEER ON DRAUGHT AT THESE CONCERTS.

"the beer that's brewed"

THE FALL RIVER LINE

OCCUPYING THE
LONG ISLAND SOUND ROUTE
BETWEEN

Boston and New York

Has the finest quintette of great steamboats that the world has ever seen. The

Priscilla, Puritan, Plymouth, Pilgrim, and Providence

Are the largest, best equipped, safest, and handsomest steamboats ever constructed. This route is one of the most attractive and naturally beautiful traversed by any transportation agency in the world. Trips of the Fall River Line are made throughout the year. Each steamboat has its own orchestra, and the service on each member of the fleet is maintained at the highest possible standard.

Tickets via this route are on sale at all of the principal Ticket Offices in the United States.

From BOSTON. Trains, connecting with steamers at Fall River in 80 minutes, leave Park Square Station, New York, New Haven & Hartford Railroad (Old Colony System), daily at 6 p.m.

From NEW YORK. Steamers leave Pier 19, North River, foot of Warren Street, daily at 5.30 p.m.

S. A. GARDNER,   GEO. L. CONNOR,   O. H. TAYLOR,
Superintendent,   Passenger Traffic Manager,   General Passenger Agent,
NEW YORK.   NEW HAVEN, CONN.   NEW YORK CITY.

HOTEL LANGWOOD,

Middlesex Fells Reservation.

WYOMING STATION, B. & M. R.R.

NOW OPEN.

Twenty minutes by rail from Boston. Sixty trains daily. Hotel coaches meet trains each way. Four hundred feet above sea level. Beautiful rides, drives, and walks. Golf links, tennis courts, and ball grounds.

For plans and prices address:

F. W. GASKILL, Manager,

Telephone, 40 Melrose.   Melrose, Mass.

THIRD SEASON.

3 Ideal Outings

Personally conducted by
F. R. COMEE,
Music Hall,
Boston.

	1.	2.	3.
Boston Leave	July 2	July 15	August 19
Arrive	July 13	July 31	September 4

No. 1. Ten days. **Saratoga, Lake George,** 2,130 miles from **Buffalo** to **Duluth**, and return on the steamer "**North-Land**" through the **Great Lakes, Erie, Huron, St. Clair,** and **Superior.**

Nos. 2 and 3. Sixteen days. Exactly alike. 700 miles' ocean sail to **Norfolk** and **Baltimore.** Over **Alleghany Mountains** and a day in **Chicago.** Up **Lake Michigan** and three days at **Mackinac Island.** 1,546 miles on steamer "**North-West**" to **Duluth** and return to **Buffalo** through the **Great Lakes, Niagara Falls** to **Toronto.** Across **Lake Ontario**, through the **Thousand Islands**, and down the **St. Lawrence River** to **Montreal** and **Boston.**

No country in the world can duplicate the journey of **1,065 miles in one steamer on fresh water** from **Buffalo to Duluth** through the Great Northern Lakes. These "Ideal Outings" are not cheap trips, as they are too extensive, trip No. 1 covering 3,000 miles, Nos. 2 and 3, which are exactly alike, covering 4,000 miles, and with only one night in a sleeping-car. There need be no fear of seasickness, as frequent experience has proved the Great Lakes to be unusually smooth in July and August. We travel first-class in every way. The parties are strictly limited, as it is impossible to secure equally good accommodations for a large number. The fatigue of too steady travel is avoided by from one to three days' rest at Old Point Comfort, Chicago, Mackinac Island, Duluth, Niagara Falls, Saratoga, etc. The average temperature through the Great Lakes in midsummer is 60°. No tourist who has made the journey has yet expressed disappointment; on the contrary, all are amazed at its extent and beauty.

SEND FOR CIRCULARS.

Allsopp's

ENGLISH ALE.
"The Red Hand Brand."

Protection for Ale Drinkers.

There is a strong and growing feeling abroad that all breweries should protect consumers by doing their own bottling. Allsopp's Ale is the only brand to-day that is bottled by its makers.

Sold at these concerts.

SATURDAY, JULY 1.
CLOSING NIGHT.

PROGRAMME.

1. MARCH, "Tabasco" — Chadwick
2. OVERTURE, "Semiramide" — Rossini
3. WALTZ, "Dei uns zu Haus'" — Strauss
4. SELECTION, "Faust" — Gounod

5. MARCH, "Cruiser Harvard" — Strube
6. OVERTURE, "Rienzi" — Wagner
7. TRIO for Harp, Violin, 'Cello — Oehlschlägel
   (Messrs. SCHUECKER, ONDRICEK, KELLER.)
8. HUNGARIAN RHAPSODY No. 2 — Liszt

9. WALTZ, "Blue Danube" — Strauss
10. SELECTION, "Serenade" — Herbert
11. AMERICAN PATROL — Meacham
12. MARCH, "Stars and Stripes" — Sousa

The *only* Lithia Water sold at these concerts.

Hygeia Lithia Water

Sparkling and Still.

By its use you will avoid the germs of disease which natural MINERAL WATERS are liable to contain.

For Sale at these concerts and by

S. S. PIERCE CO.

The purity and keeping quality of the Tannhaeuser Export under all changes of temperature, its uniform excellence being guaranteed, together with its nutritious properties, make it the most pleasant, delicious, and convenient beverage for home consumption.
Put up in corked bottles, and packed in casks of 10 dozen white flint pints, and 6 dozen amber quarts.

Highest Awards wherever exhibited.

FOR SALE AT THESE CONCERTS.

FAMOUS TANNHAEUSER EXPORT BEER

The finest Light Beer Extant. Brewery Bottling. Favorite of Connoisseurs.

Pure,   Palatable,   Perfect.
B. & E. Philadelphia Ale on Draught.
FOR SALE AT THESE CONCERTS.

The BERGNER & ENGEL BREWING CO.'S N.E. Depot,
508 and 510 Atlantic Avenue, Boston.
Telephone 3805.   SOL. BACHARACH, Manager.

M. Steinert & Sons Co.,

STEINERT HALL BUILDING,

No. 162 Boylston Street, corner Carver, Boston.

STEINWAY & SONS,

| HARDMAN, | GABLER, |
| EMERSON, | SINGER, |

PIANOS.

The Æolian, Aeriol, Orchestrelle, and Pianola.

THE ÆOLIAN
AND
THE PIANOLA
FOR SUMMER HOMES.

At this season of the year we receive many orders for these instruments for Summer Residences, and therefore beg to call attention to our extensive assortment now on display, especially suited for this purpose.

The ÆOLIAN meets the requirements of country homes, furnishing, as it does, music suitable for every occasion. It practically takes the place of an orchestra — music for dancing — orchestral concerts, — in short, music of every style and description is always available.

The PIANOLA will appeal to many on account of the very little space it occupies. It will play any kind of a piano, and can also be used upon a rented piano without the slightest injury. For the above reasons it is bound to be very popular for small cottages.

We are glad to be able to announce that we can furnish PIANOLAS with no more than a week's delay, and, at times, the day the order is given.

Persons not familiar with these instruments are cordially invited to call at our warerooms and hear them, or a descriptive catalogue will be mailed free upon application.

M. STEINERT & SONS CO.,
Steinert Hall,   162 Boylston Street,   Boston.

ANHEUSER-BUSCH BREWING ASS'N,
ST. LOUIS, MO., U.S.A.

BREWERS OF HIGH=GRADE BEERS EXCLUSIVELY.

Black and Tan.		Faust.
Michelob.		Pale Lager.
Muenchener.		Anheuser Standard.

Served at the Music Hall Concerts.

Also at all first-class hotels, clubs, and bars, and on all Pullman and Wagner cars and ocean and lake steamers.

JACOB WIRTH,   Wholesale Dealer,   Boston, Mass.

THE MUSIC HALL
PROMENADE CONCERTS

BOSTON, FRIDAY, JUNE 30, 1899.

SUMMER SEASON.
Vol. XIV. No. 46.

PUBLISHED BY
C. A. ELLIS,
MUSIC HALL.

SMOKE "LA CELESTINA," THE BEST ALL-HAVANA CIGAR. DANIEL FRANK & CO.

SMOKE THE POPULAR "BARRISTER" CIGARS AT THE POPULAR CONCERTS.

THE MUSIC HALL... Promenade Concerts
FOURTEENTH SEASON.

C. A. ELLIS, Manager.   F. R. COMEE, Assistant Manager.

Mr. GUSTAV STRUBE, Conductor.

FRIDAY, JUNE 30.
REQUEST NIGHT.

PROGRAMME.

1. MARCH, "Tannhauser" . . . . . Wagner
2. WALTZ, "Kaiser" . . . . . Strauss
3. OVERTURE, "Martha" . . . . Flotow
4. SELECTION, "Cavalleria Rusticana" . . Mascagni
5. MARCH, "U. S. Volunteers" . . . Strube
6. OVERTURE, "Mignon" . . . . Thomas
7. TWO MOVEMENTS from "Peer Gynt" . Grieg
8. INTRODUCTION, "Lohengrin" . . . Wagner
9. GROSSMÜTTERCHEN . . . . . Langer
   Violin Solo, Messrs. ONDRICEK and HOFFMANN.
   The audience is respectfully requested to preserve silence during the performance of this number.
10. OVERTURE, "Fra Diavolo" . . . Auber
11. WALTZ, "Coquetry" . . . . . Waldteufel
12. MARCH, "Runaway Girl" . . . . Van Baar

Saturday, July 1, Closing Night.

To secure satisfactory service, patrons are URGED by the Management to report PROMPTLY any inattention. Complaints made so late that patrons cannot recall either the number of the table or the waiter are obviously useless.

YOU CAN
Have your last season's outfit dyed or cleansed and refinished so it will look like new, by our French process. Why discard soiled clothing when it can be overhauled and worn as second best? You can

RELY ON
Our methods of cleansing, and need not hesitate to trust us with articles of the most delicate textures.
We dye or cleanse and refinish PROPERLY, *all* materials of household use and clothing of all kinds.

LEWANDO'S
W. Crosby, General Manager.
French Cleansers, Fancy Dyers, Fine Launderers.

PRINCIPAL OFFICES:
17 Temple Place, Boston.
479 Fifth Avenue, New York.
*Established 70 years.
Largest in America.*
Bundles called for and delivered.
Telephones in all offices.

In no other way
are men as wasteful and extravagant as in cigar smoking—because cigars are thrown away half smoked half the time.

BETWEEN THE ACTS
Little Cigars
are just right for all short smokes. They light right, they burn right and taste right. Have you ever seen them? At all stores: 10 for 10 cts., or, as they are for sale here, you can try them to-night. Tell the waiter to bring you a 10-cent box of "Between the Acts." They will add to your enjoyment of this concert.

Now the rage of the LONDON Concerts and Drawing-rooms:

YOU AND I, by Liza Lehmann, . . . 60c.
KING CHARLES, by M. V. White, . . 60c.
LIKE VIOLETS PALE, by F. Allitsen, . . 60c.
WHEN THE WORLD IS FAIR, by F. H. Cowen, 60c.
QUEEN OF MY LIFE, by E. T. Lloyd, . 60c.

BOOSEY & CO.,
9 East 17th Street,   New York.

DRINK
VAN NOSTRAND'S
BOSTON CLUB LAGER
SOLD AT THESE CONCERTS.

NORFOLK CABINET

LAGER BEER
A Particularly Fine Lager for Family Use and Clubs.
Bottled in the most careful manner at our own bottling department, and sold by the S. S. Pierce Co. and all other leading grocers in New England.

Other Brands in Bottles:
"Norfolk India Pale Stock Ale."
"Norfolk Extra Golden Ale" (blue label).
"Norfolk Standard Lager."
Our "Cabinet" and "Bismarck Brau" are the most popular refreshments at these concerts.

HABICH & CO.
H. W. HABICH,   Telephone, 86 Roxbury
EDWARD RUHL.   or 1152 Boston.

ESTABROOK & EATON'S MARGUERITE PERFECTOS, 10c. EACH. CONCHAS, 10c., 3 FOR 25c., SOLD AT THE "POPS."

THE ICE-CREAM SERVED AT THESE CONCERTS IS FURNISHED BY WEBER, 25 Temple Place and 33 West Street.

MUSIC HALL PROMENADE PROGRAMME.

PUBLISHED EVERY EVENING DURING THE SUMMER SEASON.

NOTICE TO ADVERTISERS.

The advertising columns in the Programme are controlled SOLELY by F. R. Comee, Boston Music Hall Box Office, to whom all communications should be addressed.

The United States Hotel,

SARATOGA SPRINGS, N.Y.

Under a continuous management for 25 years.

Without a peer in its appointments, service, and liberal management.

The largest structure of its kind in the world.

Built entirely of brick.

The Hotel and court cover over seven acres.

For further information, rates, etc., etc., address

GAGE & PERRY,
Proprietors,
UNITED STATES HOTEL,
Saratoga Springs, N.Y.

Colonial Beer...

The Beer that's Brewed in Glass.

PURE, CLEAN, PALATABLE.

Order a Bottle.

SOUTHER BREWING CO.,
919 Parker Street,
Roxbury, Mass.

VEUVE CHAFFARD

PURE OLIVE OIL.

IN HONEST BOTTLES.

The Peer of all Cigarettes.

Save the band label on each box for valuable premiums.

::: ALSO :::

Monopol

High-grade Egyptian Cigarettes.

No. 8A Khedive,
No. 16A Nadine,
No. 8A Egyptian Belles,
No. 70A Princess Lillian

On sale at these concerts and all first-class dealers.

OCKENHEIMER BERG, Near Bingen, GERMANY. On the Rhine.

PHILIP KRIM'S

OWN IMPORTATION OF

Rhine Wines,

FOR 30 YEARS AT

163 Shawmut Avenue.

OUR WINES SOLD AT THESE CONCERTS.

HERRICK, COPLEY SQUARE, Telephones 608 and 950 (Back Bay), CHOICE TABLES for Music Hall "Pops."

D. LEIDEN'S SPARKLING MOSELLE,

The only Sparkling Wine sold at these Concerts.

SHINNECOCK

The Perfection of

Scotch Whisky

Sold by
S. S. PIERCE COMPANY.

SATURDAY, JULY 1.
CLOSING NIGHT.

PROGRAMME.

1. MARCH, "Tabasco" . . . . Chadwick
2. OVERTURE, " Semiramide " . . . . Rossini
3. WALTZ, "Bei uns zu Haus' " . . . . Strauss
4. SELECTION, " Faust" . . . . Gounod
5. MARCH, "Cruiser Harvard " . . . . Strube
6. OVERTURE, " Rienzi " . . . . Wagner
7. TRIO for Harp, Violin, 'Cello . . . . . . Ochischlagel
   (Messrs. SCHUECKER, ONDRICEK, KELLER.)
8. HUNGARIAN RHAPSODY No. 2 . . . . . Liszt
9. WALTZ, " Blue Danube " . . . . Strauss
10. SELECTION, " Serenade " . . . . Herbert
11. AMERICAN PATROL . . . . Meacham
12. MARCH, "Stars and Stripes " . . . . . . Sousa

THE HAYWARD,
16 and 22 Hayward Place.
LADIES' AND GENTS' CAFÉ. Open until 1 a.m.
Table d'hôte dinner, including bottle of wine, 75c.,
served from 5 to 8.30 P.M.

SCIARRETTA'S NEAPOLITAN TRIO give concerts daily
from 6 P.M. until 1 A.M.

Signor SALVATORE SCIARRETTI, Lyric Tenor,
Is highly endorsed by Vice-President Garrett A. Hobart, Chauncey M. Depew,
Eugene Ysaye, Raoul Pugno, Jean Gerardy, and many other prominent people.

SMITH & KERRISSEY, Proprietors.

M. S. Ginger Ale.

We desire to advise the public that hereafter the

Codman & Hall Co.,

opposite new South Station, will be our sole New England Agents for our carbonated preparations,

GINGER ALE,
SARSAPARILLA, Etc.,

all of which are made with water from the famous

MYLES STANDISH SPRING,

at South Duxbury, Mass.

L. BOYER'S SONS,
90 Wall Street, NEW YORK.

"AMERICA'S FINEST PRODUCT."

Bartholomay's "APOLLO"

LAGER BEER IN BOTTLES.

Sold at these Concerts.

ALBRECHT & KOELLNER,
SOLE AGENTS,
Telephone, Boston 1751.   295-305 A Street.

Also Agents for the " Crystal Rock " Mineral Water.

PURE BEER

Harvard BREW. CO'S $1000.⁰⁰

PURE BEER

Sold at these Concerts,
IN BOTTLES ONLY
20¢ PER BOTTLE.

TABLE LINEN USED AT THESE CONCERTS THE L. K. HUSTED LAUNDERING COMPANY, 27 and 29 BROADWAY, CHELSEA, MASS.
LAUNDERED BY

Inglenook Vineyard.

The only California Wines sold at these Concerts.

❧❧

THE CODMAN & HALL CO.,
Opposite the South Union Station.

Sole Agents for New England.

IND. COOPE & CO.'S English Ale.

THE SECOND LARGEST BREWERY IN ENGLAND.

Brewers of the finest *light quality* ale. Very highly endorsed by the medical profession. : : : : :

❧❧

THE CODMAN & HALL CO.,
Opposite South Union Station.

Sole Agents for the United States.

DRIN
only th

PURE

WHIS

If you want p
and richne
flavor, try
only gen
and origin

OLD KENTU
TAYLOR,

Eight years old
own distillation
guaranteed p
Bottled and shi
direct from
warehouses by
None genuine w
out our signa
on bottle labels.
ware of imitat
For
indige
ailments requ
stimulants, O
KENTUCKY T
LOR has
superior.
Sold by all
class drugs
grocers, and li
dealers.

Wright & Tay
Distillers,
Fine Kentuck
Whiskies,
Louisville, K

Hirshfield &
New Englan
Agents,
31 Doane Stre
Boston.

Instruct your waiter to bring a bottle of **Pfaff's "Monogram" Lager.**

If you will do this, it will not be necessary for us to expatiate upon the good qualities of our production.
YOU CAN JUDGE FOR YOURSELF.

H. & J. PFAFF BREWING COMPANY,
Telephone 2608.   16 ARCH STREET, BOSTON.

TRY THE "COLUMBIA BRAND" VIENNA SAUSAGES.   SERVED HOT OR COLD AT THESE CONCERTS.

They cannot sell you here
Canadian Club Whisky,
Ruinart Champagne,
Royal Liqueur Scotch,
Carstair's Philadelphia Rye,
Fort Hill Bourbon,
Alhambra Sherry,
All of which you will find
of excellent quality;

But you can get

Kaiser Water,

the most refreshing of all
table waters,

Chateau d'Arsac Clarel,
N. Johnston & Sons' Medoc,
and
California Inglenook Clarets.

SUPPLIED BY

CODMAN & HALL
COMPANY,

WINE MERCHANTS,
Opposite New South Station.

IN ALL THE WORLD
NO TRIP LIKE THIS!!

2,500 MILES THROUGH THE

GREAT LAKES

ON THE

FLOATING PALACES
"NORTH-WEST" and "NORTH-LAND"

Send for circulars to

F. R. COMEE,
Music Hall, - - - - - - BOSTON.

COAL   Best Quality
AT
Lowest Prices

METROPOLITAN COAL COMPANY,
No. 30 Congress Street.

WILSON BELFAST GINGER ALE
and
Champagne Kola
are sold at these concerts.

DRINK
WILSON CHAMPAGNE KOLA.

It produces energy, activity, and force. Its medical virtues are endorsed by physicians.

The **Wilson** is acknowledged to be America's purest spring water. Bottled only in glass at the spring. North Raymond, Me.

In making our BELFAST GINGERALE we use only the purest ginger.

Beware of imitations.

Drink the **Wilson** and you are sure of the best.

Wilson Spring and Hotel Co.,
45 Arch Street.
Telephone 3129, Boston.   Boston, Mass.

THE FALL RIVER LINE

OCCUPYING THE LONG ISLAND SOUND ROUTE BETWEEN

Boston and New York

Has the finest quintette of great steamboats that the world has ever seen. The

Priscilla, Puritan, Plymouth, Pilgrim, and Providence

Are the largest, best equipped, safest, and handsomest steamboats ever constructed. This route is one of the most attractive and naturally beautiful traversed by any transportation agency in the world. Trips of the Fall River Line are made throughout the year.

Each steamboat has its own orchestra, and the service on each member of the fleet is maintained at the highest possible standard.

Tickets via this route are on sale at all of the principal Ticket Offices in the United States.

From **BOSTON**. Trains, connecting with steamers at Fall River in 80 minutes, leave Park Square Station, New York, New Haven & Hartford Railroad (Old Colony System), daily at 6 p.m.

From **NEW YORK**. Steamers leave Pier 19, North River, foot of Warren Street, daily at 5.30 p.m.

S. A. GARDNER, Superintendent, New York.
GEO. L. CONNOR, Passenger Traffic Manager, New Haven, Conn.
O. H. TAYLOR, General Passenger Agent, New York City.

HOTEL LANGWOOD,

Middlesex Fells Reservation.

WYOMING STATION, B. & M. R.R.

NOW OPEN.

Twenty minutes by rail from Boston. Sixty trains daily. Hotel coaches meet trains each way. Four hundred feet above sea level. Beautiful rides, drives, and walks. Golf links, tennis courts, and ball grounds.

For plans and prices address:

F. W. GASKILL, Manager,

Telephone, 40 Melrose.   Melrose, Mass.

THIRD SEASON.

3 Ideal Outings

Personally conducted by **F. R. COMEE,** Music Hall, Boston.

Boston	1.	2.	3.
Leave	July 2	July 15	August 19
Arrive	July 12	July 31	September 4

No. 1. Ten days. **Saratoga, Lake George,** 2,130 miles from **Buffalo** to **Duluth,** and return on the steamer "**North-Land**" through the **Great Lakes, Erie, Huron, St. Clair,** and **Superior.**

Nos. 2 and 3. Sixteen days. Exactly alike. 700 miles' ocean sail to **Norfolk** and **Baltimore.** Over Alleghany Mountains and a day in **Chicago.** Up Lake Michigan and three days at **Mackinac Island.** 1,546 miles on steamer "**North-West**" to **Duluth** and return to **Buffalo** through the **Great Lakes, Niagara Falls** to **Toronto.** Across **Lake Ontario,** through the **Thousand Islands,** and down the **St. Lawrence River** to **Montreal** and **Boston.**

No country in the world can duplicate the journey of 1,065 miles in one steamer on fresh water from **Buffalo** to **Duluth** through the Great Northern Lakes. These "Ideal Outings" are not cheap trips, as they are too extensive, trip No. 1 covering 3,000 miles, Nos. 2 and 3, which are exactly alike, covering 4,000 miles, and with only one night in a sleeping-car. There need be no fear of seasickness, as frequent experience has proved the Great Lakes to be unusually smooth in July and August. We travel first-class in every way. The parties are strictly limited, as it is impossible to secure equally good accommodations for a large number. The fatigue of too steady travel is avoided by from one to three days' rest at Old Point Comfort, Chicago, Mackinac Island, Duluth, Niagara Falls, Saratoga, etc. The average temperature through the Great Lakes in midsummer is 60°. No tourist who has made the journey has yet expressed disappointment: on the contrary, all are amazed at its extent and beauty.

SEND FOR CIRCULARS.

Allsopp's

ENGLISH ALE.
"The Red Hand Brand."

Protection for Ale Drinkers.

There is a strong and growing feeling abroad that all breweries should protect consumers by doing their own bottling. Allsopp's Ale is the only brand to-day that is bottled by its makers.

Sold at these concerts.

SEND FOR CIRCULAR
...OF...
IDEAL ..
OUTINGS
...THROUGH THE...
GREAT LAKES

Address

F. R. COMEE,

MUSIC HALL, BOSTON.

The *only* Lithia Water sold at these concerts.

Hygeia Lithia Water

Sparkling and Still.

By its use you will avoid the germs of disease which natural MINERAL WATERS are liable to contain.

For Sale at these concerts and by

S. S. PIERCE CO.

The purity and keeping quality of the Tannhaeuser Export under all changes of temperature, its uniform excellence being guaranteed, together with its nutritious properties, make it the most pleasant, delicious, and convenient beverage for home consumption.

Put up in corked bottles, and packed in casks of 10 dozen white flint pints, and 6 dozen amber quarts.

Highest Awards wherever exhibited.

FOR SALE AT THESE CONCERTS.
FAMOUS TANNHAEUSER EXPORT BEER

The finest Light Beer Extant.   Brewery Bottling.   Favorite of Connoisseurs.

Pure,   Palatable,   Perfect.

B. & E. Philadelphia Ale on Draught.
FOR SALE AT THESE CONCERTS.

The **BERGNER & ENGEL BREWING CO.'S** N.E. Depot,

508 and 510 Atlantic Avenue, Boston.

Telephone 3805.   SOL. BACHARACH, Manager.

M. Steinert & Sons Co.,

STEINERT HALL BUILDING,

No. 162 Boylston Street, corner Carver, Boston.

STEINWAY & SONS,

HARDMAN,   GABLER,
EMERSON,   SINGER,

PIANOS.

The Æolian, Aeriol, Orchestrelle, and Pianola.

THE ÆOLIAN
AND
THE PIANOLA
FOR SUMMER HOMES.

At this season of the year we receive many orders for these instruments for Summer Residences, and therefore beg to call attention to our extensive assortment now on display, especially suited for this purpose.

The ÆOLIAN meets the requirements of country homes, furnishing, as it does, music suitable for every occasion. It practically takes the place of an orchestra — music for dancing — orchestral concerts, — in short, music of every style and description is always available.

The PIANOLA will appeal to many on account of the very little space it occupies. It will play any kind of a piano, and can also be used upon a rented piano without the slightest injury. For the above reasons it is bound to be very popular for small cottages.

We are glad to be able to announce that we can furnish PIANOLAS with no more than a week's delay, and, at times, the day the order is given.

Persons not familiar with these instruments are cordially invited to call at our warerooms and hear them, or a descriptive catalogue will be mailed free upon application.

M. STEINERT & SONS CO.,
Steinert Hall,   162 Boylston Street,   Boston.

ANHEUSER-BUSCH BREWING ASS'N,

ST. LOUIS, MO., U.S.A.

BREWERS OF HIGH=GRADE BEERS EXCLUSIVELY.

Black and Tan.	Faust.
Michelob.	Pale Lager.
Muenchener.	Anheuser Standard.

Served at the Music Hall Concerts.

Also at all first-class hotels, clubs, and bars, and on all Pullman and Wagner cars and ocean and lake steamers.

JACOB WIRTH,   **Wholesale Dealer,**   **Boston, Mass.**

THE MUSIC HALL PROMENADE CONCERTS

SMOKE "LA CELESTINA," THE BEST ALL-HAVANA CIGAR. DANIEL FRANK & CO.

SMOKE THE POPULAR "BARRISTER" CIGARS AT THE POPULAR CONCERTS.

PUBLISHED BY
C. A. ELLIS, MUSIC HALL.

BOSTON, SATURDAY, JULY 1, 1899.

SUMMER SEASON. Vol. XIV. No. 47.

YOU CAN
Have your last season's outfit dyed or cleansed and refinished so it will look like new, by our French process. Why discard soiled clothing when it can be overhauled and worn as second best? You can

RELY ON
Our methods of cleansing, and need not hesitate to trust us with articles of the most delicate textures. We dye or cleanse and refinish PROPERLY, all materials of household use and clothing of all kinds.

LEWANDO'S
W. L. Crosby, General Manager.
French Cleansers, Fancy Dyers, Fine Launderers.
PRINCIPAL OFFICES:
17 Temple Place, Boston.
479 Fifth Avenue, New York.
*Established 70 years.
Largest in America.*
Bundles called for and delivered.
Telephones in all offices.

THE MUSIC HALL :: Promenade Concerts
FOURTEENTH SEASON.

C. A. ELLIS, Manager.   F. R. COMEE, Assistant Manager.

Mr. GUSTAV STRUBE, Conductor.

SATURDAY, JULY 1.
CLOSING NIGHT.
PROGRAMME.

1. MARCH, "Tabasco" . . . . Chadwick
2. OVERTURE, "Semiramide" . . . . . . Rossini
3. WALTZ, "Bei uns zu Haus" . . . . . . Strauss
4. SELECTION, "Faust" . . . . Gounod
5. MARCH, "Cruiser Harvard" . . . . . . Strube
6. OVERTURE, "Rienzi" . . . . Wagner
7. TRIO for Harp, Violin, 'Cello . . . . Oehlschlägel
   (Messrs. SCHUECKER, ONDRICEK, KELLER.)
8. HUNGARIAN RHAPSODY No. 2 . . . . . . Liszt
9. WALTZ, "Blue Danube" . . . . Strauss
10. SELECTION, "Serenade" . . . . Herbert
11. AMERICAN PATROL . . . . Meacham
12. MARCH, "Stars and Stripes" . . . . . Sousa

To secure satisfactory service, patrons are URGED by the Management to report PROMPTLY any inattention. Complaints made so late that patrons cannot recall either the number of the table or the waiter are obviously useless.

HERE ARE A FEW NAMES FROM OUR LIST OF COMPOSERS:
ENGLISH.— Stephen Adams, F. H. Cowen, S. Liddle, C. V. Stanford, A. C. Mackenzie, R. H. Walthew, H. R. Shelley, Goring Thomas, Frances Allitsen, Maude V. White, Edward German, Mary Carmichael, Liza Lehmann, etc.
FRENCH.— C. Chaminade, Jane Vieu, L. Denza, P. Delmet, Hemberg, Guy d'Hardelot, De Leva, F. P. Tosti, etc.
ITALIAN.— F. P. Tosti, P. Mascagni, G. Puccini, G. Verdi, Don Lorenzo Perosi, etc.

THE MOST REPRESENTATIVE PUBLISHING HOUSE IN AMERICA.
BOOSEY & CO., 9 East 17th Street, New York.

Knowledge differs from Experience.
You may know "all about"

BETWEEN THE ACTS
Little Cigars

but have you ever tried them yourself? Do you know how desirable they really are—how good they are—how economical they are—how convenient they are—how satisfactory they are? You can know—once for all—by having the waiter bring you a 10-cent box of ten—to smoke now—to-night—while you are enjoying this concert. They are for sale here.

BEST BEER BREWED

DRINK VAN NOSTRAND'S
P. B. ALE
SOLD AT THESE CONCERTS

LAGER BEER
A Particularly Fine Lager for Family Use and Clubs.

Bottled in the most careful manner at our own bottling departments, and sold by the S. S. Pierce Co. and all other leading grocers in New England.

Other Brands in Bottles:
"Norfolk India Pale Stock Ale."
"Norfolk Extra Golden Ale" (blue label).
"Norfolk Standard Lager."
Our "Cabinet" and "Bismarck Braeu" are the most popular refreshments at these concerts.

HABICH & CO.
H. W. HABICH. | Telephone, 56 Roxbury
EDWARD BUHL. | or 1132 Boston.

ESTABROOK & EATON'S MARGUERITE PERFECTOS, 10c. EACH. CONCHAS, 10c., 3 FOR 25c., **SOLD AT THE "POPS."**

THE ICE-CREAM SERVED AT THESE CONCERTS IS FURNISHED BY WEBER, 25 Temple Place and 33 West Street.

MUSIC HALL PROMENADE PROGRAMME.
PUBLISHED EVERY EVENING DURING THE SUMMER SEASON.

NOTICE TO ADVERTISERS.
The advertising columns in the Programme are controlled SOLELY by F. R. Comee, Boston Music Hall Box Office, to whom all communications should be addressed.

The United States Hotel,
SARATOGA SPRINGS, N.Y.

Under a continuous management for 25 years.

Without a peer in its appointments, service, and liberal management.

The largest structure of its kind in the world.

Built entirely of brick.

The Hotel and court cover over seven acres.

For further information, rates, etc., etc., address

GAGE & PERRY,
Proprietors,
UNITED STATES HOTEL,
Saratoga Springs, N.Y.

Colonial Beer...
The Beer that's Brewed in Glass.
PURE, CLEAN, PALATABLE.
Order a Bottle.
SOUTHER BREWING CO.,
919 Parker Street,
Roxbury, Mass.

All The
IMPORTED CIGARS
Sold At These Concerts Are Supplied By The
S. S. PIERCE COMPANY.

The Peer of all Cigarettes.
Save the band label on each box for valuable premiums.
::: ALSO :::
Monopol
High-grade Egyptian Cigarettes.
No. 8A Khedive,
No. 6GA Nadine,
No. 9A Egyptian Belles,
No. 70A Princess Lillian
On sale at these concerts and all first-class dealers.

OCKENHEIMER BERG,
Near Bingen, GERMANY. On the Rhine.

PHILIP KRIM'S
OWN IMPORTATION OF
Rhine Wines,
FOR 30 YEARS AT
163 Shawmut Avenue.
OUR WINES SOLD AT THESE CONCERTS.

HERRICK, COPLEY SQUARE, Telephones 608 and 950 (Back Bay), CHOICE TABLES for Music Hall "Pops."

GREAT WESTERN CHAMPAGNE

—————— A natural, genuine champagne, of the finest quality produced in America.

Sold by Wine Merchants, Grocers, and Druggists.

Music Hall, Winter Street and Hamilton Place.

Boston Symphony Orchestra,

Mr. WILHELM GERICKE, Conductor.

Nineteenth Season, - - 1899-1900.

OPENING CONCERT,

Saturday Evening, October 14, 1899.

AUCTION SALE OF SEASON TICKETS FOR THE

Friday afternoon Public Rehearsals.
$12 tickets, Monday, September 25, 1899, at 10 A.M.
$7.50 tickets, Tuesday, September 26, 1899, at 10 A.M.

Saturday evening Concerts.
$12 tickets, Thursday, September 28, 1899, at 10 A.M.
$7.50 tickets, Friday, September 29, 1899, at 10 A.M.

THE HAYWARD,
16 and 22 Hayward Place.

LADIES' AND GENTS' CAFE. Open until 1 a.m.

Table d'hôte dinner, including bottle of wine, 75c., served from 5 to 8:30 P.M.

SCIARRETTA'S NEAPOLITAN TRIO give concerts daily from 6 P.M. until 1 A.M.

Signor SALVATORE SCIARRETTI, Lyric Tenor, is highly endorsed by Vice-President Garrett A. Hobart, Chauncey M. Depew, Eugene Ysaye, Raoul Pugno, Jean Gerardy, and many other prominent people.

SMITH & KERRISSEY, Proprietors.

M. S. Ginger Ale.

We desire to advise the public that hereafter the

Codman & Hall Co.,

opposite new South Station, will be our sole New England Agents for our carbonated preparations,

GINGER ALE, SARSAPARILLA, Etc.,

all of which are made with water from the famous

MYLES STANDISH SPRING,

at South Duxbury, Mass.

———

L. BOYER'S SONS,

90 Wall Street, NEW YORK.

"AMERICA'S FINEST PRODUCT."

Bartholomay's "APOLLO"

LAGER BEER IN BOTTLES.

Sold at these Concerts.

ALBRECHT & KOELLNER,
SOLE AGENTS,

Telephone, Boston 1751. 295-305 A Street.

Also Agents for the "Crystal Rock" Mineral Water.

PURE BEER

Harvard BREW. CO'S $1000.⁰⁰

PURE BEER

Sold at these Concerts IN BOTTLES ONLY

20¢ PER BOTTLE.

Inglenook Vineyard.

The only California Wines sold at these Concerts.

❦❦

THE CODMAN & HALL CO.,
Opposite the South Union Station.

Sole Agents for New England.

IND. COOPE & CO.'S English Ale.

THE SECOND LARGEST BREWERY IN ENGLAND.

Brewers of the finest *light quality* ale. Very highly endorsed by the medical profession. : : : : :

❦❦

THE CODMAN & HALL CO.,
Opposite South Union Station.

Sole Agents for the United States.

Instruct your waiter to bring a bottle of **Pfaff's "Monogram" Lager.**

If you will do this, it will not be necessary for us to expatiate upon the good qualities of our production.
YOU CAN JUDGE FOR YOURSELF.

H. & J. PFAFF BREWING COMPANY,
Telephone 2608.   16 ARCH STREET, BOSTON.

TRY THE "COLUMBIA BRAND" VIENNA SAUSAGES. SERVED HOT OR COLD AT THESE CONCERTS.

They cannot sell you here
Canadian Club Whisky,
Ruinart Champagne,
Royal Liqueur Scotch,
Carstair's Philadelphia Rye,
Fort Hill Bourbon,
Alhambra Sherry,
All of which you will find
of excellent quality;

But you can get

Kaiser Water,

the most refreshing of all
table waters,

Chateau d'Arsac Claret,
N. Johnston & Sons' Medoc,
and
California Inglenook Clarets.

SUPPLIED BY

CODMAN & HALL COMPANY,

WINE MERCHANTS,
Opposite New South Station.

IN ALL THE WORLD
NO TRIP LIKE THIS!!

2,500 MILES THROUGH THE

GREAT LAKES

ON THE

FLOATING PALACES
"NORTH-WEST" and "NORTH-LAND"

Send for circulars to

F. R. COMEE,

Music Hall, - - - - - BOSTON.

COAL

Best Quality
AT
Lowest Prices

METROPOLITAN COAL COMPANY,
No. 30 Congress Street.

WILSON BELFAST GINGER ALE
and
Champagne Kola
are sold at these concerts.

DRINK
WILSON
CHAMPAGNE
KOLA.

It produces energy, activity, and force. Its medical virtues are endorsed by physicians.

The **Wilson** is acknowledged to be America's purest spring water. Bottled only in glass at the spring, North Raymond, Me.

In making our BELFAST GINGER ALE we use only the purest ginger.

Beware of imitations.

Drink the Wilson and you are sure of the best.

Wilson Spring and Hotel Co.,
45 Arch Street.
Telephone 3129, Boston. Boston, Mass.

"THE RECOGNIZED FAVORITE OF ALL BEERS."

Schlitz

THE BEER THAT MADE MILWAUKEE FAMOUS.

HIGHEST AWARD FOR PURITY.

Sold at these Concerts. JOS. GAHM & CO., N.E. AGENTS. 125-127 PURCHASE ST.

THE ONLY BEER ON DRAUGHT AT THESE CONCERTS.

" the beer that's brewed "

THE FALL RIVER LINE

OCCUPYING THE
LONG ISLAND SOUND ROUTE
BETWEEN

Boston and New York

Has the finest quintette of great steamboats that the world has ever seen. The

Priscilla, Puritan, Plymouth, Pilgrim, and Providence

Are the largest, best equipped, safest, and handsomest steamboats ever constructed. This route is one of the most attractive and naturally beautiful traversed by any transportation agency in the world. Trips of the Fall River Line are made throughout the year.

Each steamboat has its own orchestra, and the service on each member of the fleet is maintained at the highest possible standard.

Tickets via this route are on sale at all of the principal Ticket Offices in the United States.

From BOSTON. Trains, connecting with steamers at Fall River in 80 minutes, leave Park Square Station, New York, New Haven & Hartford Railroad (Old Colony System), daily at 6 p.m.

From NEW YORK. Steamers leave Pier 19, North River, foot of Warren Street, daily at 5.30 p.m.

S. A. GARDNER, Superintendent, NEW YORK.
GEO. L. CONNOR, Passenger Traffic Manager, NEW HAVEN, CONN.
O. H. TAYLOR, General Passenger Agent, NEW YORK CITY.

HOTEL LANGWOOD,

Middlesex Fells Reservation.

WYOMING STATION, B. & M. R. R.

NOW OPEN.

Twenty minutes by rail from Boston. Sixty trains daily. Hotel coaches meet trains each way. Four hundred feet above sea level. Beautiful rides, drives, and walks. Golf links, tennis courts, and ball grounds.

For plans and prices address :

F. W. GASKILL, Manager,

Telephone, 40 Melrose. Melrose, Mass.

THIRD SEASON.

3 Ideal Outings

Personally conducted by
F. R. COMEE,
Music Hall,
Boston.

	1.	2.	3.
Boston Leave	July 2	July 15	August 19
Arrive	July 12	July 31	September 4

No. 1. Ten days. **Saratoga, Lake George,** 2,130 miles from **Buffalo** to **Duluth,** and return on the steamer "North-Land " through the **Great Lakes, Erie, Huron, St. Clair,** and **Superior.**

Nos. 2 and 3. Sixteen days. Exactly alike. 700 miles' ocean sail to **Norfolk** and **Baltimore.** Over **Alleghany Mountains** and a day in **Chicago.** Up **Lake Michigan** and three days at **Mackinac Island.** 1,546 miles on steamer "North-West " to **Duluth** and return to **Buffalo** through the **Great Lakes, Niagara Falls** to **Toronto.** Across Lake **Ontario,** through the **Thousand Islands,** and down the **St. Lawrence River** to **Montreal** and **Boston.**

No country in the world can duplicate the journey of **1,065 miles in one steamer on fresh water** from **Buffalo** to **Duluth** through the Great Northern Lakes. These "Ideal Outings" are not cheap trips, as they are too extensive, trip No. 1 covering 3,000 miles, Nos. 2 and 3, which are exactly alike, covering 4,000 miles, and with only one night in a sleeping-car. There need be no fear of seasickness, as frequent experience has proved the Great Lakes to be unusually smooth in July and August. We travel first-class in every way. The parties are strictly limited, as it is impossible to secure equally good accommodations for a large number. The fatigue of too steady travel is avoided by from one to three days' rest at Old Point Comfort, Chicago, Mackinac Island, Duluth, Niagara Falls, Saratoga, etc. The average temperature through the Great Lakes in midsummer is 60°. No tourist who has made the journey has yet expressed disappointment : on the contrary, all are amazed at its extent and beauty.

SEND FOR CIRCULARS.

Allsopp's

ENGLISH ALE.
"The Red Hand Brand."

Protection for Ale Drinkers.

There is a strong and growing feeling abroad that all breweries should protect consumers by doing their own bottling. Allsopp's Ale is the only brand to-day that is bottled by its makers.

Sold at these concerts.

SEND FOR CIRCULAR
...OF...
IDEAL ..
OUTINGS
...THROUGH THE...
GREAT LAKES

Address

F. R. COMEE,

MUSIC HALL, BOSTON.

The *only* Lithia Water sold at these concerts.

Hygeia Lithia Water

Sparkling and Still.

By its use you will avoid the germs of disease which natural MINERAL WATERS are liable to contain.

For Sale at these concerts and by

S. S. PIERCE CO.

The purity and keeping quality of the Tannhaeuser Export under all changes of temperature, its uniform excellence being guaranteed, together with its nutritious properties, make it the most pleasant, delicious, and convenient beverage for home consumption.
Put up in corked bottles, and packed in casks of 10 dozen white flint pints, and 6 dozen amber quarts.

Highest Awards wherever exhibited.

FOR SALE AT THESE CONCERTS.

FAMOUS TANNHAEUSER EXPORT BEER

The finest Light Beer Extant.   Brewery Bottling.   Favorite of Connoisseurs.

Pure,   Palatable,   Perfect.

B. & E. Philadelphia Ale on Draught.
FOR SALE AT THESE CONCERTS.

The BERGNER & ENGEL BREWING CO.'S N.E. Depot,
508 and 510 Atlantic Avenue, Boston.

Telephone 3805.   **SOL. BACHARACH, Manager.**

M. Steinert & Sons Co.,

STEINERT HALL BUILDING,

No. 162 Boylston Street, corner Carver, Boston.

STEINWAY & SONS,

HARDMAN,   GABLER,
EMERSON,   SINGER,

PIANOS.

The Æolian, Aeriol, Orchestrelle, and Pianola.

THE ÆOLIAN
AND
THE PIANOLA
FOR SUMMER HOMES.

At this season of the year we receive many orders for these instruments for Summer Residences, and therefore beg to call attention to our extensive assortment now on display, especially suited for this purpose.

The ÆOLIAN meets the requirements of country homes, furnishing, as it does, music suitable for every occasion. It practically takes the place of an orchestra — music for dancing — orchestral concerts, — in short, music of every style and description is always available.

The PIANOLA will appeal to many on account of the very little space it occupies. It will play any kind of a piano, and can also be used upon a rented piano without the slightest injury. For the above reasons it is bound to be very popular for small cottages.

We are glad to be able to announce that we can furnish PIANOLAS with no more than a week's delay, and, at times, the day the order is given.

Persons not familiar with these instruments are cordially invited to call at our warerooms and hear them, or a descriptive catalogue will be mailed free upon application.

M. STEINERT & SONS CO.,
Steinert Hall,   162 Boylston Street,   Boston.

ANHEUSER-BUSCH BREWING ASS'N,

ST. LOUIS, MO., U.S.A.

BREWERS OF HIGH=GRADE BEERS EXCLUSIVELY.

Black and Tan.		Faust.
Michelob.		Pale Lager.
Muenchener.		Anheuser Standard.

Served at the Music Hall Concerts.

Also at all first-class hotels, clubs, and bars, and on all Pullman and Wagner cars and ocean and lake steamers.

JACOB WIRTH,   Wholesale Dealer,   Boston, Mass.

www.ingramcontent.com/pod-product-compliance
Lightning Source LLC
Chambersburg PA
CBHW032355230426
43672CB00007B/704